Shannon,
  I hope you enjoy this!
          Love,
          Mom

              10-18-99

# CatSmart

The Ultimate Guide to
Understanding, Caring for,
and Living with Your Cat

Myrna Milani, D.V.M.

CONTEMPORARY BOOKS

**Library of Congress Cataloging-in-Publication Data**

Milani, Myrna M.
    CatSmart : the ultimate guide to understanding, caring for, and
living with your cat / Myrna Milani.
        p.    cm.
    Includes index.
    ISBN 0-8092-3024-0
    1. Cats.    2. Cats—Behavior.    3. Cats—Health.    I. Title.
SF447.M49    1998
636.8'088'7—dc21                                                97-26730
                                                                    CIP

Interior design by Mary Lockwood

Published by Contemporary Books
A division of NTC/Contemporary Publishing Group, Inc.
4255 West Touhy Avenue, Lincolnwood (Chicago), Illinois 60646-1975 U.S.A.
Copyright © 1998 by Myrna Milani
Printed in the United States of America
International Standard Book Number: 0-8092-3024-0
18    17    16    15    14    13    12    11    10    9    8    7    6    5    4    3    2    1

To Michael Snell,
agent, editor, and dear friend,
who always thought he was a
dog person—until he got a cat

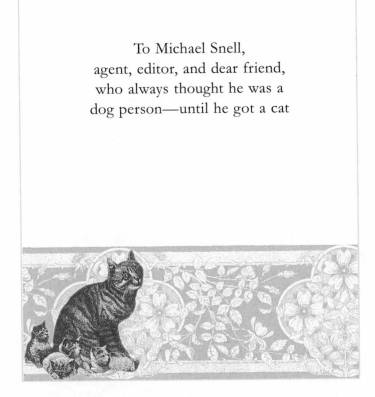

# Contents

Introduction    IX

PART I: Understanding Your Cat    I

1 A Taste of Wildness: *Recognizing the Role of the Cat's Heritage in Its Behavior*    3

2 Deceptive Packaging: *Stalking the Elusive Purebred*    45

3 A Home Within a Home: *Designing a Livable Space for Your Cat*    87

4 The Cat Keeper: *Psyching Out the Human Half of the Human-Feline Equation*    125

5 Friendly Persuasion: *Breaching the Human-Feline Gap*    167

PART II: Caring for and Living with Your Cat    205

6 Litter Box Roulette: *Troubleshooting the Number One Feline Problem*    207

7 Jungle Gymnastics: *Keeping Your Cat Physically and Mentally Fit*    247

8 A Loving Spoonful: *Selecting Healthy Feline Foods and Feeding Rituals*    289

9 Prevention and Cure: *Formulating a Feline Health-Care Plan*    331

10 Forever Feline: *Creating a Lifelong Living-Learning Program for You and Your Cat*    373

Index    411

# Introduction

Hal Archer's relationship with his cat began like many others'. "Talk about a rotten night!" he muttered to himself as he stood ankle deep in freezing slush, chipping ice off of his windshield in the airport parking lot. "What else can possibly happen?"

As if to answer his question, a scraggly cat the color of stale coffee emerged from beneath his car and studied him carefully.

"Just what I need. A darned stray," he grumbled, scrubbing the icy rain trickling down his neck with his sodden scarf.

Then for no good reason he could recall later, he turned to the cat and irritably demanded, "You could help, you know," whereupon the scruffy creature gracefully leaped onto the hood of the car and stared at him even more intensely.

Of course Hal took the cat home, where he christened her Mocha. During their 10 years together, Mocha shredded drapes and door frames and ruined Hal's leather chair. She also urinated in his closets and even once on his bed. Hal never knew whether she would eat the food he offered her or ignore both it and him. On several occasions, she bit his guests.

"All in all, I think we had a pretty normal relationship," Hal summed up for a friend who asked if he planned to get another cat after Mocha died. "But I just don't know if I want to go through all that again."

———————

Like cat ownership, authorship can be a surprising and challenging venture. About the only thing *CatSmart* shares with its predecessor, *DogSmart*, is the format. Both books first invite readers to take an intimate look at the wild and domestic species, and how breed, environment, and the relationship with the owner can affect an animal's health and behavior. Via a series of exercises, readers then evaluate their own unique pets, environments, and relationships. In the second half of the book, readers refine their personalized databases even more as they learn how to solve problems and select exercise, feeding, and health-care programs that will work best for them and their pets.

As in *DogSmart*, the prices quoted for products mentioned in this book represent a composite taken from catalogs (such as *The Pet Place*, *R. C. Steele*, *Jeffers*, *Pet Warehouse*, *Pet Solutions*, and *Cats, Cats, Cats*, among others—check for their ads in cat magazines such as *Cat Fancy* and *Cats*), pet stores, pet superstores, department stores such as Wal-Mart and K mart, supermarkets, and veterinary clinics. Most books mentioned are available from Direct Book Service's *Dog and Cat Book Catalog* (call 1-800-776-2665 or E-mail them at dgctbook@cascade.net for a copy). Finally, both *DogSmart* and *CatSmart* include information on pet disaster kits and how to perform an at-home physical, behavioral, and bond checkup.

While some of the information in *CatSmart* applies as well to dog owners, and cat owners can gain additional insights from *DogSmart*, cats constantly surprise us with their enigmatic natures as well as the endearing and frustrating ways they relate to us. Whereas many dog owners make a conscious choice to get a dog, and thus benefit from books that discuss all the factors that will ensure that they get the *right* dog, cats often have a habit of just falling into our lives.

What difference does it make? A huge difference. The way a cat arrives in its owner's life can profoundly affect the cat's health and behavior as well as the human-feline relationship. When Mocha magically appeared almost as if on cue, her arrival totally enchanted Hal. Even a cold, wet, grumpy skeptic must admit that fate or *something* special caused their two paths to intersect that dark, stormy night.

While such auspicious beginnings lend an alluring aura to even the most humble stray, such enchantment also may blind owners to remediable problems. When Mocha clawed Hal's furniture, soaked his belongings with her urine, ignored the gourmet food he offered her, and attacked his guests, Hal gave himself points for tolerating all of this.

"I don't like it at all," he told visitors to his home who commented on the destruction. "But what can you do? She's a cat." Then he'd relate the tale of how Mocha came into his life that fateful night. Other cat lovers would nod their heads in understanding: How could anyone not accept such a rare and wondrous creature, no matter how maddening her behavior? Noncat folks would do their best to keep from telling Hal that they thought he was crazier than his cat for putting up with her.

Because Hal got so caught up in Mocha's mystique, he completely overlooked the reality that underlaid her troublesome behaviors. She didn't claw his furniture to test his mettle for sainthood. Nor did she ruin his belongings with her urine to express spite or jealousy, or bite guests and ignore her food out of sheer meanness. All of these behaviors communicated important messages about her physical and behavioral needs that her owner missed. Because he overlooked these valuable clues, he made no attempt to fulfill her needs, and his tolerance doomed his cat to endure one treatable problem after another.

It's sometimes true that tolerating our pets' foibles can represent a loving response, but only if that tolerance results from knowledge of our cats' needs as well as our own. Had Hal understood Mocha's not-so-ancient solitary, territorial, and predatory wild roots, had he realized how her early life as a stray indelibly imprinted her with behaviors that would last a lifetime, he could have resolved all of her problems in no time.

As cat books go, *CatSmart* ranks far more in the "hard work" than "fluff" category. Some sections, such as those that ask you to analyze any financial, emotional, or physical limitations that may affect various aspects of your relationship with your cat, may make you feel uneasy.

"How much time can I spend caring for Mocha if she becomes seriously ill or injured?" Hal only briefly pondered the question before dismissing it. "I'll think about that when the time comes."

When the time did come, however, he wished he'd thought about it sooner.

Time and time again, the book will ask you to examine the source of your views about cats, their health and behavior, and your relationship with them: Are your beliefs and expectations based on solid knowledge about cats, or on some subjective assumption or emotion? If they result from the latter, the exercises in this book will help you to explore whether this approach works for you and your cat and, if not, how you can make positive changes.

Above all, this book celebrates the unique nature of every human-feline bond. It recognizes that good relationships exist between cats and working owners as well as between cats and folks who are home much of the time; that women and men may relate differently but equally well to cats; that the quality relationships between cats and older people, children, and singles may differ from each other as well as from those experienced by large families or people grappling with physical or emotional problems. How can we not celebrate a species with the adaptability to give so much to so many different people? How can we ever repay it?

As a dear friend once said, "Love isn't enough. It takes knowledge, too."

In *CatSmart* I hope to augment the myth and magic of cat ownership with fact and, in the process, to reveal a creature far more exquisite than we ever could imagine. This book is for anyone who ever thought about getting a cat. It's also for those whose cats enchant or trouble them, and maybe do both on occasion. And, finally, it's for a very special group of people, those who swore they'd never get a cat, or another cat, again.

"No way, forget it! Get that thing away from me!" Hal rants at the co-worker offering him the black-and-white puffball with the bright blue eyes. "Geez . . . would you look at the color of those eyes? Never saw anything quite like that. Mind if I hold him a minute?"

This one's for Hal, too.

# I

# *Understanding Your Cat*

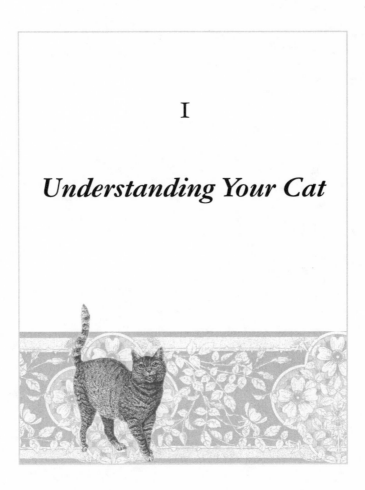

# I

# A Taste of Wildness

*Recognizing the Role of the
Cat's Heritage in Its Behavior*

When Rick Bashaw enters the brave new world of cat ownership, he approaches it with the same zest he invests in all of his activities.

"If I'm going to get a cat, I'm going to get a real cat," he announces to his neighbor, Kathy McNulty, as he scans a thick book on feline breeds.

After looking at all the pictures and reading the descriptions of the various breeds' qualities, he makes up his mind.

"It's got to be a Norwegian Forest cat." Rick's eyes glow with enthusiasm as he points to a picture of the massive creature. "Imagine a can-do cat like that right here in the city."

Kathy does imagine it, and her image doesn't quite match Rick's.

"Are you sure that's a good idea?" she asks. "There's not a lot for a cat like that to do in an apartment, plus you're gone most of the time."

"Don't be silly," Rick replies as he flips through a catalog of cat products. "I'll get it lots of toys to play with."

A few weeks later Rick gets Oslo, a three-month-old male Norwegian Forest kitten, and for the first six months man and cat live an idyllic life. Rick spends what little free time he has with his new pet and never tires of telling Oslo's many admirers about the kitten's roots in the rugged Norwegian terrain.

However, when Oslo reaches adulthood that spring, their sweet relationship turns sour. First, the cat begins waking Rick up in the wee hours of the morning, yowling plaintively, jumping at the windows, and digging his claws into the screens. Then he abandons his scratching post for the chair by the front door and then the door frame itself. Worse, Oslo starts climbing and spraying the drapes and knocking things off of shelves and counters in Rick's absence.

The final blow comes the day Rick's landlord phones him at work, shouting, "You get over here and do something about that blasted cat right now or you're outta here!"

When Rick arrives home, he encounters a knot of worried neighbors at his front door from behind which blood-curdling howls erupt periodically. When he enters the apartment, he finds Oslo rolled up in the living room window drapes, his claws caught in the loosely woven fabric. While Rick tries to free the terrified animal, the landlord storms into the room.

"What the . . ." The landlord's eyes bulge, and his face grows beet red as he surveys the havoc wreaked by the cat on the once immaculate apartment. His shouted obscenities further upset Oslo, who digs his newly freed claws into Rick's arm and neck before rocketing up and over his owner and out the door.

———————

In order to know if and how a particular cat will fit into a particular human life, we first need to explore the five most significant factors that influence the outcome of every human-feline interaction:

- the cat's wild heritage
- the cat's domestic breeding
- the human-feline environment
- human orientations toward cats
- the human-feline bond

We'll then discuss how to use this knowledge to prevent and treat the most common feline behavioral problem (not using the litter box), and to select exercise, feeding, and health-care programs that will best fit the needs of a particular cat and owner alike.

## Born to Be Wild

Building a mutually satisfying relationship with a cat begins with a knowledge of feline heritage. While this applies to our relationship with members of any species, it figures even more prominently in our relationship with cats because they pose three unique challenges to this process.

• A review of the studies of wild and domestic cats over the years makes it clear that the only certainty about cat behavior is its *uncertainty*. I blush with embarrassment at how confident I once felt about what constituted "normal" cat behavior. Now I realize that my confidence resulted from ignorance rather than knowledge.

• A comparison of wild and domestic cat behavior with that of other species quickly reveals a paradox: In many ways, cats rank as the tamest among the wild animals, and yet they remain the wildest among the tame. Given the thin, sometimes even nonexistent line between wild and domestic feline behaviors, we need to understand both.

• Cats rank as our most recently domesticated species. It would seem that the relative tameness of the ancestral wildcats should have predisposed cats to early domesticity, but exactly the opposite held true. Of all domesticated species, cats resisted human manipulation the longest. Moreover, depending on what sort of human manipulation we use to define "domestication," some scientists claim "domestic" cats aren't domesticated yet.

Before you read on, I'd like you to complete the first of a series of exercises designed to help you create a personalized database to assist you in your quest for an enjoyable, lifelong relationship with a cat. Because I'll ask you to refer to this information and expand or refine it throughout the book, I suggest you write down your answers.

Please bear in mind that no right or wrong answers exist. The goal of each of the exercises in the book is to help you evaluate your feelings about cats, any breed preferences, your environment, and the unique human-feline dynamics in your household so that you can avoid problems and choose the exercise, feeding, and health-care programs that will best meet your and your cat's specific needs.

## Wildcat Characteristic Check

List all the behaviors you like and dislike about cats. Do you think these characteristics apply to all cats? Do some apply only to wild ones? Do some apply only to domestic ones? Do you assign any specific characteristics to certain breeds? If so, list these breeds and those traits.

When Rick performs this exercise, he discovers he chose Oslo with no idea of wild or domestic cat behavior, let alone that of a purebred Norwegian Forest cat.

"I did want a real can-do cat," he admits with a sad shake of his head. "But since Oslo was a purebred, I thought he'd be fine indoors. It never dawned on me that he really was sort of a wildcat at heart."

In order to keep the domestic cat's wild heritage from ruining his human-feline domestic environment, Rick, like all other cat owners, needs to understand what domestication means to a cat.

# In the Company of Humans

Although we can't pinpoint the actual date of domestication for any animal species, leave it to the cat to generate the most controversy in this regard. Those who define domestication to mean an animal's willingness to associate with humans point to evidence found in some ancient graves near Jericho and set the date as early as 7000 B.C. On the other hand, those who define domestication as human possession and genetic manipulation surmise that this didn't occur until around 1600 B.C. Meanwhile, those who define domestication as the animal's dependence on humans for survival cite the burgeoning feral cat population consisting of abandoned pets and their offspring who fend for themselves without human assistance and claim we have yet to domesticate the cat at all.

Admittedly some owners may become involved in very needy human-feline relationships (more on this in Chapter 5), but most people's attraction to cats arises from the animal's willingness to associate with us at the same time that it retains an aura of self-containment. In other words, the idea that this animal allows us to approach it enchants us more than its dependence upon us. Rick's neighbor, Kathy McNulty, experiences the same awe he feels about the contrast between Oslo's stalking a spider and purring in his lap when she interacts with her Abyssinian, Ra.

Because this approachability or tamability plays such an important role in the human-feline relationship, we need to consider a pivotal study scientist Dmitry Belyaev conducted on silver foxes more than 30 years ago. Because the success of the Russian fox fur trade depends on humans' ability to handle these animals easily, Belyaev and his researchers set out to breed only those foxes that exhibited the most tameness.

To the scientists' surprise, however, mating the friendliest males with the friendliest females resulted in the creation of an entirely new animal. Not only did the offspring willingly interact with people like dogs, but as adults they looked and sounded different, too. They sported large ears and downy, tricolored coats, and yapped and whined like fox kits instead of full-grown animals. Also, like both domestic cats and dogs, the tamer foxes came into heat twice a year rather than annually like their wild cohorts.

This experiment revealed two important facts about animal development:

- When we breed strictly to change an animal's behavior, we automatically change its body. In other words, the animal develops as a mind-body unit.
- Breeding strictly for tameness freezes an animal in an immature state. The new foxes basically displayed the appearance and behavior of young kits.

When some people think of domestication, they think of it as a linear process humans pursue until they breed all remnants of wildness out of an animal. However, Belyaev's experiments establish the impossibility of this. Because the animal evolves and develops as a mind-body unit, as long as any remnants of the wild body type remain, the remnants of the wild mind will persist, too. In other words, as long as cats look like cats we can never eliminate their wildness completely.

"Why not?" asks Kathy as she pets Ra and mentally compares her immaculate apartment with Rick's battered home.

The answer is simple: the more a given behavior contributes to an animal's survival, the more firmly entrenched that behavior becomes. Normally we may see little obvious evidence of this, but in situations where the animal's domestic breeding doesn't provide the necessary wherewithal for survival, it will tap into these ancient reserves. Furthermore, the cat's relative newness on the domestic scene guarantees that it embodies more of its wild heritage than other domestic species.

Finally, although some people do desire to breed a totally human-dependent cat, much of the cat's allure lies in its reluctance to do our bidding. Feline ethologist (animal behaviorist) Paul Leyhausen goes so far as to suggest that, for all our talk about domesticating cats, in reality they domesticated themselves. He bases this suggestion on the lack of any historical evidence that proves humans deliberately planned to incorporate cats into their households.

"I spend all day working with people who come, sit, and stay on demand, and I'm one of them," Rick declares as Oslo ignores his owner in favor of a piece of paper flapping in the wind. "I want a pet with a mind of its own."

While many cat owners share Rick's sentiments, few want to live in cat-ravaged homes. Consequently, and in light of the cat's shallow domestic roots, it helps to understand where that wildness comes from and how it plays out in our own homes. In my experience, six wild feline behaviors create the most problems for contemporary cats in human society; cats have inherited the tendency to be:

- nocturnal
- territorial
- solitary
- predatory
- sexual
- maternal

Before we examine each of these to see how it contributes to the wildcat's survival, complete the following exercise:

## Wildness Evaluation

Consider any existing or potential cats in your life in terms of the preceding six characteristics. Which ones appeal to you? Which ones don't?

How much of your view comes from emotion? How much arises from solid knowledge of cat behavior?

When Rick and Kathy compare their answers, Rick discovers that while he attributes some of Oslo's behaviors—such as his tendency to stalk anything at the drop of a hat—to the cat's wildness, Kathy views those same behaviors in her own cat as a result of Ra's "playful" Abyssinian breeding. Given that the wildcat heritage goes back thousands of years and the modern Abyssinian breed didn't originate until the late 1800s, that's quite a discrepancy! Unfortunately for our relationship with the cat, time problems face us in other areas, too.

# The Feline Timetable

One of my favorite cat legends traces the domestic cat to a sensual liaison between a bored monkey and a lion during their long cruise on Noah's Ark. However, most scientists agree that *Felis silvestris* and *Felis silvestris libyca*—the small wildcats of Europe, India, Russia, Afghanistan, Pakistan, Iran, Iraq, Saudi Arabia, and much of Africa excluding the Sahara Desert—serve as the immediate ancestors of modern domestic cats, with the African wildcat, *Felis silvestris libyca*, contributing the lion's share to the domestic cat gene pool. Whereas scientists use the generic term "wild cats" to describe *any* wild members of the cat family, the term "wildcats" refers to a specific group of *small* cats found worldwide and from which the domestic cat evolved.

A breathtaking range of adaptability characterizes these wildcats. At least 15 different species roam Europe and the Middle East to Asia, inhabiting heath, evergreen and hardwood forests, rugged steppes, semideserts and deserts, and tropical jungles. Within a particular species, great variation also may occur. The African wildcat's striped tabby coat varies from dark gray to sandy gray-yellow, depending on whether it lives in the forests or drier areas. In addition to sporting coats that provide maximum camouflage and protection in a wide range of environments, wildcats worldwide exhibit a range of dietary preferences that ensures their survival in these diverse habitats.

Although cats can and do function in daylight, their physiology prepares them especially well for life in minimal light and what we humans consider total darkness. When cats hunt, they depend on both the food supply and the predator population. Small wildcats, sleeping in tree hollows or small caves during the day, neither compete directly for food with diurnal (light-preferring) species nor expose themselves to diurnal predators who might make a meal of them. Considering the wildcat's small size compared with many diurnal competitors and predators, this nocturnal strategy confers a definite survival advantage.

However, when a nocturnal domestic cat meets a diurnal human, problems may arise. Owner clashes with nocturnal feline behavior primarily involve one of three kinds of situations:

- stray, free-roaming adult animals
- barn kittens or others born in environments with little human interaction
- adult cats responding to the breeding season

Kathy adopted Ra from a local shelter after the Abyssinian's previous owners either lost or abandoned him in a nearby seaside resort community. The cat survived by raiding trash containers behind area restaurants and feeding on the rodents that congregated there at night. A few daytime run-ins with some irate restaurateurs further reinforced the stray cat's nocturnal habits.

Oslo, on the other hand, readily adapted to Rick's diurnal schedule until his first breeding season rolled around.

"But I had him neutered when he was six months old!" Rick protests.

Unfortunately for cat owners, the cat's territorial nature (more on this later) takes precedence over any reproductive urges, meaning that the mere presence of other cats, regardless of their age, sex, or reproductive status, will suffice to set some cats off. Thus, as soon as the local free-roaming cat population geared up for the breeding season, Oslo knew it. Perhaps he tuned in to ultrasonic "Come hither" or "Buzz off, creep" messages from other cats. Or maybe he picked up those same messages in the scent of cat urine wafting on the breeze.

"They can smell messages in urine?" Rick asks incredulously. "You're kidding!"

In fact, many animals can detect very powerful scent hormones called *pheromones* that convey a treasure trove of information even to the neutered, housebound cat who's never seen another cat since it left its mother and littermates. Moreover, the increased numbers and activity levels of cats outdoors at night during the breeding season increases the probability that these pheromones will alter the behavior of normally diurnal, housebound cats, too.

Regardless of the specific cause of the nocturnal behavior, most owners find it irritating to discover a cat perching on their heads trying to peer out the window at 2:00 A.M. Unfortunately, most owners either get up and feed the cat, hoping it will feel sufficiently grateful or satiated to let them alone, or punish it. Neither approach yields lasting results for the simple reason that both reward the unwanted behavior.

"How can punishing a cat reward it?" asks Rick as he hurriedly stashes the water pistol and rolled-up newspaper he uses to punish Oslo under a pillow.

In these late-night situations the cat seeks attention, and *anything* the owner does in response to the cat's behavior provides that. Consequently, only avoiding the cat will eliminate the behavior.

A few other changes also can help Rick to reset Oslo's clock. One, he can delay feeding his pet until last thing at night. Like many cats, Oslo sleeps after he eats. If Rick feeds Oslo when he eats his own dinner, the cat may nap afterward but then wake up ready for action in the dead of night.

Two, Rick could lock the cat out of his bedroom at night. If Oslo scratches at the door, he can put strips of double-sided tape on the door to prevent this (more on why this works later in the chapter).

Three, Rick could invest approximately $100 in a sound machine to help block out the sound of other cats outdoors as well as his own cat yowling indoors. Sound machines produce "white" noise which their manufacturers claim sounds like rain or rushing water. It also sounds a lot like static, until you get used to it, something most people do within two to three days. Because of this, some animals—and humans—respond just as well to a radio tuned to static as a sound machine. Regardless of the source, though, white noise blocks out many sounds and helps soothe animals upset by them.

Four, Rick can crate-train Oslo (a *lot* more on this in Chapter 3) so that Oslo perceives a pet carrier as his own private space. This will relieve Oslo of the burden of protecting Rick's entire home from all those free-roaming cats broadcasting their threats and desires.

Because the feline nocturnal nature can make itself known at any time, pause here and think about how you feel about the cat's unique sense of time.

---

## Feline Time Check

Think about your normal sleeping pattern. Are you a morning person or a night person? Do you work a swing shift? How does your cat's behavior fit into your schedule? If it doesn't, does this bother you? If you plan to get a new cat, when would you like it to be most active?

In addition to discounting Oslo's wild heritage, Rick forgot to ask about Oslo's previous lifestyle when he picked up his new kitten. It turned out that the Norwegian Forest cat's breeder liked to stay up into the wee hours of the morning, a schedule that served to enhance Oslo's own nocturnal nature. Oslo, of course, didn't see any of this as a problem—nighttime served as the perfect time for him to protect his domain, which was, after all, the name of the game.

## The Feline Domain

Because of its relatively recent domesticity, any cat may express other primitive behaviors in conjunction with nocturnal displays. This most commonly occurs when the cat feels vulnerable in its space for some reason. When Ra doesn't feel well, he retreats under the couch or Kathy's bed, coming out only at night to eat or drink, if then. He performs the same disappearing act when his owner introduces him to a new home or when a change occurs in her old one: a new baby or significant other—even a new rug or chair can upset him.

Why this occurs brings us to the three priorities that govern animal behavior:

- establish and protect the territory
- find food and water
- reproduce

While the cat's ultimate goal remains to add its genes to the species' gene pool, it can't do that until it finds enough food and water to support itself and any offspring. And it can't support itself and any offspring until it claims a space in which it can accomplish this goal successfully.

Imagine you're a small predator who hunts in little or no light at the same time others hunt you. What characteristics would best enable you to do this?

"You'd need to know your territory inside out, upside down, and backwards so you could locate any food as quickly as possible, as well as escape any predators," Kathy volunteers.

That's correct, and for us strongly visually oriented humans, that means noticing all of the critical landmarks, perhaps even drawing a map or taking pictures. However, such visual cues won't help us much if we need to make our way through that same space in the dark.

Although cats can see better in the dark than we can and also possess a much more highly developed sense of hearing, they don't rely much on vision or hearing to secure their space. Instead they utilize their incredible sense of smell for this purpose because scent cues work just as well in the dark as in the light and last longer than sound.

To mark their territories, cats use scent glands in their feet to lay down trails, and similar glands on the side of the face and head to mark significant vertical objects. In this way, they create a safe scent-corridor they can follow through even the most complex environment in pitch darkness if necessary.

Because cats rely on their feet to mark their territories, they like to keep them impeccably clean. This feline foot fetish gives rise to one of my favorite cat training aids: double-sided tape. (You can use loops of wide packaging tape sticky side out, but I find double-sided tape much easier to work with.) Suppose Rick wants to keep Oslo off the counter, for example. He blocks off all but a particularly tantalizing expanse of it with empty cardboard boxes, then tapes the remainder. When Oslo jumps onto the counter, he sticks, hates it, and decides to get down.

This approach offers several distinct advantages to screaming at, squirting, or smacking the cat. It works 24 hours a day, even in the owner's absence. It doesn't hurt the cat, and it creates a situation in which the animal *chooses* to stop the undesirable behavior. Not only do studies indicate that animals given a choice internalize any change faster, providing choices works particularly well with cats because unlike dogs and other pack animals, felines respond defensively rather than submissively to punishment.

In addition to secretion from scent glands, cats use urine, stool, and claw scratches to mark the boundaries of their territories. The pheromones in these secretions proclaim their species, sex, and reproductive status loudly and clearly to any other animal considering traveling through that space.

Although a wonderful system, scent marking has its limitations. Scent marks don't last forever, and it takes time and energy to refresh them. These limitations, however, become much less of a problem given another behavioral trait.

"The cat's solitary nature," Rick correctly surmises.

Because it takes time and energy to mark a territory, a smart cat marks a space only big enough to support itself and any young. Consequently, wildcats normally take a dim view of other cats in their space.

A cat's territorial and solitary natures, play such a synergistic role in feline behavior that I find it impossible to speak of one without mentioning the other. Did the cat's territorial nature lead it to become solitary, or vice versa? More likely the two characteristics coevolved over time.

Either way, there's no denying that the two behavioral traits exquisitely complement each other. In addition to diminishing the possibility of another cat's snatching a share of the limited food supply, the cat's solitary behavior reduces the chance that another cat's scent trails could confuse the resident cat as it avoids predators itself.

Within the domestic habitat where more and more cats share less and less space, two real-life incidents demonstrate what a critical role scent marking can play in feline interactions. In the first, the owner had two cats: Mable, a strict house cat, and Sable, who went in and out. Every time Sable would go out, he would immediately spray the boundaries of his territory and rub his head on prominent fence posts and trees around the yard where all the other neighborhood cats had rubbed their heads, too. When he returned home, Mable would viciously attack him, then suddenly stop and go about her business.

Although the owner feared that Mable suffered from a brain tumor, in reality the cat relied on scent to identify her feline companion. When Sable picked up the scent of other cats in the course of his own scent marking, he masked his own identity and fooled Mable into thinking that a strange cat had violated her turf when he returned. Whether the close contact during the ensuing fracas produced other scent, texture, or taste cues that triggered recognition, I don't know. I do know that when the owner washed Sable's face when he came in, that stopped the behavior for a totally unexpected reason: he hated having his face washed so much that he stopped going out!

A second thought-provoking and poignant case also involved two cats, Rose and Tulip, who had been inseparable since birth. When Tulip died suddenly at age eight, Rose retreated under the owner's bed and refused to budge.

Typically we view such cases almost romantically, saying the surviving cat grieves for the deceased one. However, I believe something far more logical—and insidious—came into play here. Because the two cats had been together from day one, I suspect Rose had no awareness of her own scent. Consequently, when Tulip died and her scent faded, Rose lost her own identity, too. Because she didn't recognize her own scent, she had to cope with two major territorial assaults simultaneously:

- the literal loss of her "other half"
- the existence of a phantom cat who went everywhere she did

Until Rose accepted the strange cat scent as her own, she barely ate or drank. Fortunately, however, this healthy, good-natured cat eventually adjusted.

Another variation on this theme may occur when one cat in a multiple-cat household leaves the household for a matter of hours or days. The ensuing attack rather than welcome upon its return may result because the cats maintain such a tenuous territorial peace that the stay-at-home cat(s) will immediately claim the departed cat's space, then view the returning animal as an intruder. Other times, scents picked up at the veterinary clinic, groomer's, or wherever else the traveling cat went may mask its identity. In the latter case, spraying all of the cats with the same scent (flea spray or a bit of the owner's cologne) may prevent the problem.

As we can see, while the feline territorial personality presents us with some of the most elegant and energy-efficient behavioral displays found in nature, it doesn't always translate into human-feline domestic bliss. Because your views of feline territoriality definitely will affect how you interact with your cat, you need to evaluate your own ideas about this primary feline behavior.

## Territorial Evaluation

Observe your own and friends' cats for signs of territorial behavior. Do certain cats appear to claim certain spots? Where are these places relative to the food and water? How do these animals react when others approach that space?

Oslo's intense animosity toward all cats, combined with his spraying and clawing of drapes and furniture near windows and doors, led Rick to correctly conclude that his pet claimed the entire apartment as his territory. On the other hand, Kathy's Abyssinian couldn't care less how many cats, dogs, or people Kathy brought home—as long as they didn't go into her bedroom. If they did, he'd either spray her bed to warn off the intruders or fight to defend the space.

In multiple-cat households, some cats may divide the space by room: "The den is Snowy's and Bourbon stays in our bedroom"—or by floor: "Hector's the upstairs cat, and Junie's the downstairs cat." Other cats will divide the house in layers, with one cat spending most of its time on the floor, a second preferring counters, lower shelves, and the backs of furniture, and the third opting for the higher terrain of closet shelves and the tops of bookcases. Indoor-and-outdoor cats in the same household may declare the entire house neutral and establish their separate territories outside; or one may claim the inside and the other the outside; or they both may claim spaces both outdoors and in. In households where cats feel comfortable with their territorial situation, the areas around the food, water, and litter box become neutral zones where the animals coexist peacefully. When cats don't feel comfortable in their territories, though, owners quickly become aware of the feline solitary nature.

## The Solitary Cat Pack

While some people doggedly insist on cramming the cat into a social behavioral mold like all other domestic species, cats just as doggedly—or rather, cattedly—refuse to conform. Because humans are social animals, often people can't comprehend what it means for a "pet" to live a solitary existence, a fact all those multiple-cat households clearly support. Even scientists who devote their lives to studying feline behavior don't claim to understand why cats interact with cats and other animals the way they do. Further complicating the picture, very few studies have been done on small wildcats, and we know nothing about the social behavior and organization of *Felis libyca*, the domestic cat's wild ancestor.

However, we do know that a solitary animal isn't *anti*-social. Obviously a strictly solitary animal could never survive because it wouldn't mate or raise its young. In reality, an almost mind-boggling degree of social diversity characterizes both wild and domestic feline behavior which, according to premier cat observer Paul Leyhausen, probably results from the cat's self-domestication.

By going this route, the cat became an opportunist capable of taking advantage of a wide range of conditions rather than a creature locked in to a rigid pattern of behavior. Other domestic species fall back on an ancestral social system when they become feral. Cats may as well, but they also may opt for a completely different form of interaction. Kathy's Abyssinian, for instance, originally lived with two other cats in a midtown apartment, but when his owners abandoned him on the beach he became a loner, an apparent reversion to his wildcat roots. Other owners tell of choosing a pet from among a herd of barn cats only to watch that animal viciously reject every subsequent cat they tried to add to their spacious quarters. Yet other people have taken in the local feline bully, who then becomes the beloved patriarch of the household's other three cats. Equally common, once-solitary house cats may join highly structured barn cat societies or loose gangs in warehouses or city dumps.

While the cat's incredible flexibility frustrates both scientists and those of us trying to understand and resolve feline behavioral problems, that flexibility does enable these animals to adjust to an equally incredible variety of social situations. Remember that establishing and protecting the territory is the cat's number one priority—taking precedence even over the necessities of finding food and water and reproduction. As a small predator as well as prey who can't count on the support of a pack or flock, the successful cat must have the elasticity to adapt to a wide range of environments both physically and behaviorally. While the cat *can* walk alone, it doesn't *have* to.

"Wait a minute!" Rick protests. "Are you saying cats can live in groups because they're solitary? That doesn't make any sense!"

It does make sense in the context of those three priorities. Animals establish and protect a territory in order to find food and water so they can reproduce. Given a limited food supply, maintaining a *relatively* solitary existence on a *relatively* exclusive territory provides the optimum solution. However, as the amount and availability of food shifts in either direction, associating with other cats might enhance the cat's chance of survival. If food becomes so scarce that the cat can't survive in its own territory, the ability to associate with another cat to ward off starvation would serve it well. Conversely, in a small area with a plentiful food supply a cat who could get along with other cats would fare better than a strictly solitary one.

A cat with social skills plus the ability to function as a solitary creature gains a distinct advantage over one born with either a strictly solitary or a strictly social orientation. Mating and rearing young would prove a trial for strictly solitary animals, and they also would suffer when the amount or location of food varied from the optimum necessary to maintain their solitary status. On the other hand, the purely social animal lacking solitary survival skills would become vulnerable when separated from the group.

Solitary animals also appear to internalize early lessons more quickly and strongly than social animals. This allows the queen (mother cat) to teach her young the basics of survival in a relatively short time, a tremendous advantage if she finds herself in a territory with a limited food supply. It also benefits the kittens, who learn to fend for themselves at an early age.

On the downside, while early internalization enables cats to learn and retain a great deal when kittens, it may create problems if these early lessons become so firmly entrenched that the cat resists beneficial changes as it grows older. This poses no problems for a kitten raised in an environment rich with varied experiences, even though it may face a life without a reinforcing pack to tell it right from wrong. However, the tendency to strongly internalize may result in permanent psychological damage for the stimulus- or learning-deprived animal. When this occurs in the wild, the animal can't adapt and it dies. When it occurs in the domestic arena, the animal requires a tremendous amount of often highly specialized support.

Because we humans rank as a social species and tend to view all members of the animal kingdom through our own eyes, we need to evaluate our feelings about solitary behavior carefully.

## Solitary Checkup

Think about the personality of the cat or potential cat in your life. Do you tend to prefer more social or more solitary feline qualities? What social or solitary behaviors attract you? Which ones bother you?

When Rick completes this exercise, he discovers that he really likes Oslo's more solitary characteristics.

"I couldn't deal with a clingy cat," he declares with certainty.

On the other hand, Kathy realizes that she merely tolerates Ra's solitary behaviors because she finds their social interactions so rewarding.

Even though Rick and Kathy view their pets' solitary natures quite differently, understanding why their pets act the way they do enables these owners to appreciate the full range of this unique feline characteristic. Once they do that, they then can tackle one of the cat's most troublesome behaviors, its predatory nature.

# The Killer Instinct

Once a cat has established and protected its territory, it turns to finding food. Hunting, killing, and eating other animals is as natural to a cat as breathing, no matter what we humans might think about it. Because evolution depends on predatory behavior, cat and mouse dance together for the benefit of both species. Furthermore, many ethologists no longer distinguish between predators who eat other animals and those who eat plants.

"Plants don't matter as much as animals!" cries Kathy, whose vegetarian diet results from her strong feelings for animals.

Maybe not to some people, but plants really do become involved in predator-prey relationships with animals that benefit plant and animal alike. However, for humans, relationships in which the predator is a bunny and its prey is a carrot don't carry the same emotional charge as predator-prey relationships between two animals.

When you ask cat haters why they don't like cats, the cat's distinction as a hunter almost invariably comes up. For all the times I've heard this complaint from cat haters (and even some cat lovers!), one particular cat hater stands out because he so perfectly typifies the peculiar hold this small creature has on even its greatest detractors.

Walt (not his real name) stopped by the clinic to speak to me about his dog one late November day. We ran into each other in the clinic parking lot where I'd just complimented another client on the beautiful tabby she was taking in for an examination.

Walt actually sneered at the woman's back.

"I hate cats because they're damn sneaky killers!" he snorted none too softly.

This all-too-common criticism came from a man heading off for a day of hunting, wearing full camouflage attire and leaning against his pickup with its requisite gun rack and high-powered rifle. The similarity between the man's clothing and the tabby's coat, and between his gun with its state-of-the-art scope and the cat's teeth, claws, and extraordinary perceptual ability almost made me laugh out loud. As much as that comparison tickled my funny bone, though, I knew Walt wouldn't appreciate it at all. I just smiled sweetly, answered his question about his dog, and retreated into the clinic to chuckle in private.

To some extent cats ask for such human contempt because, unlike dogs, who often hide their predatory natures under layers of breeding to perform more "civilized" functions such as herding or retrieving, cats remain killing machines at heart. In fact, some studies indicate that even among cats who have never seen a mouse, half will hunt the instant they set eyes on one, and many of the remaining nonhunters will quickly learn to hunt if placed with a hunting queen.

Some people abhor what they consider the domestic cat's in-your-face attitude toward hunting. Others congratulate themselves for overlooking this flaw in an otherwise perfect creature. Regardless of how we perceive this trait, we can't dispute that predatory behavior has made the cat what it is today. Only humans breed animals for functions other than those directly related to the animal's survival and well-being. Mother Nature can't afford that luxury any more than the wildcat can. Given the relative newness as well as the uncertainty of its domestication, why would a cat relinquish such a crucial survival skill, particularly since the human-offered genetic options (luxurious coats and folded ears) might confer survival *disadvantages* in the wild?

We don't know if cats ponder the political correctness of their predatory natures, but we do know that the classic feline hunting ritual consists of four basic steps:

- stalk
- pounce
- kill
- eat

Whether the cat progresses from one step to the next depends on how much stimulus it receives from the prey or the environment in the form of:

- sound
- motion
- odor

- texture
- taste

Equipped with hearing that picks up sounds in the ultrasonic range, Ra depends more on this sense to locate prey when he hunts in limited light or darkness. In the light, however, the prey's motion may first trigger the predatory dance.

Once Ra receives this first signal, he begins to stalk.

"And that irritates the heck out of me!" Kathy huffs. "He can eat a whole dish of food and five minutes later go out and stalk some poor little chipmunk."

While some people cite this behavior as proof of the cat's sadistic killer nature, in fact it provides the wildcat with a crucial survival advantage. Solitary hunters can't afford to wait until hunger overtakes them to seek food, for two reasons. First, it takes energy to hunt: the weaker the animal, the less apt it is to successfully locate and kill its prey. Second, even under the best of circumstances, cats catch their prey only about a third of the time. Consequently, if they can barely muster the energy necessary for one attempt, they probably won't be able to summon it for a second or third try.

Another reason cats stalk so readily generates the most controversy because it doesn't relate to finding food. Scientists studying different species note that predators will occasionally stalk and catch prey just to play with it. Paul Leyhausen tells of a female serval (a small wildcat) who caught a rat, carefully carried it to a crevasse, and repeatedly pushed it into the opening and fished it out again, completely disregarding stimuli from the rat that would normally propel the cat into the biting, killing, and eating steps of the predatory dance. In a variation on this theme, my shorthaired tabby, Whittington, takes great delight in hiding under the couch and waving however much tail it takes to attract the notice of a passing dog. He "fishes" for my hound and Welsh corgi from within his "cave" every bit as expertly as Leyhausen's serval.

While any cat owner who observes this type of display will readily define it as play, such a definition makes many scientists nervous. According to the long-established rules of animal behavior, animals don't really play: anything that looks like play merely reflects an attempt to master serious skills such as hunting or mating. To imply that an animal might do something simply for the joy of it prompts accusations of anthropomorphism, the highly unscientific projection of human thoughts and emotions on animals.

However, proof of how much the amount of stimulation governs play-versus-predatory-behavior lies as close as the nearest cat and cat toy. When Rick drags a felt mouse tied to the end of a string close enough to stimulate Oslo visually, the cat begins to stalk. When Rick flicks the toy a little, Oslo pounces and pins it with his front claws. Rick's tug on the pinioned toy stimulates the Norwegian Forest cat to dig his claws into it and bite it. A vigorous yank causes him to try to tear the mouse apart.

In this example, increasing motion propels the cat through the predatory cycle. More commonly, owners, prey, and/or the environment consciously or subconsciously add sounds, odors, textures, and tastes into the process, too. Even the most pacifistic owner of the most placid cat will laugh when the animal plays with its favorite toys, and feline toy preference doubtless relates to the object's odor, texture, and taste.

"You talk about wild animals conserving energy, but it seems to me this predatory dance business wastes a lot," Rick observes after a vigorous play session with Oslo.

In reality, the dance conserves energy because a decrease or lack of stimulus can abort the hunt just as quickly as additional stimulation can drive it forward. If Rick stimulates Oslo to stalk the toy, then freezes, the cat quickly loses interest and seeks some other form of amusement. Were predation a strictly on-or-off phenomenon, the cat would feel compelled to continue the unproductive game/hunt.

This predatory response also assures that prey with the sense to freeze when they spot a predator may survive. I've seen Whittington stalk chipmunks only to "lose" them when they summon the wherewithal to remain motionless rather than flee. Given a still day or a position downwind from the cat, a savvy rodent can safely freeze less than a few feet away from an oblivious feline. Then it becomes a matter of outwaiting the cat.

The stimulus-driven predatory sequence also involves appetite and quality control. When we talk about what drives Oslo from stalking to eating his prey, we're really talking about what stimulates his appetite. This aspect of normal feline behavior can precipitate all sorts of feeding problems for the domestic cat, many springing from its erroneous reputation as a fussy eater (which we'll discuss in Chapter 8).

However, such a system could benefit the cat in the wild. While wildcats will scavenge if necessary, most prefer live food. Conceivably, the amount of energy the prey exerts to avoid capture serves as a good indicator of its general health. The more vigorous the prey, the greater its nutritional value to the predator.

Although fewer and fewer people can relate to this from personal hunting experience, most can imagine going fishing. Suppose when Kathy does this, she imagines a fish languorously swallowing her baited hook and going belly up. What runs through her mind?

"That I'd rather die than eat that fish!" Kathy says with a laugh. "It was too easy, and no matter how good that fish looks, I bet there's something wrong with it."

So, even though Kathy claims that she, herself, could never hurt a fly, she can appreciate how eons of evolution enabled both predator and prey to develop patterns of behavior that benefit them both. Given the facts, how do you feel about the cat's killer instinct?

## Killer Instinct Evaluation

Consider your feelings about predatory behavior. Do they arise from emotion or knowledge? Do or could any strong negative feelings about feline predatory behavior affect your existing or future relationship with a cat? If you already own a cat, how do your beliefs about predatory behavior affect it? If you keep your cat indoors, how does it fill the time it otherwise would spend pursuing this strong feline drive? Do you play games with your cat, or does your cat make up its own games to provide an outlet for its predatory nature? How do you intend to fulfill this need in any new cat?

Like many other cat owners, Kathy takes an out-of-sight-out-of-mind approach to Ra's predatory nature. She knows he hunts when he goes out, but as long as she doesn't see him and he doesn't bring trophies home for her inspection, she ignores this aspect of his personality. On the other hand, when Rick realizes what a strong hunting instinct Oslo possesses, he begins hiding dry food in bags and boxes around the apartment for his pet to "hunt."

But will these owners find it as easy to ignore or respond to their pets' sexual natures?

# The Freudian Feline

Once wildcats establish and protect their territories and find food and water, they turn their attention to their ultimate goal: reproduction. Unfortunately, we know very little about how wildcats mate and rear their young. As humans continue to threaten their territories, wild animals get caught in a no-win situation. Those who withdraw and become even more reclusive limit their chances of attracting a mate and successfully raising their young in their ever-shrinking habitats. Those who adapt to the human presence may attract more mates, but unfortunately these mates may be domestic cats rather than other wildcats. While such interspecies breeding may enable individual wildcats to survive, it dilutes the gene pool and further undermines the chances of survival for the wild species.

Conversely, a fair amount of information about barn and feral cat reproductive strategies does exist, but it does more to substantiate the cat's tremendous range of diversity rather than define any specific feline sexual behaviors. Not only may feral, barn, and strict house cats behave differently, but also different groups of these cats may display behaviors quite different from those of similar groups in other areas. Regardless of what particular mating strategy a cat uses, though, it would probably curl the hair of any Victorian.

Even though the majority of pet owners don't intend to breed their cats and therefore have them neutered before they mature sexually, sexual behavior nonetheless may play a prominent role in the human-feline relationship, for two reasons. First, even neutered animals may respond to the breeding season. Second, because of their solitary natures, cats may respond to people as sexual partners, as well as mothers. Both situations can precipitate health and behavioral problems which a knowledge of the basics of feline sexual and maternal behavior can help prevent or treat.

"What does the cat's solitary nature have to do with how it perceives people?" Kathy asks. "After all, both social and solitary animals mate and raise young."

Although cats may form very elaborate social systems, their solitary heritage leads them to relate most intimately to other cats at two times in their lives: when they mate and when they nurse. While the social structure of feline littermates has some characteristics in common with that of dogs and other pack animals, cats don't need to depend on each other the way more social animals do.

Unlike female dogs, who come into heat approximately every six months anytime during the year, female cats collectively come into heat at the same time, usually with a primary breeding season that begins in the late winter and another, shorter one that occurs in the fall. I say "usually" because this varies from area to area and cat to cat. It also depends on the cat's lifestyle. Data from studies of free-roaming feral intact (unneutered) cats indicate more seasonality in these animals than in housebound purebred ones.

"What do domestic cats gain from going into heat at the same time?" Kathy asks. "I can see wildcats doing it so they give birth when there's plenty to eat, but domestic cats don't need to worry about that."

Kathy makes a valid point. Synchronous heat cycles offer other advantages, too, however. Cats are induced ovulators, meaning that it takes several copulations to stimulate them to ovulate. During the first days of the heat, they call (and are sexually attractive to) males, but they won't mate. Once females begin accepting males, cat sex moves rapidly from the G- to X-rated realm. A great deal of mounting (10 to 20 times a day) occurs, with or without the males penetrating the females and with or without the males inseminating the females when they do.

While the mere thought of all this copulating would make my dear departed Grammy swoon, it does serve some beneficial, albeit not fully understood, purpose. Some ethologists speculate that these multiple attempts stimulate ovulation; others say the behavior reinforces the social structure necessary to keep cats together long enough to mate. In feral animals, such mating seasons provide the most energy-efficient method for females to secure the best sires for their offspring, and for males to spread their genes in a short, admittedly often intense, time frame.

As if the numbers of mates and mating encounters alone didn't violate any Victorian sense of propriety, cats also gain distinction for the sheer exuberance of their sexual liaisons. Females yowl, crouch down, and tread with their hind feet, roll seductively, and brazenly throw themselves at male cats (or men's ankles, dogs, stuffed toys, or even table legs if no tomcats happen to be available). Males scream and viciously fight with other males, including those of other species in some cases. Some toms stay close to the female, if possible, while others merely make a brief mating stop on their way through her territory.

During pseudo- or actual copulation, the male holds the female by the neck, slides down her body (some say to get his normally backward-facing penis facing the right direction), and also treads with his back feet. Following copulation, the female lets out a blood-curdling scream and lashes out with claws extended at the male, who, also with some screaming and hissing, leaps away. Then she blissfully rolls around in the "after reaction" which appears quite similar to the catnip response. The male may or may not stay with her for another round. Although some people say the female screams in response to the pain caused by the male's barbed penis when he retracts it, the after reaction indicates that, if this is the case, she quickly gets over it.

Given these sexual practices, we can appreciate how problems may arise when cats view their owners as their mates. Consider what happens to Kathy when she rhythmically strokes Ra from the top of his head to the base of his tail. At first the Abyssinian appears ecstatic, purring and arching his back. However, if she continues, he'll suddenly grab her arm and hold her hand with his teeth.

Although these hardly seem like loving gestures, they make sense to the cat. If Kathy's rhythmic stroking elicits shadows of normal reproductive behavior, Ra responds by gripping her in the feline version of an amorous embrace. At this point, Ra perches on the very thin line separating normal feline sexual and predatory behaviors, and Kathy's reaction, not Ra's, will determine what happens next. If Kathy jerks her hand away and screams, that increased motion and sound will propel the cat from the sexual and predatory "hold" mode into the predatory "pinion and bite" mode. If she freezes, however, she may see an amazing transformation. The cat who appeared demonically possessed with his ears back and his pupils fully dilated slowly begins to relax. His ears come up, his pupils return to normal size, his jaw goes slack, and he lets go. Some cats will even shake their heads as if coming out of a trance and stagger off.

I recommend that owners use setups to extinguish this type of behavior if it occurs, even though they can avoid triggering it by not stroking the cat in that manner. This recommendation comes from years of dealing with owners who get in trouble because they carry a lot of rules around in their heads that begin, "Fluffy's a great cat as long as you don't . . ." Nine times out of ten when Fluffy nails someone, it's someone who forgot or didn't know the rules. Because others may not grasp or forgive the cat's little quirks as readily as the owner, it's safer to eliminate the behavior altogether.

Extinguishing the unwanted behavior involves using a setup in which the owner strokes the cat in the inciting way, then freezes when the animal clamps. Because only the bravest (or the most foolhardy) person can resist the urge to react when cat teeth sink into his or her flesh, I ask anyone doing this to don however many layers of whatever clothing it takes to feel absolutely safe handling the cat. For some this means leather gloves and jacket, jeans, and leather boots. One client added a catcher's mask while another opted for two pairs of jeans and gloves. Forget about looking silly. Focus on consistently responding to the cat in a neutral manner until you extinguish the negative behavior.

In a variation on this theme, Ra launches himself at Kathy when she walks across the room, biting her ankles or the back of her leg. While the ankle-biting appears more predatory than sexual, the way Ra holds her leg hints strongly at sexual motivation.

Because of the sneaky nature of these attacks, I add double-sided tape to the owner's ensemble in this situation. A well-protected Kathy covers her ankles and jeans from the knee down with the tape, then saunters seductively through the room. When Ra attacks, she freezes. Now, in addition to not receiving any stimulation from his owner to drive the reaction from the sexual into the predatory mode, Ra sticks to the tape. Granted, domesticated cats in such situations may work with mere shadows of normal feline sexual and/or predatory instinct. However, in my experience even a cat with the most shadowy grasp quickly realizes that something has gone dreadfully wrong and it had best disengage itself quickly. One habitual leg-grabber found his first encounter with the tape so distasteful, that he'd take off running when he saw or heard his owner tear off a piece of any kind of tape for any purpose!

A final twist of cat sex has tangled up more than one owner of a purebred cat. In this situation, the cat identifies so closely with the owner as its mate that the idea of having sex with another cat simply doesn't compute. Breeders tell tales of hours spent trying to shoo, cajole, bribe, and otherwise entice one cat to mate with another while the cats view each other with horror or disgust. That image seems ludicrous given the ribald orgies in which cats of more lowly breeding routinely engage, but it makes sense given the cat's maternal as well as sexual nature. However, before we delve into that, ask yourself some questions about cat sex.

## Sex Check

Once again review your image of any existing or future cats. Do any of the positive or negative behaviors on your list derive from feline sexuality? How do you feel about that? If you plan to breed your cat, how much do you know about feline breeding in general, and breeding your specific cat in particular?

Kathy definitely links some of what she considers Ra's more troublesome biting behaviors to his sexual nature. However, Rick notices only the sudden increase in Oslo's territoriality during the breeding season when many more cats roam the apartment complex. Like many other cats, Oslo considers their mere presence a territorial violation, an intrusion that concerns him far more than their reproductive status. However, none of this may prevent Ra and Oslo from viewing their owners as their moms.

# Mother Love

With its other primary drives fulfilled, the wildcat concentrates on producing and raising the next generation. Scientists assume most small wildcats give birth and raise their young in solitude, primarily because their ever shrinking habitat and numbers makes this the better survival strategy. However, in large collections of barn or feral cats, females may form their own society and even take care of one another's kittens.

Whether raised only by their mother or by her and other adult female cats, kittens enter a social world in which they interact with at least their mother and any littermates. Because the queen nurses the kittens during this period, it seems reasonable that the young associate social interaction with a readily available, reliable food supply. And, in fact, as the kittens depend less and less on their mother for food, they becomes less tolerant of each other.

During the first month of life, the kitten gets itself up and running. It comes into the world with a keen sense of smell and acute awareness of changes in pressure (called the tactile sense), exactly the senses it needs to locate the queen's breast and obtain milk. Once there, it uses its front paws to knead or tread on the breast, presumably to stimulate milk secretion. These senses, as well as its awareness of heat and cold, dominate the kitten's life during the first two weeks.

It seeks out its mother not only for nourishment, but also for warmth because it can't regulate its own temperature at this stage of development.

Many times these early kitten-queen interactions carry over into human-feline interactions. Oslo sits on Rick's lap while Rick strokes the cat's head and watches television. Suddenly Oslo's claws dig into Rick's thighs. Rick swears, leaps to his feet, dumps Oslo onto the floor, and rants about the cat's "vicious, unprovoked attack." More likely, though, Rick's stroking elicited Oslo's memories of the maternal grooming that occurred while he nursed. In response to this he began kneading, spreading his toes and digging his claws into Rick's thighs.

The sense of smell becomes fully developed by three weeks of age, followed by the sense of hearing a week later. Kittens respond to sounds by the fifth day and turn toward sounds in the environment around day 12. By the fourth week, they respond to sounds the same way adult cats do. Visual development lags the other senses somewhat, with the kittens' eyes remaining closed until roughly seven to ten days of age. Although visual development is pretty much completed by the end of the first month, too, the kittens' eyes don't completely clear for another week, and improvement in detail vision continues for another two to three months.

A fascinating glimpse of the role the environment plays in the cat's sensory development comes from a study of feline brains conducted by Robert Williams, Carmen Cavada, and Fernando Reinoso-Suarez. After the researchers determined that the brain of the average pet cat weighed 20 to 30 percent less than that of a wildcat of comparable size, they focused on the retina of the cat's eye. There they discovered that, while both wild- and domestic cats begin life with about a million retinal ganglion (nerve) cells, domestic cats lose all but about 160,000 of theirs by adulthood.

"You mean domestic cats lose almost 80 percent of their visual potential by living with us? That's terrible!" Kathy exclaims.

Maybe, maybe not. Granted it might mean that the average pet lives such a stimulus-deprived life compared with its wild counterparts that retinal ganglia and other sensory cells wither and die from lack of use. On the other hand, cutting back on sensory input also might serve as an excellent survival strategy for an animal bombarded by stimuli over which it has no control. Imagine looking out your window and seeing six times more detail and motion than you see already. Also imagine that your capacity to hear and smell all the sounds and scents in the average city or suburban environment increases to six times its current range and intensity. Most likely that would create a stimulus overload—and all the physical and behavioral problems that go with it. For people, that might mean ulcers or alcoholism; for cats it might mean chronic digestive problems or neurotic licking.

About the time kittens complete their basic sensory and physical development at four weeks of age, the queen begins bringing prey home and the kittens begin playing with it and each other. As new theories of play in both animal and human behavior emerge, it appears that the more we need to learn, the more we need to play. And young kittens do play! Then, by five weeks, they begin to kill the prey, and weaning begins. Prior to this time the mother has initiated most of the nursing sessions, but now the kittens seek out an increasingly resistant four-legged, fur-covered milk supply.

Most queens wean their kittens by seven weeks but continue nursing longer, sometimes for months. Why they do this probably relates to the fact that nursing perpetuates the social mindset that can benefit both queen and kittens in certain situations. For example, kittens living in harsh environments or hunting limited or elusive prey may need more time to learn the necessary survival skills. Kittens born into feral or barn cat populations may need additional time to develop the social skills required to get along with the group. Queens need the social mind-set nursing creates to teach their young all this.

A possible consequence of such behavior in the pet cat arena takes the form of wool-sucking. Depending on which report you read, wool-sucking is primarily a Siamese cat problem, probably caused by a lack of something in the diet, or a neurotic, compulsive behavior related to stress or an imbalance in certain brain substances. Treatments include changes of diet, dietary supplementation, behavioral therapy, and/or psychotherapeutic drugs. According to some reports, untreated wool-sucking cats will consume large quantities of wool and possibly die.

Based on personal experience and conversations with numerous cat owners, I'm convinced that the problem can affect cats of all breeds and that they may suck almost any kind of fabric. In 25 years I've yet to hear of a cat dying from a wool ball, although I suspect it could happen under certain circumstances. For example, suppose a kitten views sucking as perfectly normal behavior, because it also views the owner as its mother. Suppose, too, that the kitten doesn't feel quite comfortable in its human-centered environment; it wants and needs to learn more. Both of these feline orientations would send a strong message to the kitten to continue nursing. Barring the presence of a willing human to suck on, the kitten turns to something that either reminds it of its real mother (such as wool or another animal) or carries the intimate scent of the owner (such as pajamas or the baby's blanket—two common targets).

If the owner swats and yells at a kitten for sucking, that angry response puts the cat in a real bind because stopping the behavior runs counter to its most basic instincts.

So, what does the cat do? It may become what I call a closet sucker. Instead of relieving any tension by purring, kneading, and sucking on the object and drifting contentedly off to sleep, it waits until the owner leaves, then sucks with a vengeance. Under these circumstances, the cat tears at rather than gently sucks the fabric and could swallow enough material to create a blockage.

Most cats whose owners accept the behavior as normal and give the cat something acceptable to suck outgrow the habit by 12 to 18 months. I've owned two suckers in my life, one a barn cat kitten who sucked the fringe off a wool carriage blanket and the cotton cuff of my son's pajamas, and Whittington, a shelter kitten, who sucked and still occasionally sucks my hound's ear. Both of these kittens' mothers lived in complex environments where delayed weaning likely enhanced their offspring's survival. I don't see anything abnormal about their behavior at all.

While kittens between the ages of four and eight weeks engage in all kinds of play with their mothers and littermates, by the end of that period their focus shifts from each other to potential prey and/or inanimate objects. By three months of age, social play begins to decrease markedly, and some littermate interactions can become downright vicious.

A former cat of mine named Maggie made it crystal clear just how thoroughly a queen teaches, as well as passes on the desire to teach, her young these lessons, particularly to her daughters. Although neutered, Maggie tried desperately to teach others to hunt. I became her favorite student (or "kitten"), and she brought me an assortment of dead rodents in hopes that I'd learn the lesson. I, however, picked these teaching aides up by the tail and winged them into the woods.

After several months of this, Maggie evidently decided she needed to speak to me in my own language. But first, consider a few background details. I live in an old farmhouse with a basement wall that consists of mortarless slabs of granite and stone, a convenient entry point for any animal willing to risk an encounter with any resident cat. My kitchen counter contains a built-in chopping block that I routinely use to prepare meals. My daily ritual includes getting up before dawn to have time to write, and taking the dogs out before I turn on any lights (so I can see the stars). Then I go to the counter, turn on the light, and put the kettle on for tea.

On one particular morning, I performed this same ritual, only when I turned on the light my eyes fell on a plump rat neatly laid out on my chopping block like a Thanksgiving turkey ready for stuffing. While I stood there gawking and trying to decide whether to scream or laugh, Maggie wrapped herself around my legs, purred loudly, and looked up at me expectantly. Call me anthropomorphic, but I could almost hear that cat saying, "Hey, dummy, do you get it?" While she obviously felt inordinately pleased with herself, I didn't share her enthusiasm in the least, any more than I enjoyed winging the large rodent into the woods to join all the other dead bodies, or scrubbing my chopping block with bleach in the wee hours.

My unfeline display earned me a most disgusted look, but Maggie didn't give up. When I got Violet, my corgi, several months later, Maggie spent six weeks trying to teach the dog to hunt. Every day she'd bring home a dead mouse and drop it at Violet's feet. When the dog didn't get it, she tried a few with a little more life in them. The final blow came the day Violet happily trotted after the staggering mouse, loudly yipping and barking instead of silently stalking it. Maggie gave the dog the same disgusted look she'd given me, picked up the mouse, and took it back outside. From that day on, she treated the dog like a toy to bait and play with rather than as an equal, the same way she treated me.

Whether compelled by knowledge of the importance of maternal training or by personal experience, more and more breeders don't place kittens in new homes until they reach 12 to 16 weeks of age. Like just about everything else associated with cats, this practice elicits both boos and hurrahs. Those against it say we need to get kittens into human households during that period of maximum socialness around six to eight weeks so the animals can adapt to a social human environment. Those in favor of the delay say it takes a kitten 12 weeks to properly develop its sense of catness. I'll ride the fence here and say it depends on the cat and the breed. However, the feline sense of self as it affects the animal's health and behavior does concern me a great deal.

Consider what happened to Rick and Oslo. When Rick got Oslo at 12 weeks of age, the Norwegian Forest cat already possessed a pretty solitary view of life. While this normally would have increased his ability to cope with a greater range of environmental challenges, the fact that he was locked up in a two-bedroom apartment in a neighborhood teeming with cats produced the opposite effect. Oslo could see, hear, and smell these other cats from within his confined quarters, and those perceptions generated a tremendous amount of tension and frustration. This manifested as behavioral problems, but it could have precipitated urinary, digestive, or other stress-related medical problems just as easily. In this case, a strong, more solitary feline sense of self didn't serve this particular animal well at all.

At the opposite end of the spectrum, equally troubling problems may arise when we separate kittens from their mothers and littermates too soon. An extreme example of this occurs when well-meaning but naive people believe they can raise an orphan kitten without feline help. They don't realize that the queen's interactions with her young encompass a whole world of perceptions and skills, and that these involve sounds, sights, odors, textures, tastes, and other aspects of catness beyond human perception and comprehension. Not only that, queens also teach their young which input to address and which they can safely ignore. They also teach them what I think of as the Lesson of Degree: whether to hold or bite, and how hard to bite under what circumstances; when to freeze (versus run or fight) when frightened; when to be social, when to go it alone. A human raising a kitten can't begin to teach it all this because we remain oblivious to the complexities and subtleties of the feline world.

Consequently, kittens raised without the benefit of a good cat teacher who can imbue them with a strong sense of catness may resemble learning-disabled or even autistic children. Such learning-deprived cats live in a world assaulted by stimuli with which they can't cope because no one taught them how. An ultrasonic message from another cat overwhelms them: they overreact because they don't know how to temper their responses. All the owner sees, however, is a cat who suddenly appears possessed, who lashes out screaming and hissing when the owner tries to comfort it. "Poor baby," they say. "Thank God I rescued you. You never could have made it on your own."

While lack of feline guidance can inhibit the development of some cats' sense of self, other cats seem to be born without a clue when it comes to even the most rudimentary aspects of catness. Show them a mouse or a litter box and they stare at you dumbly or run and hide. The fact that some of these animals also react that way to their own kittens suggests that catness is an inherited as well as learned quality. Though a wild animal born into a pack possibly could gain this information over time while other pack members support it, such a wildcat never could survive on its own. On the other hand, such domestic cats do exist because some people prefer this type of animal.

This behavior may seem bizarre, but it does follow a certain logic. Recall Belyaev's foxes: the tame animals responded to people with the same lack of fear with which they responded to each other. Put another way, domestication reduces the sense of self. If we take a species like the cat initially born with a very weak sense of its solitary nature and domesticate it on top of this, we can understand how it might easily view a person as its mother and/or mate or seek to mother that person. Breed it for even more human dependency and such a cat could understandably expect its owners to show it how to use the litter box. And, in fact, I know owners of several such animals who had to do exactly that. Similarly, we can appreciate why these eternal kittens would feel reluctant to mate, let alone care for any resultant kittens. How do you feel about this?

## Feline Maternal Evaluation

This time apply all you've learned about feline maternal behavior to your list of positive and negative cat characteristics. Do the behaviors you view as positive make for an outgoing cat or a more dependent one? Why do the negative feline behaviors bother you? Could they negatively affect the cat's health and/or behavior? Could they make you feel uncomfortable?

When Rick performs this exercise, he decides to take a more tolerant view of Oslo's sucking and even gives the cat his sweatshirt to sleep on and suck in his absence. Kathy discovers that her own highly maternal views would lead her to take a kitten away from its mother too soon, just because she wants the "fun" of raising it.

When we understand the combined effects of the cat's nocturnal, territorial, solitary, predatory, sexual, and maternal behaviors, it's impossible not to admire the efficiency of the feline system. The cat comes to us possessing a repertoire of basic behaviors as elegant as the classic "little black dress" which it dresses up or down depending on the situation. The basic neck hold at its gentlest permits the queen to retrieve the straying kitten or move her litter to cleaner or safer quarters, and it enables kittens and cats to play with each other or other creatures with a touching tenderness. Increase the intensity and that same hold becomes the passionate lover's clasp. Boost it even more and the clasp becomes the territorial competitor's or predator's death grip. Treading or kneading with the front paws to stimulate milk flow gives way to treading of the back feet during sexual encounters. Roll the contented cat in a social mode on his back and he'll flatten out and gently hold your wrist and press his hind paws softly against your arm while he lovingly licks your hand. Do the same thing to a cat who considers you a mate and he'll try to right himself, grip your wrist more firmly with his front paws, hold your hand with his teeth, and tread on your lap. Try the same maneuver with a cat who views you as territorial violation, and he'll dig his front claws into your wrist, rake your arm with the back ones, and bite you. Maddening though all these variations can be, it's impossible to deny the exquisite method behind the madness.

Given all the variations that the domestic cat's wild heritage contributes to its relationship to us, it's hard to believe that the development of breeds could add even more variety, but it does. Not only that, as we'll see in the next chapter, the legends that surround cat breeds give this aspect of feline evolution its own set of inscrutable quirks, too.

# 2

# Deceptive Packaging

## *Stalking the Elusive Purebred*

As soon as Kevin and Marcy Longstreet see the white mittens on the feet of the solidly built cream-colored cat with the dark brown ears, mask, legs, and tail, they fall in love with her.

"She's gorgeous!" Marcy exclaims to the clerk standing beside the animal's cage. "I've never heard of a Birman."

"The name means 'Sacred Cat of Burma,'" the clerk explains proudly. "The people there believe that the souls of their dead holy men return to the temple in the form of these cats."

"What about the white feet?" asks Kevin.

"According to legend, a priest named Mun-Ha was killed as he prayed before the statue of Tsun-Kyan-Kse, the blue-eyed goddess in charge of priest-to-cat conversions. Mun-Ha's cat, Sinh, put his paws on his dead master's body and turned to the statue of the goddess. When he did, his white coat turned gold, his yellow eyes became blue, and his legs became brown, except for his feet which remained white because Mun-Ha's soul was so pure."

"Wow, that's really something!" Kevin studies the cat with even more admiration. "What are those white kittens in the next cage?"

"Those are Birman kittens," the clerk tells him. "Would you like to hold one?"

Several months later when the Longstreets attend a party at Marcy's employer's home, the subject of cats comes up. Naturally, Marcy tells everyone about Sing-Too, their Birman.

"Oh, I just love that solid brown color," remarks one of the guests.

"No, no, you're thinking about Burmese," chimes in another guest, trying to set the record straight. "Marcy got one of those longhaired Siamese."

"No, I think that's a Himalayan," someone else remarks. "Except they don't have white feet."

"Well, if it has blue eyes, white feet, and long hair, it must be a Ragdoll," announces someone else. "Except I never heard anything about Ragdolls being associated with dead monks."

Kevin and Marcy look at each other in confusion.

"But the clerk at the pet store . . ." Marcy starts to explain.

"You bought a kitten from a pet store?" screams her boss's wife. "How could you!"

Months later the memory of the event still makes Marcy shudder.

———————

Even though some scientists question whether we can even consider the cat domesticated, that hasn't stopped cat fanciers from developing an amazing array of feline breeds. It's not surprising that paradox attends this process. On the one hand, cats appear more than capable of surviving on their own by virtue of their solitary natures and strong survival skills; on the other hand, breeders work feverishly to develop and per-petuate cats with a distinctive look and personality—character-istics we humans find visually and emotionally appealing—rather than with characteristics that would enhance the ani-mal's survival. Not only that, even though breeders say they breed for personality as well as physical appearance, purebred show standards judge only body parts. Out of a total 100 points, the Cat Fanciers Association's Birman show standard allots 65 for head, body type, and coat, and the remaining 35 for eye and coat color. The result is that breeders take an animal with a very strong sense of survival and essentially turn it into an ornament.

"You think that's wrong?" Kevin asks as he eyes the gorgeous creature lounging on the windowsill.

Forget rightness or wrongness and instead consider how these paradoxes affect the animal's health, behavior, and relationship with its owners. Each purebred cat comes to us not only with the wildcat's heritage and incredibly adaptable behavioral repertoire, but also with traits wittingly or unwittingly bred into it by humans.

In addition to that, modern purebred cats represent works in progress in every sense of the phrase. When a co-worker says the word "Siamese" to Kevin Longstreet, he automatically thinks of crossed eyes and kinked tails, two defects theoretically bred out of the breed years ago. Unfortunately, not only didn't some breeders get the message, but also some cat lovers actually *want* a Siamese with those faults.

Obviously if the breed's appearance represents a work in progress, then, as we know from Chapter 1, so do the feline mind and personality that go with it. Consequently, each purebred cat is a point-in-time phenomenon.

Because of this, the more you know about where your cat and its breed come from, the more easily you can understand where you and your cat are headed. In the pages ahead, we'll explore the factors that wield the most influence in shaping people's ideas about, and relationships with, purebred cats. Before we do that, though, think about any purebred cats you currently own or would like to own. If, instead, you own or see a mixed-breed cat in your future, do the exercises in this chapter with that cat in mind because many mixes carry genes from purebred ancestors.

## *Purebred Checklist*

Which breeds of cats appeal to you? Why? Jot down those characteristics as well as everything you know about those breeds' histories, health, and behavior.

If your list of known facts looks a little sketchy, head to your local library or bookstore for sources on breeds that interest you. Try to examine material from authors in different countries to gain the most comprehensive view. Also, reviewing information that spans the years will give you a good idea of how much some breeds and people's ideas about them may change over time. Books such as Richard Gebhardt's *The Complete Cat Book* (Howell, 1991), Gloria Stephen's and Tetsu Yamazaki's *Legacy of the Cat* (Chronicle Books, 1990), Andrew De Prisco's and James Johnson's *Mini Atlas of Cats* (T.F.H. Publications, 1991), Mordecai Siegel's *Simon & Schuster's Guide to Cats* (Simon & Schuster, 1983), Dennis Kelsey-Wood's *Atlas of the Cat* (T.F.H. Publications, 1991), *The Cat Fanciers Association Cat Encyclopedia* (Simon & Schuster, 1995), Paddy Cutt's *Cat Breeds: The New Compact Study Guide and Identifier* (Book Sales, 1995), and Michelle Lowell's *Your Purebred Kitten, A Buyer's Guide* (Henry Holt, 1995) all serve as good starting points. Purebred cat organizations such as the Cat Fanciers Association (CFA) and The International Cat Association (TICA), local breed clubs, and magazines such as *Cat Fancy* and *Cats* also provide information about the various feline breeds.

Bear in mind that some feline resources offer lovely pictures but little in the way of text; others try to cover so many aspects of cat ownership that they treat some topics more thoroughly than others. Yet a third group offers such relentlessly glowing accounts of the various breeds' attributes that they should awaken the skeptic in every potential owner. To help sort the feline fact from fiction, let's begin by exploring how the cat's ancient history can affect contemporary purebred lore.

# The Cat Gets Religion

In spite of—or maybe because of—the fact that the cat has made the transition from wildness to domesticity of its own volition, human intervention plays a major role in the evolution of purebred animals. Human contributions fall into one of two basic categories:

- the development of feline legends and symbolism
- the development of specific breeds

No other domestic animal elicits as much human emotion as the cat. Human responses, which range from gentle ambivalence to passionate love or hatred, go all the way back to day one of the human-feline relationship. Although the cat's skill as a predator probably endeared it to early humans struggling to protect their crops and stores of food from rodents, cats enjoyed a far more mystical relationship with humans than even the most useful (or gorgeous) dogs.

Most cat lovers know that the ancient Egyptians deified the domestic cat, but few realize what a profound effect this had on human culture as well as on feline history. Prior to the domestication of the cat, the Egyptians worshiped a bloodthirsty lion-headed goddess named Sekhmut who probably owed both her existence and her temperament to the fact that lions often snacked on domestic livestock grazing along the Nile.

However, and quite befitting the feline's paradoxical nature, Sekhmut ruled not only as the Goddess of War but also as the Mistress of Healing. While this seems bizarre, a certain logic underlies it. As the mother of two once-very-rambunctious sons, I can easily imagine those ancient priests conjuring up a feminine deity who not only gave young men the go-ahead to fight each other, but also would tend their wounds and tell them how brave they were when they grew tired of it.

The image of Sekhmut supporting the combatants on the battlefield and mowing down anyone who got in her way also appealed to fighting men. According to legend, the reason she so enjoyed a good skirmish and *made* those brave warriors fight stemmed from her thirst for the blood that flooded the battlefields.

However, even the bravest warriors grow weary, and some of those resourceful fellows devised a way to trick the goddess into ending the battle: they dyed a substance akin to beer red and flooded the battlefield with it. Thinking it was blood, Sekhmut supposedly would lap up the brew until she became too drunk to continue the carnage.

It doesn't take much imagination to surmise that it was the soldiers themselves who lapped up the ersatz blood. After all, they needed Sekhmut sober to fulfill her role as the Mistress of Healing (most likely in the form of the local womenfolk), tending wounds that didn't hurt nearly so much after a few drinks.

When the small wildcat proved such a boon to Egyptian civilization, lion-headed Sekhmut underwent a major makeover and emerged as the fully feline Bastet. Bastet also maintained dual roles, but ones quite different from her predecessor: the ancient Egyptians revered her as both a virgin and a mother. Annual festivals celebrating the finer qualities of virginity and motherhood quickly became popular because they included orgiastic frenzies and the consumption of vast amounts of wine. As virginity and motherhood yielded to fertility, the cult of the cat peaked in 950 B.C. when an estimated 700,000 "worshipers" descended on Bastet's earthly base, the city of Bubastis, for what most historians agree probably amounted to little more than an extended drunken orgy. This event doubtless resulted in a few more human offspring, but it probably didn't do as much as advertised for the crops.

Most cat books end any accounts of the cat's theological significance there, or they fast-forward it to the domestic cat's complete reversal of fortune in medieval Christian Europe when it couldn't do anything right. However, few delve into the connection between the two because it still makes many of us uncomfortable. Sure, a historian might casually toss out, "Well, can't you see the correlation between Bastet the virgin mother and Christianity's Virgin Mary, and that brew-into-blood transformation and the Christian sacrament of communion?" However, such links usually don't come up in Sunday School.

If such correlations make us uncomfortable today, you can imagine the effect they had on those early churchmen trying to get a new religion up and running in a world where animal spirits played an integral part in daily life. After all, the cat wasn't some wild animal of which their fledgling flocks might catch a glimpse every now and again. It was a domestic creature who inhabited practically every barn and meadow.

So, what to do? Simple: get rid of the cats. In such a way, the cat came to claim the dubious distinction as the only domestic animal both deified and slaughtered by humans for purely symbolic reasons.

While domestic cats took a beating in medieval Western Christian societies, they attracted the homage of Eastern holy men and royalty. Ancient Chinese and Korean Buddhist monks kept cats to protect sacred documents and food stores from rodents, and some of these cats found their way to Japan where they eventually became sacred, too. However, judging from ancient artwork, the Japanese and Chinese revered the cat for quite different reasons. Japanese artists celebrated the cat's beauty and grace while the early Chinese focused almost exclusively on the animal's strength and skill as a hunter.

When specific groups of people claim a particular animal and deny outsiders access to it, they create a restrictive environment as limiting as an impenetrable mountain range surrounding an isolated plateau. Consequently, two cats brought to a monastery conceivably could have given rise to a line of cats with a specific look and temperament like the Longstreets' Birman.

Like holy men, kings or high-ranking officials could limit the breeding of particular animals as well as determine who received any kittens. The first Siamese cats in the Western world were gifts from the king of Siam (now Thailand) to the departing British consul general. The first Egyptian Mau, the only naturally spotted cat, to make it to the West supposedly belonged to a member of the diplomatic corps living in one of the Mideast embassies in Rome.

One semi-exception to this upper-class approach, the Korat, ranks as one of the oldest as well as purest breeds. Unlike the other sacred cats, Korats lived wild in the jungles of the Malay Peninsula, but they eventually spread throughout Thailand and touched the hearts of all people, regardless of position. The cats' silver-tipped blue coats symbolized wealth, and their luminous green eyes promised a fruitful harvest; a young couple could hope for no better wedding gift. So highly did the people regard the Korat that they never bought or sold these cats, but only offered and received them as the most treasured of gifts.

"No wonder more and more people want to own a purebred cat," Marcy remarks, stroking Sing-Too affectionately. "Imagine having a little piece of that history right in your own home."

Well, not exactly. We need to add a few more pieces of contemporary history to the purebred's evolutionary puzzle before we can see the whole picture. Before we do that, though, review your list of preferred feline purebreds in light of their ancient, paradoxical past.

---

## Ancient Feline History Exam

Examine your list of your preferred cat characteristics, first through the eyes of an adoring ancient Egyptian, and then as a medieval cat-hating churchman. Then do the same thing for the characteristics you dislike.

The Longstreets experience no difficulty understanding how a cat lover could worship a cat like Sing-Too given her gorgeous appearance and sweet temperament. However, taking the view of the cat hater gives them a few problems.

"At first I couldn't imagine anyone's not liking all those qualities that make Sing-Too so special," Marcy confesses. "But when I put my emotions on hold, I could see how her coat and even her personality could bug some people."

"And that was a dirty trick making us think good thoughts about a breed we *don't* like," Kevin adds. "It made me realize that all my negative feelings about slinky cats like Siamese come from one bad run-in I had with one when I was in high school."

Kevin had used that one event to create a personal legend that negatively affected his view of numerous breeds. Legends promoted by breeders can wield an equally powerful influence on people's views about a particular breed of cat.

## Modern Feline Legends

When you leaf through a cat breed book or read the breed information provided by various purebred cat clubs and associations, you can't help but feel awed by feline origins. But how much has all this captivating history *really* affected the contemporary cat's development?

While legends every bit as exotic as that of the Longstreets' Birman abound for other breeds, breeding for show and exhibition didn't become an organized activity until the first National Cat Show in London in 1871.

"You mean Sing-Too's ancestors didn't live in a temple?" Marcy looks crestfallen. "She acts so regal."

Like most other breed-related legends, a bit of fact probably does underlie the Birman legend, but the modern cat breed more than likely began many years later. Because the Birman's history reflects some of the same issues that influenced the development of other purebreds, let's examine it in more detail.

Setting aside the story of the faithful monk Mun-Ha and his devoted cat which evolved before the birth of Christ, let's jump forward to 1919 when the modern legends begin. According to one account, in that year the high priest of the Lao-Tsun Temple sent a male and a female cat to a British officer to thank him for helping several priests and their cats escape to Tibet during an uprising in Burma (now Myanmar). Another source says a greedy servant stole the cats from the temple and sold them for a hefty sum to a "Mr. Vanderbilt." Yet another claims that an unknown person sent or smuggled the cats to two men living in France. And, finally, a fourth version proclaims a Madame Marcelle Adam as the first importer of the Birman to France. Whether any of these cats could claim the legendary Sinh as an ancestor remains anyone's guess.

Further complicating matters, at least two of the accounts say that the male died during the long sea voyage, but fortunately the female was pregnant, and, it is assumed, her kittens became the foundation stock of the breed. There is no mention, however, of whether her kittens resulted from a liaison with an abandoned lover, her male traveling companion, or a shipboard mouser. Moreover, even though most accounts agree on her name, Sita, no one seems to know what happened to her.

As with many other cat breeds that developed and prospered in England and Europe at the turn of the century, World War II struck the Birman a devastating blow, and only one breeding pair survived. Through selective outcrossing (breeding between cats without common ancestors for at least three generations, such as cats of completely different breeds), Birman fanciers reestablished the breed in France by 1955. Given the Birman's coat and coloration, and the rare occurrence of the Persian's and Siamese's more common crossed eyes and kinked tails in the breed, it seems safe to say that those two breeds, or combinations thereof contributed their share to this process.

A pair of Birmans first arrived in the United States in 1959, followed by others from England and France, and even two from a temple in Cambodia. By the mid '60s, the breed had gained full show status in this country. During this time the cats' name also changed from Sacred Cat to Burman to Birman.

Whether your cat's ancestors shared its crunchies with the queen of Sheba or nefarious cat smugglers matters under only two conditions. First, it matters if you *paid* for that history. If the breed history means a lot to you, make sure you thoroughly research a particular animal's background before you buy. When the Longstreets decide to add another Birman to their family, they read as much about the breed as they can; then they talk to several breeders; then they learn to read a pedigree (a purebred animal's family tree) and pore over dozens of them. After doing all this, most people usually can find a definitive answer, if only that the modern cat's relationship to the legendary cat is exactly that: legendary.

Second, you should know your cat's *true* history if you plan to breed it. I didn't realize how rampant the selling of legends had become until I overhead a humorous remark by a young man whose cat-loving companion had dragged him from cage to cage at a show. She finally pointed to an unlabeled, unattended cat in a cage and asked, "What kind of a cat do you suppose that is?"

"It's the Sacred Cat of the Midwest," he immediately replied. "See how its gold eyes look like kernels of corn and its short brown coat looks like newly turned soil? The ancient Ohio farmers used to keep them in the fields for good luck."

So closely did this parody all the tales I'd heard that for a moment I believed him! However, while this exchange delighted me and caused me to imagine sacred cats for Detroit, Malibu, and even New Hampshire (a granite gray frosted tabby with wintry blue eyes), it doesn't negate the fact that it takes a tremendous amount of knowledge and skill to breed purebred cats properly.

While I question the ethics of breeders who deliberately concoct whimsical tales rather than reveal the whole scoop about a particular breed's roots, I find those who repeat such tales out of ignorance even more troubling. In my experience, only people who care enough to find out everything they possibly can about their cats *before* they breed them have the commitment necessary to breed healthy, stable animals. The Longstreets help no one, let alone their beloved Birman breed, if they breed Sing-Too without knowing her real history.

Because legends may constitute a large segment of the feline mystique, and because a surprising number of people who get purebred cats "just for pets" do decide to breed them, take a few moments to think of any existing or dream purebreds as the stuff of which legends are made.

## Legendary Checklist

List everything you know about the history of your existing or desired purebred. How much of this consists of solid facts? How much of it would help ensure that you add only physically and behaviorally sound animals to the purebred population should you decide to breed your pet?

When the Longstreets complete this exercise they discover that they really don't know much about Sing-Too's past beyond what the clerk in the pet store told them. Like many other owners, they didn't realize that, in spite of all of the power that legends can wield in the cat lover's world, all purebred cats owe their status to a combination of four factors:

- environmental adaptation
- mutations

- environmental restriction
- human manipulation

The first three factors act in accord with the laws of nature (or as much as human nature will allow), whereas the last one reflects conscious human intervention.

Let's examine each one of these to see what they can reveal about any current or future cats in your life.

## The Adaptable Feline

The ability to mate and bear fertile offspring remains the standard test for determining whether a particular domestic animal descended from a particular wild one. In the last chapter we learned that domestic cats' ability to mate with *Felis libyca* and *Felis silvestris* and produce fertile young leads most authorities to believe that the contemporary cat descended from these two varieties. Most also agree that, although the first domestic cats could trace their roots directly to *Felis libyca*, domestic cats with the *F. libyca* breeding introduced to Europe from Africa, Asia, and the Middle East most likely mated with *Felis silvestris* once they arrived.

Imagine a cat with the following characteristics:

- short, tawny brown coat
- pale stripes on ticked fur (i.e., composed of hair with alternating light and dark bands)
- lithe body
- wedge-shaped head
- large, pointed ears
- long legs and tail

Where would such a cat live?

"I'd bet in a warmer climate with that body style because it would make it easier to keep cool," Kevin correctly concludes.

"And someplace with a uniform terrain where they could run fast on those long legs, like a desert or other open areas that would blend with that coat," Marcy adds.

The Longstreets correctly identify what scientists consider the "warm-climate" cat form, variations of which appear in modern breeds such as the Abyssinian, Siamese, and Korat.

Now imagine a cat with these quite different characteristics:

- thick, yellowish gray coat
- pronounced vertical mackerel-patterned (ringed) stripes
- solid, muscular build
- broad, wide head
- smaller, rounded ears
- short, stocky legs and tail

What kind of environment would suit that cat best?

"That's got to be the cold-climate cat," Kevin volunteers immediately. "It's designed to conserve heat as well as blend into the woods."

Given that background, we can easily imagine those first domesticated cats with their pale stripes and short coats moving into the colder European climates. It's probable that only those with the darkest stripes, thickest coats, and stockiest bodies could survive without human assistance. They, in turn, mated with the native wildcat population to produce a domestic animal with an even more distinct striped tabby coat and a more compact body. Modern breeds such as the British and American shorthair reflect this colder-climate development.

In such a way, *Felis libyca* slowly made its way into human society, moved into harsher climates, and then remodeled itself utilizing the gene pool of the native wildcat population.

Can you see any of this ancient heritage in your cat?

## Feline Body Check

Look at your own cat(s) as well as cats in your neighborhood or those belonging to friends. Whether the cats are purebred or not, can you see the difference between the warm- and cold-climate body types?

The Longstreets easily classify Sing-Too's body type as the more muscular cold-climate type, particularly when they compare her with their neighbor's sleek Abyssinian.

Once the domestic cat nailed down the basics, though, it began to refine itself even more.

# A Multitude of Marvelous Mutations

When most of us think of mutations, we think of bizarre life forms. When most of us think of sex, we think of romantic liaisons. However, the primary advantage of sexual reproduction lies in its enhanced ability to generate mutations. While mutations may give rise to killer bees or lethal genes that kill their carriers, mutations also enable a species to respond much faster to changes in its environment.

Purebred cats owe their existence to two kinds of mutations: those that enabled the animals to survive in their geographical environment, and those that enabled them to survive in the human environment. To understand how the first kind work, suppose some Roman soldiers or Egyptian monks decide to head north to conquer or convert a few pagans and they take their warm-climate domestic cats with them for company. Once these cats arrive in northern Europe, two conditions will greatly improve the chances of the newcomers' genes making it into the local gene pool:

- their willingness and ability to mate with any local wildcat population
- the existence of mutations arising from successive domestic cat matings that will better enable their offspring to survive

We already know that domestic cats experience few problems mating with small wildcats. But what kinds of mutations would best enable a warm-climate cat to survive in a colder climate? Obviously those that enable it to adapt to the local geographical conditions. However, cats come from such a well-designed, energy-efficient, and flexible creature plan that they've succeeded in adapting to an amazing range of natural *and* human environments with fewer mutations than any other domestic species. Consequently, the modern cat remains remarkably similar to its ancestors.

For example, consider the spectacular palette of feline colors. In a famous letter to a young man about the advantages of an "experienced" woman, Benjamin Franklin noted that at night, all cats are gray. In reality, though, in terms of their genetic make-up, all cats are black, red, or a combination of the two.

"You're kidding!" Marcy laughs, pointing to Sing-Too, whose light kitten coat has given way to a creamy gold with the dark brown points and white mittens of the adult. "There's not a speck of black or red on her!"

Call it mutation magic, but from such a limited genetic palette springs the purebred cat's extensive range of colors with elegant names such as blue, cinnamon, fawn, and lavender.

Add a few more mutations, and shadings or "smokes" appear in which individual white hair shafts become tinted with another color along some portion of their length. These cats wear coats with equally heady names such as shaded silver or chinchilla golden. The tabby pattern that camouflaged the hunting wildcat comes in classic, mackerel, patched (also called torbie), spotted, and ticked varieties in purebreds, each with its own very specific definition.

Of all mutations that affected cat color, the series that produced the temperature-sensitive albino surely ranks as the most intriguing. Cats carrying this collection of genetic mutations (which probably originated in several locations simultaneously) range from pure albinos with white coats and pink eyes, to blue-eyed white cats, to those with blue eyes, a lighter coat color, and different-colored points, with the entire coat becoming darker as the environment grows colder. We can easily see evidence of the warm-climate albino series in the modern Siamese, but the solid-colored, golden-eyed Burmese hides those same genes very well. The cold-climate variation on this theme probably gave the Birman its distinctive coloration, too.

Mutations affecting the color and thickness of the feline coat could benefit an animal making the transition from a warmer to a colder climate. Even the seemingly nonfunctional temperature-sensitive albino series might give an evolutionary advantage to animals living in areas of extreme temperature variation (such as high barren planes and deserts with broiling summers and frigid winters) where a reflective lighter coat would cool them in the summer, then darken in winter to conserve body heat. In my area of New England, the bodies of some free-roaming Siamese may appear almost as dark as their points in the winter. On the other hand, put even the creamiest white Siamese body under a strong light and you'll probably see faint remnants of those ancient stripes.

A second group of mutations became part of the domestic feline gene pool strictly because they appealed to people, rather than enhanced the cat's survival. Curly coated kittens with lowly feral and barn cat roots in Devonshire and Cornwall, England, gave rise to today's elegant Cornish and Devon Rex breeds. A wirehaired mutation that occurred in a barn cat spawned the American wirehair breed. Some fanciers believed that cats car-

rying spontaneous "hairless" mutations deserved purebred status, so if a cat with fuzzy down and wrinkles appeals to you and
you enjoy bathing cats (because these cats have no fur to soak
up their natural skin oils), consider a Sphinx. Mutations that
cause ears to fold over or curl upward turned a humble stray and
another barn cat into purebred foundation stock for the American curl and Scottish fold breeds.

In fact, the idea of a spontaneous mutation's spawning a new
breed carried (and still carries) so much cachet among certain
cat fanciers that some breeders attribute changes in appearance
that occurred as the result of "off-the-record" matings between
animals of different breeds to this much rarer genetic phenomenon. For example, longhaired Abyssinians (Somalis) and Manx
(Cymrics) most likely owe their coats to unacknowledged liaisons
with longhaired cats somewhere during the development of the
breed rather than to mutations. A new breed, a longhaired Russian blue look-alike called the Nebelung, resulted from a mixed-
breed cat mating; breeding these animals with Russian blues
enhances the connection, but it doesn't change the fact that the
breed isn't a naturally occurring longhaired Russian blue.

Unlike the mutations that enabled the cat to better adapt to
its physical environment, the modern mutations owe their existence and perpetuation to the human quest for novelty far more
than to the cat's quest for survival in the wild. On the other hand,
such mutations did enable at least some cats whose earlier mutations might have hindered or completely undermined their survival in the natural world to make a relatively big splash in the
domestic feline gene pool. Obviously a cat who requires routine
bathing or grooming by human caregivers to maintain its health
wouldn't survive long on its own.

How do you feel about such genetic manipulation?

## Mutation Checkup

Think about the cat breeds that appeal to you. Do these breeds express mutations designed to enhance their survival in the natural or human environment? If you don't know, check your breed books for more information.

"Birmans definitely carry the temperature-sensitive albino series," Kevin says with a laugh. "I'd never given it a thought before, but I feel better knowing Sing-Too's color probably served a purpose at one time, even if other purely cosmetic changes have been bred into the breed since then."

While some people share Kevin's views, others don't. For sure, though, if you have strong views about any "right" or "wrong" mutations, choose a breed that supports them. Otherwise this awareness could undermine the quality of your relationship.

# Quality-Controlled Environments

Once a mutation occurs in the wild, its survival in the breed depends on the environment as much as the cat who carries it. If a mutation enables the animal who carries it to compete more successfully for food and mates in its particular environment, then the mutation will flourish—provided the environment is sufficiently restricted.

"Because that increases the probability that those carrying the mutation will mate with each other," Marcy correctly surmises.

This reality explains why the histories of many purebred cats link them to specific regions. Consider the mutation for long hair. Long hair wouldn't benefit the warm-climate cats of Africa at all, but it means the difference between life and death to those who live in colder environments. Scientists speculate that the mutation spontaneously occurred in specific areas of Turkey, Iran (then called Persia), and Russia populated by primitive nomadic peoples.

Early travelers to these high-plateau regions spoke of two varieties of beautiful longhaired cats:

- those with longer bodies, large ears, and mostly blue eyes
- those with compact bodies, shorter heads, and gold eyes

While one longhaired cat looked pretty much like another to those Europeans who had never seen any longhaired cat before, eventually the two groups gained separate status. Cat lovers referred to the longer-bodied ones as Angoras, after the capital of Turkey (now called Ankara) near where the first cats originated, and they dubbed the more compact ones Persians. The much larger, stockier body and tabby coat of the Russian cat didn't appeal to the Europeans, although it surely contributed its share to the Persian gene pool off-the-record.

The mutations that produced tailless or stubby-tailed cats also benefited from restrictive environments. These, too, doubtless occurred in many locations, but those tailless cats who lived on the island of Japan and the tiny Isle of Man (located in the Irish Sea off the coast of England) survived because of their restriction to a limited area.

The bobbed-tailed Japanese cats got an added boost when they attracted the attention of some very important people who granted them sacred status, a definite advantage when a stumpy tail might hinder balance, hunting, and mating skills in the wild. By the time even higher powers freed all cats to deal with the vermin threatening the silkworms (and thus the Japanese economy) in 1602, the gene was firmly established. Today, most of the common street cats of Japan sport bobbed tails, strongly suggesting that these animals never had to compete with long-tailed colleagues in an environment where such an appendage would provide a survival advantage.

Both the smallness and the remoteness of the Isle of Man also provided the tailless Manx with a sheltered environment, whether the mutation originally occurred there or someone brought such a cat to the island. In addition, Manx kitten tails normally span the spectrum from none to full-sized, resulting in a mixture of normal animals and those carrying the mutant gene within the same breed. This benefited the breed tremendously because breeding two "rumpy" (tailless) cats doesn't yield a litter of tailless kittens. Instead, kittens who inherit the tailless gene from both parents die before birth, and other Manx matings may produce kittens with a variety of spinal-cord and hindquarter problems. This leads many to argue that the tailless Manx can't claim purebred status because, without normal tailed animals to counter these effects, the mutation would not survive.

Other geographical restrictions played a role in the development of other breeds of cats. Depending on whom you read, the Abyssinian's characteristic coat results from its isolation either in Egyptian temples, in the jungles of North Africa, or in the British countryside. Likewise, many people in France consider the blue and/or gray thick-coated Chartreux a national treasure, and whether you believe that green-liqueur-making monks developed the breed or that the cats originated on the island of Belle-Isle-sur-Mere (probably more likely), some sort of geographical restriction permitted this breed to become established.

The British shorthair arose from hardy, feral stock brought by Roman soldiers to northern Europe two thousand years ago. Centuries later, offspring of these animals arrived in the New World, most likely brought along for shipboard rodent control by the early colonists. These first feline settlers gave rise to the two oldest North American breeds: the American shorthair and the Maine coon cat. While the American and British shorthairs remain quite similar in appearance, most experts believe that a longhaired mutation in one of the shorthaired cats brought from England gave rise to the Maine coon.

The distinctive looks of four recently introduced breeds of cats—Singapuras, Turkish Vans, Norwegian Forest cats, and Siberias—also resulted from mutations that became established thanks to geographical isolation.

The smallest entry in the purebred lineup, the Singapura theoretically owes its unique appearance to its restricted development on the island of Singapore. However, because of a fascinating history that includes three cats coming into the United States without any papers describing them, returning to Singapore as Abyssinians, then coming back to this country as Singapuras, it remains unclear whether these cats truly represent a typical street cat of the island of Singapore.

The white, longhaired Turkish Van with its colored markings on head and tail supposedly originated in the Lake Van region of Turkey. However, it seems more likely that the Armenians who settled in the Lake Van region brought these revered cats with them. Although the cats existed in the area for centuries, an added quirk of fate caused them to lose out to the native Turkish Angoras, particularly those white cats with different-colored eyes. In 1923, Mustafa Kemal Atatürk, who founded the modern republic of Turkey, designated his successor as a man bitten on the ankle by an odd-eyed white cat. Needless to say, odd-eyed cats immediately became a national favorite, as did waving one's ankles at them.

The Norwegian Forest cat and Siberia typify qualities appropriate to a very cold climate, including long, thick coats, massive bodies, and tabby markings. Currently, the Siberia just begins the process of gaining full purebred status in the United States. The Norwegian Forest cat's resemblance to the Maine coon cat troubles some, but the former's breeders claim that distinct differences do in fact separate the two.

How much of a role did environmental isolation play in the development of the kinds of cats you enjoy?

---

## Environmental Root Evaluation

Think about the different breeds of cats that appeal to you. Do any of them owe their looks to a restricted natural environment?

"It certainly seems like a temple on a mountain top would serve as a restricted environment that would establish the ancient Birman's unique features," Kevin decides after he strokes Sing-Too for a few inspiring minutes. "But it doesn't sound like that's the case with the modern breed."

While natural mutations previously needed a restrictive natural environment in order to become established, mutations that give rise to purebreds today often flourish within the confines of a cattery. Granted, this may not result in animals capable of surviving in the natural environment. On the other hand, the human-pleasing qualities bred into these animals may enhance their survival in the human environment in which most of them will live. Once we begin splashing around in the human-manipulated rather than the naturally manipulated feline gene pool, we stir up the last group of purebred cats, the derivatives.

# The Derivative Derby

Given the relative newness of purebred cats as well as the amount of outcrossing done to transform mutation-bearing barn cats into elegant feline companions over the years, it's only natural that kittens who don't look anything like the show standard periodically pop up in purebred litters. Logic says the standard should be changed to accommodate these naturally occurring animals, but logic has a way of disappearing when people start breeding animals for show. Instead, breeders used these cats to found new breeds.

The Siamese with its legend-soaked ancient past and more recent fact- and fiction-filled history definitely contributed the lion's share of this segment of the purebred cat population, to the point that one feline aficionado quipped that his idea of hell would be to find himself trapped in a room with all of the Siamese derivatives and have to name them.

However, the Siamese also claims the unusual distinction of being a derivative of itself, too.

"I know things get crazy in the cat world," Marcy jokes. "But people had Siamese cats 25 years ago when I was a kid, and they still have Siamese cats today."

True, but it's not the *same* Siamese by a long shot. At a cat show a few years ago, I overheard a conversation between a breeder and a prospective cat owner that summed up the problem facing those who recall a beloved childhood Siamese and long to own a cat just like it today.

"I'm looking for a Siamese kitten, but I don't see any," the woman in her 30s said to the first breeder she encountered in a whole row of Siamese breeders.

"These Siamese kittens are for sale," the breeder replied, pointing to the litter in a nearby cage. "And I know other breeders have kittens for sale, too."

The woman studied the long-legged, slender kittens with their wedged-shaped heads and enormous ears and shook her head.

"No, the Siamese cat I'm talking about is much stockier and has a rounder head," she explained.

"I have no idea what you're talking about," declared the breeder with certainty. "The Siamese cat has *always* looked like this."

The woman politely thanked the breeder for the information, then walked off shaking her head.

If that woman happened to go home and look up the Siamese cat in the same 1978 edition of *The American Heritage Dictionary of the English Language* that I own, she'd find a wonderful photo of the cat she remembers on page 1201. If she then looked up the Siamese in *Simon & Schuster's Guide to Cats* published in 1983, she would see that round head slowly giving way to a more triangular shape. Both of these cats, however, look like feline Mack trucks compared with the racy Siamese pictured in Richard Gebhardt's *The Complete Cat Book* published in 1991. All three cats supposedly represent *the* ideal Siamese.

How can this be? When most people think of the Siamese, they think of a blue-eyed cat with a light-colored body and darker points. However, this look originally occurred as the result of a series of mutations, and thus originally only animals who possessed those mutations displayed that coloration.

What did the original, premutation cat look like? One appealing theory proposes that it looked like the other sacred cat of Siam, the silver-tipped blue Korat, because both cats carry the gene for the blue color and have shared the same environment. Historians know this because *The Cat-Book Poems* discovered in the ancient Siamese city of Ayudha contains descriptions of both kinds of felines. Conceivably, animals displaying the semi-albino coloration attracted human attention and protection, and thus became the "indoor" sacred cats while the Korat became associated with the land. This makes sense because an almost white animal with dark brown points born into an environment where the Korat's coloration provided a survival advantage almost certainly would find itself disadvantaged when it came to concealing itself from either predators or prey.

*The Cat-Book Poems* also describe shorthaired brown cats with darker brown points and a body type similar to the Korat called the "copper" cat. Because the points of pointed cats come in different colors—including blue and brown—it's logical to expect that their body color would, too. Consequently, the blue, copper, and pointed sacred cats could reflect variations on the same theme rather than separate breeds.

However, modern cat breeders took the "Why settle for one sacred cat when you can have three?" approach. Most likely due to a lack of knowledge about genetics rather than any devious intent, the founders of the purebred cat fancy designated the creamy-colored cat with darker points *the* Siamese cat. When a brown cat with darker brown points quite similar to the copper cats found in the Tibetan monasteries arrived in the United States in 1930, a concerted effort took place to make it a separate breed, the Burmese. Tight inbreeding produced solid-colored cats with a body type much closer to that of the Korat than the Siamese. Then, in a series of events worthy of a soap opera, the Burmese dumped its Siamese heritage as best it could by expanding its gene pool with some clandestine matings, probably with American shorthairs.

Unfortunately, though, kittens broadcasting the Burmese cat's early Siamese heritage kept showing up with embarrassing regularity, sporting coats with lovely names like champagne and platinum as well as blue.

So, what to do?

Because the Burmese standard, like its Siamese predecessor, denied such variation, breeders assigned these animals to a new breed called the Malayan. Four years later and after a bitter struggle among the breeders in various cat fanciers organizations, genetic reality prevailed and the Malayans got absorbed back into the Burmese breed again, but as a separate division.

The Malayan breed theoretically provided a place to put the "wrong-colored" solid-colored kittens who showed up when "pure" Burmese cats mated. But the Burmese folks still had to figure out what to do with all those pesky kittens who kept showing up with Siamese points.

Enter the Tonkinese (presumably named after the Bay of Tonkin for reasons as obscure as those that resulted in the

Malayan's name) which, rather remarkably, was established as a *new* breed rather than an offshoot of an existing one. I fell in love with the first Tonkinese I saw in the '70s, then later credited it with the first of several Siamese-derivative-related brain deteriorations I experienced in the following years. This cat was a lovely solid champagne color and looked quite like—Dare I say it?—a solid-colored Siamese.

However, faster than I could say *Felis libyca* three times, two things happened. First, a cat lover named Daphne Negus brought the aforementioned *Cat-Book of Poems* to the attention of the Western world in the 1970s, an event that most likely precipitated the massive remaking of the Burmese and Siamese that began at that time. Second, I started seeing the more common pointed rather than solid-colored Tonkinese, both of which confused my poor brain even more.

However, luckily at that point, the Siamese-derivative circle began to close. If you want a fuller-bodied, rounder-headed Siamese like the one you grew up with in the '50s and '60s, then get yourself a Tonkinese. But if you want a cat that looks more like the original warm-climate mutation, get a Siamese. And if you come across a breeder who says Siamese cats *always* looked the way they do now, just smile knowingly and move on.

If you like the Siamese color but prefer the cold-climate body type, consider the Himalayan, a Siamese-Persian cross. On the other hand, if you like the svelte warm-climate body type but not the colors of the Siamese points, consider a colorpoint shorthair which will tiptoe through your tulips on cream, red, tabby, and every other color of little cat feet that breeders come up with. On the third hand (Siamese derivatives make you say things like that), if you don't like points at all, check out the oriental shorthair, whose sleek body comes garbed in a full range of solid colors.

Persians also spawned derivatives, but not nearly as many as the Siamese. We can attribute some of this to the fact that Persians of different colors developed such different looks that they're shown in seven different divisions: solid, shaded, smoke, tabby, parti-color, bicolor, and Himalayan.

"Wait a minute!" Marcy interrupts. "I thought a Himalayan was a cross between a Siamese and a Persian. How can they be shown as Persians?"

Theoretically, breeding true (i.e., producing kittens that all look like the parents) for a specific number of generations earns a cat the rank of a purebred. The Himalayan fulfills this criterion as a Persian in some associations, as does its longhaired version, the Kashmer.

"You lost me again." Kevin shakes his head. "If the Himalayan breeds true, where do the solid-colored ones come from?"

The same place the solid-colored Siamese come from, the breed gene pool.

From all of this, we can see that *purebred* can mean different things to different people. Moreover, given the limited size of the gene pools that some breeders manipulate to create a specific look, pet-quality kittens who *don't* meet show standards actually represent the most valuable animals in a litter. Although show-quality cats may go on to win ribbons, those who deviate from the show standard provide solid proof of the breed's ability to adapt and change. While some breeders might strive to produce only show cats, prospective cat owners should view such offerings with skepticism, especially in breeds that encourage extremes in appearance. Such uniformity often results from such tight inbreeding that medical problems become inevitable.

One final breed, a wild Asian leopard cat and domestic cat cross called the Bengal, bears mention because it represents a form of human manipulation that sets a most troubling precedent. Given the domestic cats' rather tenuous claim to domesticity and the small wildcats' increasingly tenuous existence in their ever-decreasing environments, crossing wild and domestic cats to create new breeds, such as the Bengal, offers the worst to both populations. Such crosses will further dilute the small wildcats' already shrinking gene pool and hasten their demise.

Any added wildness in the domestic animal hardly bodes well for animals who find themselves confined in our homes, anymore than it bodes well for their prey if we allow our pets to run loose. Trying to occupy the mind of a cat with years of domestic breeding in its past can try the patience of the most devoted apartment dweller. Turn a semi-wildcat loose and any local wildlife as well as other cats could pay the price. For many owners, meeting the needs of such an animal can prove overwhelming. Not long ago I saw an ad in a local paper that demonstrates the price these animals must pay when we breed for ourselves rather than for the cats: "Free Bengal. Needs room to roam. No kids."

With both ocicats and Egyptian Maus in the domesticated spotted purebred lineup, further diluting the wildcat gene pool to produce another spotted cat hardly seems warranted.

Time to see how much you know about the last batch of purebreds.

## Derivative Diagnosis

Summon the image of any purebred cat who intrigues you and ponder what any other breeds may have contributed to its heritage. Make a list of those breeds. Then list what you know about them.

"Well, that yielded a big zero," Kevin says with a chuckle, looking at his wife's equally blank sheet of paper. "It's like you said: the more we know about purebred cats, the less we know."

"Maybe up to a point," Marcy counters. "But when I think about Sing-Too as a cold-climate cat with possible outbreeding to colorpoint longhairs, it makes me see things in her I never noticed before. Sure, I kind of miss the idea of her ancestors living in a temple. On the other hand, those complex modern roots of hers are pretty exotic, too."

Indeed they are, as are the complex personalities that go with those roots.

## The Inner Cat

Another purebred cat paradox stems from many breeders' simultaneous knowledge and naïveté about genetics. As Belyaev's experiments demonstrated, breeding strictly for temperament can grossly alter physical appearance. And it seems safe to say the opposite also holds true: breeding strictly for looks can alter temperament. However, much breeding occurs as if an animal's body and mind function as two completely separate systems. The idea that a breeder can change coat or eye color or hair texture without changing any other physical attributes, let alone temperament, permeates the purebred fancy. Unfortunately, media coverage of genetic advances often gives the mistaken impression that if we breed problems into an animal, we just need to locate the gene responsible, snip it out, and replace it with a good one.

Time and time again, however, nature makes it quite clear she doesn't operate that way. When breeders focus just on external appearances, they can create internal disasters that will take a lot more than a bit of cutting and pasting to correct. Some people, like Kevin, still associate Siamese cats with crossed eyes and kinked tails. While reputable breeders eliminated this problem, an increased prevalence of heart disease in Siamese indicates yet another one. As previously mentioned, Manx can beget young with a variety of spinal and rear-end problems. Mate two Scottish folds exhibiting those prize-winning folded ears and you can get kittens with crippling joint problems in addition to the ear problems that may plague all members of this breed. The so-called Peke-faced Persians with their flattened faces may suffer from all sorts of eye, mouth, teeth, and upper respiratory problems related to this extreme look. Abyssinians and their long-haired counterparts, the Somalis, may succumb to kidney disease. As purebred cats become more popular and more effort goes into studying them, no doubt scientists will discover more breed-related problems in the future.

While purebred dogs also suffer the negative effects of short-sighted breeders who fail to view the animal as a total being, the fact that some people breed dogs for function as well as looks tempers these effects somewhat. Breeders of working dogs may know nothing about how a particular series of genes that govern coat quality and eye color may affect physical soundness, but they do know whether their dogs possess the wherewithal to perform in the field. If the animals lack the physical soundness and stamina to hunt, retrieve, or herd, the breeders don't breed them. Other dog breeders use obedience and other competitive sports to weed out the physically and mentally unsound animals.

Unfortunately, not only do no similar programs exist to test physical soundness in cats, many breeders want to put as much distance between their elegant felines and the cat's functional hunting roots as possible. The idea of a group of shaded silver Persians involved in timed hunting trials borders on ludicrous. Even if breeders would consent to such tests, the breed hardly exudes wild killer instincts.

However, such wasn't always the case. Some accounts of those first cat shows in the late 1800s and even of those held well into this century describe an almost Roman circus atmosphere, with some spectators coming to view the human bloodshed as much as the cats. Older show enthusiasts swap stories about a time when breeders routinely wore heavy leather gloves to pass their cats to judges who, in turn, handled the animals like fur-covered time bombs. Many of those early show cats were the offspring of semiwild creatures from restricted environments who lived by their wits bred to others of like kind to preserve their physical characteristics.

Most likely market pressures more than anything else led breeders to focus on temperament as well as looks. Even the most objective judge might award the blue ribbon to the more docile cat with slightly too long ears rather than the one with perfect ears who bit the judge's hand. Similarly, after a while whatever joy owners get from bragging about their cat's pedigree can't compensate for the pain and suffering experienced when they try to feed and groom the little demon.

Regardless of all this, no purebred cat standard includes a standard for temperament. Consequently, when you read about a particular purebred cat's personality in any breed book, you need to take it with at least a grain of salt, if not a lot more.

Still, some personality differences do exist between breeds. Even the most exuberant Persian probably won't come close to the activity level of a Siamese or Abyssinian, and most Persian owners are glad about that. Anyone who ever tried to groom an active Persian can tell you why a more mellow temperament best suits this breed. In my experience, Persians, Siamese, and their derivatives lack a sense of "self" and "catness" compared with American and British shorthairs, Maine coons, and Norwegian Forest cats, most likely because of the tremendous amount of human manipulation of the Persian and Siamese breeds compared with the others. Veterinarians more frequently speak of Siamese suffering from separation anxiety when parted from their owners, and Persians appear to have the weakest grasp of normal elimination behavior, something we'll discuss in detail in Chapter 6.

While some cats, notably the Siamese and their derivatives, do express themselves more often and loudly than other cats, I must wonder about the human factor here, too. Personal observation leads me to conclude that the nature of some cat calls inspires people to answer back. This, in turn, rewards the behavior and stimulates the cat to "talk" some more. As long as the owner enjoys this exchange, no problems arise. However, sometimes owners who yowl back at the cat who yowls at them and vice versa reach a point where they complain, "Why doesn't that darn cat ever shut up!"

Given that nature programs cats to view us as their moms, it makes sense that we set the stage for behavioral displays. Noisy people beget noisy cats, and yowling at a yowling cat to stop yowling most likely won't stop the behavior and could make it worse.

However, for as much as prospective owners yearn for pure-bred personality profiles and for as much as champions of particular breeds and writers of cat books might wax ecstatic about a particular breed's great love of kids, dogs, other cats, or apartment living, such blanket statements simply don't apply.

Before learning how to get around all this, pause here and think about your real or dream cat's personality.

---

## Feline Personality Analysis

List those personality traits you associate with certain purebred cats. Where does your view come from?

Like most other people's, Kevin's and Marcy's beliefs about purebred cat personalities come from personal experience with a few cats of a particular breed. Kevin's view of Siamese as "neurotic" goes back to the cross-eyed, kinked-tailed cats who populated the town where he grew up, including the one who bit him. Moreover, all of those cats came from the same breeder, hardly a broad breed view! Conversely, the Longstreets shout the praises of all Birmans based on Sing-Too, whose pet store background would appall many "serious" breeders. However, when they decide to get another cat, they vow to do it right.

# The Right Cat Stuff

With so many variables to contemplate among purebred cats, how can anyone hope to find the right cat? Nothing surpasses the value of talking with people who own the kind of cat you admire, as well as veterinarians, breeders, groomers, and other animal-care specialists who work with those particular cats.

Good breeders will encourage you to interview people who have bought their kittens, and will furnish names and phone numbers for you to do so. When you contact these people, ask about the cat's health and temperament. If you can, visit these owners and see how their lifestyle matches your own. A glowing report from a single owner with loads of time to tend a cat's special needs doesn't mean much if you're a busy wife and mother who works full-time and attends classes or other activities four nights a week. If your present or future household contains kids, dogs, and other cats, don't forget to investigate how any prospective dream cats might interact with them.

Also try to get the names of people who own cats spanning all ages. Some cats experience more problems as kittens but then grow out of them. For example, some lines of Persian kittens experience more problems with ringworm, a fungal infection, which they then outgrow. However, people with immunodeficiency problems would want to avoid these lines because humans can catch this disease from infected cats. Other breeds or lines may enjoy healthy kittenhoods but develop serious problems as they get older. Your own veterinarian or the one who cares for the breeder's animals can give you further insight into this aspect of your dream breed.

As you collect your data, look for any trends: Do both owners and veterinarians speak about skin, ear, urinary, or other problems? Do any comments about the breed's activity level bother you? For example, if you picture your perfect cat snuggled up beside you while you watch television or read, any remarks about the cat's getting into everything or loving to play "tricks" should prompt you to demand further explanation. While some owners delight in a cat who unrolls the toilet paper and swings from the chandelier, others don't share this view.

Regardless of your lifestyle, be extremely cautious about getting a cat because you feel sorry for it. Cats who make us feel sorry for them inevitably do so because they exhibit problems. While such animals can become wonderful pets for people with the time, money, and knowledge to resolve these problems, those without such prerequisites can only make the animal's situation worse.

Along those same lines, bear in mind that there's no such thing as a free cat, and especially not a purebred one. Even if a breeder offered to give you the healthiest, happiest kitten in the litter because you're such a swell person, that kitten would still need care. While that may mean only routine vaccinations and neutering, it also could include special food, grooming, or a lot of other breed-specific activities that can add up over time.

Currently some animal behaviorists hope to develop a kitten personality test that parallels those used for pups. Unfortunately, the cat's solitary and predatory nature as well as the developmental variation among breeds would seem to negate this. However, one basic rule does seem to hold true: avoid the extremes. Don't lose your heart to the tiny little ball of fuzz huddled in the corner or the furry terror who climbs up your leg. Recall what we said about the durability of early kittenhood experiences: kittens raised without the companionship of other cats or in traumatic environments may acquire behavioral problems that persist their entire lives. All the love in the world won't change that fact.

Because both extremes may respond aggressively when stressed, they require owners with the knowledge, time, and skill to provide the special kind of environment such animals need. If you don't have that, aim for the kitten in the middle—the one who looks curious, neither too clingy nor too aloof.

As far as males versus females, it depends. For every person who insists the females of one breed are more loving, you'll find another who maintains the males claim that distinction. Here again, talk to people who own or work with them. You may find that the males in one line act more cuddly while the females win those honors in another.

Are you considering adding a second or third cat to your household? Despite the amount of conflicting advice on the subject, I think I can safely offer four suggestions. First, be extremely leery of any breeders who tell you their cats adore other cats. While this may be true, developing such a line would require altering one of the cat's most basic instincts. Moreover, just because the new cat adores all cats doesn't mean your old cat will adore it. Two, introduce a kitten to an existing adult cat if possible because kittens tend to trigger social rather than territorial responses in older animals. Three, choose animals whose personalities contrast rather than match, pairing a "people cat" (a Siamese or Persian or their derivatives) and a "cat cat" (an American shorthair or a Maine coon). While both types of animals can make wonderful pets, their different personalities can limit competition and conflict. Four, talk to people who have the kinds of cats you want to mix, and compare their lifestyles and animals with your own situation.

While all of this may seem complicated, remember that any new cat represents an average 12-year investment. People who can't find the time to ensure the selection of the best cat to meet their unique needs will have a long time to rue this decision!

## Right Stuff Check

Think of your existing or dream cat as a mind-body unit. What personality traits do you consider "must-haves"? Do these take precedence over a certain look, or does the look mean the most to you? Imagine yourself seeing a tiny kitten huddled in the corner of a cage. How do you feel about that? What knowledge and skill do you possess to own such a cat? If you plan to add a second cat, what kind of animal would best meet your existing and new cats' needs as well as your own?

"When I tried to answer those questions, I wound up more confused than enlightened!" Marcy Longstreet protests. "How can I ever find the right cat?"

Because so much subjectivity surrounds the purebreds, it may take a while to weed out which feline factors you value the most. Suppose the Longstreets love the whole Birman package but want to add a cat of a different breed to their household. In that case they need to know what makes Sing-Too so different from other breeds as well as those qualities she shares with those other cats. If this exercise raises other questions and issues you never considered before, don't feel frustrated. That just proves you're learning to think about cats in new ways. As far as where to go for answers, the sources remain the same:

- books
- breeders
- people who own the kinds of cats you like
- veterinarians and other animal-care specialists

## The Right Cat Source

Regardless of what kind of cat you get, a few basic principles apply to where you get your new cat. First, the animal's space should be clean and odor free. Caged animals should have clean litter boxes, clean bedding, and fresh water. Very young kittens should be with their mothers or other adult cats. Second, the breeder or caregiver should adhere to a consistent and reliable schedule for handling caged animals and exposing them to people, other animals, and the routine events of daily life (ringing phones, slamming doors, etc.). Third, the environment shouldn't be extreme; kittens raised in chaotic, stressful environments as well as those raised in stimulus-deprived ones may experience serious problems such as aggression or excessive dependency and the stress-related physical problems that go with these.

Finally, the person selling or placing the animal should willingly provide the names of other owners, as well as any information you need to help you decide if this cat will fit you and your lifestyle. If you're considering a pet store or shelter, call area veterinarians for information on the quality of the animals and the care these places provide.

When people actually set out to acquire a purebred cat (as opposed to one acquiring them), they turn to one of four sources:

- casual breeders
- professional breeders
- pet stores
- animal shelters

The term "casual breeder" refers to people who get a purebred cat, like it for some reason or maybe just want to recoup the cost of it, breed it to another of the same breed, and sell the kittens. Needless to say, some of these folks have little or no knowledge of genetics or show standards, so buying one of these kittens can be an iffy proposition. On the other hand, such matings can produce sound pet-quality animals that come as close to type as many people desire.

Because casual breeders tend to sell most of their animals locally, potential buyers often can learn a great deal about the health and behavior of these animals from other owners, veterinarians, and groomers. These breeders also tend to charge less, an advantage only if you get a healthy, well-behaved animal that meets your needs.

Professional breeders strive to create animals as consistently close to the show standard as possible. These people function as the best sources of animals for those who want to show and breed their new pets. To find the right breeder, attend cat shows in different areas sponsored by different clubs and associations, talk to as many breeders of your dream cat as you can, and observe your dream breed being shown and judged.

Good professional breeders will do everything in their power to help you integrate your new pet into your household, and they'll also take back a kitten or even an adult animal if you can't keep it for some reason. They do this because they truly love their cats and want to ensure that their animals always get the best of care. While no one should buy a cat with the idea that he or she can dump it back on the breeder if it becomes an inconvenience, situations do arise when even the best-intentioned owners discover they can't keep a pet. Under those circumstances, knowing that the breeder will take the animal back can mean a great deal.

Marcy took a lot of grief from her boss's wife for buying a purebred cat from a pet store, but how much of that was warranted? It depends. One thing is certain: you'll pay top dollar for a cat from a pet store, as much as and often far more than you'll pay a breeder. Then the question becomes, what does this money get you? In the Longstreets' case, it got them a cat they adore and a pedigree.

An old saw reminds us that a purebred dog without papers is a mongrel, and the same holds true for cats. Whether the pedigree means anything to the Longstreets or not, that's what they paid top dollar for. Whether they got a good deal depends on what they plan to do with their pet. If they just want to enjoy her and she's a healthy, well-behaved animal, they'll probably feel they got their money's worth. On the other hand, if they decide to show her and discover that pedigree in no way guarantees that she's show quality, then they'll feel cheated.

While good breeders can serve as valuable sources of information about their specific animals and will take them back if problems arise, pet stores seldom offer this service. Most provide a limited guarantee of some sort, usually one that covers only medical problems. Some pet store clerks know little about cats and even less about specific breeds, so information about a particular kitten's or cat's origins may be sketchy at best. Some stores advertise kittens as "locally bred" to avoid the stigma attached to those purchased from mass producers. However, while this may sound more politically correct, it doesn't guarantee health, behavior, or pedigree.

Animal shelters serve as another common source of cats, with the numbers of purebred animals showing up in those facilities increasing every year. Of all the animal sources, shelters often can provide the least amount of information regarding their charges, and this can create problems for prospective owners who lose their hearts to a purebred adult shelter animal.

Consider the facts. Someone somewhere likely paid money for that cat. That means that a very good chance exists that the cat didn't work out for some reason. If the cat looks healthy, that usually means the cat has behavioral problems, most commonly not using the litter box. In fact, at an exhibit of shelter cats mounted by an organization known for getting thorough histories on all animals given up, 90 percent of the adults didn't use the litter box. That doesn't mean that such animals won't make wonderful pets, but it does mean that they require special homes as well as special handling (see Chapter 6).

A reputable shelter, like a reputable breeder, will provide you with as much information as possible and support your efforts to integrate your new pet into your household. Beware of those who appeal to your emotions, focusing on the cat's sad tale of woe or implying a one-way trip to the great cathouse in the sky if you don't adopt it. Also, so-called no-kill shelters may strike some people as more caring; however this holds true only if these organizations maintain the staff and facilities to give ill or otherwise problematic animals the proper care. If they don't, then this policy jeopardizes the health and behavior of all the animals in the shelter.

In the future I expect to see more breed rescue groups that take in cats of one specific breed with the idea of finding new homes for them. Like shelters, these can vary greatly in the quality of animals they offer and the service they provide. Like well-run shelters, the best provide a valuable service and may enable people who might not otherwise be able to afford a purebred cat to own one. At worst, they serve as collection agencies that bounce cats from household to household with no regard for resolving any existing feline problems or matching the right cat to the right person.

Unlike dealing with the kitten who shows up on your doorstep demanding you make an immediate decision, there's no need to give in to your emotions when purchasing a purebred cat. Rather you should use your emotions to compel you to choose the best source for the kind of cat you want. Once you select a clean, healthy facility operated by knowledgeable people you trust, your chances of finding your perfect kitten or cat will increase dramatically.

Just as the natural environment can affect a breed's biology and behavior, so can the home in which a cat or kitten lives with its owners. In the next chapter we'll explore what makes a human household a feline haven.

# 3

# A Home Within a Home

*Designing a Livable Space for Your Cat*

Al and Penny Liebermann can barely contain their joy when they move into their new home, an attractive row house with a minuscule front yard facing a grassy common.

"I'm sure Marlow will love this place as much as we do," Al confidently tells his wife as they watch the Japanese bobtail exploring the living room.

"With so much more space here than in the old apartment, I think we should get him a playmate," Penny suggests as the cat disappears up the stairs. "A new home and a new pal should solve all of his problems."

"Let's give him a few weeks to settle in," Al counters. "You know how he hates changes."

A week after this discussion the Liebermanns join other residents for a neighborhood block party.

"What an unusual-looking cat," remarks one of their new neighbors, Jon Sandford, when he spies Marlow peering out the window. "What kind is it?"

"He's a Japanese bobtail," Penny answers, then goes on to tell her new neighbor about the breed's history.

"I guess a cat like that must cost a lot," Jon remarks when Penny concludes describing Marlow's many purebred virtues.

"About $78,500," Al Liebermann says with a laugh, shaking his head ruefully.

"You're kidding!" Jon studies Marlow with new respect.

"Not at all," Al continues. "We actually got him as a wedding present, but he did $3,500 worth of damage to our old apartment and we got evicted. Then we bought this place for $75,000, thinking more space would make us all happy. At the rate he's going, though, he fully intends to destroy it, too!"

---

A decade ago, the idea of providing environmental enrichment for cats would have struck most people as a joke. Recently, however, two factors have made this an increasingly valid consideration.

First, we know from the preceding chapters that establishing and protecting the territory ranks as the number one animal priority and that cats display solitary or social characteristics depending on their environments. When we add the fact that more and more pet and feral cats inhabit our cities, suburbs, and countryside, behavioral problems naturally arise: the more cats, the less space per cat, and the greater the chance of territorial conflicts.

Second, owners and veterinarians daily confront more medical problems that resist traditional treatments and do appear to result from environmental stress. While giving a cat medication for a urinary tract infection usually solved the problem in the past, now more cats suffer from painful, chronic urinary problems with no clear physical cause. Other cats lick themselves raw, while still others succumb to intermittent digestive upsets. The fact that some of these behavioral and medical problems improve or even completely disappear when the environment changes strongly suggests that we need to pay more attention to the space in which our feline companions live.

Further complicating matters, although few cat lovers will admit to strong emotional views about feline environments, just ask them whether they think people should keep their cats indoors or allow them to run free, and watch the fur fly! For every person who ranks not confining the cat as the epitome of inhumane and irresponsible pet ownership, another ranks confinement as the ultimate in cruelty.

"How can someone think that letting cats run loose is okay?" Penny Liebermann asks as she studies all the vehicles and other outdoor distractions that could get her beloved Marlow into trouble.

While her remark makes perfectly good sense to her, it does so only because she divorces all of Marlow's problems from his environment. Instead, she sees his clawing the furniture and woodwork as a result of his "high-strung temperament," and his recurrent medical problems as related to a faulty diet or "some bug" he picked up somewhere.

At the opposite end of the spectrum, owners like the Liebermanns' neighbor, Jon Sandford, view keeping a cat indoors as completely wrong-headed. Jon would never consider doing this to Sheba, his shorthaired tabby. However, Jon does concede that strict confinement might be necessary for the purebreds because of their "flighty temperaments and frail health," a description most cat breeders would vehemently challenge!

In reality, though, just as cats' interactions with other cats and humans run the gamut from solitary to social, so their environmental needs may encompass a wide range of conditions. Many housebound cats live long and happy lives, as do many of those with access to the outdoors.

"But on the average, cats kept indoors *do* have longer life spans than those who go out," Al correctly adds.

"Maybe," Jon concedes. "But given the choice between a short, happy life and a long boring one or one filled with medical and behavioral problems, which would you prefer?"

Before these two cat lovers come to blows, let's look at the different factors that make a human house a cat home and what we can do to give our cats the best of our combined worlds.

## Home, Sweet Feline Home Check

Make a tour of your home and its surroundings on a typical weekday and weekend with your cat in mind. What kinds of activities occur in the area around your home? Do you consider these activities cat-friendly or hostile? Inside your home, note any objects or areas you consider off-limits. What would you do and how would you feel if your cat violated these spaces? Describe what you consider a perfect cat haven in your house.

When the Liebermanns perform this exercise they discover that even though they thought they allowed Marlow to go anywhere he wanted in their home, they really didn't mean it. While they both want the cat to stay off of the counters and tables, they encourage him to sit on shelves that don't contain any breakable objects. On the other hand, Jon expects Sheba to stay on the floor and off of all furniture except her cat bed, but he permits her to go anywhere she likes outdoors.

But what runs through Marlow's or Sheba's mind when they think about the ideal home? We can only guess, but it seems a safe bet that their thoughts center around the ease with which they can establish and protect what they consider an acceptable portion of that space. Whether the cat can do this, though, depends on both the physical and the behavioral makeup of that particular environment.

The feline space consists of four components:

- setting
- structure

- furnishings
- inhabitants

Because each of these factors possesses the potential to enhance or undermine the cat's health and behavior as well as the human-feline relationship, we need to examine them in more detail.

## Welcome to Cat Country

Except for those few cats who live aboard ships or trains or other movable spaces, cats inhabit urban, suburban, and rural settings like most people, with each area offering its own advantages and disadvantages. The first step to evaluating a cat's space, then, involves getting the big picture before focusing on the residence itself.

"I did that!" Jon proclaims vigorously. "One of the reasons I bought this place was the big grassy common where Sheba could play."

While Jon ultimately selected his home in the planned community with his pet in mind, he made that decision after he had narrowed the field to residences within a short drive of the computer company where he works. Because the Liebermanns look forward to starting a family soon, they zeroed in on the planned community's playground and the area's excellent schools and day-care facilities. Somewhat irrationally, but not all that uncommonly for pet owners, they also assumed that the best neighborhood for any future children would provide the best for their feline baby, too. Unfortunately, neither Jon nor the Liebermanns evaluated this setting in terms of the amounts and kinds of stimuli it might generate for their pets.

Chapters 1 and 2 introduced the cat as an extraordinary, recently domesticated animal with the sensory skills necessary to survive in the wild. Oblivious to this heritage, many owners will take in a stray cat or kitten or adopt one from a shelter and expect it to adapt immediately to apartment living, automatically shrinking its worldview such that it remains perfectly content within those limits. These people often express shock when their pets respond dramatically to inhabitants or events that occur in the cat's own home. When they learn that their furry friends might also respond to inhabitants and events on the streets surrounding the building and in the park 15 stories below, their mouths drop open in surprise.

A few years ago I received several calls from the media when a study of the fate of "high-rise cats" caught their attention. Veterinarians in metropolitan areas periodically see cats who leap or fall from apartment balconies and windows, sometimes from great heights. The fact that those cats who fall one or two stories often sustain much more serious injuries than those who fall from much higher levels intrigued some scientists, and they decided to study this phenomenon. The report that tickled the media's fancy concluded that, at greater heights, cats flatten their bodies like flying squirrels, floating rather than falling to the ground. Falls through shorter distances, however, don't allow the cat sufficient time to assume this lifesaving posture.

While most veterinarians viewed this as a medical issue, the media—at least those jovial talk-radio hosts who called me—wanted to know *why* high-rise cats were jumping in the first place: Should apartment-dwelling owners worry about their cats' committing suicide? Given the tongue-in-cheek nature of the media coverage, I couldn't offer much in the way of concrete information. Nonetheless, the behavior continues to intrigue me. I can easily envision some of these animals becoming so entranced by birds flying by at eye level that they leap at them with nary a thought about what lies below. I imagine others assaulted with such a dazzling amount of tempting stimulation that they similarly forget to look before they leap to investigate it more fully.

But do some cats, who lack the physiological or behavioral ability to ignore or escape from certain frightening or frustrating stimuli over which they have no control, literally become so overwhelmed that they take a flying leap in an effort to relieve the tension? I honestly don't know.

"That's why we moved out to the suburbs, to get away from all that," Penny remarks. "Someday we'd like to move even farther out into the country."

When urban dwellers become aware of how external input might negatively affect their pets' health and behavior, a common response urges them to move to somewhere with more space for the animal. Apartment dwellers dream of condos solving all of their problems; condo dwellers pray for the wherewithal to buy a house in the suburbs; suburban home owners save for a place in the country.

While new settings sometimes miraculously solve an animal's problems, that doesn't happen as often as many pet owners would like to believe. Suburban and rural settings might not offer the *same* attractions and distractions as metropolitan areas, but they do offer as many, if not more.

Consider the planned community in which the Liebermanns live. Although it's hardly a bustling metropolis, a steady stream of residents, visitors, and service people routinely walk or drive by their home. Five days a week, workers construct more homes on the other side of the green. Six days a week, the whistling letter carrier ambles up the Liebermanns' front walk, the brass mail slot clanks open, and mail falls to the floor. Seven days a week the newspaper hits the front door with a dull *thwack!*, one or more children or adults ring the doorbell soliciting funds for some worthy cause, and Al and Penny plus any service people, friends, or family members to whom they've given permission to enter their home come and go at will. Depending on the season, street sweepers or snowplows will pass by, as will trick-ortreaters, carolers, cyclists, roller skaters, or softball and card play-ers on their way to and from the community center.

While Al and Penny think of their community as a serene haven compared with the city in which they work, shy Marlow views it quite differently!

When the Liebermanns and Marlow visit friends who live on what Al and Penny consider a blissfully quiet farm, a completely different collection of stimuli awaits their feline companion. Instead of the sounds, scents, and sights of human traffic and activities, Marlow hears those emitted by domestic and wild ani-mals. Sheep bleat, foxes scream, and wild turkeys call; scent marks of wild animals mingle with those of horse and cow manure; hawks soar overhead, and rabbits and field mice scurry through the meadows.

Another aspect of environmental settings sure to gain impor-tance in the years ahead concerns the presence of any threatened or endangered species in the area upon which a cat might prey. Recently, an Australian legislator called for the removal of *all* cats from the country, citing their devastating effect on the native ani-mal populations. In another instance, shortsighted town planners granted a less than environmentally concerned developer per-mission to build on the edge of a natural preserve that protected threatened rodent as well as bird populations. Not only were the development's residents required to keep their cats strictly indoors, but they also were expected to trap and eliminate any loose cats found on their property. Needless to say, the resultant public outcry turned this pastoral setting into a very noisy place!

Every environment comes furnished with its own unique sources of natural and man-made sensory signals. If the animal can't deal with those, it becomes the owner's responsibility to make the necessary changes to ensure that it can. As the num-ber of cats continues to increase, more people will turn to systems such as Cat Fence-In, a device that keeps cats in their yards and other cats out. (You can call them for a free brochure at 702-359-4575.) Cabana Systems, which we'll discuss in the next section, currently is developing a screened gazebo that connects to the owner's home with a short tunnel, giving the cat free access to this large, safe area outdoors. Kali-Ko Cathouses offers an assortment of portable covered plastic playpens that provide the cat with a safe space outdoors. (For further information on this system, call their kennel consultant at 800-658-5925.)

Before reading on, take a tour through your cat's country and get a cat's-eye view of your neighborhood.

## Setting Evaluation

Walk around your neighborhood or acreage, keeping the cat's incredible sense of hearing, smell, and motion-sensitive vision in mind. What kinds of things could attract or distract your cat? Does the setting become more active at certain times of the day or week? What seasonal changes occur that might affect your pet?

When Jon Sandford and the Liebermanns tour their neighborhood, they view the same characteristics quite differently. The other cats who Jon sees as potential playmates, the Liebermanns view as sources of disease and bad habits. Jon sees the grassy common as a place where Sheba can chase butterflies and play with the local children. To the Liebermanns it represents a place where Marlow could hurt himself or people could abuse him. As opposite as these views may appear, both contain some element of the truth. The important thing is for owners to sort the fact from the fiction.

As we'll see, much as these owners' views of their environments may differ, their cats' behavioral responses to those settings may differ a great deal more.

# The Behavioral Setting

Setting can affect the cat's physical and psychological well-being and the human-feline relationship for two different behavioral reasons. First, recall that the cat's solitary nature leads it to internalize early experiences much more strongly than social animals do. Like the city mouse who felt out of place when she visited her country cousin (and vice versa), cats raised in one setting may experience difficulty when moved to another.

A common example arises when caring people take in strays from the mean streets or rugged wilderness and try to make house pets out of them. Although some of these cats do relish the change, many find the new environment traumatic to the point that they become destructive and even leap at doors and windows in an attempt to escape.

Consider what happens when the Liebermanns cat-sit for the free-roaming Sheba when Jon goes to Europe for a month. Al and Penny decide to keep Sheba indoors for two reasons:

- They don't think any cat should run loose outdoors.
- They're terrified that something will happen to Sheba while she's under their care.

On their very first day as cat-sitters when they go to feed and play with Sheba at Jon's home after work, Sheba streaks out the door the instant they open it, then refuses to come when they call her. To add to their misery, the Liebermanns discover that during her confinement the normally well-behaved cat shredded the drapes, knocked a Waterford vase off of the mantel, and sprayed Jon's bed with urine. Because the Liebermanns failed to appreciate that Sheba's territory included the area around Jon's home as well as the structure itself, they created a situation far more hazardous to her health and behavior than if they'd followed her owner's usual routine.

On the other hand, when Al gets so fed up with Marlow's destructive behavior that he boots the bobtail outdoors one Saturday morning, the cat huddles under a rosebush, trembling in fear. Nothing in his indoor upbringing, first with a doting breeder and then with the Liebermanns, has prepared him for this. When a neighborhood dog comes bounding up to play with him, Marlow panics and bolts into the street, directly into the path of an oncoming car, something the street- and dog-savvy Sheba would never do.

The cat's strong territorial nature also can determine whether a particular setting will enhance or undermine its health, behavior, and relationship with its owner. Remember that establishing and protecting the territory takes precedence over eating, drinking, and reproduction. Consequently, anything threatening about the area surrounding his home can interfere with Marlow's appetite as well as his relationship with his owners. Given these negative effects, we can appreciate why he would attempt to relieve this stress any way he can.

"How do cats relieve stress?" Penny asks, thinking of the deep-breathing exercises she does to accomplish that goal.

It appears that cats relieve tension by taking it out on their environments or on themselves, depending on their personalities. Unfortunately because veterinary medicine, like human medicine, rarely considers personality as a factor in disease, no concrete data on this connection exist. However, discussions with veterinarians and cat owners suggest that more extroverted cats will vent their frustration on the house or its furnishings if something in the environment threatens them, while more introverted animals may lick themselves, vomit, or experience seizures or other chronic medical problems.

How do you think your specific environment does or could affect your cat's behavior?

---

## Environmental Review

Make a second tour around your property or neighborhood, this time bearing in mind any existing or dream cat's roots and personality. How does the environment complement these? Note any environmental factors you think might cause problems for your pet.

On their second tour of their neighborhood, the Lieber-manns think about the secluded cattery near the ocean where Marlow spent the first eight months of his life.

"No wonder he feels threatened here!" Al exclaims as he steps aside to allow a rhythm band from the day-care center to march by. "Even though this place seems a lot quieter to me than our apartment in the city, I can see now that it's not that much better for him."

When Jon conducts this same exercise, he decides the stim-ulus load in the planned community equals that of the busy dairy barn where Sheba spent her first few months. He also realizes that luck more than anything else enabled her to learn how to cope with the traffic when he turned her loose as a youngster.

Once we learn how to evaluate the bigger environmental pic-ture from a feline perspective, we need to take this process indoors.

## Kitty Architecture

In an article entitled "Facilitating Pet Ownership Through Improved Housing Design" (*Journal of the American Veterinary Medical Association*, September 15, 1996), urban planner Virginia Sandford Jackson makes a compelling case for the need to pro-vide quality environments for pets as well as people. Rather than proposing this as a warm, fuzzy, animal-loving alternative, the author points out that these changes make sense for very prac-tical reasons. Pet-friendly housing improves the quality of the ani-mal's life, and that, in turn, decreases the likelihood of problems. Because problem animals may destroy private property as well as become public nuisances when their owners turn them loose or abandon them, housing approaches that take the animal's needs into account make sense. While most of Jackson's recom-mendations apply primarily to dogs, one warmed the cockles of my garden- and cat-loving heart: interior courtyards. What a delight they would be to cat owners! However, until that happy day when everyone shares Jackson's enlightened views, it behooves owners to evaluate their homes with an eye toward providing feline-friendly spaces to head off any problems.

According to most etiquette books, people should greet any stranger at their doors with a smile that compels the caller to introduce him- or herself and state the reason for the visit. However, Marlow could care less about this human social amenity. A typical scenario begins to unfold when a volunteer seeking donations for the local hospital knocks politely, clears his throat, and prepares to deliver a cheerful greeting when Penny Liebermann cracks open the door. She begins to smile, then suddenly lunges and shrieks, "Yii!!!! Don't let the cat out! Al, quick, Marlow's out!"

Al streaks past the startled visitor and disappears into the wintry night in his shorts and T-shirt. The visitor may feel shocked by this display, but he may also consider it a normal part of fund-raising in suburbia. In fact, one fund-raiser told me she finds that such pet owners often end up making a sizable donation, perhaps to buy the volunteer's silence regarding the event.

However, if you prefer to project a more genteel image and want to keep your cat indoors, pay close attention to any exterior doors in your home. Screen doors offer extra protection for those occasions when you don't have time to ascertain the cat's location before opening the door. Doors that open into mud rooms or enclosed foyers separated from the rest of the house by an interior door also permit more gracious greetings.

Owners who lack screen doors or other protected entryways sometimes try to prevent feline escapes by barricading the door in one way or another. However, such devices rarely stop the cat but do present a safety hazard for others in the household who might need to exit quickly. Mats that shock the cat can turn a simple behavior problem into a neurotic one 10 times more difficult, if not impossible, to resolve. Because of this, it makes more sense to train the cat to stay away from the door.

However, training cats to stay away from doors poses its own special problems. For one thing, cats tend to respond defensively to punishment. Consequently, if the Liebermanns swat Marlow every time he gets too close to the door, they may wind up with a cat who bites them as well as bolts. One trainer suggests using the same door-slamming technique recommended for dog owners in which the owner opens the door a few inches and then, when the animal starts to charge it, slams the door hard. While the combination of the shock and sound makes this technique very effective for dogs, the cat's small size and relative speed make it hazardous. By the time Penny slams the door, Marlow may be halfway through it already. Granted, this might keep him away from the door, but only because his injuries will keep him away from everything.

Most owners fare better using a combination of distraction and aversion techniques. To do so, owners set up the cat so they can control the entire event, thereby guaranteeing the consistent response necessary to ensure lasting change. At a prearranged time, someone knocks on the door, and one member of the household distracts the cat while another lets the visitor in. Effective distraction devices include favorite toys and noise-makers, balls, and crumpled balls of paper. Some owners use food treats, but for reasons we'll discuss in Chapter 8, I prefer that owners avoid this approach if possible. If the owner consistently creates the positive distraction every time someone comes to the door, soon the cat will seek out the toy rather than the door when any door-related activity occurs.

Owners of persistent door-lungers may need to cover the floor in front of the door with several strips of double-sided tape to further discourage the cat. The taped area should be narrow enough that any people can easily step over it, but sufficiently large to discourage the cat from jumping it.

One clever owner used the dreaded vacuum cleaner to keep her cat away from her apartment door. Her pet hated the appliance so much that the mere sight of it would send the animal scurrying in the opposite direction. In conjunction with this, the owner evolved a greeting ritual that occurred in the kitchen rather than at the door in the living room. She instructed any visitors to ignore the cat when they entered until they removed their coats and moved to the kitchen. Once there, they happily called the cat and greeted him fondly when he came. Now as soon as he hears her or anyone else at the door, he scurries to the kitchen and waits there for his special greeting.

Owners of cats who go in and out almost always rate a cat door as one of the best investments they ever made. Cat doors come in a wide variety of shapes and sizes to fit every need. Some fit into screens, others into windows, sliding doors, or French doors. Other doors admit only cats wearing a special "key" that triggers the door's electronic lock mechanism. Some doors can only be locked or open, while others can limit the cat's access to one direction or the other. Still other doors have indicators that tell owners whether the cat is out or in. As the number of cats continues to grow and environmental concerns increase, I suspect cat owners will increasingly opt for pet doors that open into secure outdoor areas as the best solution. (For a crash course in many of the options available, call Pet Doors U.S.A. at 800-749-9609 and request a catalog.)

Whether cats spend all of their time or only part of it indoors, they like to be able to see what's going on outside. This doesn't necessarily mean they'll spend a lot of time looking outside if owners provide this opportunity. However, it's almost a sure bet it will bother them if they can't. As much as Marlow may cringe at what happens outside the Liebermanns' home, he spends a great deal of time hanging on the window frames peering outside. He'd probably prefer to sit on the windowsills, but the Liebermanns' windows don't have sills, so the curious cat digs his front claws into the lower window frame and his back ones into the wall below and hangs instead. Although passersby snicker at the worried cat face peering at them, his owners see nothing humorous about their gouged window frames and walls.

Fortunately for cat owners, even though few architects may think about cats, other creative folks do, and more products for feline structural environmental enhancement pop up every day. Because tension in indoor cats can occur when the animals can't determine the origin of the sensory input, one of my favorite additions is the Thrill-of-the-Wild or Cabana Lookout offered by Cabana Systems. Cats can sit in this easily installed screened bay-window insert and get a panoramic view of what's going on outside from within the safety of their own homes. (Call 800-273-1338 or visit Cabana's Web site at http://www.cabana.com for further information on these window inserts.)

Several companies offer shelf assemblies to broaden small sills enough to accommodate furry feline bodies. However, you should keep a few cat-safe points in mind when considering these products. First, make sure the shelf fastens securely. When Marlow makes a running leap onto the budget model the Liebermanns purchase, the shelf collapses, dumping the cat on the floor and splitting the frame. Second, while some of these shelves come with luxurious coverings, that's an advantage only if you can easily remove them for washing or replacement. If not, the shelf can become a source of infection as well as an eyesore. For older cats or those who experience difficulty jumping, Avcon Products (phone: 714-530-4828) offers Kitty Walk which consists of a series of steps up to a window perch.

If you're handy with tools, you can construct your own cat-sized shelves and affix them to walls next to windows or in areas where your cat(s) can enjoy perching unmolested by humans and animals alike. In addition to enabling pets to look out previously inaccessible windows, these shelves can relieve territorial stress in another way. Recall that cats in multiple-cat households may establish their territories in layers. Owners of homes without built-in or freestanding shelving to enable their pets to do this can provide this same benefit by affixing cat-sized perches to the wall. People lacking carpentry skills can contact CatCliffs at 800-555-7367 for a brochure describing their premade window, wall, and corner perches.

Truly lazy persons like me who live in narrow-silled homes can place solid tables or other pieces of furniture in front of the window and put a cat bed or folded towel on it. I use an antique trunk for this purpose, with Whittington's bed at one end, some potted geraniums at the other, and ferns hung from the ceiling above. In addition to looking out the window, he bats at the ferns when the wind stirs them and considers my weekly plant watering ritual a wonderful event which he observes with great interest.

What kinds of wall coverings provide the most compatible human-feline habitats? More than a few owners curse the day they opted for cork, burlap, or other fabric coverings, although their pets delight in shredding them. One paradoxical variation on that theme came from a piano teacher who shared an apartment with her cat. She carpeted one wall strictly for soundproofing but discovered another unanticipated advantage: her cat adores literally climbing the wall. Because the cat previously climbed the curtains and drapes, the owner considered this a marvelous improvement.

Easily washed painted plaster or plasterboard (sheetrock) walls with wooden framework remain the universal favorite of cat owners. While we don't normally think of cats indulging in food fights or otherwise making a mess, they do mark walls, door frames, and doors as well as furnishings with their scent. A careful observer will see little gray smudges at cat-head height on my front, cellar, and bathroom doors. Other cats mark other doors; some mark window frames or areas where walls meet. One lesson pet owners quickly learn is that more expensive, higher quality washable paint will more than pay for itself in the long run. Depending on the room and the color, satin or semigloss finishes may provide additional cleaning benefits without the loss of aesthetic appeal.

For those cats who mark exterior corners of walls often and vigorously enough to wear off the paint, attaching a Cat-a-Comb to the area may spare the walls. This device consists of two small plastic panels that the owner glues to the walls at the juncture. The panels contain combs for the cat to rub against as well as pouches the owner can fill with catnip to attract the cat. Whether these work depends on whether the cat will accept combing rather than marking and whether it responds to catnip (not all cats do).

One of my favorite feline accessories (also carried by Pet Doors U.S.A.) goes by the name of Cat Hole. Cat Hole is an arched interior cat opening designed to provide cats access through closed interior doors, a blessing for owners who keep the litter box in chilly basements, or in closets away from stool-eating dogs and curious toddlers. The removable arch comes with a snap-in brush to pick up hairs when the cat passes through it as well as "fat cat" adjustments to accommodate cats up to 22 pounds.

As far as flooring goes, cat owners agree that washable wood, tile, or vinyl with washable rugs always beats wall-to-wall carpeting. Cats do vomit and get diarrhea; they also get fleas and shed. While carpeting hides cat hair better than wood, vinyl, or tile, it's a lot easier to sweep or vacuum hair from a hard, smooth surface than from a textured fabric. Also, though many cats won't use carpet-covered scratching posts (more on this later), a fair number will zero in on carpeting on stairs or by doors or windows as ideal places to dig and claw. While wall-to-wall carpeting can be repaired, less-than-perfect results as well as the cost lead many cat owners to opt for other floor coverings.

A final consideration when evaluating your home or a potential new one as a cat haven involves delving into its feline history. For example, in addition to going from a very serene setting to a hectic city as a young kitten, Marlow had to contend with the fact that the people who occupied the Liebermanns' city apartment before they did owned a cat who sprayed urine in the bathroom and owners' bedroom. Naturally when the inexperienced, frightened young cat moved into such a place, every instinct urged him to mark those same spots to claim that space as his own. Had the Liebermanns known about the previous feline inhabitant's habits, they could have thoroughly cleaned these areas before bringing a cat there.

A second historical fact to ascertain when moving into a place vacated by pet owners is the time between their departure and your intended arrival. More than a month passed between the day the former occupants moved out and the Liebermanns moved in and added Marlow to their household. During that period the many flea eggs shed by the previous feline tenant hatched and grew very hungry. The instant Marlow walked in they attacked, and the poor cat had to deal with this irritation in addition to everything else. Consequently, if you plan to buy or rent in areas with flea problems, you can save a lot of time, money, and frustration by treating your new home for fleas *before* you move in.

Time to make a tour of your home to see how its basic structure measures up as a cat house.

## Structure Check

Walk through your home and survey the doors, windows, walls, floors, and any other permanent fixtures. If you own a cat, what evidence of your cat's presence do you see? How do you feel about this? What structural changes would make your home more cat-friendly for any existing or dream cat?

When the Liebermanns conduct this exercise, Al decides to build some shelves to provide Marlow with a better view of the world outside their home. Penny decides it makes more sense to use a cherished handmade rug as a wall hanging rather than constantly yell at Marlow for digging at it on the floor. Meanwhile Jon decides to add a cat door to allow Sheba access to his home even when he's not there.

Once we evaluate the setting and the structure itself, we need to examine our furnishings with our cats in mind.

## The Well-Appointed Cat House

A former client once described the decor in her home as "Early American Cat with Feminist Overtones." When I asked her what that meant, she replied, "I have a lot of period pieces covered with cat hair, but I don't care." While such a statement might curdle the blood of an antiques collector, it typifies those made by owners who have achieved a decor that balances their own and their cats' needs.

Unfortunately, most owners come to such conclusions following often highly emotional confrontations with their pets. When the Liebermanns bought their first furniture, they didn't own a cat, so the idea of how a cat would respond to it never crossed their minds. When Penny saw a couch that appealed to her, unlike an experienced cat owner she didn't think, "No way! That color will show every cat hair, plus hair will stick to that fabric like ticks on a hound!" Instead she agreed with the clerk that the navy blue couch with its loosely woven fabric would surely become the focal point of the Liebermanns' first home.

And, once Marlow moves in, it certainly does.

"Get off that couch, you hair ball!" Penny routinely yells at the cat while she tries to pick his white hairs out of the fabric.

"Take that, you furry demon!" Al shouts as he blasts Marlow with a water pistol when he spies the bobtail clawing the corner of the couch yet again.

Contrary to what some people may want to believe, cats do not shed and claw because they made a pact with the CatDevil to do this eons ago. All but the hairless cats (who leave grease spots) naturally shed, and all cats naturally claw, too. Daily grooming can reduce the amount of free-floating hair, but few cat lovers find the time for this, and rogue hairs would still escape anyhow. Consequently, it makes sense to select furnishings that take this reality into account.

"Like what?" asks Penny, looking at the shabby remains of her once lovely focal point. "I don't want a white couch with orange and black spots."

Although the idea of a mackerel tabby hassock or a seal-point recliner does have its appeal, such drastic solutions aren't necessary. The ideal cat-resistant upholstery possesses two characteristics:

- a hair-hiding pattern
- a fabric with a hard, smooth finish

People who prefer light-colored cats should stick with light-colored fabrics; those who favor dark-colored animals should select their furnishings with that in mind. Those who live with multiple cats or see multiple cats in their futures should consider subtle patterns that include the colors of that particular feline palette. Think herringbone rather than bold stripes, and lots of little geometric shapes or flowers rather than a few large ones, to confuse the eye and make any hairs appear part of the pattern.

Not only can the right color and pattern do wonders to hide cat hair, a fabric with a hard, smooth finish will make it easy to clean up the hair that inevitably will fall. Also pay attention to where your cat prefers to snooze on your furniture. Even though cats often give the impression that they sleep *everywhere*, in reality most have a few favorite spots. Placing pillows with removable, matching fabric covers, towels, or other cat-friendly pads in these areas will spare the furniture. One pad manufacturer claims that its ultrasoft hand-washable fibers also carry an electrostatic charge that traps hair, dirt, and dust. Although such a thought warms the housekeeper's heart, that charged surface might not appeal to all cats.

Smooth, dense fabrics also help discourage clawing, another major bone of contention between owners and their feline companions. While all the anti-clawing approaches from declawing the cat to covering the corners of furniture with clear plastic protectors work, they treat clawing as a problem rather than as a natural behavior. However, cats claw for perfectly legitimate behavioral and health reasons, and we need to understand these in order to make an intelligent decision about how to deal with this "problem."

Chapter 1 discussed how wildcats use claw marks to claim their territories. They also use this process to sharpen their claws. They need these sharp claws to pinion their prey before they can kill it as well as to protect themselves. Obviously, a wildcat with dull claws won't last very long in the wild.

Owners usually don't object to cats' using their claws to defend themselves unless they scratch people. However, few owners take a similarly tolerant view of cats who claw to establish or protect a territory within their homes. And although owners typically evaluate clawed furnishings in sentimental ("I inherited that chair from my grandmother!") or financial ("That couch cost $1,500!") terms, the location and composition of the clawed objects can tell us a great deal more.

Cats clawing to mark their territories usually select objects based on their *significant locations* rather than on their composition. Thus, when Marlow feels threatened by something outdoors, he may shred the exterior door frame or the wall beside it and completely ignore the otherwise enticing couch positioned against an inside wall. However, when the Liebermanns move that same couch next to the door, the cat claws this more foot-

and claw-friendly object instead. Very shy cats or those threatened by something within the household often will focus their clawing on areas such as the stairways (if the owners sleep or spend most of their time upstairs), bedroom door frames, or objects in these sacred spaces.

In addition to using their claws to mark their territories, cats claw because they *need* to do so for health reasons. In order to keep the claw healthy, cats follow a two-step nail-grooming process that includes:

- removing the outer layer of the claw as needed
- sharpening the claw points

Examination of a cross section of a cat claw under a microscope reveals that it grows in layers, sort of like an onion. Periodically cats shed the worn outer layer and expose a fresh new one. In order to do this, they dig their claws into an object up to the base of the claw and pull down to peel the outer layer off. Sometimes owners find these shed bits of claw around favorite scratching areas. Other times they remain oblivious to this phenomenon until problems arise.

For example, one day Jon notices Sheba limping. When he examines her front paw he discovers that the claw of her "thumb" has thickened and grown right into her foot pad, creating a painful abscess. In this situation, the position of the claw at the side of the foot prevents Sheba from properly grooming it when she marks her favorite narrow fence post outdoors. The layers build up, and the claw becomes longer and longer until it eventually grows right into her foot and an abscess forms. Jon's veterinarian treats the infection and shows Jon how to routinely check her feet, remove any excess claw layers, and clip these claws.

"Isn't he afraid he'll cut her nail too short and make her bleed?" Penny asks. "I did that once to my parents' dog. What a mess!"

Unlike with dog nails, you can easily see the blood vessel in most cat claws, and it's easy to avoid. If you've never noticed it, gently press a cat foot between your thumb and index finger to expose the claws. Then shine a small flashlight or penlight through one of the claws from the opposite side. You'll see the vessel clearly, as well as how the nail tapers to a point. Owners who clip their cats' claws either remove that tapered part with standard nail clippers or use special cat nail clippers to do the job.

Sometimes older cats with arthritis or those with medical problems will stop scratching and develop claw problems, too. This lack of self-care may lead to infections at the base of the nail or to a generalized thickening of the claws to the point that the cat can no longer retract them. Worse, the exposed claws can get caught in carpeting and upholstery and cause a nasty fall. Regular feline pedicures designed to remove the excess layers and keep these areas clean will prevent this problem.

Once we realize why cats claw, we can appreciate the need to provide them with a proper place to do this if we want to keep them from ruining our furnishings. The traditional approach recommends buying or building a carpeted scratching post, rubbing it with catnip or some other attractive substance, and then sitting back and watching the cat use it.

I can hear experienced cat owners chuckling already. While this approach will work with young kittens and older animals accustomed to clawing carpeting, it usually won't work for those who already prefer the corner of the couch or chair. Not only do Marlow's early experiences play a major role in fixing his clawing preferences, so does feline common sense. Given the choice between the densely woven carpeting on his new scratching post and the loosely woven fabric on the couch, the cat will choose the latter every time because it better enables him to dig his claws in deeply enough to pull off those outer layers.

What happens when Marlow wants to sharpen the points of his claws? Granted, the carpeting on the scratching post certainly beats the fabric on the couch for this job, but it doesn't come close to that little patch of the wooden door frame he's been clawing for months.

In this situation, the Liebermanns will fare much better if they cover the carpeted scratching post with a fabric similar to that on the couch.

"But he'll claw through that in no time!" Al protests.

True, he may. But upholstery remnants cost a lot less than couches. Not only that, as Marlow claws at the fabric-covered post, he'll become accustomed to the feel of the carpeting beneath the fabric, and then the carpeting itself as the fabric gives way. Eventually he may come to accept the carpeting completely.

"What about sharpening his claws?" Penny reminds us. "He was using the door frame for that."

Cats who prefer wood for this activity often will accept pieces of whole or split logs. Cats who habitually claw vertical sections of furniture or door frames adapt more easily to split logs securely fastened to the wall at the same height. One creative cat owner rolled a large section of a sawed-off tree stump approximately two feet in diameter by two feet high into her family room, where her cats spend most of their time. Here it serves a dual function as a scratching post and magazine holder even though few of her guests realize this.

For those cats who prefer plasterboard, cardboard, or other unusual scratching materials, the goal remains to provide something as similar to the preferred object as possible, then to slowly wean the cat to something else if desired. While some owners see providing the cat with its own cat-sized piece of plasterboard or a cardboard box to shred as giving in, others see it as a way to meet the pet's special needs without allowing it to destroy their homes.

When it comes to clawing, cats always prefer secure objects, a requirement many commercial scratching products fail to address. While carpeted or sisal scratchers that hang on doors or sit on the floor may appeal to owners, cats may not use these because they move when the animal applies sufficient pressure to perform the necessary grooming ritual. Aside from throwing the cat off-balance, this may result in painful twisting of the trapped claws. Because of this, less stable objects work best when introduced to young kittens, who then can develop the necessary skills to compensate for any motion as they get older.

After installing an alternative scratching object in the significant location next to the original target, the owner places a layer of double-sided tape on the original target to discourage its use. Owners who hope to shortcut the process by only discouraging the cat from one area without supplying it with a more acceptable one run the risk of the animal's merely switching its attention from one piece of furniture or door frame to another. One owner who routinely blasted her cat with a squirt gun when it even thought about clawing a prized antique love seat was horrified to discover that the cat started using the back of an equally valuable antique chair kept in a spare room. By the time she realized this, the cat had damaged the chair beyond repair.

How do your furnishings stack up as cat bait?

---

## Furniture Evaluation

Walk through your home again, evaluating your furnishings in terms of any existing or dream cats' behavioral and health needs. Does the position or composition of any of these pieces make them more likely to attract negative feline attention? What could you do to prevent such problems?

Although the Liebermanns conducted this third tour based on the assumption that Marlow ruined *all* of their furnishings, their new knowledge made it clear that he concentrated most of his attention on a few objects that carried a strong behavioral charge. Because Sheba established her territory outdoors, Jon finds little evidence that his furnishings affect his cat one way or another. On the other hand, like all cats, Sheba definitely responds to the presence of people and other animals in Jon's home.

# Moving Violations

Nothing in a cat's environment influences it as much as its human and animal companions and neighbors. Because we'll examine the unique characteristics of the human-feline relationship in depth in the next two chapters, we'll limit our discussion here to other animals.

Ironically, many people shifted from dog to cat ownership during the last 20 years because pack-oriented dogs experienced troublesome behavioral and medical problems when changing human lifestyles resulted in their being left home alone all day. At that time, the solitary, nocturnal cat who didn't mind being left alone (because it slept most of the day) seemed like the ideal pet.

In fact, had we permitted the cat its solitude, the domestic cat population would probably experience a lot fewer problems today. However, as social animals as well as often linear thinkers who envision ourselves at the "top" of the animal kingdom, we humans just couldn't resist the temptation to reshape this unique creature in our own image, as we did—and do—all other domestic animals. When Marlow begins destroying the Liebermanns' first apartment, the idea that loneliness causes this behavior immediately occurs to Penny because *she* would feel lonely under those circumstances, and soon that belief becomes firmly entrenched. She sees the solution as giving Marlow another cat for company. The idea that other animals might *cause* the bobtail's behavior never crosses her mind.

"My mom has two cats who love each other," Penny says in defense of her position.

Such utterly true statements always make me wonder why I don't stick to human-canine problems. Indeed, sufficient numbers of cats do live together in perfect harmony to make a convincing case for the evolution of the cat from a solitary to a social species. However, far more of the medical and behavioral problems plaguing contemporary cats result from the presence of too many cats than from too few. Moreover, those cats who do live peacefully together probably owe their peaceful existence to their environments as much or more than to their feline genes.

"Are you saying people shouldn't have more than one cat?" Penny asks somewhat sharply while Al bobs his head up and down to nudge me toward an affirmative reply.

Penny's question warrants a rousing, "It depends," which won't please either her or Al. However, it *does* depend. We already noted that, even though cats may have very precise ideas regarding how much space they need in order to feel comfortable, they don't always readily share that information with us. More often than not, owners discover that Cat One considers Cat Two an intruder rather than a charming companion and many times owners might not relate this to the cat's territorial nature at all.

For example, when Jon takes in a stray and Sheba begins clawing his bedroom door frame, he first attributes her behavior to jealousy. This causes him to lavish more affection on her to prove he loves her just as much as ever. When the behavior continues, however, he decides her spiteful, mean nature compels her to get even with him by destroying his home.

Compare Jon's experience with what happens when the Liebermanns add a second Japanese bobtail to their home. Marlow hisses and swats at the kitten and refuses to allow it anywhere near the food, water, or litter box. When the Liebermanns isolate the new kitten in a spare bedroom, it cries and refuses to eat and drink. Within a matter of weeks, both cats come down with upper respiratory infections, and Al and Penny wind up medicating them in addition to trying to get them to at least tolerate, if not like, each other.

Why did these resident cats view the addition as a territorial violation rather than as a new playmate? The answer takes us back to that most basic imperative: the need to establish and protect the territory. In Sheba's case, she found the new adult sufficiently threatening to feel compelled to claim Jon's bedroom as her own. While Jon viewed this behavior as spiteful and mean, Sheba saw it as protecting something very special to her. Meanwhile Marlow's sheltered, solitary upbringing led him to claim the entire Liebermann home as his own; he viewed *any* addition to it as a threat.

What about cats and dogs? In spite of all the old husbands' tales about people or animals fighting "like cats and dogs," dogs and cats fight far less often than cats fight with each other. Why this occurs goes back to the cat's territorial nature. Domestic cats and dogs may share the same physical space, but they don't use it the same way, any more than a person and a cat use the same space the same way. These differences permit a certain compatibility that doesn't exist when animals of the same species compete for the same resources in the same way.

Even a dog and cat raised together to the point that their owners say the cat thinks it's a dog or vice versa will usually hang on to enough of their distinct identities that they avoid the kinds of conflicts that occur between members of the same species. My own experiences mirror those of other multiple-species owners. My cat Whittington sucks on my hound Watson's ear, and he sleeps on the dog's blanket beside my bed as well as in his own cat bed on the trunk—but never on my bed or on any other piece of furniture. He also plays with Watson, cornering the dog (who outweighs him by more than 40 pounds), lunging at him, and trying to sink his claws into the dog's woven nylon collar so the dog can drag him through the house.

Prior to Whittington and Watson, I owned another dog who dragged my Siamese cat around the house by the head. While such behavior might shock noncat folks, it's a fairly common canine-feline interaction. Aside from the game's giving the cat a wet, slippery head, it did my pet no harm. Moreover, she invariably initiated the game, rubbing up against the dog's muzzle and batting him with her head. After observing these and other cat-dragging dogs for years, I consider this a shadow of the retrieving instinct that compels adult wild dogs and cats to carry their young. In the contemporary version, the animals use this same instinct to create a game as crucial to their survival in a relatively unstimulating human environment as the original instinct was for their ancestors in the wild.

Cats also will form relationships with pet rabbits, mice, rats, fish, reptiles, amphibians, and even birds. The younger the cat when introduced to these animals, the more likely it will respond to them as playmates rather than prey. However, the range of response is so tremendous that owners who envision nonfeline companions for their cats should view any warm, fuzzy stories about such interspecies relationships with a fair amount of skepticism as regards its applicability to their own households. Just because it works for one cat and one parrot doesn't mean that it will work for all. Unfortunately, some cats will suddenly turn on once-gently-handled playmates of other species because of seemingly unrelated events in the household. For example, one evening during a party, Marlow attacks the Liebermanns' $1,500 parrot. While it seems like a totally unprovoked, vicious attack to the Liebermanns and their guests, in reality the sound, motion, scent, and other stimuli generated by the party propelled the skittish cat into the predatory mode. When the bird ran toward Marlow squawking as usual, the overstimulated cat bit the parrot rather than held it as he had in the past. The bird's frantic attempts to get away plus its screams of pain, combined with the shouts of the Liebermanns and their guests, caused the cat to bite harder—a perfectly logical but nonetheless tragic response.

Pause here and give careful consideration to any existing or future pets who live or might live with you.

## Inhabitant Check

Think about any other nonhuman inhabitants in your home and their known or suspected relationships with any cats in your life. Which inter-species behaviors bother you? Which ones do you enjoy? If you foresee other pets in your future, how do you intend to introduce them to your cat?

"I only have Sheba now, but I want to get another pet in the future," Jon murmurs thoughtfully as he works on the exercise. "I really want a dog, but I thought Sheba would hate one, since she hates cats. Now I plan to explore that option more seriously."

"Not me!" exclaims Penny. "I want another cat!"

Penny's response is typical to say the least. Studies continue to show that the average American cat owner owns more than one cat. The challenge then becomes providing a true home rather than just a space for those animals.

# Making a House a Home

Many multiple-cat owners begin as single-cat owners who discover they enjoy the experience so much that they go searching for a second feline companion. After all, the average cat weighs less than 10 pounds: How much trouble could it be compared with that 70-pound dog who ate the couch and then snacked on the meter reader?

As the number of cats continues to grow, multiple-cat owners, breeders, and shelter personnel may even pressure single-cat owners to get another pet. That same excess cat population also guarantees that at any time a feline temptation can show up on the doorstep or in the arms of a sobbing, wheezing friend who's allergic to it. Given that reality as well as the increased numbers of other animate and inanimate territorial challenges with which the average cat must deal in the average human home, we need to consider what we can do to help our pets live comfortably in such an environment.

If someone had told me 10 years ago that I'd advocate free-access crate-training (FACT) for cats, I would have rolled on the floor laughing. True, I knew the advantages of teaching dogs to accept a fiberglass pet carrier as a haven into which they could retreat when events overwhelmed them, but cats? Never! Cats were even more of a freedom symbol than dogs, such a potent symbol that we didn't even require owners to license them, even though it made every bit as much sense to do so as it did to license dogs. The idea that a cat would want, and *need*, a clearly defined personal space seemed ludicrous.

However, after talking to thousands of cat owners at numerous cat-related events all over the country, I came to the conclusion that while we humans might view cats as most adaptable to the human environment, the increased numbers of behavioral and medical problems plaguing our favored felines didn't support that view. Then the obvious question became: What kind of microenvironment do cats seek out in our homes? In order to answer that question, I turned to the cats themselves.

When cats feel comfortable in their homes, they perch and sleep out in the open, on windowsills or shelves, in cat beds, or on human beds or other furnishings. When they don't feel comfortable, they seek out more secluded quarters.

"How can Marlow not feel comfortable here?" Al wants to know as he observes Marlow's lush cat bed and other cat paraphernalia.

Like many cats, Marlow's discomfort arises from two sources:

- the environment
- his specific personality

We already saw that the clash between Marlow's pastoral early upbringing and the bustle of his subsequent city and suburban settings led to stimulus overload. Whether his more timid nature or the environment caused him to develop that personality remains one of those chicken-egg phenomena that leads me to urge prospective cat owners to select stable kittens from environments as similar to their own as possible. However, once the amount and kind of environmental stimulation exceeds the cat's ability to cope with it, the animal naturally will seek some way to retreat from it. Marlow would hide in empty grocery bags or burrow under the newspaper or sweatshirt Al left on the floor.

"Oh, look, he's playing," they'd laugh. "Isn't that the cutest thing!"

However, playing cats don't retreat into or under objects and curl themselves into tight, motionless little fur balls to make themselves appear as small and nonthreatening as possible. They bounce and leap in or under the object to elicit sound and motion to trigger the play/prey response.

Once I realized how many cats, and particularly those with problems, displayed this retreating behavior, it seemed logical to provide them with a safe, secure space to which they could retreat at will. Initially, the idea of crate-training a cat ran so counter to the conventional wisdom that I didn't even consider it. Instead, I recommended that owners leave paper bags and upside-down boxes with openings cut into them in their bedrooms or other secure places for their pets to hide in when the going got rough. Those desiring more permanent as well as aesthetic cat havens could turn to a wide variety of commercially available products. Many cat condos include carpeted hidey holes for shy animals. Fuzzy sheepskin cat tepees provide snug sleeping quarters at the base and a hole at the top for escape. One fabric version of the paper bag has an inner layer that crinkles when the cat moves.

As I analyzed many of these products as potential havens for stressed cats, however, I saw problems. While multiple openings do make for great cat games, they also can make life miserable for the animal trying to avoid an overly playful or aggressive feline companion. Similarly, havens that make noise every time the cat moves may delight the stable animal but make the stressed one even jumpier. As if Marlow didn't have enough to worry about with the street sweeper and all those free-roaming cats in the neighborhood, now he must contend with the fear that his slightest motion will trigger a sound that alerts his foe.

Even when cats did adapt well to these havens, their owners couldn't easily move them to a different environment. We live in a mobile society. Not only will most people move at least a few times in their lives, they also take vacations, go on business trips, and visit family and friends. When we do this, more and more of us want to take our cats along. If we don't take our cats to visit Aunt Esther and Uncle Harry, we may take them to the kennel instead. We also take them to the veterinary clinic for routine care, as well as when they become ill or injured.

"Given the cat's highly territorial nature and its need to feel comfortable in its space in order to eat and drink normally (and thus remain healthy), wouldn't it make more sense to provide the animal with a safe haven the owner could easily transport?" I asked myself after another eight-hour stint listening to owners complain about problems obviously related to stimulus overload. Once that critical question was raised, the idea of feline free-access crate-training seemed so glaringly obvious that I couldn't imagine why I hadn't thought of it before.

A small pet carrier big enough to hold the cat, a comfy blanket or an old sweatshirt, and a small litter box, if necessary, placed in the owner's bedroom or another sacred space puts it all together. For this purpose, I personally prefer the smaller fiberglass or plastic dog carriers that consist of top and bottom halves and a door that can be disassembled for easy cleaning. Some owners use wire pens covered with a blanket, while others find that their cats prefer fabric carriers.

Aside from providing the cat with a safe personal space within the owner's home, FACT ensures that wherever that carrier goes, the cat's private space goes with it. Where Marlow used to disappear under Aunt Esther's couch and refuse to come out all weekend, now he can explore her home *at will*, then scurry back into his crate if something upsets him. When the Liebermanns move, Marlow's home goes with him. Rather than reverting to nocturnal behavior, feeling constantly on edge, and eating little, if anything, until he lays down the necessary scent trails in their new home, he can safely eat, drink, and relieve himself in his private space until he accomplishes that goal.

"That sounds great in theory," Al admits, "but Marlow *hates* his carrier."

Like more than a few other adult cats, Marlow came to this conclusion following a familiar sequence of events. From the time they got him, the Liebermanns placed Marlow in his crate only when they needed to take him to the veterinary clinic. Consequently, he associated the carrier with a car ride that terrified him so much that he often urinated and drooled during it. He also related it to sitting in an unfamiliar room surrounded by other animals and all kinds of threatening sounds, sights, and odors, and to being poked, prodded, and stuck with needles by strange people, or worse. It's not surprising that, after a few such episodes, just the sight of the carrier caused him to take off in fright. Then to all of the other negative associations, the cat could add fleeing his increasingly irate owners, who chased him through the house and eventually trapped him and stuffed him into the carrier.

So, what to do? Because of the many benefits conferred by FACT, I recommend that owners take the time to eliminate any carrier-related negative associations. For cats like Marlow with strong aversions, this may mean thoroughly cleaning and even replacing carriers soiled by frightened animals in the past. Then it becomes a matter of gradually accustoming the animal to the carrier under positive conditions.

For example, after the Liebermanns dismantle and thoroughly clean Marlow's carrier, they put only the bottom half of it on the hope chest at the foot of their bed where he likes to sleep. They line the bottom with Al's old, unlaundered (and thus intimately scented) sweatshirt and an old sweater of Penny's. They feed their pet and otherwise interact with him positively and quietly in that space. After Marlow grows accustomed to this, they add the top; once he accepts that, they put on the door.

While the Liebermanns can shut the door if necessary to transport Marlow or confine him for his own safety, keep in mind that a carrier should provide a private, personal space to which the cat enjoys free access at all times. You're not creating a jail! This open-door policy means that when visiting children stretch Marlow beyond his limits, he can retreat to his crate on the chest at the foot of his owners' bed. Also, children find it much easier to understand and accept the concept of "Don't bother Marlow while he's in his house" than "Stay away from the cat."

Depending on the strength and duration of any negative cat feelings, it may take from one month to as long as six months to get a cat to claim this space as its own. For owners with outgoing, healthy, well-behaved pets, that may seem like too much work. However, even the most happy-go-lucky, well-behaved, healthy cat may long for a snug familiar haven when moved to a new home, when the new baby or significant other enters the scene, or when the cake burns and sets off the smoke detector and scares the poor animal out of its wits. For animals who experience chronic behavioral and/or medical problems, anything that reduces territorial stress will pay big dividends.

While FACT can do wonders to relieve stress in older animals, crate-trained kittens gain an additional benefit. Based on the wide variety of feline reactions to space, it appears that how much personal territory cats need to feel secure gets set in their furry little heads at a very young age. As we discussed earlier, some cats seem perfectly content with a single room to call their own, whereas others need a whole floor, and yet others need to claim the entire house and all 10 acres around it. Unfortunately, as clear as these space limits may appear to them, we often don't realize they even exist until we exceed them.

I got my first crash course in this subject from a client who lived blissfully with 17 cats in a small mobile home. She became a local legend because of her marvelous way with cats—until she took in the 18th stray. Apparently, those particular 17 cats constituted the critical mass for that particular environment. Why, is anyone's guess. When she added the 18th, she precipitated a feline meltdown. Fifteen of the original 17 cats began clawing as well as spraying everything in sight. Worse, removing the last cat, with the most heartfelt apologies to the others, did no good. The owner had to retrain all 17 cats, a monumental task for even the most ardent cat lover.

If we FACT kittens, however, the carrier becomes their private space, and the rest of the house becomes shared space. Consequently, single cats don't need to worry about establishing and protecting their owners' entire homes. When the plumber comes, crate-trained Marlow retreats to his carrier in his owners' bedroom. Compare this with Sheba, who considers the upstairs bathroom in Jon's home part of *her* space. When the plumber works there, she feels pressured to assert her claim on that space. That may mean marking it or even attacking the intruder.

Crate-training cats in multiple-cat households also avoids the uncertainties that exist when cats establish their territories on their own. While these animals may appear to live in perfect harmony with each other and their environment, their owners can't predict how their pets will respond to a change. As with my client in the mobile home, one seemingly insignificant event can cause the whole social structure to collapse.

Think about your household and its activities as they may create or alleviate stress in your cat(s).

## Stress Test

What kind of stress relievers would you consider using in your environment? If you own or envision owning more than one cat, how do you think your pets relate (or will relate) to each other? How will you feel if they don't get along? If you discovered that your cats threaten each other far more than they enjoy each other, what would you do?

"When I did this exercise, I really had to think a lot about my beliefs," Penny confesses thoughtfully. "I'm positive my mom's cats love each other, and crate-training seems so unnatural. And yet, when I think about how Marlow destroyed this place, the idea that he's doing that because he's upset bothers me, too. I don't want him to live like that. Still . . ."

Mixed feelings such as these plague many cat owners and undermine the success of even the most well-conceived training, exercise, feeding, and medical programs. While knowledge of our environment and our cats' territorial nature can go a long way to relieve stress in our feline companions, whether we make changes and whether they will work depends as much on our half of the human-feline equation as on the cat's half. That being the case, let's delve more deeply into one of the most fascinating human-animal relationships in the world.

# 4

# The Cat Keeper

*Psyching Out the Human Half of the*
*Human-Feline Equation*

When Donna Fairchild's husband, Jim, presents her with an
American shorthair kitten, she can't believe her eyes.
"Such a tiny little baby kitty!" she exclaims as the kitten
burrows into the sleeve of her sweater.

Although Courtney, the Fairchilds' daughter, votes for "Squeaker"
and "Tiger" and Jim favors "Butch," Donna insists that the name "Baby
Kitty" perfectly describes their new pet.

Within a year Baby Kitty grows into a formidable feline hulk whose
futile attempts to burrow into Donna's now much-too-small sleeves
never fail to reduce his owner to giggles.

"What a silly little mama's boy you are," she croons softly to him as
he wraps his paws around her neck, butts his massive head against her
chin, and purrs rapturously.

However, outdoors Baby Kitty leads quite a different life. The
instant he appears, every bird and rodent on the Fairchilds' half acre
flees in terror. As he silently stalks his victim through the thick
undergrowth bordering the property, his powerful muscles propel him
effortlessly but relentlessly toward his latest target.

Late one night Baby Kitty's normally ignored life as a ruthless killer intrudes on Donna's cherished image of him. First, she senses the big cat next to her head on the pillow. Then, as she struggles to separate dream from reality, she feels his body begin to contract spasmodically. The first feline retch catapults her into full wakefulness.

"No! Don't! Get off the bed, you idiot!" she shrieks.

But it's too late. By the time Donna turns on the light, an odoriferous trail of semidigested but still distinguishable mouse parts adorns her pillow and drips over the edge of the bed to the floor.

"You monster!" she screams when her bare foot slips on something wet and warm on the rug and she slams into the wall.

While Donna staggers to the kitchen for cleaning supplies and Jim struggles heroically to suppress his laughter, Baby Kitty saunters down the hall, burrows under the covers on Courtney's bed, wriggles up beside her, and almost instantly falls asleep.

------

Of all the words used to describe cats over the centuries, my favorites remain "inscrutable" and "paradoxical." As with the ancient Egyptians first coming to grips with this latest addition to the domestic animal lineup, the Fairchilds' response to what they consider Baby Kitty's enigmatic, mysterious, unfathomable, or perplexing behavior spans the spectrum from enchantment to revulsion. And just about the time they think they've figured him out, he does something to turn their theories upside down. No sooner did the image of Baby Kitty dancing with a sunbeam convince Donna that he wouldn't dream of hurting a flea than her furry baby turned into a killer of terrorist proportions.

While such an awareness might make the prospective or new cat owner a little uneasy, those who have owned many cats and even the scientists who study cats don't fare much better. As I compared the information I compiled for this book with other cat-related material I've accumulated over the years, it became clear that for as much more as we now know about cats, in a way we know less.

"How can you know more but know less?" asks Jim as he picks cat hair off his sweater the morning after the late-night debacle. "That doesn't make sense."

It does make sense, because humans and cats keep consciously and subconsciously evolving in ways that affect our relationship with them more than with other domestic species. Up until the 1970s, many people associated cats with women and feminine traits, whereas dogs traditionally assumed the role of man's best friend. The idea of a male public figure's proclaiming his affection for cats ranked on a par with the American Kennel Club's adding a lilac point Birman to its logo.

Nonetheless, an enigmatic, mysterious, and still unfathomable (and thus quite catlike!) change occurred with the dawning of the Age of Aquarius. When researchers Claire Budge, John Spicer, Boyd Jones, and Ross StGeorge showed more than five hundred college students pictures of a thirtysomething man or woman alone, with a dog, or with a cat and asked them to rate these individuals, the students rated the man with the *cat* as nicer, more stylish, and more athletic than that same man pictured alone or with the dog. On the other hand, those same students awarded higher ratings to the woman with the *dog*.

If the idea that people's views of cats have changed dramatically over the years surprises you, you're in good company. It surprised the researchers, too. However, no one has fully explained how this shift in human orientations toward cats affects the human-feline bond. It surely has affected it, but it may take a while to understand the exact nature of these changes.

In spite of this enigma, we do know that one aspect of the human-feline bond affects virtually every aspect of our relationship with the feline half of the equation: the remaking of the cat as a social species. In terms of the human-feline bond, at the heart of this issue is the question: Is the cat actually evolving into a more social, pack-oriented creature like all other domestic animals, or are we imposing this image on it because that's how we view our interactions with all animals?

"I'd never force Baby Kitty to give up his catness just to please me!" Donna Fairchild protests earnestly.

Perhaps not knowingly, but given the cat's status as our most primitive domestic animal coupled with its maternal/sexual nature, could we unwittingly alter our cats' behaviors as well as their relationships to us by the way we treat them?

The first step in our journey to answer this question involves an overview of the major ways people interact with cats. For convenience, I divide these into three broad categories:

- the cat as furry baby (anthropomorphic view)
- the cat as furry robot (chattel view)
- the limited interspecies partnership (integrated view)

Although we'll discuss each view separately, owners may adopt any one or even a combination of two views, depending on the situation. Because these views have the potential to enhance or undermine the human-feline relationship, it helps to recognize their unique characteristics.

Before learning to do that, however, contemplate your relationship with any existing or future cats.

## Dream Cat Relationship Checklist

Review your notes about any existing or dream cat's personality, this time paying attention to how you *feel* about these different qualities. Where do those feelings come from? Past experiences? Experiences shared by other cat owners? Books, advertisements, or other media?

When Donna reviews her feelings about cats, she decides Baby Kitty fits her image of the perfect cat—"Except I wish he were more cuddly like my mother's Persian and didn't hunt," she adds when Jim reminds her to be totally honest. On the other hand, Jim finds the big cat's independent streak and prowess as a hunter to be two of Baby Kitty's most redeeming qualities.

"I don't think I could live with Baby Kitty if he really was a big baby," he confesses.

In keeping with the paradoxes that characterize the human-feline relationship, though, when the Fairchilds think about adding another cat to their household, they envision a mellow Persian who prefers to stay indoors, a cat quite the opposite of their beloved Baby Kitty.

Once owners recognize the different kinds of feelings that may affect their relationships with their cats, the next step is discovering the source of those feelings.

## Furry Feline Humanoids

In my experience, only the most repressed people can ignore the surge of maternal (or paternal) feeling that numbs all rational thought when soft, silky cat fur tickles human skin or a little pink cat tongue affectionately rasps human fingertips. In fact, a survey of cat owners conducted by the Massachusetts Society for the Prevention of Cruelty to Animals revealed that only 24 percent of those interviewed acquired their pets as the result of a conscious choice. Most cat owners, I among them, found themselves sharing their homes with a cat as a result of circumstances that run the gamut from the ridiculous to the sublime. Unfortunately, the very nature of these acquisitions can set us up for highly emotional relationships with our cats.

Consider how Baby Kitty wound up living with the Fairchilds. A co-worker of Jim's originally purchased the American shorthair from the Garden of Eden Pet Store because she felt sorry for the little kitten sitting all by itself in the great big cage. However, when she took him home, her significant other immediately began sneezing and wheezing and threatened to move out if she didn't get rid of the cat. The next morning she took the kitten to work, with the idea of returning him on her lunch hour, but then she got called out to an emergency meeting and asked Jim to keep an eye on the little fur ball for her.

A newly emerging cat man, Jim closed the door to his office and let the kitten out of the carrier, felt the softness of kitten fur and the roughness of cat tongue, immediately lost his heart, and declared, "I bet Donna would *love* this kitten."

When Jim repeated Baby Kitty's tale to his wife, she immediately envisioned the Garden of Eden Pet Store as a subsidiary of the Black Hole of Calcutta, Jim's co-worker's significant other as a cat hater, and the co-worker as a spineless blob for refusing to keep such an adorable little creature.

"Poor little baby," she cooed to the kitten. "I'll make it all up to you."

From this scenario we can see how easily people can project their own ideas and beliefs onto an animal, an approach scientists refer to as anthropomorphism. However, even anthropomorphism isn't what it used to be when I began writing about human-feline relationships 15 years ago. Then most animal behaviorists considered viewing animal behavior in terms of human behavior as the ultimate scientific sin. The image of a frivolous, overweight, older woman dripping with diamonds and simpering over a toy poodle with painted toenails, or babbling nonsense to a Persian cat lounging on a satin pillow, served as a potent negative image for anyone who would dare challenge the scientific standard.

However, increased research of the human-animal bond as well as a growing respect for long-ignored studies demonstrating how we and animals affect each other's physiology and behavior slowly but steadily eroded this image. By 1995, a study conducted by the American Animal Hospital Association found that 61 percent of the pet owners surveyed consider their pets members of the family, and more and more scientists accept the value of empathy when studying other species. In addition, the emergence of evolutionary psychology—which applies the principles of animal behavior to humans—further fuzzes the line separating human and animal behavior.

The crux of the anthropomorphic view, however, doesn't lie in either its prevalence or its acceptance by the scientific community. What matters is whether the feelings and beliefs that humans project onto animals result from solid knowledge of that animal and themselves or from pure emotion.

For example, when Donna Fairchild joined the ranks of those many accidental cat owners, she unfortunately succumbed to what I call the Saint Francis Syndrome, envisioning herself as saving Baby Kitty from a fate worse than death. Although the cheerful kitten showed no evidence of abuse, his new owner created a fictional history for him that included all kinds of neglect.

"Here, Baby, eat more so you'll grow big and strong," she coaxed him, offering food from her own plate as he sat in her lap while she ate. "I'm sure those horrible people didn't feed you well at all!"

By the time Baby Kitty celebrates his fifth birthday, he suffers from intermittent diarrhea and other diet-related problems, all of which Donna blames on his traumatic life before she got him rather than her own faulty beliefs and injudicious feeding practices.

In this situation, Donna's emotions give rise to a feeding program that undermines her pet's health. Had she talked to the previous owners first or, better, accepted her veterinarian's evaluation that Baby Kitty's glossy coat and overall healthy appearance didn't support her view, she could have spared her cat all of the problems related to her loving, but erroneous, beliefs.

Anthropomorphic views arising from human emotions also can take a terrible toll when cats become ill or injured. While this can create problems with any animal, it especially does so with cats, who may respond quite negatively to treatments that humans and other domestic animals tolerate easily. When Baby Kitty limps home after one of his hunting sprees, Donna automatically gives him baby aspirin twice daily for the pain. Not only do the cumulative effects of the drug make him seriously ill, the medication does nothing to treat the puncture wound that caused the limp.

"I understand what you're saying about bad anthropomorphism, but what about the good anthropomorphism?" Donna wants to know.

When we share a common ground with our cats based on knowledge rather than emotion, something magical can occur. As a new veterinarian, I quickly learned this difference from my clients, including an old curmudgeon named Isaac and his equally tough old cat, Boy.

"Somethin's troublin' Boy," Isaac announced as he placed the enormous gray tiger on the stainless-steel table between us.

I dutifully examined the cat from head to tail while Isaac watched me intently and Boy stoically endured the entire process. When I concluded the procedure, I confidently pronounced Boy in perfect health. When the owner remained unconvinced, I ran a battery of diagnostic tests, all of which supported my original conclusion.

"Yer wrong," Isaac flatly rejected all of this. "We'll be back."

Two weeks later he returned, and everything about Boy's demeanor practically screamed, "Sick cat!" This time the lab tests confirmed that his pet suffered from a serious viral disease.

That and similar experiences over the years have convinced me that owners can know their animals so well that they can detect changes sooner than the most skilled professional and the most sophisticated equipment. While love no doubt plays a role in the development of this extrasensory perception, it does so because it inspires owners to learn as much about a particular cat and their relationship with it as possible. By stretching the limits of what they know about their cats' needs as well as their own, they greatly increase the chance that they'll quickly notice any changes.

Before continuing, ponder any anthropomorphic elements that exist or could exist in your relationship with any present or future cats.

---

### Anthropomorphic Self-Analysis

Review your description of your ideal cat, and put an "A" beside any qualities that reflect your personal beliefs about cats and what's good for them. Does your orientation result from emotion or solid knowledge? Mark those based on emotion with an "E" and those that result from knowledge with a "K."

When the Fairchilds review their list, they discover that many of their beliefs about what constitutes perfect American shorthair behavior arise from how they *think* Baby Kitty should act rather than any solid knowledge of the breed.

"I just assumed all purebred cats would be placid and cuddly babies like my mom's Persians," Donna confesses. "But now I realize that maybe that's not true."

"The more I thought about it, the more I realized that I used my folks' barn cats as the standard for Baby Kitty's behavior," Jim admits after he completed the exercise. "We always expected them to be able to take care of themselves."

Jim's ideas about his pet bring us to the second way people view cats.

# Furry Feline Robots

The subject of treating cats like chattel, or objects, shouldn't automatically trigger images of animal abuse as it tends to do for many cat lovers. Rather, a *lack* of emotion characterizes the chattel orientation, whereas people who abuse animals often anthro-pomorphically project their own feelings of self-hatred and inad-equacy on their targets.

Like anthropomorphic views, views of cats as chattel may spring from either human emotion or solid knowledge.

"How can you develop an unemotional view emotionally?" Jim reasonably wants to know.

To understand how this can happen, let's examine the five basic forms the chattel view takes in the human-feline relationship.

First, we see the classic chattel-oriented person who uses a cat for self-enhancement. While these owners can occur in any environment, they most commonly crop up on the purebred show circuit, where they view their cats as pedigrees, ribbons, and championships. If the cat doesn't perform in a manner they believe reflects positively on them or if it requires that they put more into the relationship than they get out, they get rid of the animal.

A second, more common variation of the chattel theme takes the form of a laissez-faire attitude that springs from the wide-spread belief that cats can take care of themselves. Owners who wouldn't think of letting their dogs go outside without supervi-sion will let the cat out with nary a second thought.

"You think that's wrong?" Jim asks as he watches Baby Kitty stalking a butterfly.

I can say unequivocally that no one should let a cat outdoors without at least a second thought. So many variables can come into play when owners do so that they should evaluate their own and their specific cat's needs as well as any environmental fac-tors before making this decision. For example, the Fairchilds acquire a timid Persian, Nadia, who cowers in the doorway while Baby Kitty eagerly streaks into the yard. For Jim to nudge Nadia out the door based on his belief that cats can take care of them-selves hardly ranks as caring, knowledge-based behavior.

"What about ignoring Baby Kitty when he kills a mouse rather than flipping out the way Donna does?" Jim counters.

In this third variation on the chattel theme, the ability to view the cat's behavior objectively can definitely benefit the cat and the owner's relationship with it. Consider the facts:

- Cats are natural hunters.
- The majority of outdoor cats are going to hunt.
- Most cats who hunt eventually kill something.
- Cats who kill something may eat it or bring it home.
- Cats who bring their prey home may put it in their owner's bed or on the rug in front of the kitchen sink.
- Cats who eat their prey may throw it up in the house.

Given this reality, it makes sense for owners to accept hunting behavior and its consequences unless they're willing to confine the cat and fulfill these needs some other way. In Baby Kitty's case, Donna's carrying on every time he makes a kill or throws up mouse guts doesn't faze the big cat in the least. On the other hand, such owner histrionics in response to what the cat perceives as normal feline behavior may set a less confident cat up for stress-related medical or behavioral problems. When Donna screams at Nadia for urinating on the rug by the kitchen door to claim her territory, the poor cat gets so upset that she develops diarrhea.

In addition to the chattel approach enabling owners to cope with normal feline behaviors that they find troublesome, it can benefit those whose pets succumb to serious illness or injury. Suppose that one day Baby Kitty gets hit by a car. Anthropomorphic Donna becomes so caught up in how she would feel under the same circumstances, or if it happened to a human loved one, that she falls completely to pieces and can't remember a single thing Dr. Renfrew, the veterinarian, says.

Compare this with what happens when Donna adopts a chattel view under these same circumstances. In this instance, she puts all of her emotions on hold so she can understand everything Dr. Renfrew tells her about Baby Kitty's condition, and she can ask meaningful questions about the treatment. Once she gets the situation under control, she might break down and have a good cry, but not until she knows the nature of her cat's injuries and the kind of care he requires.

Fourth, owners may adopt the chattel approach when their own lives become so hectic that they lack the time for any but the most rudimentary interactions with their pets.

"Then they shouldn't own a pet," Donna huffs derisively, hugging Baby Kitty tightly to her chest.

When Donna makes this statement, she forgets about the week when Courtney came down with the flu, Jim broke his leg, and her car's transmission died. She doesn't remember whether she fed herself that week, let alone the cat. Other times a special holiday, a major project at work or school, or human additions to or deletions from the household may cause us to put our relationship with the cat on automatic pilot for a while. All cat owners do this at one time or another, and most cats graciously accept the situation and find other ways to amuse themselves.

The one exception takes the form of those cats with whom their owners have created highly anthropomorphic relationships. If Donna constantly fawns over Baby Kitty, cooking him special treats and developing special play rituals that take up most of the day, when circumstances make it impossible for her to do this, her pet will feel abandoned. Some animals may refuse to eat or drink under these circumstances, thereby setting themselves up for medical problems.

Often the owners don't fare much better. Donna feels so guilty about not cooking Baby Kitty's special "din-din" when she returns home after another exhausting day at work preparing for her company's annual meeting that she can't fall asleep that night. The next morning she breaks down in tears when her pet races out the door with barely a glance in her direction.

Can you imagine situations in which a chattel view could either enhance or undermine your relationship with your own pet?

---

### Chattel Self-Analysis

Review your description of the perfect cat, relationship, and programs with a view toward any items that reflect chattel views. Do these views result from solid knowledge (K) or from emotion (E)?

Jim's list supports his new awareness that his views about cats taking care of themselves stem from his childhood on a farm.

"We had lots of barn cats, and it seemed like they took care of themselves pretty well," he remarks. "On the other hand, they weren't born in a cattery and spoiled rotten by Donna like our new little Persian."

In this situation, Jim's orientation was knowledge-based to some extent for one of his cats, but it was totally emotion-based for the other. Because Baby Kitty's personality, background, and breeding made him comparable to some of the barn cats Jim knew as a child, Jim could logically draw these conclusions. On the other hand, this same belief sprang from pure emotion and wishful thinking when he applied it to Nadia.

Like all human orientations toward animals, the appropriateness of the chattel view for a particular human-animal combination in a particular situation should remain the key consideration. The same holds true for any other limits we impose on the interspecies partnership, too.

# The Integrated Interspecies Partnership

When I first began writing about people's relationships with their pets, I called the third human orientation toward animals the bonded view. This sprang from a belief that I shared with other veterinarians, trainers, and behaviorists that we could *create* a solid bond between an owner and an animal simply by keeping that animal well behaved and healthy. However, surveys of owners indicated that we had it backwards: the existence of a solid bond, not the lack of one, leads owners to seek help when problems arise. While improving an animal's health and behavior may enhance a relationship, it won't create a bond between an animal and its owner if one doesn't already exist.

The existence of a solid bond also may cause owners to accept even the worst behavior or medical problems in their pets: "I know my mom wouldn't put up with all of her cat's problems if she didn't love him so much," Donna Fairchild assumes, voicing a sentiment familiar to many pet owners. However, this sentiment may reflect something other than love if the owner merely chooses to tolerate rather than treat correctable problems.

This greater insight now causes me to use the term "integrated" to describe the third human orientation, because those who adopt it integrate an awareness of their own and their pets' limits into the relationship. All owners place limits on their relationships with their cats, but those who take an integrated approach consciously establish limits that best meet their own and their pets' needs. Unlike anthropomorphically and chattel-oriented owners who seek to increase or decrease their emotional involvement with the animal, those who adopt an integrated approach seek to knowledgeably define the boundaries of the relationship. While these limits may take many forms, the majority fall into one of four broad categories:

• financial
• time
• emotional
• physical

Take a few minutes to consider these limits as they may apply to your cat(s).

## Limit Check

Think about your relationship with your existing or dream cat. Can you imagine anything that your pet could do or that could happen to your cat that you simply couldn't accept? What would you do under these circumstances? Don't forget that no right or wrong answers exist, and that the more effort you put into this evaluation, the more it will benefit you and your cat.

When the Fairchilds perform this exercise they, like many owners, claim they can't imagine anything they wouldn't do for Baby Kitty.

"Our love for him is limitless, unconditional, just like his love for us," Donna states, repeating the often-heard owner's claim.

While this notion sounds so good that it echoes throughout the pet-owning population, it reflects far more fantasy than reality. In order to avoid the negative effects a lack of knowledge about limits can create in your relationship with your pet, let's explore each of the four categories—financial, time, emotional, and physical—in more detail.

# The Greenback Barrier

Imagine that Baby Kitty gets hit by a car which shatters his front leg. When Donna discovers her injured pet, she rushes him into Dr. Renfrew's veterinary clinic screaming, "Do everything you can!"

Taking her at her word, Dr. Renfrew not only does everything within the limits of his modern facility, but he also calls in a board-certified veterinary orthopedic specialist to perform some highly specialized surgery on the shattered limb. Any rosy glow Donna feels about her furry baby's recovery drains right out of her several days later when she receives the cat, orders to keep him strictly confined for at least eight weeks, and a bill for $1,789.56.

In this situation, Donna's anthropomorphic view of her cat combines with her failure to acknowledge any limits she places on the relationship to set her up for a nasty shock as well as a deadly blow to the Fairchild family budget. Her anthropomorphic orientation led her to respond to Baby Kitty's injuries the same way she did when Jim broke his leg: Do everything possible. However, unlike Jim, Baby Kitty isn't covered by the comprehensive health insurance package provided by his employer. Like many other pet owners, Donna had no idea when she begged the veterinarian to do everything for Baby Kitty that "everything" can cost quite a lot, even in the smallest veterinary clinic.

Donna's failure to acknowledge that certain financial limits did apply to her relationship with Baby Kitty definitely complicated an already complicated situation. Had she recognized her limits beforehand, she could have explored other options when the crisis occurred.

"Like what? Let Baby Kitty suffer?" she asks as she stares at the bill in her hand. "What choice did I have?"

In reality, Donna had several choices. For one thing, a large portion of that bill covered the cost of the orthopedic surgeon. Dr. Renfrew could have done the surgery much less expensively himself, but the cat may have limped, something the veterinarian didn't think Donna would find acceptable given her anthropomorphic view of her pet. Consequently, he didn't raise this possibility, and she didn't either.

Nor did Donna choose to ask for an estimate of what the surgery would cost. Because she thinks of Baby Kitty as a member of the family, she'd never put a dollar value on him any more than she would on Jim or Courtney. Some owners likewise don't raise the issue because they fear others will look down on them if they do. Granted, a few veterinarians or veterinary technicians might try to make owners feel like insensitive meanies for bringing up the issue of cost, but the majority will appreciate the honesty and try to work within any stated limits.

A third option available to Donna was working out a monthly payment schedule to cover the cost of the treatment. However, because she chose to give in to her emotions and ignore the family's limits, she triggered a set of events that undermined her relationship with the veterinarian ("Why didn't he tell me how much this was going to cost!") and her husband ("You spent *how much* on that cat?").

And how did this lack of acknowledgment of financial limits affect Donna's relationship with her pet? Although she claimed that her great love for Baby Kitty caused her to do what she did, she blames him for all the problems created by the hassles of keeping him indoors, not to mention the cost of his treatment: "You'd rather have chicken breast instead of spaghetti, Baby? Tough. It's *your* fault we can't afford anything better."

Whether you adopt a stray or spend thousands for the offspring of a champion show cat, that pet will cost you money. The old adage holds true: *There's no such thing as a free cat.* Unfortunately, financial considerations rarely rank as a top priority with prospective or existing cat owners. As noted before, cat ownership comes as a surprise to most people. Jim Fairchild never even thought about getting a cat until he opened the cat carrier his co-worker unceremoniously plopped down on the corner of his desk that fateful day. As with many others in this situation, such a small interval of time elapsed between when Jim considered himself a prospective cat owner and when he actually became one that he didn't even notice the transition.

Also, cats come in such deceptively small packages compared with most dogs that their cost may seem irrelevant. When I conducted educational presentations at cat shows, I spent my free time wandering through the show halls observing people as well as cats, and I saw the results of this packaging phenomenon at work all the time. My favorite episode involved a middle-aged man whose L. L. Bean boots, jeans, and corduroy sports coat practically screamed, "Golden retriever!" As I perused an assortment of cat paraphernalia, I first became aware of him peripherally, as he moved toward, then away from, a cage housing one of the most heart-stoppingly beautiful litters of Maine coon kittens I'd ever seen. In fact, I'd fled those very kittens for the safety of a makeshift boutique filled with kitty T-shirts and earrings lest I fall hopelessly in love with one of those endearing fur balls myself.

In retrospect, I probably should have tried to warn him, but I got so caught up in the unfolding drama that I didn't say a word. Instead I watched him hovering around that cage of kittens like a moth courting a flame. The instant I heard him politely ask the breeder if he might look at the kitten with the hairy ears in the corner, I knew he was a goner.

"Oh, you mean the one with the gorgeous ear tufts." The breeder's tinkling laugh reminded me of Glinda the Good Witch in *The Wizard of Oz*. "He's a grand-looking little fellow, isn't he?"

While the kitten nosed the gentleman's cuff, I easily imagined him working the math: *"Let's see, my golden retriever cost $350 and weighed 15 pounds when I got him. That's, umm . . . roughly $23 a pound. How much could a little thing like this cost?"*

At least I assume that's what he thought because he suddenly announced, "I'll take him," and I can't imagine anything else that could have produced the look of stunned horror that momentarily flitted across his face when the breeder replied, "That'll be $950."

Later I saw the new owner stagger out of the show hall with kitten, carrier, litter box, one bag each of clumping, scented, and environmentally sound litter, food (four different brands of canned and dry), and a large bouquet of bouncing cat toys on the ends of long sticks. The total bill? Surely well over $1,000.

Granted, it may cost a lot more to acquire a purebred cat from a breeder than a stray from the local shelter, but *any* cat costs money. Exactly how much depends on many factors that we'll explore in the chapters ahead. However, even though cat owners may cite lack of money as the reason why their cats developed serious problems ("I couldn't afford all those expensive tests"), a lack of knowledge rather than money causes far more problems. Owners who get themselves into costly problems with their pets commonly lack knowledge in three key areas:

- how much they can afford to spend to acquire and maintain a cat
- how much it actually costs to acquire and maintain a cat
- how to reduce those costs by avoiding or preventing medical and behavioral problems

While the gentleman who lost his heart to the Maine coon kitten needed to decide only whether to pay for his new addition by check or with his American Express or Visa card, most of us aren't so lucky. I've watched prospective owners at shows, in pet stores, and in animal shelters extracting well-worn and folded emergency funds from secret compartments of their wallets, or pooling funds with friends to pay for a cat. While that may mean that these folks *really* want that cat, the fact remains that, if they can barely muster the funds to buy it, their chances of funding its proper care run from slim to nonexistent.

Worse, unlike the man who got a healthy, beautiful, well-tempered Maine coon for his investment, some people spend money they don't have for cats or kittens, not because they really want them, but rather because they feel sorry for them for one reason or another. If they can barely scrounge up the funds to pay for an animal with physical or behavioral problems, they'll probably have a tough time coming up with the money to treat those problems properly.

In general most cat owners take one of three approaches to feline finance:

- They deny any financial limits and hope they never become an issue.
- They react emotionally.
- They critically analyze any cat-related issues in terms of how much they can afford to spend.

While some owners sail through 13 to 15 healthy cat years without ever giving a thought to cat-related expenses, other owners don't fare so well. We already saw what happened to Donna Fairchild when she denied any financial limits the day Baby Kitty got hit by a car. That denial produced a negative shock wave that rippled through virtually every aspect of her relationship with her pet.

When Donna actually held the bill for Baby Kitty's care and no longer could deny any financial limits, she responded emotionally. She ranted, she raged; she blamed Dr. Renfrew, the orthopedic surgeon, herself, and the cat. Other owners vent their emotions immediately. They request an estimate for neutering, then swear and slam down the phone when they get it. They scream at the breeder for charging more than they can afford. They curse the cat for developing an allergy to the cheapest cat food.

The most successful cat owners, on the other hand, care enough to consider whether they can afford to get a cat, or add another one. The day Baby Kitty enchanted Jim, the new owner forced himself to control his emotions long enough to calculate whether the Fairchild budget could accommodate a pet. Then he called Dr. Renfrew for estimates of first-year expenses such as kitten vaccinations, worming, and neutering. Unlike some naive owners, though, he also considered the cost of lifelong care and requested estimates for any recommended preventive care (annual checkups, boosters, flea control, etc.). Then he factored in the cost of food and litter based on discussions with other cat-owning co-workers. Then, and only then, did he act on his initial impulse to take the cat home to Donna. However. although Jim's approach enabled him to unemotionally tally the cost of maintaining a *healthy* cat, he neglected to consider—or discuss with his wife—how much they could afford to spend if their new pet became seriously ill or injured.

This brings us to the third kind of knowledge all cat owners need: how to reduce costs by preventing problems. Another basic truth of animal ownership puts it in a nutshell: *It always costs less to prevent problems than to treat them.* People who know the basics about cats, their particular breed(s) and individual cat(s), their environment, and their relationship with their cats gain two distinct money-saving advantages:

- They're less likely to select problem animals.
- They can detect early signs of change and treat little problems before they become big ones.

"That's all well and good, but I don't see how that applies to Baby Kitty's getting hit by a car," Donna counters. "I never saw him anywhere near the road until I found him lying in it."

From a purely economical point of view, it makes sense for anyone who believes that cats should run free to consider how much they can spend treating any injuries the cat may incur during its unsupervised romps. It also makes sense to know as much as you can about the cat's outdoor environment to make sure it's as cat-safe as possible.

One of the Fairchilds always accompanied Baby Kitty when they first got him, and they never saw him go anywhere near the road. However, because they knew little about feline behavior, they didn't realize that he would claim that space and feel very strongly about protecting it as he grew older. When the family who lived across the road from the Fairchilds added a cat to their menagerie, Baby Kitty began to cross the road routinely, seeking evidence of the interloper.

"I told Donna and Jim they should keep that cat inside," Donna's mother insists as she strokes her obese Persian. "That would've solved all their problems."

Maybe, maybe not. As we know from previous chapters, some cats adapt quite well to a housebound existence, while others experience stress-related medical and/or behavioral problems that can cost their owners a great deal of money. Consequently, there's no substitute for knowledge of the cat, the environment, and the relationship.

All this talk of expensive show cats and budget-breaking veterinary bills might give the impression that only the financially secure can claim the joys of cat ownership, but that's not the case at all. Some of the healthiest, best-behaved animals belong to people on very limited budgets. However, these people recognize that they can't afford to ignore little problems until they become big ones, any more than they can cut corners when it comes to preventive care. Instead of taking Baby Kitty to Dr. Renfrew once a year to have his teeth cleaned or taking him only when a tooth becomes infected, Donna learns how to brush her cat's teeth at home. Not only does this help keep her cat healthy, it saves her quite a bit of money, too.

What financial limits do or could affect your relationship with your cat?

---

## Feline Financial Analysis

Examine your checkbook entries or monthly bank statements for the past year. How much extra cash do you have to spend on a cat and its upkeep? If you barely make it from paycheck to paycheck but still want a cat, what items would you be willing to forgo for your cat? If your cat developed problems, how much could you afford to spend for treatment? What kind of payment options would best fit your budget?

Some people who want a purebred pet willingly give up a vacation or season tickets to a sporting event to pay for it. One former client on a very strict budget called her cat Lucky Strike because she gave up cigarettes to pay for him and his upkeep. As it turned out, her own health improved so much that Lucky wound up saving her more money than he cost her!

Incorporating any children in the household into the budgeting process can also pay big dividends. Children who contribute part of their allowances or do odd jobs around the house or neighborhood to earn money to purchase and care for their pets gain a much more responsible view of pet ownership than those whose parents foot the bill for everything.

Evaluating any financial limits does take time, but time also constitutes another investment quality that cat ownership entails, one equally worthy of owner consideration.

## The Furry Timepiece

A fair number of cat lovers believe that their cats can tell time. The owners of these clever felines describe how they routinely set their electric alarm clocks for six or seven in the morning and, when a power outage silences the alarm, the cat jumps onto the bed, yowls, or even smacks the owner at one or two minutes past the appointed hour. In typical cat fashion, however, while some cats do learn not to awaken their working owners on weekends, others take fiendish pleasure (or so their owners insist!) in awakening them early on these days, too.

These stories point out that, like everything else that affects the human-feline relationship, both cat and owner observe certain time limits. It's understandable that its status as our only nocturnal domestic animal can throw a few curves into the cat's relationship with daylight-loving, diurnal humans.

Contemporary cat owners also experience an increasing number of time idiosyncracies. The instant the alarm sounds, the

Fairchilds begin gearing up for the day, while Baby Kitty stretches languorously and lazily begins grooming himself. In addition to his owners' daily rituals—fixing breakfast, packing lunches, going to work or school—just about every day holds something extra. Donna attends aerobics class at least two evenings a week, Jim belongs to an investment club and plays on a softball team, and Courtney takes ballet and piano lessons in addition to playing soccer and basketball. On any given day, the Fairchilds' schedule also includes grocery or other shopping, medical and dental appointments, car inspections and oil changes, haircuts, school conferences, or other meetings. Their weekend calendar bulges with notes about charity car washes, bake sales, outings with friends or relatives, and other activities.

Consequently when the idea of getting a pet came up, a cat seemed the ideal choice.

"Everyone knows that cats practically take care of them- selves," Jim naively repeated the truism that's doomed more than one contemporary human-feline relationship.

The idea of cats as get-it-and-forget-it pets probably goes at least as far back as Rudyard Kipling's classic "The Cat That Walked by Himself" in which the author describes the cat as "neither friend nor servant" like other domestic animals. As pre- viously mentioned, we social humans don't easily accept the cat's solitary nature, and, like much other cat-related literature, Kipling's tale vacillates between celebrating and chafing at the cat's unique relationship with people.

The Fairchilds fare no better. One day they thank their lucky stars that they don't need to worry about walking or training Baby Kitty as they would a dog, because they simply don't have the time to do that. The next day they berate him because he wants to play when they want to sleep, or he wants to sleep when they want to play with him.

How much time does a cat take? It depends on the individ- ual. Prior to Baby Kitty's untimely encounter with the car, his upkeep required remarkably little time. Because Jim and Donna didn't want to deal with a litter box, Jim installed a cat door that allowed Baby Kitty to come and go as he pleased. Feeding the cat fell to Courtney, and she simply filled his bowl with dry food every morning so he could eat whenever he wanted. Initially she also filled his water dish daily, too, but he much preferred to drink out of the sink or toilet. At first this bothered Donna, but she let it go because it didn't seem to harm him and trying to stop the behavior seemed like more trouble than it was worth. Total time investment: about five minutes a day.

For those who own in- and outdoor cats who don't use cat doors and do drink water out of a dish, the time investment increases. Depending on the weather and my schedule, I open the door for Whittington between four and twenty times a day. I fill a large stainless bowl with water which he shares with the dogs. Not only does he drink from this bowl, but he also enjoys playing in it, so I must add the time it takes me to clean up the water he splashes on the floor. Still, it adds up to less than a half hour a day even on those days when he finds the water bowl particularly tempting.

Like many other owners of shorthaired felines, I don't spend much time grooming my cat. Often pressed for time myself, when I stroke Whittington I check the quality of his coat and skin while communicating how much I enjoy his company (more on this in Chapter 10). If I notice a cloud of cat hair floating upward when I do this, I get out the brush.

On the other hand, this approach would never work on the majority of the longhaired breeds. When the Fairchilds first added Nadia to their household, they never found the time to accustom the Persian to grooming. Soon this oversight set a vicious cycle in motion. Because the cat resisted grooming, the owners grew to dislike it, too, and groomed her even less. In no time, Nadia developed mats at the base of both ears and on her tummy that so irritated her, she dug and scratched at them.

After a harrowing three hours during which Jim held the struggling cat and Donna tried to cut the mats with manicure scissors, the Fairchilds gave up and took their pet to a professional groomer. The groomer suggested clipping the cat down completely and then accustoming her to grooming, first with stroking, then with grooming gloves (special gloves with rubberized nubs that remove loose hair), and finally with a comb and brush. However, before they began that daily ritual, the groomer suggested they take Nadia to their veterinarian to determine the cause of the red splotches on her skin. When Dr. Renfrew confirmed that Nadia's skin had become infected under those mats, he prescribed a medicated shampoo and antibiotics.

In this scenario, the owners' failure to find a few minutes to groom their cat regularly translated into hours spent trying to rectify the negative results of that decision. Which brings us back to two familiar themes:

- The more you know about your cat, your environment, and your relationship, the more quickly you can recognize changes and prevent problems.
- Preventing problems not only saves money, but also time.

The most important, but also the most often overlooked, time investment new cat owners can make is the time they devote to gaining knowledge about cats. Unfortunately, between the cat's reputation as a trouble-free pet and an increasingly sophisticated veterinary profession that offers seemingly magical cures for medical and behavioral problems, a lot of people falsely assume they've covered all the bases. However, I can say without hesitation that even the best medication is only as good as the owner's ability to get the drug into the animal as prescribed. Drugs that miraculously kill disease-causing organisms when given twice daily for 10 days may yield infections *resistant* to those same drugs if the owner medicates the cat only once a day, skips a few days' medication, or stops medicating the cat after a week instead of 10 days.

Call me Dr. Gloom-and-Doom, but I prefer to think of myself as Dr. Prevention when I ask owners to envision the worst thing that could possibly happen to their cats and then review their schedules to see how much time they could free up to resolve this problem. Although the Fairchilds initially found such an idea too horrible to even consider, after Baby Kitty's accident they could think of little else. The cat's eight weeks of strict confinement, not to mention his tremendous aversion to these new limits, wreaked havoc with the Fairchilds' schedule. Suddenly, they found themselves rearranging all their activities around the cat, a major sacrifice that Baby Kitty seldom appreciated. However, after that wretched experience, their view of how much time it takes to own a cat changed dramatically.

"In retrospect, we should have done things a lot differently," notes Jim as he supervises Baby Kitty's first forays outdoors following the accident. "Now I'd make sure any new cat has a litter box and knows how to use it. Second, I'd accustom it to a fiberglass carrier. Third, I'd pay closer attention to changes occurring in the neighborhood—in both the human *and* animal populations. I had no idea how much these could affect so many different aspects of Baby Kitty's health and our relationship."

How do you intend to cope with any time crunches your cat may generate?

## Feline Time Check

Imagine an average weekday, Saturday, and Sunday in your household. How much time can you realistically devote to your cat without feeling pressured? If something happened to your cat, how much additional time could you free up for its care? If no extra time exists, what cat-care alternatives could you use?

When the Fairchilds first completed this exercise, their view of Baby Kitty as a cat who could take care of himself led them to dismiss its importance. However, after his accident they took it much more seriously because their failure to consider their time limits earlier ended up costing them a great deal of time and money later. Unaccustomed to life as an indoor cat, Baby Kitty signaled his discomfort by clawing the furniture and spraying urine on the drapes. He also spent a great deal of time trying to get out—hardly the quiet rest the orthopedic surgeon ordered!

After coping with one time- and money-consuming event after another, the Fairchilds decide to take advantage of Dr. Renfrew's day-care option. Donna drops Baby Kitty off at Dr. Renfrew's every morning on her way to work and picks him up on her way home. The Fairchilds also rearranged their schedules so that someone always remained home evenings or weekends during his recovery, a major feat given their complex lives. On the other hand, they also used this opportunity to make changes that would ensure they and their pet would never need to experience such a hectic schedule again.

Needless to say, all of this gave the Fairchilds an opportunity to evaluate the emotional limits of their relationship with Baby Kitty, too.

## Emotional Boundaries

In addition to eliciting the full spectrum of anthropomorphic- and chattel-oriented emotions common to all species of domestic animals, cats evoke a range and intensity of human emotional responses evoked by no other species. Moreover, expressing one's innermost negative feelings about cats publicly doesn't carry nearly the stigma that expressing similar feelings about dogs would. I still maintain my original view (set forth in *The Body Language and Emotion of Cats*) that how people respond to what they perceive as different or novel will determine how they respond to cats. If they dislike and distrust novelty, they'll dislike and distrust cats. If novelty attracts them, cats will attract them.

Additionally, feline nocturnal, solitary, maternal, sexual, and predatory behaviors color human emotions about cats because they serve as a constant reminder of these aspects of ourselves. And just as it stuns the fictional Alice when Dinah, her well-behaved prim and proper Victorian kitten, becomes the diabolical Cheshire Cat after Alice falls down the rabbit hole into Wonderland, so some of us find these four-legged reminders of our subconscious selves unnerving, too.

On the other hand, contemporary cat owners who enjoy cats and embrace their differences may experience an openness and honesty quite unlike that known to most dog owners. This realization came to me when I began giving public presentations to cat owners. My experience talking to dog owners had prepared me for mixed audience participation based on what people believed they could reveal about their pets' behavior and their relationship to their animals without incriminating themselves.

For example, dog owners rarely will admit in public that their dogs relieve themselves in the house. The thinking goes that "Any idiot can housebreak a dog," and therefore any person who can't do this obviously lacks some gray matter. Consequently, when I address this issue in a presentation and even actively solicit questions, it's a rare dog owner who will raise his or her hand and admit that the resident canine experiences this problem. However, after the presentation, these same people will beckon to me from behind potted plants, or lurk in stairwells or parking lots awaiting my arrival, only to blurt out in hushed tones and with many a nervous glance over their shoulders that, "Herbie does it." They feel so embarrassed that they can't even say what Herbie does, but their tortured expressions say it all.

Compare this with what happened the first—and every succeeding—time I brought the subject of house soiling up to a group of cat owners. I solicited input from the audience as usual, fully expecting them to don serene Buddha smiles like the dog folks. Instead, hands shot up all over the place.

"My cat pees on my socks," a well-dressed woman in the front row cheerfully admitted.

"No kidding," chimed in a man from the row behind her. "Mine much prefers to spray my wife's shoes."

"Hah, you think that's something!" boomed a voice from the back of the room. "My cat takes a dump on my pillow every night!"

"Don't you just want to kill him when he does that?" came another voice.

"Oh, hell, yes! Want to wring his scrawny neck every time it happens," boomed the voice from the back of the room with a hearty chuckle. "Can't imagine what I'd do without him, though."

On and on it went, a mind-boggling display of cat-elimination one-upmanship accompanied by raucous laughter and much good-natured kidding. Unlike their canine-owning compatriots, these folks didn't feel the least bit inferior about owning a cat with behavioral problems or confessing their most antifeline feelings about these displays. To most of them it constituted a perfectly normal and, depending on the behavior, even a *fun* part of owning a cat.

However, while giving our cats that much emotional leeway certainly beats burning them at the stake and crucifying them the way some medieval Europeans did, it can create problems, too. Recall the Saint Francis Syndrome: Even the most positive emotions can't overcome the problems created by lack of knowledge.

In addition to unabashedly confessing their pets' most angelic as well as demonic behavior, cat owners may maintain very strong feelings about certain feline qualities. A former client of mine cared only for white cats, even though she knew cats of this color may experience more medical problems. Similarly, for every person who hates black cats, one exists who adores them.

"How can you stand living with a Persian?" one of Donna's co-workers asks when Donna proudly displays Nadia's picture. "I couldn't stand a cat with so much hair."

In addition to feline looks' eliciting strong human emotions, so do behavioral characteristics. Although the Fairchilds find Nadia's quiet demeanor the perfect contrast to Baby Kitty's exuberance, many visitors to their home align themselves with one cat or the other.

"I'd give anything to have a little fireball like this," one visitor sighs longingly as Baby Kitty leaps onto her shoulder and nibbles her ear.

"I'd shoot him if he belonged to me," vows another, scrubbing cat drool off her neck.

"What a gorgeous little creature!" another visitor gushes over Nadia. "Such a perfect little lady."

"Why don't you trade that dust mop in for a real cat?" scoffs another when Nadia scurries off the instant she sets eyes on the man.

Although we might feel compelled by some inner sense of feline democracy to proclaim that we like *all* cats, in reality most of us don't. Most of us maintain, albeit often unacknowledged, strong feelings about various facets of feline appearance and behavior. Unfortunately, we usually don't become aware of these emotional limits until the cat does something to exceed them.

For example, Jim dismissed his feelings about disliking long-haired cats—or rather their long cat hairs—as inconsequential until he found himself becoming irritated at Nadia every time he discovered one of her silver hairs decorating his clothing, a not infrequent event. Whether we believe Jim's response to be justified or not, the fact remains that it *will* affect his relationship with his pet, which in turn will affect her health and behavior.

How do we know this? Ivan Pavlov (of bell-ringing, drooling dog fame) conducted two experiments that demonstrated the profound effect people can exert on the mind and body of animals. In one, he monitored a dog's heart rate while the animal rested alone and as it responded to the arrival and presence of one of Pavlov's assistants. As expected, the dog's heart rate increased when the assistant entered and the animal greeted him. However, not only did the dog's heart rate return to normal, it dropped even lower while the dog was in the assistant's company than when that person left. Pavlov referred to this phenomenon as the *effect of person*, and we know from later studies that the opposite also holds true: Animals can exert a positive effect on human physiology simply by sharing the same space.

In a second experiment, Pavlov wanted to study the pain-reducing properties of morphine on his dogs. However, morphine also causes dogs to vomit before becoming sedated. When he began his experiments, Pavlov would inject his dogs, they'd throw up, and then they'd fall asleep. However, quite to his surprise, soon the dogs would vomit and fall asleep when they saw him merely preparing the morphine.

The idea of fooling the body into behaving as if it had received a drug was called the *placebo effect*, a phenomenon the scientific and medical communities either ignored or dismissed as charlatanism. These people simply couldn't accept that an animal or person could respond to the mere thought of the treatment as well as the treatment itself and therefore missed evidence of the extraordinary healing properties of the human and animal minds.

Granted, we could never conduct Pavlov's morphine experiments on cats because, again typical for the species, they react exactly the opposite of dogs, becoming greatly excited rather than calmed by the drug. However, other experiments over the years indicate that cats do respond to both the effect of person and the placebo effect.

These and similar human-animal bond and mind-body experiments loudly and clearly communicate that how we feel about our cats does affect them. Therefore, the more we know about our emotional limits, the more readily we can strengthen those that work and eliminate those that don't. Moreover, we can use these limits as guidelines when we get a new cat.

Pause here momentarily and consider those feline characteristics that attract and repel you.

## Emotional Limits Check

Review your list of positive and negative feline qualities. Which ones carry the greatest emotional charges? Are these positive or negative charges? Where do these feelings come from? How do they affect your feelings about the cat(s) displaying them?

Like many cat fanciers, the Fairchilds thought they loved all cats. However, by the time they completed this exercise, they realized that didn't quite hold true. Courtney mentioned a dislike of "noisy cats like Ms. Holmquist's Siamese," a reference to a neighbor's cat whose yowling also irritated Jim but delighted Donna. Although I say coat color doesn't mean that much to me, I must admit I'm a sucker for blue (gray) cats and fully intend to get a blue British shorthair if fate ever sees fit to allow me to pick a cat instead of having one sneak into my life.

Once owners recognize how any financial, time, and emotional limits may affect the human-feline relationship, an evaluation of any human physical limits will complete the picture.

# Physical Limiting Factors

Considering that the average adult cat weighs between 8 and 12 pounds, it may seem somewhat ridiculous to contemplate any human physical limits with respect to cats. After all, even petite Courtney Fairchild can pick up hulking Baby Kitty. However, as someone who works with both aggressive dogs and aggressive cats, I can state with some authority that trying to do something to a cat who doesn't want that something done will pose as much of a challenge as trying to do the same thing to a 90-pound rottweiler. In fact, given the choice between the rottweiler and the cat, I know a lot of big brawny guys who'd rather take on the dog.

While many people do prefer cats because of their comparably small size, most people also find strange adult cats more intimidating than kittens. Those who feel this way definitely should purchase or adopt young rather than full-grown animals, for several reasons.

First, recall that one of the tenets of the human-animal bond is that owners who fear their animals communicate that fear to them in countless ways. These people hold themselves differently and move less smoothly, two characteristics that the cat's highly developed motion-sensitive vision can easily perceive. Additionally, that old saying about animals sensing fear has some basis in fact. Remember that when frightened many animals, including humans, secrete very powerful scent hormones called pheromones, and the cat's highly developed sense of smell enables it to detect these readily.

When owners knowingly or unknowingly communicate their fear to their pets, that affects the animal's response to them. Like us, animals can take one of three paths when frightened:

- freeze
- flee
- fight

Suppose the Fairchilds obtain Nadia from a breeder just a week shy of her second birthday. Without thinking, Donna places the cat in Courtney's lap. Because this cat looks so different and acts so differently from the gregarious Baby Kitty, Courtney feels insecure and freezes. Sensing the child's fear, the Persian becomes fearful, too: her pupils dilate, and she flattens her ears to make herself appear smaller. However, Courtney thinks this makes the cat look scarier than ever. She leaps up and dumps Nadia onto the floor. At this point, we can hope either that the cat freezes when Courtney runs, or that Nadia runs away from the frightened child. If the cat opts to fight, the already troubled relationship will take a possibly disastrous turn for the worse.

Compare this with what happens if Courtney encounters Nadia as a frightened 12-week-old kitten. In this situation, the child's heart goes out to the animal. She talks to Nadia softly and moves very slowly lest she frighten her new pet more. When Nadia lashes out, Courtney feels sorry for her pet and makes a snug haven for her in a cat carrier, vowing to respond even more gently and patiently until her new pet overcomes her fear.

Perhaps sensing our fears or ambivalence, Mother Nature makes young animals more appealing than older ones. With their proportionately larger heads and eyes, young mammals of all species tug at our heartstrings more readily than animals with adult proportions. On some primitive level, they seduce us to care for them, maybe even in spite of our better judgment. That being the case, it makes sense for people who feel physically incapable of handling a cat—or who classify anyone in their household in this category—to get a kitten rather than an adult.

Unfortunately, that recommendation directly conflicts with some recommendations regarding pets for people with certain diseases or on medications that impair the human immune response. Those recommendations urge individuals with such problems to get adult cats rather than kittens because the latter may carry more parasites and diseases. However, people with physical ailments seeking an adult cat must also bear in mind that many adult cats wind up in shelters or in search of new homes because of behavioral problems.

While some might argue that a cat with behavioral problems poses no threat to human health, I disagree. First, not using the litter box ranks as the number one feline behavioral problem (which we'll discuss in detail in Chapter 6), and a house fouled with feline urine and/or feces hardly constitutes a healthy environment. Second, living with such a cat can produce a tremendous amount of stress, particularly if the new owners believe they saved the animal from an untimely death at a shelter. Because of the negative effects that stress may add to these people's already compromised immune response, it would seem most unwise to adopt an adult cat without full knowledge of its behavioral as well as medical history.

Time and again in our discussion of the human-feline relationship, it boils down to an almost mystical quality known as *presence*, that special aura that comes from a combination of knowledge, confidence, and respect. To me, presence functions like a spiritual black belt, enabling even the frailest person to respond in a manner that can calm and reassure even the most fractious animal. While some people like to believe they were born with a "way with animals," more often this results from confronting animals in controlled situations where they can respond with confidence.

Cat owners who yearn to develop presence but don't feel quite sure of themselves still may do so. If you consider yourself among them, first put on however many protective layers you need to feel 100 percent comfortable handling that kitten or cat. If that means a thick flannel shirt, a leather jacket, two pairs of leather gloves, three pairs of jeans, boots, and a catcher's mask, so be it. As confidence in your cat and yourself grows, you can always shed these extra layers. On the other hand, it can take forever to heal the damage a scratch on the hand can do to the mind of someone who didn't quite trust cats in the first place.

Remember: prevention always takes less effort than treatment. If you, or anyone else in your household, feel physically vulnerable around cats, don't deny that the problem exists or hope it will magically disappear. Instead, do whatever you need to do to enable you to interact with that animal without fear.

## Cat Owner's Physical Checkup

Review your own health history and that of anyone else in your household. Note any problems that a cat's presence might aggravate. Do these physical limits lead to any fears about handling cats? Do the fears arise from concrete knowledge or emotion?

When Jim initially contemplated taking Baby Kitty home to his family, he thought long and hard about Courtney's allergies. However, her pediatrician assured him that as long as Courtney really wanted a cat (which she did) and as long as the Fairchilds took some recommended precautions, the new addition should pose no problem. Just to be on the safe side, though, Jim and Donna made sure that Courtney wore protective clothing and that they supervised her first interactions with their new pet until everyone felt confident Courtney could both handle him properly and trust him.

One final note about bringing animals into homes with folks under medical care. Some health-care professionals who know little or nothing about the many benefits of the human-animal bond see animals solely as sources of disease. If you really want a pet and your physician refuses even to discuss the issue, check with other health-care professionals. Many hospitals and nursing homes have instituted pet visitation programs, and the folks who run them may have the data you need to make your case to your physician. Perhaps they can help you convince your physician that a visit from a well-behaved "therapy cat" once a week or so would really boost your spirits. Barring that, these people might be able to refer you to other physicians who can better meet your needs.

People with physical ailments seeking to maintain a quality life with their pets or those with healthy pets who would like to participate in visitation programs can contact the Delta Society at 289 Perimeter Road East, Renton, Washington 98055-1329. Those with Internet capacity may contact the society via E-mail at deltasociety@cis.compuserve.com or visit their home page at http://www.deltasociety.org for further information.

# The Human-Feline Balancing Act

No cat owner maintains a black or white view of his or her pet. Not only may the Fairchilds treat Baby Kitty or Nadia like a furry baby or an animated robot on any given day, they also may apply different limits to their relationship with their pets. While it's true Jim and Donna gasped in horror when presented with Baby Kitty's surgical bill, once they got over the shock, they also realized how much the cat meant to them. In other words, they realized that their emotional limits did allow them to make that amount of financial investment.

Not only do our orientations toward our cats change daily, but they also change over the course of the animal's life. Owners who may respond very anthropomorphically to young kittens may lean more toward more chattel views as their pets get older. All of the Fairchilds pampered Baby Kitty when he first entered their lives, but Jim grew fiercely proud of the cat's great hunting and other survival skills as the shorthair matured. On the other hand, Jim found the contrast between Baby Kitty and shy Nadia so profound that he babied the Persian even more as she got older.

For most owners, financial limits are linked to employment, and these, too, may wax and wane during the cat's life. The same new job that originally made Baby Kitty financially feasible suddenly vaporizes when Donna's company downsizes and she finds a pink slip included with her paycheck. The family reassesses their feline budget and decides that the benefits of feeding the cat a good-quality food make that food a cost-effective investment. However, they replace expensive chemical flea control with daily vacuuming, and professional grooming with a flea comb.

Time limits also change. Courtney's braces come off, she gets her driver's license, and she discovers boys. Her parents reach a point in their careers where they don't feel obligated to work long hours anymore. Quick pats to cat heads as owners rush in and out of the house yield to long evenings spent reading or watching television with the cats curled beside them.

Within the pet-owning population we also see what the human behavioral scientists refer to as *ageism*. Those who succumb to ageism relate to the cats differently as the animals get older, simply because they're older. One day Donna decides Baby Kitty shouldn't go out because "he's too old," rather than because the cat did anything that indicates he no longer can handle this experience.

Most commonly, owners who respond this way become much more anthropomorphic as the animal gets older, to the point that their reactions may undermine the animal's health as well as the relationship. One owner I know became so obsessed with her older cat's urinary problems that she dashed to the litter box every time she heard the cat using it. Her sudden, anxious appearance so upset the poor animal that he didn't want to use the box at all!

While some owners do succumb to ageism as their pets grow older, more often their emotional feelings about cats gradually evolve over time. As noted earlier, unlike dogs, cats seldom evoke neutral emotional responses: people who don't like cats *really* don't like them. However, for those willing to give a cat a try, emotional limits may expand over time. Originally when cat ownership surpassed dog ownership, logic said this occurred because the solitary cat fit better in a society where people spent less and less time at home. However, in no way are cats little dogs who use litter boxes, so it didn't seem likely that those who truly desired a canine presence would find a cat an acceptable substitute.

While some owners didn't, many others did—often much to their surprise. Although I can't prove my hypothesis, I can easily imagine the man in the golden retriever ensemble who paid $950 for a Maine coon kitten as a first-time cat owner. Moreover, I can imagine his becoming so enchanted by this undoglike creature that he even questions his sanity at times.

The reason this image comes so easily to mind is simple: I've seen it happen so many times. When Jim Fairchild first laid eyes on Baby Kitty, he felt something he'd never felt for a cat before, something so unsettling that he told himself he got the kitten for his wife rather than for himself. But by the time Baby Kitty reached a year of age, anyone who knew the family knew Baby Kitty was Jim's cat.

Finally, owner physical limits also shift and change with time. We grow older just as our pets grow older. The addition of a significant other, a new baby, or another pet may completely alter our view of the cat. Owners who evolve intricate rituals with a pet may find them impossible to maintain when they themselves become ill or injured.

In all of these situations, the critical issue relative to the health of the cat and the human-feline relationship isn't the rightness or wrongness of any changes, but rather whether the owner recognizes these changes and has the knowledge to respond effectively to them. During the time that cat and owner spend together, their lives will change many times, and each change potentially will alter that person's view of the animal for good or ill. Once we recognize that, and how we view cats in general and our own cats in particular, this knowledge serves as a critical cornerstone as we lay the foundation for a healthy, long-lasting relationship.

---

## Changing Limits Evaluation

Imagine yourself and your cat(s) over the next 10 years. How might any changes you foresee affect your view of your pet? Do you feel yourself becoming tense when you think of your cat's getting old? What changes in your own life might affect your financial, time, emotional, or physical limits? How could these affect your relationship with your cat?

When Courtney Fairchild completes this exercise, she realizes that she spends less time with the family cats as she grows older. However, she also realizes that she treasures their presence on the bed beside her every night more than ever. Meanwhile, as Jim and Donna envision themselves and their cats getting older, their views shift more toward quality-of-life considerations. They realize they'd spare no expense to save the life of a healthy young cat struck down by a treatable illness or injury. However, they don't feel that way about incurable diseases or even some curable ones that might befall an old animal, a view their daughter's emotional limits won't allow.

Granted, such introspection may prove a bit unsettling. However, once you nail down your orientation and any limits, you'll find it much easier to breach the human-feline gap, the subject of our next chapter.

# 5

# Friendly Persuasion

*Breaching the Human-Feline Gap*

Nothing inspires Frank Mallard more than the view of the rustic deck and rolling fields visible through the sliding door of his home office.

"Much as I hate doing the end-of-the-month bookkeeping, that view makes it all worthwhile," he tells his wife, Karla. "That and the breeze coming through the screen."

One day as Frank struggles with a new computerized bookkeeping program the family cat, an ocicat named Hootie, walks across the deck, sits outside the screened door, and meows politely to be let in.

"Go away," Frank orders the cat sternly. "I've got work to do."

When Hootie meows politely a couple more times, Frank continues to ignore her. Finally and with nary a trace of emotion, the cat slashes the fabric screen with one murderous swipe of her claws, glides into the room, and jumps into Frank's lap just long enough to establish eye contact. Then she jumps down and saunters upstairs.

"Frank, you'll never believe what just happened," Karla calls down the stairs less than a minute later. "Hootie came into our bedroom, ripped open the window screen, and jumped out onto the roof!"

Before Frank can process this report, however, Hootie leaps down from the roof to the deck railing, then takes up her position outside the slashed screen door and meows politely again.

Almost as if in a trance, Frank gets up and opens the door.

———————

Once we comprehend the basics of the cat's wild and domestic heritage, of our shared human-feline environment, and of our particular orientation toward cats and any limits we place on our relationship with them, we can use this information to analyze even as seemingly bizarre interactions as the one the Mallards experienced.

More or less.

"What do you mean, 'more or less'?" Frank asks as he contemplates the ruined screen and the ocicat now contentedly sleeping on the corner of his desk with that brain-frying mixture of love and contempt experienced by many cat owners on occasion.

Theoretically we can look at the domestic animal response as composed of five layers ranging from the most contemporary and complex to the most primitive (both chronologically and behaviorally):

- human-animal bond
- individual
- breed
- domestic
- wild

Typically when social domestic animals encounter a new or threatening situation, they first call up the *human-animal bond* program. When someone bangs on the Mallards' front door, Peony, their golden retriever, barks once and sits quietly as taught. Other dogs who lack this training move to the second layer, expressing various *individual* traits to relieve the tension.

One of Peony's more dominant littermates barks ferociously while another, submissive one chews his feet. Yet another sibling retreats to the third—*breed*—layer, picking up her ball and carrying it to the door for the visitor to throw so she can retrieve it. Dogs who find nothing in their breed heritage to meet their needs will call up the *domestic* layer, which essentially compels them to respond like immature wild pups, whining or displaying other puppy behaviors to relieve the stress. If that doesn't resolve the tension generated by the situation, they respond like *wild* adults.

While we can clearly see this linear progression at work in dogs, the contemporary cat's recent self-domestication, coupled with its breeding for looks rather than function, can thwart this sequence every step of the way. Someone knocks on the Mallards' door. What did her owners teach her about this?

"Nothing that I can recall offhand," Frank admits. "Sometimes she runs upstairs, sometimes she sticks around, sometimes she goes out the door when whoever knocked comes in. That's how cats are."

From this we can see that, whatever else the bond may contribute to human-feline interactions, even the most rudimentary training that we consider a must for dog ownership often plays no role at all when it comes to the cat.

What about the individual layer? Unlike dogs who automatically try to position themselves relative to any visitor according to the principles of pack structure, cats don't maintain any such internal rules. Consequently, while some may respond either dominantly or submissively, others may display solitary rather than social behavior and do neither. Moreover, they may respond in one way to the visitor today and in a completely different way tomorrow.

While cat breeders may describe at great length how their particular breed differs from all others, the recent domestication of the cat and even more recent evolution of breeds doesn't provide the average cat with much of a database here, either. An oci-cat like Hootie may react more energetically to a visitor than a Persian would, but maybe not.

Dogs who act like wild pups tend to act more submissively and vocalize more, opting for anything from sharp alarm yaps to beseeching whimpers and whines. Immature wild kitten displays fall in the sucking, kneading, and purring range; and, aside from the Siamese and some of their derivatives, vocalization doesn't play nearly the role in their relationship with us that it does in our interactions with other social animals. Consequently, more-extroverted cats in this mode may leap into the visitor's lap and begin kneading and purring, whereas more-introverted ones may streak into the owner's bedroom and dive under the bed to suck on a fuzzy toy either then or after the visitor departs.

Cats who "revert" to the wild adult cat mode—basically the strong, silent type—don't behave that unusually. In this mind-set, establishing and protecting the territory becomes the primary drive. Hootie marches right up to the visitor and rubs her face on his legs and ankles to mark him.

"What a wonderful cat!" exclaims the visitor. "She's so friendly."

Another less confident cat in this same mode might spray the visitor with urine, while a third might make a beeline for the owner's bedroom or the baby's crib and spray these instead.

However, even though we can roughly map out parallels between canine and feline responses, feline responses often lack the consistency of canine ones. Whereas Peony almost inevitably responds to the same visitors the same way, a cheerful welcome from Hootie today in no way guarantees the same treatment tomorrow. Furthermore, behaviors that seem firmly entrenched in young animals may change dramatically as they get older.

For example, when the Mallards got Hootie as a young kitten, her relationship to them closely resembled what they experienced with their dog. However, as she grew older, she became less cuddly and more aloof. The caption of a delightful cartoon of a woman describing her relationship with her cat sums up this common feline phenomenon perfectly: "We used to be very close, but now we're just friends."

One final ingredient in the human-feline bond stew takes the form of the cat's self-domestication which enables it to respond in totally unique ways. Whereas Peony will sit patiently at the door and bark to be let in year after year, one day Hootie decides she's had enough. Not content to just rip the screen, she rips *two* screens in a complex display that exceeds anything her owners taught her, at the same time that it communicates a message they completely understand. Put another way, Hootie's behavior reflects an advanced form of communication with her owners that goes beyond the *human-defined* limits of the human-feline bond.

Some cat owners might consider this a perfectly common feline phenomenon. How do *you* feel about it?

---

## Relationship Evaluation

Think about what you consider the most perfect human-feline relationship. List its qualities. What does the cat contribute to this? What do you contribute? What qualities do you consider definite must-haves for human and/or cat? What human and/or feline qualities do you believe would harm your relationship irreparably?

When Frank and Karla perform this exercise, like many cat owners they discover a curious fact: in spite of everything, they think they and Hootie have a wonderful relationship.

"True, she does some things—like that screen business—that drive me nuts," Frank admits. "But strange as it sounds, the fact that she actually did something so diabolically clever makes me like her even more."

"I honestly can't think of anything she could do that would upset me, except maybe bite someone," Karla adds. "Not me or Frank, but a stranger or a child."

The Mallards agree that their relationship with their cat indicates genuine affection for Hootie, and that providing her with any necessary veterinary care as well as suitable food and fresh water, and letting her in and out more or less on demand fulfill their obligations to this satisfying relationship. If for some reason they couldn't do that, they believe they would relinquish the right to own a cat.

Because the cat's unique nature makes it difficult, if not impossible, to apply any hard-and-fast rules to our interactions with it, let's turn the Mallards' town into a cat shrink's paradise and see what their neighbors' problematic relationships can teach us about the human-feline bond. However, before we do that, we need to consider a major shift in the human-feline population that makes such an unusual array of human-feline relationships possible.

## The New Millennium Cat

Of all the new types of cats that pop up, the largest group receives the least attention and doesn't rank as a breed at all: the housebound cat. Housebound cats come in all breeds, sizes, shapes, and colors. On the other hand, like purebreds, the housebound cat can and does display some idiosyncrasies not found in feral animals or those who go in and out freely. Among all of its idiosyncrasies, though, its *total* dependence on the owner to fulfill *all* of its needs heads the list.

In the preceding chapters we explored the nature of some of those needs, and in following chapters we'll discuss specific ways owners may fulfill these within the context of their own needs and any limitations. In this chapter, we need to examine how this dependency can affect the bond between owner and cat. To do that, we need to understand how certain cats became house-bound in the first place.

While some people point to the increased number of pure-breds as the reason for the increased number of strict house cats, four other human factors also come into play:

- changing human lifestyles
- increased owner guilt
- elitist views of animal ownership
- anthropomorphic and chattel views

First, the increased popularity of cats as pets paralleled the entrance of more women into the workforce and the increased number of households with no one home during much of the day. People who care about their pets feel uncomfortable leaving them outdoors to fend for themselves for 8 to 10 hours at a stretch, if not longer. Because a housebound social dog left alone could experience a great deal of stress as well as do a lot of damage, a housebound cat seemed like the perfect pet for this new generation of working owners.

Second, and close on the heels of the first, absent owners as a group feel more guilty about what happens to their pets than those who stay or work at home. Even if their cats succumb to an infection that every other cat in the neighborhood comes down with, these owners tell themselves it wouldn't have happened if they hadn't left the cat alone all day. A surprising number of these owners accept a wide range of correctable behavioral problems with comments such as, "He does it because he misses me so much" or "She's getting even with me for abandoning her every day."

When I first began working with owners of animals with behavioral problems, I felt frustrated when one owner rejected every solution I offered for her cat's relatively simple clawing problem, saying it wouldn't work for her pet. Only with time and experience did I realize that, just as some people believe owning a sickly or ill-mannered animal makes them superior people, others who spend a lot of time away from home believe they don't deserve a healthy, happy pet. Once that belief takes hold, they'll consciously or subconsciously do everything in their power to support it.

A third factor that complicates life for housebound cats springs from a long-standing societal view of pet ownership that flies in the face of reality. Human-animal bond studies indicate that people who society traditionally maintains have the least right to own pets—people who are physically, mentally, or emotionally impaired—benefit from a pet's presence the most. The idea of denying pet ownership to them rests on nothing more than pure, centuries-old arrogance, but such thinking still influences our ideas about what constitutes responsible pet ownership today. In reality, though, we all feel physically, mentally, or emotionally impaired at one time or another, and we all treasure our pets even more at those times. Nevertheless, for some people more than others, the idea that they must work especially hard to prove their worthiness as pet owners remains firmly entrenched.

Finally, we know from Chapter 4 that some owners who know little about cats often believe they can do no better than to treat their pets like furry little humanoids. Others assume that cats can take care of themselves and pay little attention to them at all. Because feline needs differ so dramatically from human ones, owners with anthropomorphic and chattel views understandably experience more problem relationships with their cats than do than those with knowledge of both their own and their cats' strengths and limitations.

When we put this all together, we wind up with a unique as well as potentially explosive human-animal bond situation. In the feline half of the equation, we see a housebound animal who instinctively may relate to its owner as its mother in a situation where it depends totally on that owner to fulfill its every need:

dependence squared. The human side yields increasingly stressed owners who need their feline companions but feel guilty and unworthy to own them, and who seek to alleviate these negative feelings by treating their pets either anthropomorphically or as chattel: a lack of knowledge cubed.

When a dependent kitten meets a kindhearted but unknowl-edgeable owner, the combination can make Dr. Frankenstein's relationship with his homemade monster look like a match made in heaven. As Dr. Frankenstein discovered, neither participant in such liaisons fares too well.

Take a few minutes now to analyze your own feelings about the human influences in the human-feline relationship before reading on. Although these feelings play a particularly important role with housebound cats, they can affect any human-feline relationship. Moreover, even the most venturesome in- and out-door cat may opt to spend most or even all of its time indoors as it gets older or if environmental changes occur. Many cats go outdoors only in the summer; others may instantly become house cats when a new dog or cat moves into the neighborhood.

---

## Armchair Bond Analysis

Once again consider your relationship with any existing or future cat. How do you think your lifestyle benefits or undermines your relationship with your pet? How much of a role does guilt play in your interactions with your cat? How would you define a "good" owner? Do you fulfill this def-inition? Note any anthropomorphic- or chattel-oriented elements in your definition.

"Hey, give us a break!" Frank complains. "Can't you give us a list of possible answers we can just check off?"

While I like to make things as easy for pet owners as possi-ble, the fact remains that too many people get into trouble because they latch on to someone else's database instead of creating their own. I know all too well from working with both clients and students that any list will lead some to accept my suggestions as the *only* right answer, even though these answers may not apply to their particular cat and situation at all.

Frank bites the bullet and thinks about his relationship with Hootie and comes up with some facts that surprise him.

"I didn't realize how much of a role guilt plays in our relationship," he admits after some quiet contemplation. "I bet I sometimes feel as guilty about letting her out as other owners feel about keeping their cats inside all the time. What if she got hurt out there? Once that guilt creeps in, and even though I know better, I jump to all kinds of anthropomorphic conclusions about what she thinks about me."

Considering that the Mallards experience an excellent relationship with their pet, we can understand how owners who lack a comparable amount of knowledge about their own situation can get themselves and their cats in a lot of trouble. In general, we can classify these problematic relationships in one of two broad categories:

- unnaturally dependent
- symbolic

Let's pop in on some of the Mallards' neighbors now to examine how their human-feline relationships evolve and the consequences for the participants.

## The Owner Who Loved Too Much

Anyone who knows Evelyn Jacobs knows she loves cats. If you asked these people how they know they'd say, "Because she puts up with so much from that darned cat of hers."

"I know Dudley has problems," Evelyn admits after graciously acknowledging yet another round of compliments about her devotion to the exotic shorthair. "But I just can't abandon him when he needs me so much."

Indeed, Dudley does need Evelyn a great deal. In addition to periodic digestive upsets and urinary tract infections, the cat attracts upper respiratory viruses like a magnet. The staff at the PetCare Veterinary Clinic jokes about naming an examination room in his honor because they see him so often for one ailment or another. However, they take even his most minor problems very seriously because they dread the thought of hospitalizing him.

"They kept him there once, and he almost died without me," Evelyn explains, wringing her hands at the memory. "The veterinarian called it 'separation anxiety,' and it was so horrible I vowed never to let him get that sick again. Now I watch him constantly and take him to the clinic the instant I notice anything unusual at all."

———————

At first glance, it appears that Dudley is one lucky cat for finding an owner like Evelyn who tolerates his many problems. However, let's add a few more facts to this relationship résumé:

- Dudley's breeder prides himself on breeding animals for physical soundness as well as looks.
- None of Dudley's litter mates experience any health problems.
- Evelyn got Dudley the week after her divorce became final and three days after her old cat died.
- She picked the most timid kitten in the litter

When we add these details to the picture, what initially looked like a cat problem suddenly becomes a bond problem. By selecting a kitten she defined as "needy" and then showering him with attention in an effort to distract herself from her divorce and the death of her old cat, Evelyn made herself the center of Dudley's world. In turn, the cat did likewise. However, for as much as this helped Evelyn through a difficult time, it had dire consequences for her pet.

"Just because she babied him?" Karla Mallard asks. "But he was such an adorable little puff ball when she got him, I would have done the same thing. Anyone would have."

While Mother Nature does imbue most young creatures with adorable characteristics guaranteed to entice most adults to care for them, feline separation anxiety invariably results from a cat's overdependence on its owner. Two perfectly normal feline behaviors conspire to create this situation:

- the kitten's tendency to perceive humans as its mother
- the cat's strong territorial nature

"But how can perfectly normal cat behaviors create such horrible problems?" Frank wants to know.

In cases of separation anxiety, the owner makes him- or herself such a major part of the kitten's life that that *person* rather than the physical space becomes the animal's territory. Granted, such relationships do have some advantages.

"I can take Dudley anywhere," Evelyn boasts. "As long as he's with me, he's happy as a clam at high tide."

However, the disadvantages of these relationships far outweigh this advantage. While these cats may appear quite happy in their owners' presence, they fall completely to pieces away from them, to the point of becoming severely depressed. Remember that establishing the territory takes precedence over eating and drinking; when Evelyn leaves, Dudley's appetite vanishes. It probably doesn't bother Dudley not to eat or drink from the time his owner leaves for work until she returns home nine hours later. However, this could spell trouble for him under two conditions.

- if disease-causing organisms lurk in the neighborhood
- if he suffers from some ailment and needs to keep his strength up to shake it off successfully

In the first case, the stress undermines Dudley's immune response and makes him an easy target for any hot virus, bacteria, or parasite seeking a host. Once that happens, he can't fight off the infection as effectively as a more independent cat because doing so requires energy, and that energy comes from food. Because of this we can appreciate why these animals may experience chronic or recurring medical problems.

When Evelyn decides to go off for a week's vacation, life becomes even more complicated for Dudley because not eating and drinking for seven days will definitely create health problems. Nor will it matter whether she takes him to the very best kennel, hires the world's best cat-sitter to care for him in her home, cooks all of his favorite foods in advance for the cat-sitter to feed him in her absence, or leaves pages of instructions about his care: no Evelyn, no territory, no food or water.

One ironic twist also may plague these relationships. The combination of the intense emotional charge Evelyn assigns to Dudley plus his highly negative response to hospitalization for a relatively minor ailment causes her to become obsessed with keeping him healthy. Unfortunately, this causes her to hover around him, constantly observing his every bite of food or lap of water, his every trip to the litter box. Let even a hint of a cat cough or sneeze escape him, and she grabs him and examines him thoroughly, prying open his mouth to look at his throat and shoving a thermometer up his rectum. While routine at-home examinations (which we'll discuss in Chapter 10) have many benefits, Evelyn goes overboard. Pretty soon Dudley finds himself in a horrible bind: even though he can't live without her, her tense presence makes him more tense himself.

A final blow strikes these animals when their owners refuse to assume responsibility for this situation. After basking in the glow of others' nominations for sainthood for not going anywhere without Dudley, Evelyn meets Mr. Right and decides to fly away to Tahiti with him for two weeks.

"I'm sure Dudley will be fine when I'm gone because he knows how important this is to me," she tells the apprehensive kennel owner as she and her new beau dash off to catch their plane.

Other owners who boast that their cats would die without them discover much to their surprise that their pets really would, and that may mean treating *all* medical problems at home, no matter how serious. When Dudley succumbs to a severe infection, Evelyn must take him to the veterinary clinic twice daily for treatment, and then take him back home to nurse him and monitor his progress there. After three sleepless nights, she feels as sick as her cat.

Before reading on, complete the following exercise to gain insight into your own feelings about this aspect of the human-feline bond.

## Sainthood Checkup

Imagine yourself and any existing or future cat on a typical weekday and weekend. What kinds of human-feline activities come to mind? When you think of doing something with/to your cat that would prove how much you love it, what comes to mind?

When Evelyn performs this exercise, she always sees herself intimately interacting with her pet. In her mind the ideal cat sits in her lap and follows her everywhere she goes. When she thinks of proving her love, she imagines spending even more time grooming him and brushing his teeth.

Compare Evelyn's responses with the Mallards'. Frank and Karla immediately think of Hootie's antics and the silly games they play with her.

"I can't think of anything Hootie would love more than for us to bring home a new box or bag for her to play in," Karla answers after some thought. "Of course, she loves it when we hide her old toys, too."

Owners of cats who experience separation anxiety unwittingly or deliberately make their cats exclusively dependent on them to fulfill some human need. While Evelyn quickly loses her saintly status once we know the whole story, the fact remains that such relationships can easily ensnare loving owners who lack knowledge of basic feline behavior.

However, sometimes owners can become as dependent on their cats as their cats become on them.

## Two Hearts Beating as One

D uncan Foucault, the neighborhood grouch, lives a block away from Evelyn with his equally touchy cat Styx, a black shorthair with smoldering green eyes. In addition to their temperaments, owner and pet share two other characteristics.

"I'm fat and diabetic, and so's my cat," Duncan announces in a tone that practically dares anyone to disagree with him.

Who could possibly disagree? One look at man and beast makes it quite clear that both carry extra pounds, and a peek in the owner's fridge reveals both his and his pet's supply of insulin.

Duncan's wife, Lorena, expresses mixed feelings about the unusual relationship.

"I'm sure the fact that Duncan cares so much about Styx makes him more conscientious about taking his own medication as well as treating Styx," she admits. "But no one but Duncan can handle the cat, and neither one of them sticks to a diet. Every time one of them has a problem, I can't help but think of the other. What will happen to Duncan if something happens to Styx? What will happen to Styx if something happens to Duncan?"

———————

Like separation anxieties, cases of so-called behavioral and/or medical codependencies remain rare, but veterinarians increasingly encounter this phenomenon in both dogs and cats. In cases of a strictly behavioral codependency—the aggressive owner with the aggressive pet, the timid owner with the timid pet—we can see how this could happen. While opposites may attract us sometimes, we humans just as often lose our hearts to an animal who reminds us of ourselves. Most likely Duncan didn't think, "I like that obnoxious kitten because he reminds me of myself," any more than shy owners think, "I want that little wimp in the corner who acts just like me." Instead, Duncan picks the kitten with the most "spirit," and shy folks zero in on "sweet" and "quiet" pets. Once we pick the kitten soul mate, the maternal human-feline bonding process takes over to reinforce whatever behaviors we find appealing.

"So, what's wrong with that?" Karla Mallard wants to know.

There's nothing wrong with that, provided the cat's behavior doesn't create any problems. For example, Duncan considers it a great game when, as a kitten, Styx lunges at his hands and Duncan barely whisks them out of the way in the nick of time. However, visitors and acquaintances unfamiliar with the game wind up with nasty bites and quickly come to dislike and avoid the cat, a turn of events that makes him even less sociable. At the same time, Styx's bond with Duncan grows stronger, fueled by the many snacks Duncan shares with his cat, who, he insists, "is the only one who *really* understands me." By the time Styx reaches seven years of age, he has a well-established reputation as a fat, nasty cat only Duncan can handle.

At this point, we can say that as long as Duncan can supply Styx with an environment in which the cat can express his grouchy temperament in acceptable ways, no problems exist. However, if the behavior leads to lawsuits from visitors attacked by the cat or if it undermines the cat's health, then this particular behavioral codependency doesn't work.

"You're not going to tell us that grouchiness causes diabetes in cats, are you?" Frank asks skeptically.

Not at all, but research indicates that obesity can contribute to this ailment. Thus, all those snacks Duncan shares with his pet do play a major role in this codependent relationship.

Styx's personality comes into play in other ways, too. First, Duncan shares his food with Styx to celebrate their special bond based on their similar "spirited" temperaments. Duncan never gives food to the couple's other cat, a Siamese Duncan considers a fawning baby, and that cat maintains its svelte appearance. Had Duncan not shared a special behavioral bond with Styx, he probably wouldn't have overfed him, either, thus sparing Styx at least obesity, if not diabetes.

Second, Styx's personality complicates the diagnosis of his medical problem from the very beginning. Dr. McCandless at the PetCare Veterinary Clinic dreads seeing the animal because she knows the big cat will viciously fight everything she tries to do for him. Worse, after tussling with Styx to get the necessary blood samples to confirm her suspicions that the cat suffers from diabetes, she can't say for sure that all the physiological changes that occur when an animal struggles won't give rise to any abnormal test results as much as or more than any medical problem would.

Third, Styx's personality definitely undermines his treatment because no one but Duncan can go anywhere near the cat. Consequently Styx's health, like his behavior, becomes inextricably linked to his owner's. If anything bad befalls Duncan, Styx's days are numbered, too.

On the human side of the coin, Duncan doesn't fare much better from this codependency. Although he adores his "one-man cat" when both of them are hale and hearty, when they develop medical problems, he finds himself in a bind. He doesn't want to change his way of interacting with his pet because he finds their particular bond most satisfying, plus he feels that both he and Styx need this special relationship to help them cope with their ailments. On the other hand, Duncan does worry about what will happen to his cat if he himself should require hospitalization. In fact, during one such hospital stay, Duncan became so anxious about Styx's welfare that his physician sent him home lest his emotional state worsen his condition.

The leap-and-bite game that so appealed to owner and cat also creates problems when Duncan becomes ill. Not only can't he avoid Styx's claws and teeth as easily as in the past, any wounds become more easily infected and take longer to heal. While Duncan could train his pet not to attack using the method described in Chapter 1, he thinks this would be cruel after promoting and enjoying the behavior all those years. Moreover, even though he knows that both he and Styx should stick to the diets recommended by their respective doctors, food treats play such an important part in the relationship that Duncan can't bear to change that, either.

"I can understand how behavioral codependencies come about, but what's the deal with the medical ones?" Frank asks. "Did the owner's lousy eating habits make the cat sick?"

Although it seems logical that those same bad habits that undermine human health will also undermine animal health if the owner involves the animal in them, the facts don't bear this out. Many healthy people own animals with medical problems, and many healthy pets bring joy to their sick owners. It does seem reasonably safe to say, however, that codependent problems result from synergistic human and feline physical, behavioral, and bond combinations with *the* right (or wrong) owner somehow finding *the* right (or wrong) cat. But, until that happy day when both physicians and veterinarians can accurately evaluate their respective patients' problems in this light, we can only speculate on the cause.

These cases point out another amazing paradox about cats. On the one hand, we have an animal quite capable of making it on its own in the wild. On the other, we have one who can mimic its owner's most subtle behavior or physiology, even to the point of destroying itself.

This brings me to one final anecdote regarding what may or may not be a variation on the codependency theme. At a cat show several years ago, a boisterously cheerful woman asked me what kinds of vaccinations her new kitten, a lovely little oriental shorthair, would need.

I rattled off the list and ended with, "Panleukopenia, also known as feline distemper."

"No, I don't want to give him that one," the woman interrupted with a very sincere smile.

"Why not?" I asked, thinking that maybe some previous cat of hers had reacted badly to the vaccine.

"Because I want him to be as mean as possible," she declared triumphantly.

Her response so surprised me that I automatically gave her the medical facts about distemper, including that it had nothing to do with making an animal nasty.

"Oh, then I'll have it done," she assured me, then thanked me for my help and disappeared into the crowd.

I've encountered naive owners of Doberman, rottweiler, or other pups purchased for "protection" who erroneously assume that vaccination for a disease called distemper will make their dogs too nice for this sort of work. However, these people almost invariably struck me as edgy enough that the rest of us probably needed protection from them, which an aggressive animal surely would supply.

"Wait a minute! How does an aggressive animal protect others from the owner?" Frank interrupts, then suddenly laughs. "I get it! Because no one bothers going anywhere near a person with an aggressive animal!"

Correct. In this situation owners can use the nasty animal as the reason no one wants to interact with them. ("You can't fire me, because I quit!") However, most of us probably wouldn't want to cultivate a friendship with someone who tolerates or reinforces negative animal behaviors. While we might question the owner's ability to handle the animal more than anything else, that distrust automatically carries over into other areas. Consequently, although people can't put "Beware of Human" signs in their yards or windows to alert others of any antisocial tendencies, alerting others to the presence of a nasty animal can serve the same purpose.

Given all this, the fact that the cheerful woman at the cat show wanted a mean cat flabbergasted me. Did she harbor some dark inner core that I couldn't divine? Did she intend to wreak havoc on some former spouse or beau who dumped her for being too nice? Did her sister own a mean cat and she had to own an even meaner one? Could she actually want a cat for protection? What could possibly motivate such a seemingly nice person to want a mean cat? Why not just get a mean cat? Why consciously set out to make a nice one mean? I honestly don't know the answers to those questions, but that conversation reminds me that when it comes to people and cats, the oddest relationships can be the rule rather than the exception.

Before we continue our tour through the Mallards' unusual neighborhood, evaluate your feelings about medical and behavioral codependencies.

## Codependency Checkup

Think again about that ideal relationship with a cat. How much of a role does the idea that your cat is like you play in it? Do you want your cat to reflect only your best qualities, or does the idea that you might share the same weaknesses appeal to you, too?

"There's no denying that Styx appealed to me originally because his personality was so much like my own," Duncan admits. "And I can honestly say that our having the same disease has been a godsend on more than one occasion. While I don't like the idea that I might have caused his problems, I don't know how I could have made it as well as I have without him."

When Frank Mallard examines what he considers his totally normal "undependent" relationship with Hootie, he begins chuckling.

"Now that I really think about it, so many of her characteristics that appeal to me— her diabolical sense of humor, for instance—are the same ones I enjoy in myself," he confesses with a grin. "And although I never thought about it before, it is kind of comforting when she and I both get colds the same time every year."

So, once again we can see that what can become a very serious problem may have its roots in aspects of the human-feline bond that we find enchanting.

In the previous examples, we saw how the kitten's tendency to respond to humans as its mother coupled with the solitary animal's learning pattern, which firmly fixes any early lessons, results in cats' bearing a strong resemblance to their owners in one way or another and also leads to problematic dependent relationships. Cats also can carry a potent symbolic charge for some people, an ability they've possessed without rival in the domestic animal arena ever since they first set furry foot on human turf.

## The Symbolic Cat

"How does dependency differ from symbolism?" Karla wonders as we tackle this second group of problematic relationships. "Don't both approaches treat the cat as something other than a cat?"

Think of dependency as an active process whereby the owner wittingly or unwittingly changes the animal's behavior and/or its physiology. Rather than merely reflecting the owner's beliefs, these animals actually embody them. The dependencies remind me of familiars, animals whose bodies mythical folk with special powers supposedly assumed when they wanted to move about in nonhuman form. These people gained all the advantages and disadvantages of that animal body. Thus, the witch who assumed the form of a cat—the familiar choice for witches—would gain the cat's incredible senses and agility that would enable her to spy unseen on witch-hating humans. On the other hand, she also gained the cat's small size and other feline characteristics that could prove a distinct disadvantage when she encountered a cat-hating dog.

However, treating animals as *symbols* is a relatively passive process. In this instance, people merely assign the animal and/or one of its normal behaviors a meaning. For example, the strong flocking instinct of sheep that leads them to follow the leader anywhere, even to death, became a potent Christian symbol of innocence. People traditionally link "Fido" with "faithful"; the bald eagle carries an emotional charge for Americans; millions attribute panther, tiger, or bear qualities to all kinds of athletic teams even though they may know nothing at all about these animals.

Given this human penchant for using animals as symbols, it comes as little surprise that the cat, with its unique behaviors and ability to elicit strong human emotion, ranks as one of the most potent animal symbols, if not the most potent. Not only that, the almost schizophrenic nature of the symbolism historically attached to cats also distinguishes it from other animals. While the symbolic innocence of lambs and Fido's faithfulness were passed down through the ages intact, feline symbolism has vac-illated wildly. Moreover, such wild fluctuations continue today, even among owners interacting with the same cat! The same motion Karla views as "almost poetic" when Hootie stalks an out-of-reach butterfly across the yard becomes "sneaky" when Hootie stalks a chipmunk.

To understand how this can happen, consider the symbolism that involves the cat's eyes, or rather the highly reflective structure inside the eyeball called the tapetum. As the light grows dimmer and dimmer, the cat's pupil dilates to let in more light, and the tapetum reflects that light to enhance the animal's nighttime vision. Dogs, horses, and sheep, among other animals, also possess this structure which comes in hues of brilliant metallic blue, green, and yellow. However, even though other animal eyes can reflect light, the cats' eyes alone took on a potent symbolic meaning.

"Because they were the only nocturnal domestic animals, they'd be the ones most likely to get caught in the lamplight or whatever," Frank correctly speculates.

Additionally, like other diurnal species, we humans instinctively love the sun and fear the dark, a legitimate fear for early humans given that wild animals could creep up and attack them while they slept. Hence, many ancient religions involved sun worship and focused on probable answers to the (to them) troubling question, "Where does the sun go at night?"

Imagine an ancient Egyptian hearing a noise outside his abode. His heart pounds and his pulse races. What demon of the night lurks out there? He steps outside holding his lamp high, ready to defend his home and family, and sees two bright yellow orbs of light shining up at him.

Perhaps the Egyptian's fright clouded his judgment so much that he couldn't admit that the fearsome demon of the night was only a cat. While any sensible person surely would fear a demon, what kind of a coward would fear a little four-legged, fur-covered mousetrap? On the other hand, who *wouldn't* feel awed in the presence of a god (or goddess) capable of carrying the *sun* in its head at night?

While we can never know for sure what led the ancient Egyptians to link this and other feline qualities to those of higher beings, we do know that their doing so earned the cat a revered place in their culture.

When the tapetum of the *medieval* cat caught the light, however, all hell literally broke loose, or so the medieval Europeans believed. While the god of monotheism theoretically reigns in darkness and light, visually oriented diurnal humans nonetheless persisted in fearing things that went bump in the night a lot more than those that bumped in the day. And, monotheistic theology notwithstanding, many people feel most cut off from any higher power in the "witching hours," that darkest of darkness before the dawn. Whereas the ancient Egyptians sought to relieve their fear by populating the night with friendly feline spirits whose glowing eyes assured them the sun would indeed rise again the next morning, the medieval Europeans huddled in their homes at night and declared anyone or anything afoot demonic. In the latter environment, that same flash of the feline tapetum became the gleam of Lucifer's eyes.

As we can see from these examples, all that the ancient and medieval cats did was dilate their pupils in response to the dark just like all animals, including humans, with or without a tapetum. However, this perfectly normal physiological act got the cat deified in one culture and crucified and burned at the stake in another.

"I thought you said symbolism was *passive* compared with separation anxiety and the codependencies," Frank reminds me. "Being made a god or crucified doesn't sound passive to me!"

Frank makes a valid point. However, the symbolic cat's change in status comes about as a result of the animal's expressing a *neutral* feline behavior. Compare this with the owner of the dependent animal who consciously or subconsciously reinforces a *problematic* physical or behavioral response such as fear, overeating, or aggression. No doubt many cats in ancient Egypt blithely went about doing cat things oblivious to the fact that some humans considered them godly, just as countless others no doubt romped through medieval Europe quite unaware of their demon status.

However, when these cats became trapped in the same, restricted environment with the symbol makers, their lives became complicated indeed. The adored Egyptian mouser winds up sacrificed, mummified, and buried just because its owner dies; the medieval cat trapped in a dead-end ally by club-wielding humans doesn't stand a chance.

Before we delve into how this plays out in contemporary human-feline society, consider what role symbolism plays in your relationships with cats.

## Symbolic Checkup

Summon the images of both positive and negative interactions you've experienced with any cats, then make a list of anything about those incidents that sticks out in your mind. Examine your list carefully. How many of the feline displays on it are normal ones to which you attach a symbolic meaning? How did any symbolic meaning you noted affect your response to the display and the animal?

Once more Frank winds up chuckling by the time he completes the exercise.

"I could have sworn I didn't attach any symbolism to Hootie when I started this," he laughs. "But now I have to admit I'm right up there with those ancient Egyptians some of the time, and I can commiserate with those medieval Europeans on occasion, too!"

Like Frank, most of us do treat our cats symbolically from time to time just as we dabble in dependencies. However, and as so often happens, the problem isn't that we do it, but rather that we don't realize we do. Let's take a look at just how complicated life can become for the modern house cat trapped in a symbolic relationship.

# The Four-Pawed Mirror

A few doors down from the Mallards another neighbor, Tony Bouchard, spends much of his spare time campaigning so fanatically for women's reproductive rights that even those who agree with his position duck behind the bushes when they see him coming. Tony and his wife, Marla or Marva—no one can remember her name—live with their four Siamese cats, So, La, Ti, and Do, two females and two males, all unneutered. During the breeding season Tony keeps the males and females in separate rooms, and their tortured yowls make more than a few visitors to the neighborhood wonder how the residents can sit by and do nothing while someone obviously tortures babies in the Bouchard home. Some even go so far as to make anonymous calls to the police and then learn the truth: "It's only a bunch of cats."

While some of the residents do periodically consider filing a complaint, they feel so sorry for Marva—or Marla—that they don't want to cause her any additional grief. After all, in addition to being married to a fanatic, the poor woman doesn't get much sleep, either.

———————

In this example So, La, Ti, and Do experience perfectly normal feline reproductive urges and all of the yowling and caterwauling that go with that. Normally owners respond in one of two ways to these animals:

- They breed them.
- They have them neutered.

However, Tony sees himself as a champion of reproductive rights and insists on abstinence as the proper way for civilized beings to deal with their urges. Because he doesn't want his cats to reproduce, he imposes this same rule on them and keeps them indoors so no free-roaming feline libertarians can take advantage of them.

As a result, Tony's housebound pets enjoy neither the freedom to fulfill their reproductive urges, nor the dulling of such urges that neutering confers. Instead, they live in an almost constant state of frustration several months of the year. Not only that, but the considerable stress this generates sets them up for a progression of medical conditions such as upper respiratory and urinary problems, too.

"That man should be neutered!" Karla hotly declares.

While the irrational nature of many symbolic relationships appears quite clear to those who don't share the symbolism, those involved in these interactions often don't see their beliefs as negatively affecting their pets at all. In Tony's mind, he loves his cats dearly and gives them the best possible care.

"I buy them the most expensive food, and each one has a special bed. I play with them every day, and they get the best treatment money can buy when they get sick," he boasts. "I wish I had it as easy as they do!"

When asked why he doesn't neuter his pets, Tony adamantly asserts, "It's not only wrong, it's an unnatural and unnecessarily cruel thing to do to an animal."

Another more common kind of sexual symbolism attached to cats goes by the name of the *harem effect* and befalls people who own multiple animals of the opposite sex—women own males, men own females—who fight with each other. Rather than do anything to reduce the tension between the cats, these owners dismiss the behavior with an, "Oh, they're just fighting for my attention." Sadly, that explanation completely ignores the reality of bite wounds, abscesses, and all the other problems that assail constantly battling animals.

While sexually orientated symbolism often tips in the anthropomorphic direction, other owners may attach symbolic meaning that reduces their pets to furry windup toys—or less. The latter kind of symbolism may crop up anywhere but seems more prevalent on the cat show circuit. To some extent, the very nature of cat breeding supports this orientation. Chapter 2 discussed the role genetic manipulation and the breeding of mutants plays in the purebred cat world; it also noted how show standards arbitrarily focus on physical appearance, often reflecting human emotion and preference more than any recognition of feline health and behavior.

As a result of all this, the temptation exists to show and breed cats for reasons that have little at all to do with the cats' needs. Surely we all recognize the "Winning is everything" owners who describe their cats in terms of prizes won. These people claim their cats' ribbons and trophies as their own, saying things like, "*I* won best of show in Dallas," as if the judge had stretched them out and held them above his head for all to see. Needless to say, cats imbued with this kind of symbolism don't fare too well when they stop winning!

Another kind of negative symbolism that the cat fancy elicits takes the form of reducing a cat to a body part. In cat show halls, comments such as, "I breed for coat rather than color" routinely are heard, as if the gene(s) for coat (or eye color or tail length) exist in a vacuum totally separate from the rest of the cat. The media may adore such an extremely simplistic view of genetics, but the idea of reducing an animal to a single body part makes the gap that separates the symbolic cat from its owner poignantly clear.

Yet another type of detrimental symbolic relationship earns the name of the Henry Higgins Syndrome. Owners of these cats forever try to make them into something different. Some insist on showing cats who hate shows, even going so far as to pump the animals full of drugs to calm them down or to fend off the stress-related infections to which the cats almost inevitably succumb following a show. Other owners insist that their more solitary cats do love each other dearly even though their behavior makes it quite clear they don't. Still others try to make mothers out of babies and babies out of mothers, couch potatoes out of hunters and hunters out of couch potatoes. While the particular

form the symbolism takes may vary greatly, the underlying principle remains the same: the owner takes a human belief and projects it onto the cat without any concern about whether doing
so meets the pet's physical and behavioral needs.

The final form of symbolism feeds on the owner's belief
that love will conquer all, no matter that the cat's nature and
the owner's knowledge of it might argue to the contrary. No
matter how much they may know about feline development
and the kitten's need for a good cat teacher, some people will
convince themselves that the orphan kitten *they* raise will beat
the odds, "because I love it so much." Others maintain that
their aggressive cats would never *really hurt* anyone because
"Fluffy loves me and he knows how much I dislike that sort of
behavior."

Basing a relationship on this kind of love symbolism poses
two problems. First, these owners often use love as an excuse
for not learning what they need to know to evaluate and resolve
any problems. When Tony tells visitors that he lets his sexually
primed cats yowl and pace, unable to eat and drink properly, for
days because he loves them so much, such sentiments sound
extremely hollow.

Second, such symbolism puts the responsibility for any feline
problems that arise as a result of the owner's symbolism on the
cat. When one of Tony's females succumbs to a whopping uterine infection and requires emergency surgery to save her life, he
can't believe it.

"I love you so much, how could you do this to me?" he murmurs to the barely conscious cat.

While we may chafe at the owner who sees the cat as a political statement or body part, the ones who use love in this manner can do just as much if not more damage to the human-feline
bond.

Though these particular cases may trigger a strong desire
never to reduce our own human-feline relationships to symbolic
levels, in fact we do this routinely. Frank's admiration of Hootie's

hunting ability stems far less from her controlling the rodent population than from the parallels he draws between the behavior and his own martial arts training. Paradoxically, when Hootie snuggles purring and kneading in Karla's lap, Karla's thoughts leap to her now grown daughter and the grandchild she yearns to hold. So many owners attach so much symbolism to feeding the cat that we'll devote a whole chapter to that subject.

"Well, that's just great!" Frank huffs. "How do we know if the symbolism we attached to our cats is the good or bad kind?"

Before we explore the answer to that question, review your feelings about viewing cats as symbols.

## Symbolic Checkup II

Review your comments about those aspects of your relationship with cats to which you assign a symbolic meaning. How does or could your symbolism affect your pet's health and behavior?

When Frank reviews his remarks about his relationship with Hootie, he discovers that most of them do take the ocicat's needs into account.

"But I can see that in some cases that was more luck than anything else," he admits. "And while I do attach some symbolism to her hunting ability, in no way would I care less for her if she stopped doing that for some reason."

Meanwhile, Karla detects a potential problem in her symbolism that she never noticed before.

"When Hootie snuggles into my lap and I make that maternal connection, if I happen to be eating something I automatically offer some to her, just as I would a child," she explains. "I never did that when she was younger."

Karla's revelation points us to yet another special quality of the human-feline bond, its dynamic as well as elastic nature.

# Striking the Balance

We know that every owner and every cat comes into the relationship with his or her own unique set of physical, behavioral, and environmental needs. We also know that some cats, owners, and environments allow more room for change than others. Just as houseplants need a pot big enough to permit them to grow or they'll eventually become pot-bound and die, relationships need a certain amount of leeway, too. In general, the more rigid the owner's or cat's behavior, or the more restricted the environment, the more likely relationship problems will develop.

In this chapter we've seen how, given a particular cat and environmental conditions, owners who equate human and feline needs can create an animal with little or no sense of its feline self.

"Dudley's not a cat," boasts Evelyn Jacobs. "He's a *purr*son."

If the cat possesses a sufficient sense of self to resist being crammed into this human mold, though, the relationship probably won't be a rewarding one for the owner. Before Evelyn got Dudley, she took in a stray who drove her to distraction.

"No matter what I did for that cat, he didn't appreciate it," she recalls. "I offered him food from my plate and he ignored it. When I gave him his own special pillow on my bed, he insisted on sleeping on top of the bookcase, or even outside, for Pete's sake. Instead of curling up next to me while I read or watched television, he wanted to chase bugs."

Although we can readily recognize that stray as a perfectly normal cat, Evelyn doesn't see it that way at all. On the other hand, she does see Dudley, the most timid, smallest kitten of the litter, as the most perfect companion because she can mold him to fit any image she wants. However, she doesn't realize that she can do this precisely because he lacks a sufficient sense of self to resist her manipulation.

In this situation, the owner completely overwhelms the cat with her own needs and desires to the point that he never develops a sense of self and thus becomes completely dependent on her for his identity. True, Dudley still *looks* like an exotic short-hair and even acts like one, at least in Evelyn's eyes. Whenever he deviates from that image, though, as his "mother" she persuades him to abandon the behavior.

"Don't dig in your litter like that." Evelyn claps her hands sharply as she scolds the timid kitten. "You're making a mess."

Dudley immediately stops and scurries from the box, completely ignoring his instinct to bury his waste.

"What a wonderful little boy you are!" Evelyn gushes, totally unaware that she just undermined Dudley's weak sense of cat-ness even more.

Other times, Evelyn reinforces needy behavior in the kitten because it makes her feel more needed herself.

"Did the sound of that mean old radio scare you?" she asks the kitten when a loud commercial makes him flinch. "Mommy will turn it down for you."

While all of these behaviors seem innocuous and even silly, they make it impossible for Dudley to live without his owner. Ironically, a lot of owners involved in such dependent relationships will chalk it all up to their great love for their pets.

"Dudley loves me so much he'd die without me," Evelyn tells her best friend.

Of course, because she knows nothing about normal cat behavior, she feels mortified when he almost *does* die without her.

People who share medical or behavioral problems with cats pose a completely different kind of bond problem. Deliberately or unintentionally, they and their pets become involved in a dance in which they share similarly restricted *internal* as well as external environments. Because the cat depends on the owner for treatment, how that person views his or her own problem will definitely affect the cat's health and behavior. If Duncan wants to curb his temper and adhere to his diet to help control his diabetes, most likely he'll impose the same on Styx. While such mutually supportive human-feline relationships can work for both participants, if Duncan doesn't want to treat his own problems, he most likely won't want to treat his cat's, either. More likely, he'll use his pet's problems to validate his own.

"You know how rotten it is not to eat what you want, don't you, buddy?" Duncan asks Styx as he scoops ice cream for the two of them. "Those doctors would be grumpy, too, if they had to put up with what we do."

At the opposite end of the bond spectrum we see symbolic relationships that maximize the distance between owner and pet. Again, no problems arise if the owner assigns a positive symbolism to the cat that doesn't restrict the cat's behavior. Frank adores Hootie's prowess as a hunter because it reminds him of his own competitive spirit, a trait he credits for his success in business. That his business success has nothing to do with his cat's hunting ability doesn't affect Hootie in the least. She goes about her hunting quite oblivious to the connection Frank makes between his own and her behavior.

On the other hand, when Tony Bouchard imposes his rigid reproductive politics on his cats, they do suffer physically and behaviorally from both their restrictive owner and their restricted environment. Similarly breeders who see cats as prizes or body parts pose no problems to healthy cats in a fulfilling environment. However, if those people focus on coat or body type and ignore the rest of the cat, these animals will suffer from this symbolism every bit as much as the breeding animal confined to a cage for its entire life.

From this we can see that owners need to strike a balance when it comes to how much distance they place between themselves and their pets. If we lean too far in either direction, we risk denying our pets their unique feline natures as well as denying ourselves all the benefits of a mutually rewarding bond.

Given that fact and the awareness that cats have the potential to re-create the feline behavioral wheel at the drop of a whisker, it may seem as if every cat owner teeters on the brink of bond disaster every minute of every day. However, millions of owners experience wonderful relationships with millions of cats without giving a thought to what makes their relationship so special or how it came about.

Consider the Mallards' relationship with Hootie. Their daughter fell in love with a kitten she saw at a friend's home during a slumber party her junior year in high school. She brought the kitten home, and all went swimmingly. Why? The Mallards radiated that one quality that can make or break any human-animal relationship: presence.

All humans and animals radiate an aura consisting of all sorts of sensory and perhaps even extrasensory cues that communicate a tremendous amount of positive and/or negative information to others. Those others, in turn, absorb this information (often without any conscious awareness of doing so), as well as generate their own. This interplay strongly affects how the two relate to each other. Theoretically, presence consists of both positive and negative qualities. In behavioral terms, however, presence refers to a very positive trait that's a hallmark of all successful relationships.

Even though both people and animals with presence stand out from the crowd, most of us can't precisely define the phenomenon. Yes, it embodies all of the definitions assigned to it by the dictionary: presence does refer to qualities such as "bearing" and "grace." Those who possess it move in the world with a certain confidence and assurance.

"Don't cats always move that way?" Karla asks as Hootie lightly springs into her lap and stomps down a nap nest.

Happy, healthy cats do, but not those who feel vulnerable. The vulnerable animal acts hesitant, tentative, and even jumpy, its entire demeanor radiating tension. The same thing happens to people, too. Owners who feel unsure about themselves or their cats communicate this to the animal in a thousand subtle ways.

Because we know that we and our pets can affect each other's physiology merely by sharing the same space, any human body language most likely won't go unnoticed by the cat, any more than a person would miss the message communicated by a cat with bristled fur. While more aggressive cats may exploit this lack of owner presence, more timid ones may feel even more apprehensive around these people. Meanwhile, very young animals may feel compelled to mimic the owner's behavior if no other cats share the household to teach them otherwise.

Another definition of presence refers to the physical space immediately surrounding a great person, such as "in the presence of the king." Owners and animals with presence radiate an aura that affects the area around them, too. Put an owner and a cat with presence together and the two interact in a way that makes one plus one equal more than two. It can be downright spooky, evoking thoughts of the supernatural. Whether you believe in such phenomena or not, the result is both *super* and *natural*.

Cats and owners with presence generate such a strong sense of self that they don't feel threatened by those not like them, including each other. This sense enables them to detect and adapt faster to changes in themselves, the other, and/or their environment than those lacking this quality. Where does it come from? How do you get it? I firmly believe it results from solid knowledge combined with love.

"That sounds wonderful," Evelyn admits after she aborts her vacation to Tahiti with Mr. Right to care for Dudley. "But how do you get to that point when you're having problems?"

Most owners who experience problems with their pets really do love them. It's lack of knowledge that does them in. Consequently, the first step toward resolving problems is to objectively define and evaluate the problem in terms of yourself, the cat, the environment, and the relationship in as much detail as possible. When Evelyn asks the who, what, when, where, how, and why questions and examines her answers in terms of what she's learned about cats in general, Dudley in particular, their environment, and their relationship, she discovers that many of his problems either are actually her problems or constitute perfectly normal feline behaviors.

"The real problem was that I didn't realize babying him would make him so dependent, any more than I accepted that cats naturally dig in their litter," she remarks after she completes her fact-finding mission.

If Evelyn decides it's a cat problem, she makes a list of what signs Dudley displays. "Dudley pees in my bedroom" is a legitimate sign; "Dudley hates me" isn't. Don't forget to note all physical as well as behavioral signs. Evelyn gets so upset by the sight of Dudley urinating on her rug that she doesn't even notice how much more water he's been drinking lately.

"I felt horrible later when Dr. McCandless told me that he had an infection that caused him to drink a lot more water," Evelyn confesses later. "Poor little guy was sick, and stupid me, I yelled at him."

Next Evelyn examines the environment. What changes have occurred that may have precipitated the problem? At first she sees nothing askew.

"I haven't bought any new furniture or moved anything around," she notes as she walks from room to room in her house. Then she gets to the bathroom and sees the towel mounded up on the edge of the tub. "Oh! My boyfriend has been staying over a lot more lately!"

That realization causes Evelyn to analyze her relationship with Dudley. When she does this, she quickly discovers how drastically both the amount of time she spends with her pet and the kind of interaction she experiences with him have changed since she met Mr. Right.

"Before, I treated Dudley like my baby, but then I expected him to start acting like an independent cat the instant my own life changed," she groans disgustedly at herself. "What a rotten owner I am!"

If Evelyn stops the process at this point, the guilt will assault her, and she might even ditch Mr. Right. If so, she and Dudley will become even more dependent on each other. However, if she reaches this point and recognizes both her own and her cat's needs and looks for a way to meet them both in their changing environment, then she takes the first step on the road toward a more mutually rewarding relationship with her pet. Once she does that, both she and Dudley will also take a first step toward developing presence.

All owners form some kind of a bond with their cats. Some owners feel that as long as the relationship meets their human needs, that's all they have to worry about. However, a relationship that meets the needs of only one of the participants isn't a relationship at all. Making a cat dependent to the point where we forget about all its own unique behavioral and physical needs reduces it to a dim shadow of ourselves. Seeing a cat as a reflection of some human belief or need uses the cat as little more than a mirror. While both orientations can add depth to our own feelings, if they don't take the cat's needs into account, they comprise a solo venture. We may own the cat, but we don't relate to it: we don't share each other's presence.

## Bond Tune-Up

Given all you now know about your cat, your environment, yourself, and your relationship, consider any problem(s) you've experienced with your pet. If you don't have a cat, think about problems experienced by cat-owning friends. Who has the problem—the cat, the owner, or both? What exactly is the problem? When, where, and why does it occur? How do you feel about this problem? Does it undermine your relationship with this cat?

After Evelyn analyzes her and Dudley's considerable problems and turns her attention to her feelings about them, she discovers something that surprises her a great deal.

"Considering how much I contributed to this, I thought I'd feel really miserable and guilty," she confesses after she completes the process. "But as I took in all that information about cats, the environment, and myself and applied it, I felt I was learning so much that would help both me and Dudley that I really enjoyed myself."

The more we need to know, the more we—and our cats—need to play. Evelyn's genuine love of her pet led her to seek solid knowledge when problems arose, and out of that came presence and the enjoyment it embodies, two qualities that will ensure a lasting and mutually rewarding human-feline relationship.

Now that you understand what makes cats and our relationship with them so special, let's apply that information to solving the number one feline behavioral problem. Then we'll see how understanding the special human-feline relationship can help you select the best exercise, feeding, and health-care program for your pet.

# II

# *Caring for and Living with Your Cat*

# 6

# Litter Box Roulette

## *Troubleshooting the*
## *Number One Feline Problem*

For six years Tasha, a lovely Russian blue, lives in perfect harmony with her owner, Sara Volcano. When Sara moves into a retirement community, she voluntarily gives the cat to her son and daughter-in-law, Ian and Katie Volcano. All goes well for a while and then one day, while Ian and Katie rush to get ready for work, Tasha squats and urinates on the bathroom rug.

"Oh, poor baby! You must have a bladder infection!" exclaims Katie. "I'm making an appointment to take you to the vet's right now."

Sure enough, within days of starting the medication, Tasha stops peeing on the rug . . . but continues peeing on the bed in the guest room. However, Katie doesn't discover this second site until weeks later when she prepares the room for another visit from her brother, his children, and their dog.

"You spiteful little brat!" Katie screams at the fleeing cat while Ian tries to swat the animal with a rolled-up newspaper. "You know Sara made that quilt for us! You know how much she loves you! How could you?"

A few days later, the Volcanos notice Tasha repeatedly using her litter box. At first this pleases them, but when they replace her litter with shredded white paper towels as their veterinarian suggested, they discover blood in her urine.

"How could we have been so stupid!" Ian berates himself angrily. "The poor cat never got over that infection. She's been sick all along!"

The owners wallow in guilt while the veterinarian gives Tasha a thorough (and expensive) workup to discover the cause of the problem.

"Everything checks out fine," the doctor assures them when they come in to pick up their pet. "It must be behavioral."

Katie and Ian look at each other and then at Tasha, too confused to speak. They take their pet home, relieved that she suffers from no medical problem, but frustrated with the thought of living with urine-soaked furnishings. However, the behavior suddenly stops and the owners eventually forget all about it—until six months later when Tasha starts peeing on the bathroom rug again!

---

Whenever I speak to a group about feline behavior, I try to cover all the wonderful idiosyncrasies that make this species so fascinating. I also allot time at the end to answer questions about these many behaviors. Invariably, though, the majority of the questions boil down to, "Why doesn't my cat use the litter box?"

After listening to my umpteenth reply to the umpteenth variation on this theme, a colleague cheerfully asked, "Have you ever considered changing your name to Dr. Cat Pee?"

That remark and my awareness of the increasing number of owners grappling with this problem made me vow to write a whole chapter on the subject. No feline behavior generates more negative emotion and undermines the human-feline relationship more; no behavior causes the abandonment and death of more household pets.

Look at what happened to Ian and Katie. In addition to feeling frustration, anger, revulsion, guilt, and remorse, they must cope with the stench, the ruined furnishings, criticism from others for putting up with the behavior, and any human health hazards posed by the problem. Although Ian and Katie experience no health problems themselves, Ian's mother suffers from a disease that undermines her immune response. Consequently, Tasha's habit of urinating on the guest room bed could have medical repercussions for the family.

As is so typical for the cat, the more we know about animals who don't use the litter box, the less we seem to know. Traditionally cats displaying this behavior were divided into two groups:

- those with medical problems
- those with behavioral problems

Theoretically, each group exhibited its own set of signs which rated its own specific treatment. As in human medicine, problems designated as "medical" often generated more compassion and understanding than those labeled behavioral. The old thinking defined a person or animal who succumbed to a medical problem as a victim who warranted our sympathy, whereas those with behavioral problems chose not to do the right thing for some reason.

As more and more cats began to experience this problem over time, it became clear that medical and behavioral problems don't constitute an either/or, but rather an "and" situation. Every medical problem contains a behavioral component, and every behavioral one can lead to medical problems. Moreover, every problem has a bond component, too.

To see how this works, let's evaluate what happened to Tasha with respect to the Big Three animal drives:

- establish and protect the territory
- find food and water
- reproduce

First, Tasha begins peeing in the spare bedroom following the first weekend visit by Katie's brother, his two kids, and their dog, which the cat views as a major territorial threat. The stress created by their presence also causes Tasha to eat and drink only the barest minimum, leaving her vulnerable to physical problems. Next she must deal with the trip to the veterinarian and her owners' grabbing her and stuffing pills down her throat twice a day. Later, when her owners discover the urine in the guest room and yell at her, she feels even more vulnerable. This, in turn, compels her to mark her territory even more and eat and drink even less, further stressing her immune response and increasing her susceptibility to urinary tract problems. Meanwhile, she also keeps returning to the bathroom rug because Katie's detergent didn't completely remove the urine scent from its rubberized backing. When Katie discovers this, owners and cat can go through the same vicious cycle all over again.

As urination and defecation problems have become more and more common, new waste-related terminology has emerged. The current scientifically, medically, and politically correct terminology for displays involving urine and/or feces that the cat deposits anywhere but in the litter box for any reason is *inappropriate elimination*. No matter what this phrase adds to—or subtracts from—our understanding of the problem, it does make it easier to discuss the subject in polite society. That's good because wherever two or more cat owners meet, the subject almost always comes up. Katie would never consider mentioning that Tasha pees—or takes a leak, or poops—on the bed when she discusses cats with other cat lovers at a picnic hosted by her boss. However, she quickly becomes involved in a discussion of inappropriate elimination.

To get a comprehensive picture of the many factors that combine to create a cat who doesn't use the litter box (or "practices inappropriate elimination"), we shall don our cat detective hats. In this role we'll seek to answer the questions *what, who, when, where,* and *why* to help you prevent or treat this most common and troublesome feline problem. While we'll apply this process to inappropriate elimination, it works equally well for all feline problems.

Before reading on, though, evaluate your feelings about this number one feline behavioral problem.

## Elimination Evaluation

Imagine yourself discovering urine or stool somewhere outside your cat's litter box. What is your immediate reaction? How does this make you feel about the cat? How does your response make you feel about yourself? How much of your reaction arises from solid knowledge? How much of it reflects pure emotion?

"The first time Tasha didn't use the box, I was convinced she had a medical problem, and I was willing to accept that," Katie reports. "I get bladder infections myself and know how painful they can be. But when she started going in the guest room, that really made me angry."

"Whether there's a legitimate medical reason for it or not, just the thought of urine or stool anywhere but in the litter box disgusts me," Ian frankly admits. "I don't care what causes it. I just want it stopped as soon as possible."

"To me it's all part of cat ownership," Ian's mother, Sara, offers. "You take the good with the bad."

Like most owners, Katie, Ian, and Sara feel strongly about their personal viewpoints. Also as with most owners, their comments indicate little concrete knowledge of the underlying causes of the cat's problem. To rectify this situation, let's begin our investigation by taking a closer look at the liquid and solid evidence of the alleged crime.

# The Evidence

Surprising as it may seem to many contemporary cat owners, up until a few years ago, reports and studies of inappropriate elimination focused strictly on urine in three forms:

- sprays
- puddles
- drops and dribbles

The cat detective would see the spray and declare, "Ah ha! That cat is marking his territory." The sight of a puddle, drops, and dribbles outside the box immediately pointed toward bacteria, viruses, and other medical causes as the culprit.

Given that all animals mark their territory with their stool as well as their urine, it seems odd that owners rarely mentioned stool outside the litter box. When it occurred, they almost invariably linked it to some sort of a "bowel problem," even if the stool appeared perfectly normal.

Two reasons could explain this. First, the idea of a cat's pooping on the bed so violates the centuries-old image of the fastidious feline that owners of these animals conceivably could have feared to publicly acknowledge the behavior, lest they and their pets incur the disgust of others. Sara's neighbor kept the fact that his cat periodically left "stool presents" on his bed a secret from everyone but a few of his most trusted friends, cat lovers all. Naturally Sara wouldn't think of sharing the news of this animal's indiscretion with her waste-phobic son and his wife.

If ignoring the behavior didn't work, owners of cats who defecated outside the box probably gave the animal up, offering some totally unrelated excuse such as, "I'm allergic to it." Many of these owners surely did this all the while praying that some miracle would keep the behavior from recurring in any new home. Doubtless, other owners experiencing this problem abandoned their pets along the side of the road.

However, while closet poopers may have existed right along, we can't discount the possibility that the rise in reports of such inappropriate elimination means it's a relatively recent phenomenon. Such behavior could result from changes arising in two different quarters:

- the cat
- the environment

We'll discuss both of these in more detail. For now, suffice it to say that marking with stool requires more energy than marking with urine.

"Seems pretty equal to me," Ian remarks dubiously. "Tasha spends about the same amount of time in the box, regardless of what she produces."

While that may be true, it usually takes a cat less time and energy to locate water and convert it to urine than to catch prey and convert it to stool. This could explain why cats would rely more on urine, reserving stool for more serious marking. The fact that frightened mammals will lose control of their bladders first and their bowels second also supports this speculation.

Another possible explanation centers around visibility. Although cat urine has a very pungent odor, it becomes invisible when sprayed on trees or on the ground. On the other hand, a pile of stool makes a strong visual as well as olfactory statement.

In addition to determining whether the evidence consists of urine, stool, sprays, puddles, drops, dribbles, piles, or dibs and dabs, cunning cat sleuths check for amount and physical appearance: Big puddles or little ones? Bright yellow, almost colorless, or pinkish urine? Large, smelly piles, or discreet little dollops? Rock hard, runny, or just-right nuggets? Such clues can provide your veterinarian with valuable information about any medical component of the inappropriate elimination.

If the cat urinates on carpeting that makes it difficult to determine the liquid's color, blot it up with white paper towels and examine the towels. If the cat urinates in the litter box as well as elsewhere, replacing the litter with shredded white paper towels or white stryofoam "peanuts" will make it much easier to determine color. Periodically using this makeshift litter also serves as an excellent way to monitor cats prone to urinary tract problems that result in bloody urine.

"Surely you're joking!" Ian blanches at the mere thought of such scrutiny when the veterinarian first suggests it.

True, such observations come more easily to veterinarians than to many cat owners. On the other hand, the more information the Volcanos can collect, the more accurately they can define exactly what Tasha is and isn't doing. If they couldn't bring themselves to do this, they'd need to either pay someone else to collect these necessary clues for them or attempt to diagnose and treat the problem without these essential facts. While the latter might strike Ian as more aesthetically pleasing, it offers the least chance of finding a lasting solution.

Finally, even though most of us consider *anything* deposited outside the box troubling, the fact that the cat deposits only urine or stool or both can provide a valuable clue to both the cause of and the solution to the problem.

Throughout this book, I've often asked you to imagine various aspects of your relationship with your cat. This technique, called *imaging* when used in medicine and sports, serves as a very effective way to dry run potential events that you find problematic for any reason. For some people, consideration of waste products falls into that category. When Ian uses imaging, he needn't contend with the odor of stool or urine, stimuli that trigger a maximum negative emotional response. Nor does Katie need to deal with all the negative feelings that attend the awareness that she must clean up any mess. By summoning an image of the urine and stool without these factors, the owners can practice responding in a more objective way. Then when they encounter the real thing, they can collect solid data instead of negative emotions.

Use your imaging skills for the following "Evidence Analysis." As with all the exercises in this book, don't worry about giving right or wrong answers. Even if you decide you know nothing about your pet's urine and stool and don't want to, you're better off than someone who doesn't give the subject a thought until problems arise.

---

## Evidence Analysis

Summon an image of an existing or future cat. Now imagine its normal urine and stool. What do they look like and smell like? Next imagine your pet's abnormal urine and stool. How do these differ from the normal products? If you can't answer these questions, how do you feel about that?

Because Katie and Sara count litter box cleaning among their present or past duties, they both have very accurate impressions of Tasha's normal and abnormal urine and stool.

"I can't say much about the color of Tasha's urine because we normally use a clumping litter that rolls itself into a little ball when she goes on it, but I do recognize what I consider a normal size, number, and odor of those clumps as well the amount, odor, and consistency of her stool," Katie reports. "If there's a change in any of these characteristics, I do notice it, although I might not do anything about it."

Sara nods in agreement. Ian's highly negative, emotional response to his pet's wastes, on the other hand, leaves him clueless about this aspect of pet ownership.

Now that we can understand the *what*, we need to take a closer look at the *who* of inappropriate elimination.

# The Feline Suspect

In the past, cats who didn't use the litter box were divided into two basic groups: those with behavioral and those with medical problems. Those classified as having behavioral problems were primarily intact (unneutered) males spraying urine during the breeding season. Those experiencing medical problems were usually neutered males and females.

At the time, studies proclaimed that castration would eliminate 90 percent of the spraying problems in male cats. During this same period, other studies also indicated that neutered males experienced a higher incidence of urinary tract infections that would cause them to urinate outside the box. The scientific community labeled spraying by intact males and an occasional female as "behavioral," and everything else "medical." Within the medical realm, neutered males seemed more prone to urinary problems that led to blockages of the urethra (the narrow tube connecting the bladder to the exterior opening) than their intact cohorts.

For a while, this rather simplistic view appeared correct. Male cats for the most part stopped spraying when neutered, and all the others got better on medication or a combination of medication, surgery, and dietary management.

However, such no longer holds true. Males and females, intact and neutered, now leave puddles of urine and piles or little nuggets of stool of varying consistency, as well as spray urine, to mark their territories. Cats with urinary tract problems still leave puddles, drops, and dribbles, but those with bowel problems tend more toward diarrhea. In all of these cases, though, the once clear line separating behavioral from medical inappropriate-elimination problems has grown fuzzier and fuzzier.

Based on input from cat owners and veterinarians, it appears that Persians and Himalayans and longhaired mixes thereof mark with stool more frequently than other breeds. It also appears that

cats tend to mark with urine *or* stool, just as they tend to succumb to chronic urinary *or* intestinal problems, but not both.

Most likely, these particular breeds' use of stool to mark
relates to their relatively tenuous grasp of normal elimination
behavior. More owners of animals with this breeding describe
elimination rituals that include the cat's digging at the wall or
floor, eliminating in the box, then digging at the wall or floor
again, rather than digging a hole in the litter, eliminating in it,
and then covering the waste. Such behavior raises the specter of
a cat who instinctively relates digging to elimination but doesn't
grasp exactly how, so it does the best it can. Whereas predators
no doubt would kill off those who so obviously broadcast their
presence in the wild, owners of pampered house pets seldom go
to that extreme.

While some breeds, such as the Abyssinian, may experience
more renal (kidney) problems, no breed appears to contribute
more or less than its share to the population that doesn't use the
litter box. As noted in Chapter 2, so much variation in temperament and even physiology may occur from one line to
another within a breed that it makes sense to ask about the incidence of elimination problems in the specific line that captures
your fancy before you buy.

Many owners of cats who don't use the litter box describe
their animals much as the Volcanos describe Tasha.

"She's quiet and a little shy around strangers but very loving
around us," Katie lists as the Russian blue's most prominent
traits.

"And smart as a whip as well as a sweetie," Ian adds proudly.
"In fact, if she weren't such a wonderful cat, I doubt we'd have
put up with her peeing."

One exception to this sweet, somewhat introverted feline
profile remains purely speculative at this time. Although we lack
both sufficient numbers as well as studies of more recent entries
into the purebred arena such as the Norwegian Forest cat, Sin-

gapura, and other native (as opposed to genetically manipulated) breeds from specific geographical locations, owner input suggests that these breeds might not feel quite as inhibited as others when it comes to marking their territories. The same also holds true for domestic-wildcat crosses such as the Bengal.

Unlike the typical inappropriate eliminators whom owners commonly describe as lovers rather than fighters, members of these more primitive, less genetically manipulated breeds may mark simply as a matter of course, just as they would in their native, outdoor environments, and not because they feel vulnerable. Also, unlike with members of older and more established domestic breeds, the concept of eliminating in a litter box might not be firmly entrenched in their furry little heads. Because all of the treatments aimed at stopping marking focus on reducing or eliminating the stress that precipitates it, and the behavior doesn't appear stress-related in these animals, treating them poses a major challenge.

How old are cats who don't use the litter box? That depends on why they don't use it. The behavior may occur in young animals who never grasped the litter box basics in the first place. Kittens raised without the benefit of an adult feline teacher and those kept in crowded quarters without a box or only a dirty one may opt for the floor or rug. Physical defects of the urinary or intestinal systems that prevent the kitten from controlling urine or bowel movement also may lead to accidents outside the box.

Discussions with owners suggest that cats whose temperament and/or environment set them up for elimination problems begin to show signs during the first breeding season following maturity, roughly around a year to 18 months of age. Medical problems and/or increased territorial threats also may cause once trustworthy feline senior citizens to begin eliminating in areas other than the box. Nevertheless, virtually any cat of any age can display the behavior at any time, given the right combination of factors. Tasha experienced no problems whatsoever until Sara gave her to Ian and Katie. All the changes this precipitated in the cat's once peaceful and predictable life made the Russian blue feel vulnerable.

Before reading on, think about your cat as a potential litter box shunner.

---

### Feline Eliminator Evaluation

Conjure up the image of your ideal cat. What characteristics on your list—breed, personality, age, early experience—might set your pet up for elimination problems?

It takes the Volcanos mere seconds to realize that their highly intelligent, but quiet and a bit shy Russian blue is a prime candidate for inappropriate elimination of one sort or another.

"I can see how Tasha could get hit with a urinary tract infection any time, but why wouldn't she mark all the time?" Katie wants to know.

In order to answer that question, we need to explore the *when* of inappropriate elimination first.

# To Pee or Not to Pee

When Tasha initially stopped using her litter box, two reasons led the Volcanos to dismiss the behavior:

- They really didn't want to think about it all.
- They hoped it wouldn't happen again.

Given this ostrichlike approach, they missed the valuable information they could have gleaned by asking the question, "When does the inappropriate elimination occur?"

Many times owners neglect to answer the easiest time-related question: Does the cat *always* eliminate outside the box, or only *sometimes*? If the cat always eliminates outside the box, then the owner can move on to an examination of where it goes. However, many cats eliminate both in the box and somewhere else, and, in these cases, knowing when the cat doesn't use the box can help solve the mystery.

Cats with painful urinary tract conditions will urinate whenever the painful urge strikes. Sometimes this will occur in the middle of the night if the animal awakens in discomfort and can't make it to the box in time. However, it also may occur after eating, drinking, or a play session, or during or following stressful events.

Other cats urinate or defecate outside the box only at night. Three reasons could explain this behavior. First, because free-roaming outdoor cats tend to revert to their nocturnal roots, an indoor cat threatened by the presence of such rovers will feel more pressured to mark at night. Second, indoor cats who are highly attached to their owners also feel more vulnerable when their owners sleep, and this, too, can lead to inappropriate elimination. Third, if owners punish the cat for not using the litter box but do nothing to relieve the cause of the problem, the animal may wait until the owners go to bed before displaying the behavior.

"Can't the owner just whack the cat the next morning?" asks Ian sheepishly.

It seems highly unlikely that Tasha would connect her late-night marking and Ian's angry outburst the next morning. More likely she'll link his anger to whatever she was doing at the time he punished her. If she happened to be eating, drinking, or grooming herself, such after-the-fact punishment may cause her to feel stressed any time she indulges in these perfectly normal activities. Thus, not only does such punishment do nothing to teach Tasha to use the litter box, but it can create other behavioral and medical problems for her, too.

In cases of urinary tract problems, the when of the initial incident may differ considerably from that of successive soiling events. Originally, Tasha's infection causes her to urinate on the bathroom rug because that's where she was when the urge hit her. When Ian and Katie begin punishing her for doing that, however, she goes there only in their absence.

Compare this pattern with that of a marking cat whose initial elimination coincides with the presence of what the animal views as a territorial threat: a new home or significant other, a new cat in the neighborhood or household. When Katie's brother descends on the Volcano household with his kids and dog, Tasha feels pressured to mark the bed once used by Sara, her beloved previous owner. Because the Volcanos rarely use this room, Tasha could eliminate in this area at any time with little chance of discovery.

Inappropriate elimination also increases during the breeding season when the cries and pheromones of free-roaming animals may stress the housebound pet. I also get more calls about cats' not using the litter box after the Christmas holidays, although the relationship here appears a little murky. While all the comings and goings at that time of the year certainly could lead to more stress-related marking as well as urinary problems, a significant number of these owners complain of long-standing elimination problems. In these cases, I suspect that comments from holiday guests—"Yuck, this place stinks!"—or the owners' inability to invite holiday revelers to their homes because of the smell triggers the request for help at this time.

Along those same lines, a strong suspicion exists among some who study this problem that urinary problems and/or marking escalate when tension exists among the human occupants of the household. Little hard data support this suspicion because few, if any, owners who take a cat to a veterinarian for urinating on the bed consider the question, "How are you and your spouse getting along?" either medically or politically correct.

Despite any hard evidence, however, some of these feline problems do disappear almost magically when someone moves out or in, when the cat moves to a new home, or when the owners provide their pet with some way to get away from the people. Sadly, but understandably, owners experiencing emotional trauma themselves may come to depend upon the cat even more for comfort at those times. Not only does this increase the pressure on the cat, but it also decreases the probability that these people will provide the animal with a more serene environment until they achieve the same for themselves.

Does the timing in your life and environment lend itself to creating inappropriate elimination problems for your cat?

### Elimination Time Check

Recall your description of an average weekday and weekend in your household, and also the changes that occur during the year (holidays, vacations, visits from friends, etc.) Then list the changes that occur in your neighborhood on a daily, weekly, and seasonal basis. How does your cat respond to these changes? If they upset your cat, what could you do to relieve that tension?

When Ian and Katie complete this exercise, they quickly realize that Tasha's problems did initially follow a seasonal pattern.

"That's why we let it go at first," Ian recalls. "When it suddenly stopped, we thought everything was fine."

Now that we understand the what, who, and when of inappropriate elimination, we need to investigate *where* and *why* it occurs.

# Variations on the Litter Box Theme

Most cat owners notice specifically where their cats go outside the litter box if this behavior occurs in one significant area such as on a bed, right inside the front door, or dead center on the rug in the upstairs hall where owners inevitably step in it as they stagger to the bathroom in the middle of the night. Owners whose cats eliminate in more than one place, on the other hand, often refer to this pattern as "everywhere" or "all over the house."

Normally, however, the behavior doesn't occur everywhere, and a critical analysis of where the cat deposits its stool or urine can provide valuable clues about the cause of the problem. In general, inappropriate elimination occurs in two basic locations:

- in the immediate vicinity of the litter box
- in specific areas away from the litter box

Cats who eliminate in the vicinity of the box may adopt one of four approaches:

- urine *and* stool always deposited beside the box
- urine *or* stool always deposited beside the box
- urine and/or stool periodically deposited over the edge of the box
- urine sprayed on the walls by the box

Cats who consistently eliminate near the box usually do so because they don't like something about the litter or the box. They'd really like to use it—they know they should—but something keeps them away. Litter heads the list as the most common "something" that drives a cat away from the litter box. Cats with litter aversions typically fall into one of three categories.

First, if the litter differs sufficiently from what the cat used previously, the animal may reject it. Former free-roaming cats accustomed to using a clean patch of dirt or sand every time they felt the urge may find a box filled with even the most expensive litter a poor substitute. These cats will go right next to the box unless the house contains plants in pots of sufficient size so that the cat can use them instead. In this situation, using dirt or sand in the litter box, then gradually mixing it with litter over time, may solve the problem. (Cover any flowerpot tops with double-

sided tape to keep the cat out of them during this process.)
While most cats will accept a trade-over, some maintain such
firmly entrenched litter preferences that it takes less time and
energy to meet these preferences than to try to change the cat.

Second, for every new litter on the market with an additive
guaranteed to make it smell like a rose garden or roll up in a ball
and flush itself down the toilet, we can find a cat who's allergic
to it. Litter allergies may produce a wide range of signs, including sneezing, wheezing, coughing, runny eyes, or itching skin.
Cats allergic to clumping litters may lick and chew their paws,
behaviors that owners may dismiss as normal grooming until the
animal licks itself raw. Replacing the litter with plain sand or
shredded white paper towels often will disclose whether the litter poses the problem. Also, observing the cat for changes in its
behavior when switching from one brand of litter to another for
any reason will enable owners to pick up signs of problems
before they get out of hand.

Third, some cats take a Goldilocks view of litter and will
refuse to use boxes with too much or too little litter to meet their
needs. To determine if such preferences affect your cat, fill a box
about half full of litter, then tip it so that the amount varies from
shallow at one end to deep at the other. Observe where in that
gradient the cat prefers to go, then fill the whole box to that level.

As far as litter boxes go, many cats and their owners don't
share the same views at all. My database of cat paraphernalia
includes an amazing assortment of litter boxes from the most
high-tech (a self-cleaning, computerized one for $199) to the
most discreet (a litter box disguised as a piece of furniture for
$129.95). Hooded litter boxes that the animal enters through a
cat-sized opening are currently in vogue, but many cats don't
share their owners' enthusiasm for them. I suspect that two reasons account for most feline aversions to these:

- cleanliness
- negative associations

Let's face it: no one enjoys cleaning a litter box, and many people will do just about anything to avoid that task. For those who prefer the out-of-sight-out-of-mind approach to feline waste but lack a remote cellar corner in which to sequester a standard litter box, a covered one makes an acceptable compromise. Add the fact that some covered boxes now contain space for deodorizers, and owners can avoid seeing *and* smelling the unsavory contents.

However, the cat expected to use such a box doesn't fare so well. What the owner views as an aesthetically pleasing color-coordinated, floral-scented feline accessory, the cat may view as a dark, dank, kitty gas chamber.

Unfortunately, the tops of covered boxes also make convenient places to store objects such as pooper-scoopers and other cat-related paraphernalia. This, in turn, gives rise to tales of cats who abandoned their hooded boxes once and for all when an object moved or fell on the box while the cat was relieving itself inside.

Within the uncovered-box realm, cats with arthritis or other medical problems may find the sides of some boxes too high. Cutting a cat-sized notch in one side to permit easier entry will resolve this problem. (Be sure to smooth the edges after you do this.) The shallow cardboard trays that form the base of cases of soda and other beverages make excellent disposable litter boxes for these animals, too.

Some cats with or without medical problems find the standard litter box too small and confining. Offer them a larger plastic sweater storage box, though, and they'll often hop right in.

If the cat deposits only urine *or* stool outside the box, it may belong to that small group of felines who want two boxes, one for urine and one for stool. In the single-cat household, this poses no problem: simply get the cat two boxes. However, in multiple-cat households, life gets more complicated. If one cat wants a number one and a number two box and another cat will do any number in any box, then, aside from keeping the cats in separate areas, the best solution is using multiple boxes with a small amount of litter and changing that daily.

Stool and urine that periodically drape or dribble over the edge of the box in a manner reminiscent of Salvador Dali usually signals a dirty box. When Tasha uses her litter box, she cares far more about keeping her feet clean than where her waste winds up in the box. This deep-rooted behavior occurs because the scent glands in feline feet play such a crucial role in the wildcat's survival.

However, this behavior plays out quite a bit differently in the average litter box–sporting household. Consider one very common litter box ritual. As Ian cleans the box, Tasha observes her owner's every move. The instant he finishes, she leaps into the box and urinates—even if she just did so minutes before Ian cleaned the box. Over the next few days she'll work her way out from that initial spot, always with a mind toward keeping her feet on clean litter. Eventually she reaches a point where her feet remain on clean litter, but her rear end hangs over the edge of the box, as do any eliminated wastes.

Like most cat owners, the Volcanos tuck Tasha's box in a corner so they won't accidentally kick it and send it skittering across the floor. However, this effectively limits the area of the box Tasha can use as she works her way from the center to the sides. Moving the box away from the wall will enable the periodic waste-draper to work toward all four sides of the box equally and may eliminate the problem. Other times, more frequent litter replacement does the trick.

Cats who spray urine on the walls around their boxes pose a bad news/good news situation for their owners. Obviously, cat urine dripping down the wall ranks as bad news for most cat owners. The good news is that the behavior indicates a feline willingness to spray/mark in the box rather than on the drapes or corner of the bed.

The traditional "cure" for this behavior involves putting aluminum foil or something else on the wall that would make a distracting sound when the urine hit it. However, even when it works, distracting the cat does nothing to address the underlying stress that precipitates the marking behavior. More than a few owners who opt for this route later discover that their cats simply start spraying somewhere else.

Offering the cat a high-sided box represents a far more behaviorally sound solution. While some sprayers will accept hooded boxes, owners must keep these spotlessly clean, which the structure of some of these boxes makes difficult. High-sided boxes, such as one called the Potty Jo, contain a cat-sized notch in one side that permits easy entry and exit. A cat-loving friend of mine uses a less expensive 20-gallon plastic storage container for this same purpose. She likes it because she keeps the litter box in her bathroom and she can snap on the lid when company comes. If her cats can't negotiate the higher sides as they get older, she'll cut a notch in the side of the container for them.

Fortunately, cat lovers adore challenges, so I don't feel the least bit hesitant to ask you to ponder any existing or future cat's litter box basics.

## Litter Box Checklist

Observe any existing litter, litter box(es), and their location, or review your ideas about any litter, litter boxes, and proposed feline elimination sites for any future cats. How many of your ideas about these subjects reflect solid knowledge of your cat and its preferences?

If you selected a particular litter box because you liked its color and a particular litter because you admired its packaging, and your cat religiously uses the box, don't feel guilty. On the other hand, if your cat doesn't use the litter box and exhibits any of the inappropriate elimination patterns discussed, you need to raise your litter and litter box consciousness. A good place to start is with the previous owner or breeder.

"Oh, I'm so sorry I forgot to tell you," Sara apologizes profusely when Ian calls about Tasha's litter box and litter preferences. "Tasha hates covered boxes and would rather die than use that sparkly litter that smells like lilacs. And make sure you put the box some place out of the way, but well lit. She *hates* using the box in the dark."

Though such preferences may sound bizarre, responding to such feline quirks may mean the difference between owning a cat who uses the box and one who doesn't.

Cats who eliminate in the vicinity of the box make it a simple matter to determine where the cat is relieving itself. However, other times the answers to the questions, "Where is the cat going?" and "Why there?" require further investigation.

## In Search of the Elusive Do-Do

While no owners like the idea of their cats eliminating anywhere outside the box, most do look more kindly upon those animals who eliminate *near* the proper place. Logic says these cats at least know where they're supposed to go, even if they don't go there. Unfortunately, some owners use that same logic to conclude that any cat who begins eliminating away from the box has somehow forgotten the most basic litter box facts.

As a result, this second group of cats must cope with a double dose of negative human emotion. Not only do their owners chafe because of the presence of urine and stool in the wrong place, they also label the cat stupid or spiteful because it can't even remember where it's supposed to go.

Regardless of what their owners may think, most cats who eliminate away from their boxes display a fair amount of intelligence and no spite when they choose their alternate spots. Basically, cats who eliminate away from the box choose locations that:

- better meet the cat's physical needs
- offer greater privacy
- carry a high emotional charge

The first two behaviors involve the presence of both urine and stool, whereas the third involves one or the other. Unfortunately, in all of these cases owners unaware of normal feline physical and behavioral needs find it difficult, if not impossible, to understand what the cat attempts to communicate by its choice of location.

"We already talked about litter boxes and litter," Katie points out as she monitors Tasha's activities lest the Russian blue sneak into the guest room again. "What other kinds of physical needs are there?"

Although we don't normally list cleanliness as a feline behavior, per se, most people do attribute this characteristic to cats more than any other domesticated species. And rightly so. However, some owners find the mere idea of litter boxes so repugnant that they put them in the farthest corner of the basement or otherwise hide them, and then rarely clean them.

The location of the box, in and of itself, may create problems if the cat can't easily get to it. Litter boxes in areas that require the use of stairs may stymie kittens or cats who never developed stair-climbing skills. Older animals with arthritis and younger ones with muscle or skeletal injuries may opt to leave puddles and piles at the top of the cellar stairs rather than risk descending a narrow staircase into a dark basement. Animals with kidney and other medical problems, or those on medications such as cortisone that cause them to drink and urinate more frequently, may need a box on every floor or at both ends of a large single-story home to meet their special needs.

Decorative litter box concealers that completely cover the box may function more as insurmountable obstacles than attractive cat paraphernalia in some situations. Some cats simply lack the necessary coordination and strength to push open a door, let alone leap up to one and push it open. After plowing through the door and tumbling headfirst into the litter, the cat may decide it's just not worth the effort.

Owners who don't clean the box and who also make that box difficult to find and use give their cats two reasons not to use it. Some of these animals wind up urinating and defecating in the owner's bathroom, sometimes on the rug, but more often in the sink or tub. While this behavior completely revolts the average owner, a certain feline logic may underlay it. Given the choice between a box in a remote location that the owners might clean once a week, if that, and a sink or tub they'll doubtless clean the instant they discover the incriminating evidence, which spot would a fastidious cat select?

While no studies of this exist, it also seems logical that, given their tendency to relate to their owners as their mothers, some cats also eliminate in the bathroom because that's where their owners go.

In either case, offering the animal a clean box in the bathroom coupled with leaving about an inch of water in the sink or tub usually solves this problem. Owners who don't want the box in the bathroom can *gradually* move it to another location acceptable to the cat as well as the owner once the cat routinely uses it.

Similarly, not regularly cleaning a hooded box or one kept in a decorative enclosure may doom such an aesthetically pleasing setup. Imagine yourself a cat who wants to keep its feet clean. How anxious would you feel about jumping through a door into a litter box containing God only knows what? A cat so unfortunate as to land in its own waste gets a very strong message to go somewhere else. Once this occurs, owners may need to accustom the cat to using a clean, unconcealed box first, then reintroduce the concealed one.

Some cats also object to using litter boxes located too close to their food and water. This also makes sound behavioral sense because few animals will soil in the area where they eat or sleep. From day one, a wildcat mother licks her kittens to stimulate them to urinate and defecate, and then she consumes the wastes in order to keep the nest clean. As the kittens grow older, she moves them if their quarters become fouled, and she teaches her young to bury their urine and feces. While domestication has weakened this instinct in many animals, it does still occur in some cats.

Many owners note with interest and gratitude that cats who eliminate in places other than their litter box will use boxes placed in pet carriers, as discussed in Chapter 3. However, I suspect this occurs because the inappropriate elimination resulted from the stress related to the box's previous location, our next elimination topic.

## Feline Physical Facts Evaluation

Evaluate any existing or proposed litter boxes as they relate to your cat's physical needs. Could an older cat use these as easily as a younger, more agile one? Do you keep the box clean? Does any scattered litter come anywhere near the animal's food or water?

When the Volcanos complete this exercise, they realize that they thought only of themselves when they selected a location for Tasha's box.

"I'd be happy to move it," Katie admits, "but Tasha makes such a mess with the litter, and she won't use a covered box."

Aside from the aforementioned high-sided boxes, Katie can purchase special litter-catching rubber mats to place around Tasha's box or use a standard doormat for this purpose. Other owners place a fuzzy bathroom rug they can easily shake out or wash under the box to catch flying litter as well as wipe cat feet clean. Still other owners prefer putting a standard box within a larger one to limit the amount of litter scatter. Unfortunately, however, some owners could offer their pets the most perfect litter box in the cosmos and it still wouldn't solve their cat's inappropriate elimination problems.

# Cats with Bashful Bladders

The largest group of cats who both urinate and defecate away from the box live in households with other cats. In wildcat terms, when we ask two cats to use the same litter box, we essentially ask them to claim the same small space. While their excrements may look like just wee-wee and doo-doo to us, those substances can also proclaim, "Stay out! If I catch you here I'll knock your furry block off!" While many house cats don't interpret litter box contents in this manner, shyer cats who must share a box with more aggressive ones may elect to seek out a closet, little-used room, or corner of the basement in which to relieve themselves in peace.

Other times, the presence of dogs or young children (or immature adults) in the household who torment or intimidate the cat while it uses the box causes the problem. Many dogs find cat stool a tasty snack and will hover over the defecating feline. Their presence scant inches from the defecating cat can serve as a major impetus for some cats to relieve themselves elsewhere.

Because these cats want to relieve themselves in the right place but can't, they often select alternate locations that offer not only a certain amount of privacy, but also something that will double as litter. I recall one cat who zeroed in on a stack of papers in the owner's attic, shredded them, and neatly covered his waste with the shreds. Unfortunately, the cat chose a stack of treasured family documents for this purpose. Another cat shredded clothing, while still others went in boxes filled with styrofoam "peanut" packaging material.

Because this form of inappropriate elimination does at least reveal what the cat considers an acceptable location, the most logical solution involves thoroughly cleaning the area (more on this later) and placing a litter box there or as close to that area as possible. While most cats will begin using the new box immediately, sometimes those with long-standing problems develop a preference for their makeshift litter. In these cases, the owner must gradually switch the cat from the substitute to what the owner considers a more acceptable litter.

## Privacy Check

Think about the location of any existing or proposed litter boxes. How might their placement affect your cat's need for privacy? How accessible are these spaces to other animals or people who might intimidate your cat? If you own more than one cat, do their personalities lend themselves to peaceful litter box coexistence, or would multiple boxes better meet their needs?

"I told my brother not to let his kids and dog bother Tasha while she was in her box, but now I realize that was silly," Katie remarks after she considers the box's less-than-ideal placement in the mud room. "They were in and out of that room the whole time they were here. Even if they didn't want to stop and get to know her better—which they all did because they don't have a cat—they would have disturbed her with their comings and goings."

Owners considering adding a second cat should provide a second box, too. That way if any conflict arises, the cat who feels intimidated can use the second box rather than the closet.

However, even when we supply our cats with the cleanest, most acceptable litter in the perfect litter box located in the ideal place, we can't guarantee that the cat won't eliminate in other areas for purely emotional reasons.

# Elimination Hot Spots

The final group of inappropriate eliminators urinate *or* defecate in locations that carry a strong emotional charge. These areas include:

- bathrooms
- bedrooms
- beds, cribs, or furnishings frequently used by the owner
- clothing, toys, or other articles belonging to the owner
- family rooms, offices, or other spaces where the owner spends a lot of time
- hallways containing doorways to significant rooms
- in front of exterior doors

"Hey, we already talked about cats going in the bathroom," Ian points out when he scans the list.

True, but our earlier discussion pertained to cats with urinary tract problems who get caught short and just happen to go there, then return to that area because of the scent, and those who urinate *and* defecate there because of some aversion to the litter box or litter. Now we're going to look at cats who urinate *or* defecate in the bathroom—or any other of the areas listed—to claim that space as their own and to signal their willingness to fight to protect it if necessary.

Always bear in mind that these distinctions may prove arbitrary at best. What begins as pure territorial marking may lead to medical problems because animals who feel pressured to mark will strain to produce the urine or stool to accomplish this task. Tasha relieves herself in her litter box and moments later hears a free-roaming cat outdoors: she strains to summon the urine to mark the guest room bed. If she feels repeatedly pressured throughout the day or night, she may strain more and more, to produce less and less urine, which eventually may even contain blood. Cats who mark with stool may begin with formed stool which gradually becomes looser and looser.

"But why do they go in the bathroom?" Katie asks, pointing to the first item on the list.

Like all of the other hot spots except hallways and just inside or on exterior doors, the bathroom carries particularly intimate owner scents. In the owner's absence, a frightened animal may gravitate toward that space because it offers the greatest amount of comfort. Because of this, the cat would naturally want to protect that area first and foremost.

"What about the cats who go in the halls or by the doors?" Ian asks. "Don't they feel strongly about those areas, too?"

Hallway markers tend to share strong ties with more than one family member. Consequently, rather than indulging in the time- and energy-consuming task of marking multiple areas, they'll mark a common space such as a hall. When such sacred spaces occur both upstairs and downstairs, these animals will mark the top or the bottom of the stairs. Cats who leave piles, sprays, or puddles near exterior doors signal their willingness to protect the entire house from real or imagined outdoor threats.

In general, where a cat marks serves as a good indicator of its degree of confidence in its ability to protect the space. Those who mark just inside exterior doors express a higher degree of confidence than those who go in a hallway, dead center on the family room rug, or under the dining room window. Unlike those willing to protect entire floors or rooms, cats who mark the bed, clothing, and toys will fight only to protect those they hold most dear.

Given all this, we can appreciate why an older or shyer cat may suddenly begin marking when a new cat moves into the neighborhood or the owner's home, or when other significant changes occur in the household. Rather than expressing jealousy or spite, the animal merely shrinks its territory to a more manageable size. By the same token, a cat who moves into a home previously occupied by other cats—or even other animals—may mark any place where the previous inhabitants did to claim this space as its own.

"But why do they keep doing it?" Sara wants to know. "Especially once they realize how much it upsets us."

Cats keep doing it because it works. No matter how much the Volcanos may jump up and down, scream, blast Tasha with water pistols, or smack her with rolled-up newspapers, the fact remains that the dreaded visitor with his dreaded children and dog *didn't* return. The big scary motorcycle that roars down the street every night *doesn't* burst through the walls and destroy her and her beloved owners. Thus, because protecting her territory takes precedence over everything else—including getting yelled at, squirted, or whacked—Tasha will continue doing it unless her owners do something to relieve her of that responsibility.

Before we discuss what the Volcanos and other owners can do to treat the various causes of inappropriate elimination, take a few moments to consider your feelings about territorial marking.

## Feline Marker Evaluation

Imagine yourself discovering that your cat has marked your bed or a treasured object. What's your immediate reaction? How do you feel about it? How do you feel about your cat? How do you intend to deal with any negative feelings?

The majority of people who perform this exercise admit that, even knowing what they now know about territorial marking, the very thought of their pets urinating or defecating on their belongings makes them very angry. The more honest among them admit that they can only hope the cat doesn't happen to walk by when they discover the done deed, because they'd find it difficult not to lash out at the pet. This, in turn, makes them feel incredibly guilty. As we noted before, though, guilt serves no useful purpose unless it spurs the owner to make meaningful change.

"The thought of Tasha peeing on the bed in the guest room made me so mad, I scared myself and Katie, too, not to mention the cat," Ian admitted later. "That's why we decided to do everything in our power to make sure it never happens again."

Before the Volcanos begin to make the necessary changes, they need to examine one final clue in the feline elimination mystery.

## The Diet Connection

Talk to anyone whose cat suffers from urinary problems and the issue of diet probably will come up. When these problems first began occurring among pet animals, male cats who suffered from urinary blockages got the most attention because such blockages created life-threatening problems. Because many of these cats ate dry food, many researchers believed a connection between diet and urinary tract problems existed. One theory maintained that cats who ate dry food often drank less water. Cats who drink less and produce less urine will more likely experience a blockage if they encounter the bacteria or a virus that creates the mucous or gritty sandy debris that may occur in an affected animal's urine.

Other researchers said, "No, it's not the fact that the food is dry. It's the minerals in the food that cause the problem."

Because the mineral content shows up as "ash" on pet food labels, for a while cat owners sought to feed their cats, and especially the males, the food with the lowest ash content.

Then another batch of studies attempted to further define which specific minerals caused the problem. Researchers eventually established a link between urinary tract problems and the magnesium content of the food. However, before the low-magnesium link had time to register with owners, it yielded to one that attributed the problem to the kind of urine the diet produced. At that time, the urine of many cats with urinary problems contained debris that formed only in a urine with a basic pH.

"So," concluded the scientists, "if we feed cats a food that produces an acidic urine, we'll solve the problem."

Such thinking gave rise to all those foods that claim to reduce feline urinary problems by lowering urinary pH, the scientific measure of a substance's acidity. Alas, as the number of problems associated with a too-basic urine declined, those related to a more-acid urine increased. As if all this weren't bad enough, studies now indicate that more and more cats of both sexes succumb to urinary tract problems not caused by bacteria or viruses, and the cause of these current problems remains unknown.

Even though the signs associated with urinary tract problems and theories explaining them have changed over time, one fact remains: cats who eat dry food experience a higher incidence of urinary problems than those who eat canned food. While some-day scientists may discover a specific nutritional link, the obvi-ous behavioral one already exists.

"Because establishing and protecting the territory takes precedence over eating and drinking, cats who don't feel com-fortable in their space will only eat and drink the minimum amount," Sara concludes, making the correct connection.

And because dry food contains a maximum of about 10 per-cent moisture compared with a minimum 75 percent in canned foods, cats who eat dry food will consume even less water under stressful circumstances.

Consequently, while it appears incorrect to say that diet *causes* the urinary tract problems that may lead a cat not to use the lit-ter box, it makes sense to ensure that these animals drink suffi-cient amounts of water in addition to decreasing or eliminating any stress-producing environmental factors. We'll delve into ways to enhance fluid intake in Chapter 8, and turn our attention now to relieving environment stress.

## Dietary Evaluation

Think about what you feed any existing cat(s) or plan to feed any future ones. Do you maintain any food phobias based on previous ideas about urinary tract disease? Would you change your cat's diet based on what you know now? Why or why not?

"I guess we should feed Tasha canned food," Katie admits after she ponders this latest piece of the inappropriate elimination puzzle. "But she prefers to nibble throughout the day, and canned food gets stale. I'd rather focus on relieving the stress so she feels more comfortable drinking."

That decision brings us to the final step in the process of preventing inappropriate elimination.

# Making a Clean Sweep

When the Volcanos think of relieving the stress in their household, their minds automatically jump to the different ways they can help Tasha feel more secure in their home.

"For sure, she needs a private space where she can get away from it all," Ian declares. "We'll get her one of those carriers and put it in our bedroom."

Although free-access crates can do much to relieve tension, cats who soil outside the box may require more stringent measures than this. A first critical step that many owners often overlook is cleaning up the evidence.

Regardless of why a cat urinates or defecates outside the box, once it does so, any residual odor of those substances will attract it like a magnet and compel it to go there again. To reduce this temptation, don't use any cleaning products that contain ammonia. Because urine contains ammonia compounds, such cleaning agents will attract rather than discourage the cat from using that area. Also avoid highly perfumed cleaning products or those that contain phenols (such as Lysol) that could trigger feline allergic or toxic reactions.

When Katie noticed the urine on the floor next to the bed in the guest room, she blotted it up, then sprinkled the area with baking soda and let it sit for several hours to absorb any residue she might have missed. Finally, she thoroughly cleaned the area with a solution composed of three parts water to one part white vinegar. While some experts recommend only the use of the vinegar solution, the increased numbers of cats on diets designed to create an acid urine argues for a combination of acidic (vinegar) as well as basic (baking soda) agents to neutralize the full urine spectrum.

This standard home remedy works well on nonporous surfaces such as finished wood and vinyl—particularly with a cat who makes a strong connection between elimination and the box and who eliminates outside the box for unique reasons (such as a medical problem the owners notice and treat immediately).

However, if it doesn't work the first time or if the cat soils rugs or porous furnishings, using enzyme-containing agents specifically designed to clean up urine and feces stains and neutralize their odors will save a lot of time and money in the long run. In response to the increasing numbers of house-soiling cats, new products claiming to do the job appear almost daily. A quick rule of thumb when selecting one: you get what you pay for. Neutralizers (such as Cat Off, Feline Odor Eliminator or F.O.N., Outright, and Nature's Miracle) that destroy odors cost more than substances that merely mask them so that humans (but not cats!) can't smell them. Some products remove stains but don't neutralize odors, and *vice versa*, in which case you'll need to buy two products to get the job done.

When enzyme-containing neutralizers don't work, they almost invariably fail because the owner didn't use sufficient amounts of them. Another quick rule of thumb: use one and one-half times as much neutralizer as the amount of waste you want to clean up. For urine on a rug, that means *soaking* the entire area, clear through any pad below the rug. That also means soaking the padding on couches or mattresses. Because these products average about $5 for eight ounces, a real temptation exists to use less rather than more. However, given the way these products work and the cat's incredible ability to detect the scent of even a few molecules of unneutralized urine or stool, skimping actually costs more in the long run.

In addition to cleaning up all traces of the evidence, Ian and Katie put Tasha in her crate with a litter box when they're gone or when they can't watch her constantly. Most cats curl up and go to sleep when relieved of the responsibility for protecting the territory. Those few who still feel pressured to mark can go in only one place: the litter box. Thus, this technique teaches them that they should both eliminate and mark in the box, two associations that don't come naturally into most marking cats' furry little heads. Once sprayers get the hang of standing in the box in the crate to spray, they can be offered a high-sided box.

"I like the idea of free-access crate-training, but I don't like the idea of confining an animal," Sara confesses. "Can't I just confine the cat to the laundry room or keep it away from the areas where it messed?"

Many cats appear to recognize two calming states—total freedom or total confinement—with anything between these two generating, rather than reducing, tension. Total freedom means a cat door that the cat can use as it pleases to escape stressful situations indoors or explore troublesome ones outside. Total confinement means a space big enough for the cat, a blanket, food and water, a litter box, and a toy or two. For many animals, locking them in a powder room or pantry practically *guarantees* they'll mark because the confinement offers the worst of both worlds: they can't determine the nature of any threat outdoors, and they can't hide from it. Owners who opt for such a compromise also should provide a crate or other haven for the animal to use in this limited space.

In addition to thoroughly cleaning the soiled areas, blocking off rooms or storing rugs and other items on which the cat urinated or defecated until the cat forgets about them may work. However, the success of this approach totally depends on the owners' willingness to clean these areas scrupulously and keep the cat away from them for as long as necessary. Owners who don't fulfill these requirements not only won't solve the problem, but will actually make it worse.

If the area can't be blocked off or if the rug can't be removed, placing an object on the spot so the cat can't get to it may serve as a deterrent. For example, the Volcanos place a nightstand over the spot on the guest room carpet where Tasha urinated. Putting a place mat or newspaper over previously soiled areas and placing the cat's food and water dishes there also may discourage some animals from eliminating in these areas.

Cat doors connected to secure outdoor areas—even small outdoor cages—may relieve the tension caused by other cats in the household or by something outdoors. Just being able to get away that little bit may calm cats who feel threatened by other cats—or people or animals—in the household. For cats who feel threatened or frustrated by events outdoors, the ability to make a quick trip outside to see what's going on or to mark may relieve the tension.

Note that the success of all of these alternatives depends on the existence of a secure space for the cat within the household. If one doesn't exist, the cat denied access to the original target will find someplace else to mark, or it will mark any articles placed over the original spot.

Owners of spraying cats also should use protective covers on any electrical outlets anywhere near the target area. Cat urine sprayed in an exposed outlet may cause a short circuit and start a fire. While that might put an end to the cat's inappropriate elimination, less drastic and equally effective methods to achieve this goal exist!

"How long does it take to break the cycle?" Sara asks the question on the mind of every owner of every inappropriately eliminating cat.

Another behavioral rule of thumb: the longer the cat has displayed the behavior, the longer it will take to resolve it. I recommend keeping cats away from previously soiled areas or articles for twice as long as the period of soiling. If the Volcanos feel confident that Tasha didn't urinate on the bed in the guest room until that weekend six weeks ago when Katie's brother visited, that means keeping the guest room door firmly closed for 12 weeks after thoroughly cleaning the affected area.

Owners who can't determine exactly when the problem started should keep the cat away from the previously targeted areas for a minimum of four months. If that period will end during the breeding season, I ask owners to continue with any restrictions until after that seasons ends. I know from experience that previous markers who mind their pees and BMs during the off-season may break their training during this more stressful time of the year.

Cats crated in the owners' absence should adhere to the same four-month timetable. In this situation, I ask owners to create a low-keyed ritual that includes scooping the cat up and placing it in the carrier with a neutral phrase like "Kennel up, Tasha." Giving the cat a special toy it receives only at these times further reassures it. As noted previously, placing the carrier in some comforting space such as the owner's bedroom, and drawing the blinds and using a sound machine or radio to generate white noise further help create a safe haven for the cat. When the owners return, they reverse the process, neutrally greeting the cat, releasing it, and removing the toy.

At the end of the designated period, the owners go through the same kenneling ritual, but they just close rather than lock the door. The cat could get out if it wants; however, most animals choose to remain in their carriers until their owners return.

Finally, owners of multiple cats who inappropriately eliminate as a result of territorial clashes can take heart even if they find the idea of crate-training unacceptable for some reason: packing everyone up and moving to a new home may solve the problem. Many times such problems arise because owners bring in cats over a period of time, forcing the new cats to claim previously claimed space. By moving to a new territory at the same time, all the cats start out equal. I'd still recommend crate-training everyone before the move to limit the disputes. However, some owners unwilling to do this report that, after a few hair-raising spats, the animals divvy up the space and settle down.

In situations where owners don't provide their cats with private space, though, the probability that external threats such as the breeding season or a visiting repairman will disrupt the peace runs high. When this occurs, these owners must go through the additional work of determining which one of the cats displays the problem behavior as well as analyze all of the other factors necessary to resolve the problem permanently.

Regardless of what approach an owner takes with the cat who eliminates inappropriately, any solution must meet the cat's as well as the owner's needs. Unless it meets both, at most it can do only half the job.

Time to reflect on how you'd treat an inappropriate elimination problem if it occurred in your pet.

## Treatment Evaluation

Consider all the different approaches suggested for the treatment of feline inappropriate elimination. Which ones appeal to you? Why? Which ones don't? Why?

When Ian and Katie review their feelings about the various treatments, they discover that they focus on quite different issues.

"I don't like the idea of putting my rugs or other items away for months," Katie announces with certainty. "I'd much rather keep a constant eye on Tasha when she's loose and crate her when I can't watch her."

"Not me!" Ian declares emphatically. "I'd much rather store items or completely block Tasha's access to anything she might even *think* about urinating on, plus I'd rather crate her than risk her messing again."

"I could never crate an animal, especially not Tasha," Sara proclaims with equal conviction. "I'd rather stay home 24 hours a day and watch her like a hawk for as long as it takes to solve the problem."

While we may agree or disagree with these views, the fact remains that owners must take them into account when choosing a solution. If any solution—no matter how proven—runs counter to Katie's, Ian's, or Sara's beliefs, they won't implement it consistently and it won't work for them. Because problems related to inappropriate elimination tend to be more long-standing than others, consistency and owner commitment to the process play an absolutely crucial role. Consequently, selecting a treatment based on solid knowledge of the cat's needs as well as the needs of the cat's owner(s) offers the greatest chance of success.

Now that you know how to untangle one of the most complex problems that cat owners can face, designing the best exercise program for your cat will be mere child's play.

# 7

# Jungle Gymnastics

## *Keeping Your Cat Physically and Mentally Fit*

Artists Julie Krinos and Erica Kidder prize few of their possessions more than Limo, the sleek black kitten they adopted from the local shelter.

"He's so active, though, we go nuts trying to keep up with him," Julie confesses as she lunges for the crystal vase that a velvety paw sets teetering toward oblivion.

"We should have named him Tornado," Erica, an award-winning weaver, puffs as she charges after the furry comet streaking toward her loom. "I had no idea kittens could move so fast!"

Five years later, the couple describes Limo's early search-and-destroy missions to Max O'Neill, a friend contemplating getting a cat.

"Nothing was safe around him," Julie recalls. "Once when I was preparing a collection of watercolors for an exhibit, he shredded one and tracked paint on four others. What a mess!"

"Another time he unraveled a wall hanging I'd spent weeks working on," Erica comments, adding another item to Limo's already lengthy rap sheet. "All in all, it's a wonder we made it through that period."

Julie vigorously nods her head in agreement.

"Thank God all he does now is eat and sleep," she remarks, stroking the obese animal they now affectionately refer to as Blimpo rather than Limo.

All the way home after that visit, Max tries to reconcile what he'd just seen and heard with his own ideas about the feline companion he hoped to get.

"I don't want a cat tearing up my home," he declares with certainty. "But I don't want a fat blob, either."

He stops and waits for the light to change at the busy intersection near his apartment building.

"There's no way I could let a cat outdoors in all this traffic, and I can't afford to move anywhere else." He sighs heavily as his dreams of owning a cat begin to vaporize. "Isn't there some way a cat can get enough exercise in a small space without destroying it?"

When Max verbalizes those same concerns to a friend who lives in the suburbs, he becomes even more confused.

"My cats can go in and out whenever they choose, but all they do is sleep and eat," the friend complains. "I don't see that it makes any difference where you live. That's just the way cats are."

Max was still pondering this aspect of cat ownership a week later when he found the cutest little kitten huddled in the doorway of his apartment building.

––––––––––

Neither Julie, Erica, nor Max would argue with those experts who contend that pets who exercise regularly remain healthier and experience fewer medical problems than those who don't. They'd probably even agree with those studies that indicate that regular exercise also helps build the animal's confidence and decrease stress, both of which decrease behavioral problems, too. They'd most likely also see the value of "mind-body" rather than just physical exercise programs. However, how does one achieve this with a cat?

Dog owners may pick and choose from an amazing array of exercise options, many specifically designed to meet the needs of particular breeds. Cat owners, on the other hand, often must fend for themselves, a task made more frustrating by the fact that many of our ideas about what constitutes feline exercise also seem to arise more from legend and folklore than reality. However, because obesity ranks as the number one feline nutritional problem (more on this in Chapter 8) and given the fact that behavioral problems rank as the foremost owner concern, wise owners must answer the question, "What comprises quality exercise for my pet?"

Like many owners, Julie and Erica think of cats as self-exercising. They viewed Limo's kittenhood antics as a phase he would pass through and rejoiced when he finally did. However, because of the role the mind-body connection plays in health, this limited approach generates problems for their pet down the road. Later, not only must Limo cope with all the medical ailments that attend overweight, those extra pounds make him feel sufficiently vulnerable that he begins marking his territory, too.

Other owners, like Max, want the best for their pets but have no idea where to begin. Because any exercise program must meet your own needs as well as your cat's, reflect a moment on what feline exercise means to you.

## Feline Exercise Evaluation

Think about yourself, your cat, and your environment as they relate to exercise. Do you see yourself as a more active person or a couch potato? What about your cat? What could you do to help your cat get a healthy mind-body workout in your home?

When Julie and Erica first looked at this exercise, they laughed. They couldn't imagine how their own attitudes about exercise could affect their pet. Moreover, after Limo's destructive youth, they felt no desire to stimulate him to become more active again. But when their veterinarian tells them that Limo's weight coupled with his mild heart condition could lead to more serious problems, they see the matter of exercise in a whole new light.

"In the past I just ignored the subject," Erica frankly admits. "I knew Limo was gaining weight, but as I got older, I tended to gain myself, so I didn't give it much thought. Then when the vet said that about his heart, it dawned on me how little exercise he gets."

"Except when he gets into trouble," Julie adds, recalling all the past damage done by the cat.

"I can relate to that," Max concurs as he strokes Minnie, his new calico kitten. "I want Minnie to get the right amount of exercise, but I don't want her to wreck my place. Plus I'm so busy most of the time. And it's not like I can enroll her in obedience classes or one of those other dog activities, is it?"

As is the case with many cat lovers, when Erica, Julie, and Max try to evaluate feline exercise needs, they discover they don't know where to begin. How can we possibly meet the needs of an animal designed to hunt within the limits of the average owner's home and lifestyle? What goes through the average cat's mind as it strives to fill its time? As always, the best answers come from the cats themselves.

## The Feline Athlete

When dog lovers tell me of their plans to get a sporting or working dog, I always recommend they attend field, herding, or other events that demonstrate the quality of the canine mind that goes with the look these people admire. I then suggest they involve their pets in exercise programs that provide the same degree of mind-body challenge. Unfortunately, cat lovers can't rely on such organized events for clues regarding their pets' similar needs. However, several items in my collection of cat factoids and memorabilia do provide some insight into the fantastic range of the feline mind-body.

Item One: A report in the March 3, 1993, *Seattle Times* described a cat who learned not only to relieve himself in the toilet, but also to flush it when he finished. Alas, the bored animal so enjoyed the latter activity that he flushed three thousand gallons of water through the system in a month's time. According to a friendly plumber, that's anywhere from 400 to 2,000 flushes!

Item Two: An article in *Cats* magazine ("Living on the Edge" by Jill Carey, July 1996) tells of Toby, an orange tabby who swims, surfs, rides motorcycles (wearing goggles, leather hat, and vest), bicycles, and takes bubble baths, among other activities he shares with his owner. Toby didn't start out to become a star. He just wanted to go everywhere his owner did. One day when his owner decided to take a dip after a jog down the beach, Toby went right in after him.

Item Three: About five years ago, a woman in California confided that her Siamese cat would open the owner's jewelry box, remove all of her gold chains, drag them to the dining room, and line them up in straight rows on the dining room table. My immediate (internal) response was, "Oh, sure!" However, because the woman appeared both intelligent and sincere, I added her tale to my files. Over the years, I've heard more and more stories about cats playing with and/or stealing jewelry as well as money. The jewelry prize goes to a cat who spirited away his owner's diamond ring and hid it somewhere in her 10-room house.

Two facts about these feline thieves intrigue me. All of them stole only the best jewelry, and never less than a 20-dollar bill, with the latter giving rise to visions of cats saving up for trips to Tahiti. Perhaps cats with lower aspirations exist and their owners either don't notice any losses or attribute it to leprechauns. After all, surely "The cat stole my subway token" ranks right up there with "The dog ate my homework" when it comes to excuses! Second, the feline-filching trend began on the West Coast and made it to the East about two years later, a pattern I noticed with other behaviors, too.

Item Four: About the time the jewelry phase hit the East Coast, the West Coast cats got into socks. The first sock wave consisted of cats who laid down trails using their owners' socks, which they rummaged out of clothes hampers and laundry baskets. The trail laying invariably occurred in the owner's absence or during the night, and the owners inevitably claimed that the cats looked embarrassed when caught red-pawed. While some cats insisted on using family members' socks or even those belonging to one specific person, others eagerly accepted their own personal collections of socks stored in special baskets thoughtfully provided by their owners.

The second sock wave upped the ante even more. Not only did these cats lay down sock trails, but they also *matched* the socks. Needless to say, I can hardly wait to see what they will do next!

While these and countless other stories delight us, they also can teach us a great deal about what it takes to keep some cats amused. Furthermore, even though these displays appear extraordinary and quite unrelated to anything most of us would consider "normal" cat behavior, they do have a certain primitive logic.

Consider the flushing and surfing cats. The feline aversion to water appears more myth than fact. Given their choice between a fresh flowing brook or a stagnant pool, feral and free-roaming pets will opt for the former just as wildcats will. This attraction for water carries over into many house cats who enjoy playing with as well as drinking fresh water in sinks, toilets, tubs, and showers, to the point that many owners now tell of cats teaching themselves to turn on faucets as well as to flush toilets.

Stealing jewelry, money, or socks could represent variations on the ancient theme of retrieval behavior via which wild queens move their kittens to new quarters. Jewelry might attract cats because of the noise it makes when they bat or drag it, and money most certainly could emit scents that might entice the animal. Items such as dirty socks that carry the intimate scent of the owner would seem logical surrogate "kittens" to carry about, as would any socks the cat claims as its own.

"What about lining up those gold chains or laying down sock trails?" Erica wants to know. "That hardly sounds like normal cat behavior."

True, but recall that the cat's self-domesticated status means it can improvise more easily than other domestic species. We know that cats come preprogrammed with the knowledge to lay down scent trails and a certain level of retrieving behavior. Could some intelligent, bored cats apply these ancient skills to contemporary objects to achieve a completely different purpose in the same way an orthopedic surgeon may utilize the basic principles of gardening and carpentry when repairing a shattered limb?

Unfortunately, until that lucky day when we humans become smart enough to understand how cats think, we can only guess. However, these and other feline testimonials make it clear that individual cats exhibit activity preferences just as people do.

Does breeding affect exercise needs and preference? We do know that some cats, like some people, tend to gain weight faster than others. Controlling your pet's food intake and implementing a regular exercise program can head off this problem.

Certain lines of cats seem to enjoy retrieving and/or catching objects more than others. At one time, more owners of female Siamese and Siamese derivatives reported this behavior, but now I hear of its occurring in many breeds as well as mixed breeds of both sexes. Retrieving cats often will display the behavior when given small objects they can easily pick up. Some take a fancy to small spongy or crumpled paper balls, whereas others prefer to retrieve furry objects. A writer friend's cat only carries off her pens, which he deposits in specific areas in her home.

We also know that much feline play mimics predatory behavior and that certain lines and breeds possess stronger hunting instincts than others, although most will learn to hunt if taught. Kittens raised in barns or in- and-outdoor environments almost invariably will follow just about anything that moves. Purebreds from a long line of cattery cats may require a little interspecies tutoring. However, owners of even the most disinterested Persians report successfully teaching their pets to stalk and pounce on toys using a regular program of teasing. Admittedly, some of these cats initially appear to go after the toy more out of irritation than in fun, but eventually most come to enjoy the game.

This brings us to how the cat's age can influence its exercise. We already noted that we often don't even think about exercising kittens because they seem constantly on the go. However, we also know that early experiences tend to become more firmly entrenched than lessons learned later in life. Consequently, if owners don't take the time to reinforce kitten behaviors—such as predatory play—that could form the foundation of a lifelong exercise program, they may find it much more difficult to teach the adult cat these same behaviors later.

Of course, cats being cats, exceptions naturally occur. Because moving kittens falls into the adult wildcat's behavioral repertoire, many times retrieving behavior doesn't show up in domestic cats until they reach adulthood. For people lucky enough to own one of these animals, few cat-owning experiences rival the feeling of enchantment that attends the appearance of this hidden talent. I can still remember the awe I felt when an orange domestic shorthair named Ray one day daintily picked up his ball, carried it to me with head held high, and dropped it lightly at my feet. For a moment I didn't know whether to laugh or cry, whether to pick up the ball and cuddle it or toss it and see what would happen. I tossed it, and a wonderful game and a memory that persists long after his passing were born.

What about cats as playmates for other cats? This idea crops up routinely as the logical solution to the lazy- or fat-cat problem. However, the cat's solitary and territorial nature, to say nothing of all those inappropriate elimination problems, makes this an iffy solution at best. If Erica and Julie get Limo a feline playmate and Limo considers the new cat a territorial violation and stops eating and drinking, he might lose weight. However, if he then succumbs to urinary problems or starts spraying his owners' bed, his sleek appearance won't bring them much joy.

Other cats can and do keep each other busy, as do companions of other species. The trick here is to select the animals carefully and give the relationship time to develop. Don't expect the new kitten or pup to turn a couch potato into a party animal overnight. Both animals need time to get used to each other before they can turn their attention to play.

Spend a few minutes thinking about how any existing or future cat's unique qualities might affect any exercise program you devise for it.

## Kitty Calisthenics Check

Observe how your own cat(s) or those you admire spend their time during the average weekday and weekend. What kinds of games appeal to the pet? If you don't indulge in formal game-playing with the cat, what does it do to amuse itself? Does it prefer to stalk objects? Does sound attract it? What kinds of sound? Does it enjoy playing with water? Balls of paper? Dangling vines or cords? Empty bags? The more detailed your list, the more specifically you can meet your pet's needs.

Because Limo hardly moves at all anymore, Julie and Erica must think back to how their pet acted as a young kitten.

"Sound and motion definitely attracted him," Julie recalls immediately. "The reason he made such a mess of my paintings was because I had one of those bird feeders that attach with suction cups on the window of my studio. He got so excited watching it, he leaped onto the table where I keep my paints and brushes and knocked everything over."

"And he used to love to climb, too," Erica adds. "We used to laugh about his being part monkey."

While such observations may seem ridiculously obvious, they provide a good starting point for these owners. The more they think about how Limo exercised, the more they realize that certain textures appealed to him more than others, as did certain rooms and times of day. Where before they systematically set about to eliminate all these preferences in order to put an end to Limo's destructiveness, they now consider ways they can incorporate these activities into an exercise plan that will meet his needs as well as their own.

After observing Minnie, Max realizes that activities that generate a great deal of sound and motion frighten the quiet little kitten far more than they attract her. However, more subtle murmurings or movements, and especially those she can control herself (such as a ball that makes a sound when she nudges it with her paw) will keep her amused for hours. As her confidence grows, her play becomes more exuberant.

Once you recognize what kinds of activities appeal to your particular cat, you can find ways to fit them into your environment, relationship, and lifestyle.

## The Feline Playground

In Chapter 3 you analyzed your home as a safe and secure space for your cat. Now you need to analyze it as a potential playground.

"That's where we got into trouble," Julie admits. "We never gave it a thought before we got Limo, and once we did, it was too late. We were too busy trying to keep him from wrecking our stuff to think about much else."

Given that lesson, how would these owners approach the problem now?

"For one thing, we'd put all our art supplies in cat-proof containers," Erica immediately volunteers. "Because we'd never had a pet, it didn't dawn on us that a kitten would find these items so irresistible."

"We'd also put away breakables or anything with sentimental value until we discovered what kinds of objects attracted his attention," Julie adds. "I can't believe how many times I screamed at Limo for knocking over that same vase and rolling it along the mantel instead of just putting the darned thing away until we taught him to stay off there. He much prefers to roll his ball around, but we never thought to get him one because we were so worried about the vase."

Like many owners, Julie and Erica discovered that the fact that they didn't consciously provide their new kitten with an environment designed for cat play in no way decreased their pet's desire—and need—to play. If owners don't give their cats toys to play with, the cats will find their own. If cat and owner are lucky, this may mean some other (human or animal) member of the household, or safe, acceptable objects such as empty paper bags and boxes. For the unlucky, however, it may mean that the cat chews on electrical cords, swings on the curtains, eats the plants, flushes toilets, or steals jewelry. While Max, like most typical cat lovers, smiles at the idea of a kitten playing on a piano keyboard, when Minnie gaily trips across his computer keyboard and zeros out a whole spreadsheet, her little game doesn't amuse him at all!

Even having some other pet or person in the household providing play and exercise opportunities doesn't rule out the need to evaluate your home as a kitty playground. While your pet might not give your collection of porcelain miniatures on the end table a second glance, that's no guarantee it won't plow right through them when involved in a fun game of tag with you or some other playmate.

Along those same lines, people who lose their hearts to two little fuzzy kittens often envision them frisking happily on the rug in the middle of the family room like two well-mannered children playing jacks. However, even two little kittens can cover a tremendous amount of ground. Moreover, we know that sometimes cats will establish their personal space at the level of windowsills or top shelves. Consequently, when cats get into a hot game of tag, the activity may take them across the back of the couch, up the bookcase, across the mantel, back down to the chair, then up and down the stairs.

In another favorite multiple-partner game, the cat lies upside down under a couch, an upholstered chair, or a hassock, periodically sticks its head out, and bats at another cat, a dog, or a person passing by. When the cat does this, it digs its hind claws into the underside of the furniture to steady itself. While some owners take an out-of-sight-out-of-mind approach to what this does to the underside of the furniture, others are appalled when they discover the damage.

Even Mother Nature herself can become a playmate, changing once-ignored objects into instant toys. My cat Whittington couldn't care less about the ferns hanging from the ceiling above his perch on the old trunk—until they sway in the breeze. Of course, I didn't know about his secret playmate until the day he gave one of my green-tressed beauties a pitiful trim. Another cat owner noticed a soiled, slightly dug-up patch on her white rug that logic and the process of elimination told her the cat caused, but why? The culprit turned out to be a prism hanging in the owner's window. During the brief period of the day when the sun struck the bauble, the cat would play with and "attack" the shimmering rainbow it cast on the rug.

If the idea of your pet's using certain objects in your home as playthings bothers you, put these items out of harm's way. If you can't do that, use double-sided tape to train your cat to stay away from them. If neither of these options appeals to you, perhaps some other kind of pet would suit you better than a cat.

Once you explore your home for items you don't want your cat to play with and eliminate this temptation, you need to consider objects that your pet could appropriate as toys. I mentioned Whittington's periodic fern attacks, the only one of my many houseplants he bothers. I can accept this because he doesn't eat the plant and he doesn't swat it all that often. However, if your cat routinely shreds and eats your plants, you should discuss this with your veterinarian. Even nontoxic plants can cause problems if those plants filter a fair amount or certain kinds of pollutants from the air. Depending on where you live, your houseplants might contain enough of these pollutants to cause your cat digestive or other medical problems. Also, cats who eat rather than play with plants might suffer from an underlying nutritional problem rather than boredom.

Whether you allow your cat to play with your socks, undies, the kids' toys, or your toothbrush remains a matter of preference. Just remember that cleanliness is next to godliness. Even if you don't mind a bit of cat drool on your socks, you should wash or replace such "human" cat toys regularly. Also beware of playthings that look like something else. This brings us back to that whole legion of objects that people drag for cats to stalk and pounce upon. The urge to do so looms so great that often we'll drag whatever we happen to have in our hands. If that happens to be a bath towel it usually poses no problem. However, if Max unthinkingly teases Minnie with the unplugged cord of the iron or electric drill, he sets her up for a double disaster. First, in the process of tugging on the cord in his absence, she might pull the appliance down on herself. Second, she might bite a cord that *is* plugged in. Erica, meanwhile, rues the day she waved an old stocking for Limo to stalk and catch: three days later the cat destroyed five good pairs of hose she'd washed and left hanging in the bathroom to dry.

Finally, as discussed in Chapter 3, the concept of environmental enrichment has gained increased popularity. As a result, more people speak of building or buying their pets a feline activity center that features multiple exercise options. However, because these centers can take up a fair amount of space, you need to consider if and how one of these will fit into your home. It won't help Limo if his owners consider his top-of-the-line feline jungle gym a pain because it's ugly, too big, or impossible to clean. If space is limited, consider an activity center such as Catnex which comes in modules you can arrange in any shape you like. Other activity centers fit on tabletops, while some specially designed cat trees fit snugly into corners. If you don't like to clean house or lack the time to do so, bear this in mind, too, when you look at self-contained activity centers in which you can leave your pet to play all day. Although some of the wooden-framed ones with carpeted perches and other accessories approach works of art, the washable plastic ones require much less maintenance to keep their fresh appearance.

Before continuing, think about your home as a kitty playground.

## Kitty Playground Check

Review your notes from Chapter 3, this time with an eye toward your home as a place for your cat to exercise. What household objects can your cat play with? Which ones would you prefer it ignored? What could you do, or would you do, to keep your cat away from these verboten objects? Can you think of acceptable objects you could add to your pet's environment? Does your cat play in any special areas of your home? Do these activities and areas meet with your approval? If not, why not?

"Even though I knew about the problems Julie and Erica had with Limo when he was a kitten, I really didn't have a kitten's-eye view of my apartment until I got Minnie," Max discloses after he completes the exercise. "A lot of my worries about her getting into my things turned out to be unfounded, but I think that was because I put *everything* out of her reach after hearing those horror stories about Limo. On the other hand, her personality is a lot different from his, too. Things that would attract him—like flapping window shades and blowing curtains—scare her to death."

Given the wide variety of objects that cats may view as toys, it makes sense to consider the kinds of objects that will give your particular pet the most complete mind-body workout.

## Playground Equipment

The wildcat's entire environment serves as both a playground and a school, and contemporary house cats can enjoy the same setup. All kittens and many adult cats view *anything* they find lying around our homes as a potential toy. This poses a good news/bad news dilemma for owners. On the plus side, the fact that cats will happily amuse themselves for hours with paper bags, boxes, cardboard rolls from toilet or wrapping paper, crumpled balls of paper or cellophane, paper clips, rubber bands, ladybugs, spiders, houseflies, dust balls, plants, clothespins, and anything else they can get their furry little paws on does feed into our notion of cats as pets who can exercise themselves.

On the minus side, however, we already noted how even the most seemingly innocuous household objects can create problems if the cat tries to eat them. And whether the cat tries to do that depends on how much stimulation it receives from the object and the environment during the play session. Thus, the dangling piece of yarn or string may pose no problem for years because the owner lives in a quiet apartment building. However, when a family with three young children moves in across the hall or a road crew begins tearing up the street outside, the additional sound, motion, and other stimulation may drive the cat from stalk-and-pounce games into actually eating the string.

So many variables come into play when cats appropriate household objects as toys that it's easier to provide the cat with acceptable, safe playthings. Nothing can guarantee that a stray bug or handkerchief left by a visitor won't capture your cat's fancy, but cats accustomed to playing with their own toys will pay less attention to those objects than animals who routinely view all of their owners' belongings as potential playthings.

Even paper bags and cardboard boxes, which I personally adore as cat toys, can pose problems. I recall several tales of kittens inadvertently carried off in the dirty laundry bag or even put out with the trash because their owners didn't realize that the animals were exploring these objects at that time. Because of this, giving the cat its own special bags or boxes, or presenting these items for play using a specific ritual that makes them different from all other bags and boxes that might be lying about (such as calling the cat and rustling the objects), serves two purposes:

- It focuses the animal's attention on its own bags and boxes.
- It reminds owners to check all bags and boxes before discarding them.

To help prevent possible problems, you also can outfit your feline playground with cat bags and boxes designed specifically for your cat's enjoyment. The fabric group includes bags that make noise when the cat moves in them, tepees with escape holes that pets can climb through, and tunnels to navigate. Cardboard box variations include the Smarty Cat School House which consists of interchangeable units with tunnels, windows, and doors that you can arrange to fit your home as well as your cat's play preferences. Another version, Mr. Spats' Lazy Cat Lodge, contains two levels, several doors, and a sunroof.

Here again, it pays to know your cat before you buy. Some cats so adore the noise made by certain cat sacks that they can't wait to rip through the fabric and discover the source of the sound. Nonwashable fabric cat bags or tunnels won't last very long if used regularly. The same goes for designer cardboard boxes. Minnie's lasts for years because she climbs through it daintily. Limo, on the other hand, uses his for a scratching post as well as a toy, reducing it to a pile of rubble within a matter of weeks.

The majority of cat toys typically elicit predatory behaviors, even though the toys may consist of nothing more than a ball of crumpled paper the owner attaches to the end of a string and drags. Manufactured versions include handheld wands with attached strings and toys, fishing reel–type devices via which owners can "cast" the toy and reel it in as the cat pursues it, and motorized systems that twirl toys for the cat to pursue. When considering such toys for your cat, make sure any strings are firmly attached. Also beware of toys with fake eyes, bows, sequins, or other decorations a curious pet might pull off and swallow. Finally, if your pet suffers from allergies or acne on its chin, stick with simple toys made from natural, minimally dyed fibers. While toy-related allergies are rare, prevention makes the most sense for animals with known allergic tendencies.

As with scratching posts, freestanding toys that cats bat require a firm anchor. When Limo gives a ball attached to a springy post affixed to a carpeted base a good slug, the whole contraption skids across the floor and crashes into the stand holding Erica's collection of handmade glass flowers. An enthusiastic swipe of a paw may cause battable toys held by suction cups to go flying, too. I purchased one such toy whose bell-containing plastic ball split in two on impact, causing me to race both cat and dog to the rolling bell and grab it before one of them ate it.

One of my favorite battables, called the Tiger Toy, consists of a plastic, wood, and nylon mobile patterned after similar devices used to exercise zoo animals. When the mobile is suspended from the sturdy hook provided, the slightest touch causes the attached mouse to dip and sway. Here again, the success of the toy depends on the owner's anchoring it firmly. The same goes for climbing ropes, which may consist of nothing more than a piece of heavy rope with knots tied along its length firmly secured to the ceiling. These make wonderful cat exercisers, particularly when hung near windows or other household activity centers that the cat might enjoy viewing from a fresh angle.

Like some scratching posts, some toys rely on catnip to pique the cat's interest. While this may, indeed, attract some cats, bear in mind that not all cats respond to catnip and those who do may not develop this capacity until four months of age or older, perhaps because it's linked more to sexual than play behavior. Consequently, you may want to test your cat's sensitivity to this substance before you invest in a more expensive catnip-dependent toy.

As far as what catnip does, the euphoric reaction it elicits in some animals looks remarkably similar to the so-called after reaction following mating. Because cats who respond to catnip may pay little attention to where they leap or roll, make sure you cat-proof the area if you offer your pet this substance. Even though cats who do respond to catnip may appear quite active while under its influence, the reaction soon wanes, and thus it doesn't serve as a reliable source of feline exercise.

Can cats become addicted to catnip? I don't recall any reports of this in domestic animals. Presumably some mechanism similar to olfactory fatigue which causes animals—and us—to become insensitive to an odor after a while comes into play and terminates the cat's response. Other cats will play eagerly with a catnipped toy for a few days, then lose interest in it completely. However, reports of wild felines becoming addicted to naturally growing hallucinogenic plants do exist. In these situations, though, the animals become so entranced by the plants that they pay little attention to establishing a territory and eating or drinking, let alone reproducing, and quickly become eliminated from the gene pool.

As mentioned, retrieving cats prefer small objects that they can pick up easily, with some favoring spongy balls that bounce high on impact while others prefer fuzzy ones. However, animals with stronger maternal instincts may find a ball's bouncing and rolling disconcerting; they much prefer toy mice or the owner's socks. Owners of retrieving cats prone to allergies should pick their pets' toys with particular care, since these animals will come in much closer contact with these objects than cats who merely bat their toys about the floor.

Owners seeking to enrich their housebound cat's environment with an activity center will find numerous ones on the market. Some of the smallest ones consist of little more than a combination of toys. For example, Max gets Minnie one that consists of a little nook with an attached scratching post, a battable mouse, and a ball in a track she can amuse herself trying to catch. Some creative owners construct their own activity centers, accessorizing their pets' crates with battable toys, then surrounding the crate with a playground of homemade toys.

"Like what?" asks Max, ever on the lookout for cost-saving options.

For starters, you can cut paw-sized holes in the top and sides of a cardboard shirt box, pop a Ping-Pong ball inside, tape the box shut, and watch your cat try to get the ball out. A variation on this theme uses a cake pan filled with a small amount of water in which float paw-sized pieces of sponge. Cats will amuse themselves for hours trying to fish these out. If you don't like the idea of your pet's winging wet pieces of sponge around the kitchen, put the pan in an empty bathtub and let your cat play with it there. One owner put her pet's crate and toys in an old child's playpen she bought at a yard sale. The plastic liner makes any mess easy to clean up, and the cat can get into and out of its playground easily. Another cat owner with toddlers also likes the playpen arrangement because her children can't get into the cat's toys or bother the animal while he's playing. Although I have never hear of a cat chewing up and swallowing chunks of sponge or balls, it pays to observe the cat when it plays to ascertain how it relates to its toys.

Commercially available activity centers come in carpeted, plastic, and wooden open versions, and screened and wire enclosed ones in all shapes and sizes. Unless accessorized with toys that arouse the cat's interest, these serve only as places for the cat to relax. The trick involves selecting the right combination of hanging battables, teasers, climbing ropes, tunnels, and ladders to stimulate your particular cat to play in your absence. Otherwise, even the most expensive and attractive activity center won't keep your pet physically fit.

While kitty videos may not induce cats to do much exercise, there's no denying that some cats find them a fascinating way to exercise their minds. You can purchase videos of birds, fish, and mice produced with cats in mind or make your own. Some owners report that their pets enjoy watching tapes of family members, other pets, and even themselves.

A final toy consideration applies to multiple-pet households. Puppies and dogs may eagerly shred and even eat toys with which a cat may do nothing more than happily bat. Consequently, if you own dogs or other pets, make sure any cat toys won't create problems for them. Similarly, toys that one cat may bat gently may stimulate two or three cats to play cat hockey, complete with full body slams and brawls. Because a thin line can separate play and predatory/fight responses and we know how sound and motion contribute to the latter, you should introduce motorized, windup, or other noisemaking devices gradually to ascertain whether they'll precipitate quality exercise or kitty knockouts.

Take a few minutes to consider your ideas about the ideal cat toys to keep your cat fit and trim throughout its life.

---

### Playground Equipment Check

Think about any existing or dream cat's personality and activity level as they could affect its exercise program. What kinds of toys would best suit your pet? Does it prefer to play by itself or with others? Is it a batter or a stalker? A retriever, a climber, or a fisher?

"Right now Limo's nothing but a lump," Julie says with a laugh. "But he used to be quite a climber when he was a kitten. And he loved to bat things around much more than stalk them."

"Minnie's not like that at all," Max chimes in. "She really likes to stalk things, plus pick them up and carry them."

Given these different feline reactions, we can see how doting cat owners may present their pets with a new toy only to discover that the animal wants nothing to do with it whatsoever. We already touched on several possible contributors to these aversions, and individual animals may experience their own unique phobias. Because of this, it makes sense to observe your kitten or cat and see what kinds of activities appeal to it, then select toys and games that complement these. However, recognizing what kinds of activities appeal to your cat and seeing if and how they fit into your specific environment takes time, and that reminds us that no exercise program will work for your pet unless it works for you, too.

# Mirror Games

Aside from those cats with free access to cat doors, most cats depend on their owners to provide them with the wherewithal to fulfill their exercise needs. For owners of in- and-outdoor animals, this may mean little more than opening the door to allow the cat to go outside to exercise and amuse itself. The owners of strict house cats, however, function as far more than door-persons—whether they realize it or not. Therefore, any anthropomorphic or chattel views these owners maintain about feline exercise definitely will affect their pets and the relationship.

For the most part the media portray cats anthropomorphically. This makes sense because the average person knows little about cats compared with other species; barring this knowledge, they impose their own beliefs on the cat. When we combine this with those lofty feline legends, it seems perfectly logical to depict cats as furry babies who do little more than sleep and eat. Whereas dog books treat us to drawings and pictures of dogs of all ages at work and play, cat books more commonly limit playful illustrations to kittens. Older cats snuggle on pillows or next to their owners, lounge in the sun, or pose in front of a wide variety of formal and informal backdrops. Or they eat.

"Sleep and eat, that's what cats do!" Erica exclaims.

While this may make perfectly good sense to many a cat owner, does it represent good *feline* or good *human* sense? Considering the cat's recent domestication as well as its predatory lifestyle, does it seem likely that this species carries couch potato genes?

Surprisingly enough, that may be true. We know that the cat evolved physiologically and behaviorally to hunt. We also know that wildcats spend most of their waking hours hunting because they usually must make several attempts before they succeed in catching their prey. Thus, Limo's ancestors became genetically programmed to spend most of their time hunting, eating, and sleeping. When owners of domestic cats relieve their pets of the burden of hunting food—as well as all the exercise involved in those unsuccessful as well as successful hunting forays—that leaves the animals with only the sleep and eat portions of the program unless their owners find some other way to channel that predatory potential.

"I never thought about it before, but Limo's life is a lot like my dad's," Julie remarks pensively. "When Dad was younger and worked every day, he was in great shape physically. But when he retired, he really put on the weight. My mom was always cooking something special for him because she was so glad to have him home. Come to think of it, Erica and I were always giving Limo treats, too, once he quieted down. And Dad was so happy not to punch a time clock, he didn't do much but sleep, eat, and lounge around like Limo, too."

In this situation, Julie's anthropomorphic evaluation of the problem after the fact helps her realize how her own beliefs contributed to her pet's lack of exercise and subsequent weight gain. Once she realizes that, she and Erica can focus on finding ways for Limo to exercise that utilize his natural tendencies.

While some anthropomorphic owners like the thought of their cats lounging about doing nothing just as their godlike ancient Egyptian ancestors did, other owners have strong ideas regarding what their pets should play with and how. High-tech owners who love gadgets may buy their cats motorized mice that whirl and twirl crazily across the rug. If the cat runs from instead of plays with these, the owners feel cheated. Other, high-energy owners may expect their cats to share their views. When Erica decides that she and Limo should lose weight together, she sets up a fast-paced exercise program for both of them.

"Come on," she says, nudging him with the toe of her sneaker when he yawns at her hand-clapping, foot-stomping attempts to get him up and moving. "Get with the program."

Even though this approach might help Erica shed a few extra pounds and keep in shape, that's no guarantee it will work for her pet.

While most cat lovers chafe at the idea of treating their pets like chattel, this probably ranks as the most common owner orientation toward feline exercise. We normally don't play with the cat because we believe it needs exercise: we play with it because doing so makes *us* feel good. If we don't feel the need or have the time to experience that feeling, well, the cat can just amuse itself.

Whether the cat *can* amuse itself depends on the cat. If your cat maintains its optimal weight and doesn't suffer from chronic or recurrent medical and/or behavioral problems, then it probably can. On the other hand, if Minnie whiles away the hours digging at the walls or herself when Max gets involved in a big project at work, perhaps she's not quite as capable of taking care of herself as he'd like to think.

"Won't free-access crate-training take care of that problem?" Max asks as he watches Minnie spend what seems like an awfully long time licking one paw.

Granted, a crate or other haven gives an insecure animal a place to which it can retreat when it becomes overwhelmed by its environment. However, the crate does nothing to build the animal's confidence so that it may live more comfortably in the owner's home. The confidence necessary to do this arises from the cat's sense of self which, in turn, depends on its ability to fulfill its function. In domestic cats, that means the animal must either successfully fulfill its predatory function or engage in some other activity that challenges its mind and body to the same degree. When Max couples free-access crate-training with a daily confidence-building playtime during which he, Minnie, and others interact positively, his once timid pet becomes more outgoing.

Recall all you discovered about your own anthropomorphic and chattel views and apply what you learned to your cat's exercise needs.

## Owner Exercise Orientations

Examine any existing or proposed feline exercise programs for evidence of anthropomorphic or chattel views. Do any anthropomorphic views arise from solid knowledge of your pet's exercise needs? Do any represent your emotional views about what constitutes quality feline exercise? Do your chattel views arise from knowledge of your cat's needs or a desire not to become involved in this aspect of your cat's care?

"Whenever I think about my orientation toward animals, it's hard not to think that there's some right or wrong answer," Erica remarks as she finishes evaluating how her view of cats in general and Limo in particular affects his exercise. "Still, I can see how both Julie and I take a mixed approach to Limo's exercise. Sometimes we look at it purely in terms of our own needs, and other times we disregard it completely."

At this point, owners like Erica must strongly resist the temptation to wallow in guilt. Sure, it would be nice if we all knew everything there was to know about cats before we got one so we wouldn't make any mistakes, but even people who spend their lives studying cats don't know everything about them. The issue isn't what you did or didn't do with this or some other cat in the past, but rather what you're going to do *now*. So, instead of feeling guilty, Erica should examine how her and Julie's anthropomorphic and chattel views influence Limo's activities, and discard those beliefs that don't meet his needs as well as their own.

Max experiences a completely different revelation when he performs this exercise.

"I don't treat Minnie like a little baby any more than I treat her like an animated robot," he announces. "But I did have some pretty strong ideas about how cats should play. Some of these came from books, but a lot were based on my fear that she'd turn into a blob like Limo."

In this case, even though Max's views of exercise resulted from a sincere desire to keep his cat as healthy and happy as possible, his failure to take her unique needs into account initially created rather than solved problems for him and his timid pet. Once he realized this, he made the necessary adjustments in his own orientation.

"Now all I need is the time to put all this into practice!" he exclaims, a sentiment echoed by many a modern pet owner.

# Kitty Playtime

A proper feline exercise program depends on two kinds of owner time commitment: time to determine the best kind of exercise for the cat, and time to accomplish it regularly. Because of the cat's long-standing, if somewhat erroneous, reputation as a pet who can take care of itself, a suggestion to set aside time to create a feline exercise program and get it up and running usually elicits polite snickers if not howls of laughter.

Most certainly Julie and Erica felt that way when they got Limo. At that time they concentrated all of their efforts on stopping what they considered his unacceptable activity, and spent hours disciplining him or booby-trapping the forbidden areas and objects that attracted him. Unfortunately for Limo, his owners didn't spend any time providing him with a more acceptable outlet for his energy. This resulted in two problems:

- They and Limo missed much of the fun of kittenhood.
- They didn't establish a mutually acceptable and reliable exercise program.

When asked to reminisce about Limo's kitten days, his owners recall it as a nightmare period during which they spent most of their time riding herd on their exuberant pet.

"I can't tell you how relieved we were when he outgrew that stage and settled down!" Erica sums up her feelings about this difficult period.

However, when Limo develops weight problems later, the lack of any exercise routine creates a double whammy for his owners. First, they must find the time to develop an exercise program that will entice a now enormously disinterested cat rather than an inquisitive kitten to stir himself. Second, they must find time in their busy schedules to implement the program long enough to get those excess pounds off their pet and ensure that the exercise will remain part of his daily routine.

Compare Julie's and Erica's experience with Max's. Like anyone who even fleetingly thinks of getting a cat, Max's heart went out to the soaking wet, shivering, tricolored fur ball huddled in the doorway. However, where Julie and Erica took a "What's to know?" approach to feline exercise when they got their new kitten, Max observes Minnie for a few days to discern what kinds of activities appeal to her. Max soon discovers that his new companion likes objects that move, but she prefers to study any potential toy carefully before she begins to play with it. Because of this, whenever Max gets a new toy for his pet, he gives her several days to get used to it before he begins incorporating it into her exercise routine.

Admittedly, Minnie's more placid temperament makes this an obvious first step, but even exuberant kittens and cats can benefit from such gradual introductions. For example, in one of their few early attempts to focus Limo's energy more constructively, Julie and Erica buy him an expensive battery-powered mouse, turn it on, and send it whizzing right at him. The toy looks and sounds so unlike anything Limo has ever seen that he takes off in fright, disappears under his owners' bed, and refuses to come out. When Max introduces this same type of toy to Minnie over a period of days, it soon becomes one of her favorites.

Or consider another favorite cat game, hide-and-seek. While most cats enjoy exploring empty bags and cardboard boxes, this game involves spreading a collection of bags and/or boxes of varying sizes around the house and hiding a favorite toy or some other treat in one of them. However, because it takes a certain amount of time for most cats to get the hang of the game, owners may need to start with only one or two bags and allow the cat to see them place the toy in the bag. They then gradually add more hiding places to the game until the cat must search the entire house looking for the hidden treasure. While a cat can amuse itself for hours once it understands the game, it takes time for the owner to teach it.

In addition to allowing cats time to become familiar with any new toys or learn new games, owners need to address the issue of the best playtime for their cats. Owners of cats allowed access to the outdoors typically equate "playtime" with "outdoor" time and give little thought to what, if any, exercise the animal gets indoors. As long as the cat remains healthy and well behaved, this approach appears to work.

However, as more and more data point to free-roaming cats as major contributors to the diminishing songbird population, *when* we put the cat out becomes increasingly important. Typically in the literature of bygone years, the nightly ritual included putting out the cat. This makes perfectly good sense because cats are, after all, nocturnal animals. Putting cats out at night also ensures that, if they hunt, they'll hunt nocturnal rodents rather than birds.

So, why do so many people let their cats out only during the day? Although some claim it's safer, statistics don't bear that out. True, a cat roaming at night might fall prey to a fox, a coyote, or another wild animal. However, far more pet cats fall prey to cars and trucks, mechanical creatures that more commonly prowl the streets during the daylight hours.

Other owners say they let their cats out during the day because they can respond quickly if something bad happens. However, many of these owners work or spend a fair amount of time away from home. During their waking hours at home, the sounds of television, radio, and other activities could easily drown out the cries of an injured cat, a sound that might wake them immediately in the wee hours of the morning.

Another variation on the outdoor time theme deals with leash-walking cats. Faced with the dual threat of cats contracting rabies from raccoons, skunks, and bats as well as preying on songbirds, more and more areas are enacting feline leash laws. While many cats can and do adapt quite well to this form of exercise, it takes time to accustom the animal to both the harness and the walking process. While the pup's strong social orientation means owners often can merely turn their backs on the leashed animal and trot off knowing it will follow, this rarely happens with cats. Owners who use such a sink-or-swim approach can not only sour their cats on this form of exercise, but also seriously hurt them when the animal resists and they drag it down the street.

Regardless of whether the cat goes out, should owners set aside a specific playtime for their pets? While it hardly seems necessary for kittens, making this part of the young animal's routine can pay big dividends as it grows older. In addition to making it easier to keep older animals fit and trim, it guarantees owners quality time spent with their pets.

"I know a lot of owners who see mealtimes as the special time they share with their pets," Max admits. "But I didn't want to do that with Minnie because I didn't want her to get fat like Limo. And though I do enjoy it when she just curls up beside me when I work, I get a real kick out of that half hour I spend tossing her toys or making up new games for her."

Owners of cats with fussy appetites often play with their pets before feeding them, using games that stimulate their pets' predatory instincts and, thus, stimulate their cats' appetites. Those whose cats get restless during the night often play with their pets just before they go to bed, thereby increasing the likelihood that these animals will sleep through the night.

In addition to thinking about how your cat will spend its time in your presence, you need to think about how it will amuse itself in your absence—otherwise you may spend a great deal of your own time cleaning up after your pet. While most cats do spend much of their time sleeping (provided they have a safe and secure place in which to curl up and do so), it's a good idea to provide them with access to some form of entertainment in case they feel the need to burn off a little energy when left alone. This may mean nothing more than a collection of safe toys or something as elaborate as an activity center.

Think about the play time you spend or want to spend with your cat, and the play time your cat spends or will spend alone.

## Clocking Cat Exercise

Review any time limits you noted on your "Feline Time Check" in Chapter 4. Do these allow time for any regular exercise program for your cat? If not, can you free up some time? Next, think about how your cat spends an average day and weekend. Can you think of ways you can incorporate an exercise program into these?

Even though Julie and Erica thought their hectic lives left little time for regular play sessions with Limo, they discovered that wasn't true.

"He always hangs around when one of us takes a bath or when we prepare a meal," Julie says with a laugh. "So, we just designated those as his playtime."

Julie and Erica float small 1½- to 2-inch cubes of sponge in the tub for Limo to fish out, blow bubbles for him to chase, and dangle towels for him to leap at. While they prepare dinner, they toss single pieces of cat food for him to retrieve, or hide them or pieces of carrot in paper bags, stacks of paper cups, or empty plastic containers for him to "hunt." They sing and chatter gaily to him, so enchanting him with their unusual behavior that he can't help but follow them wherever they go. In such a way, the once lethargic cat gets a quality workout within his owners' narrow time limits.

Max, on the other hand, sets time aside after his evening meal to play with Minnie.

"I like it because it gives me a chance to unwind at the same time it gives her a chance to burn off a lot of energy," he confesses. "When I watch her play, and laugh at her antics, I can just feel the tension drain out of me."

Given such a hefty benefit to the human spirit, anything that exercises the cat would seem more than worth its weight in gold. Fortunately, owners can enjoy such benefits for much less.

## The Cost of Playtime

Cat activities span the spectrum from the ridiculously simple to the elegantly sublime, and their prices span an equally broad range. Even cats with the fanciest pedigrees will succumb to the allure of household items, but if you don't monitor your cat's play and the animal eats a piece of string or chomps on an electrical cord, those freebies could cost you a great deal, indeed.

If you prefer that your cat plays with something more sumptuous than discarded grocery bags or appliance boxes, expect to spend $15 to $25 for premade cat sacks, tunnels, and tepees. Designer cardboard boxes range from $15 to $25 on the low end to more than $100 for a four-level carpeted version.

For less than a dollar, you can buy a sponge, cut it into 1½- to 2-inch cubes or even fish-shaped pieces, and float these in a $2 cake pan containing about an inch of water. You also can let your cat fish for an old Ping-Pong ball trapped in an old cardboard shirt box ($0). If you and your cat prefer something a bit more sophisticated, though, this same game comes premade in cardboard, plastic, carpeted, or motorized versions, all in the $10 to $20 price range.

If your cat likes to chase bubbles like Limo, you can blow him some of yours when you bathe or do dishes ($0), or you can purchase a bottle of liquid designed specifically for this purpose and a bubble blower for less than a dollar. If your pet prefers to chase beams of light, a flashlight ($1 and up) may do the trick.

However, if it prefers a smaller beam, you can cut a small hole in a piece of cardboard and tape it over the lens of your standard flashlight ($0), or you can buy a penlight for this purpose ($2 and up). Those who do public speaking note that their cats enjoy chasing laser pointers, too ($29.95 and up). As with any kind of light, the goal remains to get the cat to chase the beam, not to blind the animal, something you may need to point out to young children and certain immature adults.

All kinds of stalkables and battables fall in the $2 to $5 range, and you usually get what you pay for. If your cat plays rough, it's worth the extra cost of the sturdier toys to avoid cleaning up the stuffing or catnip that gets flung everywhere when your pet goes in for the kill. However, if your cat likes to carry its toys around or bat them under the woodstove, don't forget to make sure you can launder any expensive toys. If not, it might cost less in the long run to buy cheaper ones and replace them more often.

Handheld teasers, in which the toy and connecting string attach to a pole that the owner flicks, range from $5 to $20. In a motorized, variable-speed version called Mouse Chase ($46.99), the toy bounces and periodically changes directions. Other toys attach to freestanding bases ($5 to $15), while still others come as part of cat houses and activity centers priced $30 and up. Many of these toys come attached to "scratchable" surfaces such as carpeting or sisal, so if you can find one that fulfills your cat's clawing as well as exercise preferences, you can solve two problems at one time. The aforementioned battable Tiger Toy patterned after the exercisers used in zoos costs $20 to $25, depending on where you buy it.

At the low end of the cat-activity-center price spectrum you'll find compact plastic activity centers that include balls, teasers, scratching areas, and hidey holes in the $25 to $35 range. The lowly carpeted or sisal scratching post has spawned an incredible array of cat trees priced from $45 to more than $1,000, depending on their materials and accessories. The top part of one called the Condo Carrier can be used as a carrier, a real plus for owners desiring an alternate method of crate-training ($109.95). The aforementioned carpeted modular Catnex that you can arrange any way you like costs $24.95 to $69.95 plus shipping and handling. Movable wire enclosures with cat shelves range from $125 to $175 depending on accessories. Kali-Ko-Kathouses vinyl walk-in Purr Palace and Kathouse cost from $599 to more than $1,000. If you desire activity centers constructed of wood rather than carpeting or plastic, consider the pre- and custom-made cedar environments built by House of Cats International for $300 to $5,500.

If you plan to walk your cat, invest in a figure-eight harness ($5 to $10) which your cat can't slip out of nearly as easily as a standard collar. While you probably can walk a well-trained cat in a controlled environment using little more than a six-foot length of heavy cord (less than $1), a good $15 to $20 retractable leash will offer your pet more exercise opportunities. Using such a leash, Erica can give Limo plenty of freedom to explore the grassy meadow, but then reel him in and keep him close to her when the path takes them near shrubbery or other obstacles in which a light rope or standard leash might become entangled.

Simchavision offers bird, fish, and mice videos for $19.95 each or $49.95 for the set, plus shipping and handling. The company will even put two selections on one tape if you like, for a full two hours of feline viewing pleasure. (You can call them at 800-484-6437, ext. 4748, for further information.) If your cat prefers real birds, bird feeders that attach to the outside of windows with suction cups range from less than $10 to more than $100. While it would seem the presence of a cat face scant inches away would scare any wild birds off, this doesn't appear to occur. The birds quickly become accustomed to the cat, and many owners tell tales of their cats forming friendships with certain birds who come to feeders, and waiting eagerly for their feathered playmates' arrival every day.

Summon the memory of any financial limits you noted in Chapter 4 as you design your cat's ideal exercise program.

---

## Balancing the Exercise Books

Compare the amount you allotted for your cat and its upkeep with the cost of your desired exercise program. Can you afford the kinds of feline activities you want? If you can't, can you think of any ways you can free up additional funds or give your cat that same exercise experience more economically?

"I love the idea of those activity centers," Julie admits. "But there's no way we can afford one right now."

However, when she recalls how much Limo used to enjoy playing around Erica's loom, the two women set about designing Limo his own wall hanging, firmly attaching pieces of heavy fabric and toys to a heavy, knotted rope and sisal framework.

Given Max's limited budget and cramped space, he purchases several small, high-quality cat toys for Minnie and uses paper bags, cardboard boxes, and other items he finds about the house to amuse her.

If few owners think much about the cost of exercising their cats, even fewer consider how their own emotional limits may enhance or sabotage their pets' activities. Nonetheless our emotions can and do affect our cats' exercise programs.

# Owner Emotional Sit-Ups

Because so much of what we call cat play represents predatory displays, it has the potential to generate strong human emotions. When Minnie stalks and pounces on her toy mouse, flips it up in the air, and bats it around, Max thoroughly enjoys her antics. The day he comes home from work and finds her doing the same thing to a *real* mouse, though, he sees things quite differently.

"Bad cat!" he shouts at his terrified pet as he chases her through the house brandishing a rolled-up newspaper. "Put that poor thing down!"

Needless to say, her owner's response thoroughly confuses Minnie. Her not-so-ancient heritage strongly programs her to hunt, a trait Max strongly reinforced by the way he played with her and the kinds of toys (furry "mice," feathery "birds") he bought her. When we add her view of him as her parent/teacher, the frightened creature suddenly finds herself without any reliable reference points. No wonder she streaks off and hides!

Another emotional aspect of feline play arises when owners unwittingly or deliberately cross that sometimes nearly invisible line between play and predatory behaviors. Some owners get a big kick out of rolling their cats on their backs and "tickling" their tummies—until the cats come up and rake human arms with very sharp hind claws. Max often starts out playing low-keyed stalk-and-pounce games with Minnie, but as the two of them get into it, he feeds more sound and motion into the process. Instead of just dangling her toy, he makes it bounce crazily; instead of just chuckling, he hoots and hollers at her frantic leaps to grab it. When she makes one particularly spectacular leap, misses, and sinks her claws into his chest rather than her toy, however, he loses his temper.

In both of these situations, an understanding of the cat's predatory nature and any feelings about it would alleviate negative responses. If you can't bear the thought of your cat's hunting *anything*, theoretically that means no one should play or otherwise interact with the animal in a way that evokes such a response. However, because so much of the cat's psyche springs from its predatory nature, this approach would deprive the animal of an essential part of its nature. Consequently, prospective cat owners who maintain such views probably should consider a pet more suited to their own emotions.

Anyone who has ever watched a cat stalk a butterfly knows that cats possess infinite patience. Cat owners sometimes need a lot of patience, too, when it comes to putting together quality exercise programs for their pets. Like free-access crate-training, training a cat to accept a harness and walk on a leash takes time. Impatient owners who try to rush the process will only prolong it. Similarly, when Erica and Julie become so eager for Limo to try his new climbing wall that they pick him up and hang him on it, the fat feline dangles helplessly for a few seconds, then falls clumsily to the floor and scurries off. Compare this with his owners' allowing him time to become accustomed to it on his own terms, teasing him with pieces of rope or toys that they then attach to the lowest parts of the hanging so he can easily reach them.

If you want your cat to walk on a leash or accept a new toy or activity center, give the animal time to adjust to it. If your own impatient nature won't allow you to do this, ask a more patient friend to help you.

Another raft of negative exercise-related emotions may await the unwary purchaser of a new activity center. Whether Frank Lloyd Wright would agree or not, some of those systems are downright lovely. Thus, for many owners an activity center would seem to offer the best of all worlds, providing the cat with a safe place in which to play and owners with an aesthetically pleasing addition to their homes—until the cat begins to use it, that is. Max saves for months to buy Minnie a color-coordinated cat house with wonderful carpet, wood, shingle, rope, and sisal details.

"It looks like a piece of sculpture," he boasts to a friend.

Minnie likes it every bit as much, but not as an *object d'art*. She much prefers to scratch, rub, bat, pummel, and otherwise mutilate its many features as she plays in it.

"At first, every time she clawed at it, I cringed and had to force myself not to yell at her," Max says. "When I bought it I knew it cost that much because it was carefully designed with a cat's needs in mind, and that's exactly what she should do with it. Still, it took me a while to get over my negative feelings."

Erica and Julie had to work through even more complex emotions when Limo finally got the hang of his homemade climbing wall.

"For a while we were on an emotional roller coaster that began when we felt guilty for letting him get so fat," Erica admits frankly. "Then when Limo wouldn't use the wall hanging right away, we felt really depressed and angry at him and ourselves. But then when he got the hang of it and started tearing it to shreds, we had some pretty mixed feelings about that, too. We were really glad he was using it, but we're artists, and dumb as it may sound, we considered that climbing wall a work of art."

In both of these cases, the owners had to rethink their ideas of what constituted a quality cat gym versus a quality work of art. Until they reconciled these views, they ran the risk of allowing their emotions to undermine their cat's exercise program.

A final emotional aspect of cat exercise involves other, usually noncat owners' responses to those of us who play stupid, but fun, games with our cats. I have been known to completely forget about dusting the floor when I notice Whittington's paw zip out from under the couch and try to snag the fibers of my mop. Slowly I drag the mop back and forth in front of the couch, awarding myself points when he misses it. Silently I creep around to the end of the couch in hopes of surprising him from behind. "Aha!" I shout gleefully when a quick flick of the mop causes him to reveal *his whole head*! The phone rings, and I run to answer it.

"What are you doing?" asks a noncat-owning acquaintance.

"Oh, nothing. Just cleaning house," I say, wiggling the mop at the cat.

Sometimes it takes a great deal of imagination to come up with ways to exercise cats, and some of these can be a source of embarrassment to their owners. However, you can avoid this by testing the water with strangers first, beginning with relatively safe questions such as, "Do you have a cat?" then working up to a fuller disclosure as your new acquaintance reveals more of his or her feline feelings. That way you won't admit to someone who can't appreciate the finer points of this sort of exercise that you and your cat dance to *The Marriage of Figaro*.

Review your list of any emotional limits you think could influence your relationship with your cat and apply them to feline exercise.

---

## Exercise Emotion Evaluation

Think about all the different ways you do or want to exercise your cat. Do any of these elicit any particular emotions? Are these positive or negative emotions? What could you do to increase the positive and eliminate the negative ones?

When Max asks himself these questions, he discovers that his negative emotions arise when he expects Minnie to ignore her predatory nature.

"As long as I keep reminding myself that she's a predatory animal and how our play can affect her behavior, I'm all right," he explains as he watches Minnie clamber over her tree house. "I just need to be more objective about it."

Erica and Julie discover that they have to take Limo's needs into account as well as their own feelings. While his destruction of their lovingly constructed climbing wall initially upset them, they soon see it as a challenge to add things to it that will stimulate their pet as well as make it less of an eyesore. However, that does require a certain amount of physical as well as emotional effort.

# Huffing and Puffing with Puff

We don't usually think of exercising cats as an endeavor involving much physical strength, but owner physical limits can play a role in the creation and upkeep of a feline exercise program. The rarest consideration deserves first mention because of its implications for people with impaired immune responses. The majority of people who come in contact with the organism that causes cat scratch disease or cat scratch fever don't even know it. However, for some, a scratch, lick, or bite from an infected cat (or dog or even from a puncture wound caused by a thorn, wood splinter, or fish bone) can cause serious illness. Selecting types of play that focus the cat's attention on its toys rather than people definitely will limit the risk to immune-impaired people who own cats or who might visit cat owners' homes.

Along these same lines, a surprising number of owners allow their cats to leap on them at will as part of the exercise program. While there's no denying that these sudden leaps up from the floor or down from the top of the closet or refrigerator to the owner's shoulder do exercise the cat and delight the prepared owner, they can spell trouble for those unprepared for the assault. One of Limo's flying leaps so surprises Julie's elderly mother that she stumbles against a table and breaks her wrist. Another visitor's shriek of surprise when Limo lands causes the startled cat to rake the man's neck with his claws. What began as a meeting with a possible buyer of one of Julie's watercolors ends with a trip to the emergency room.

Owners with limited mobility can still give a cat a good workout. One cat owner I know who uses a wheelchair purchased an inexpensive child's fishing rod and tied one of his cat's toys to the line instead of a lure. When he cast his pet's furry mouse the length of his living room, his cat would charge after it at full speed. Then the owner slowly reeled the mouse in, flicking it and making it—and the cat—leap and bounce all the way back to him.

Owners with physical limitations also find that teaching their cats to play hide-and-seek can provide their pets with a great deal of exercise with minimal human exertion. Some owners always leave an assortment of boxes and bags around for their pets to explore, periodically popping a surprise into one of them to perk up the cat's interest. Others lay out a lightweight obstacle course to amuse their pets on rainy days.

Finally, we know that many cats will retrieve balls or other objects thrown by their owners. Because such games require minimal effort on the owner's part, even bedridden cat lovers can participate in this feline sport.

At the opposite end of the spectrum, excessive human physical activity or force may undermine a feline exercise program. Every time I see an owner dragging a reluctant cat on the end of a leash, I think of those reports linking aggression in dogs to cervical (neck) pain caused by owners jerking on collars. Even a child can exert enough force to topple a cat; if the person is moving when this occurs, the poor creature may sustain numerous cuts, bruises, and abrasions before the owner realizes what's happened.

Also, in the course of normal play cats eventually reach a point when they've had enough. Some may slow down gradually, whereas others may just suddenly quit. If Max urges Minnie to keep playing because *he* wants to, his overenthusiasm will turn his pet off rather than on to exercise. Similarly, if Erica and Julie feel so guilty about Limo's weight that they vow to exercise him until *they* drop, they don't help their pet develop lifelong good exercise habits.

## The Human-Feline Ball Game

The idea of exercising a cat generates ambivalent feelings in even the most loving cat owner. On one hand, Julie and Erica can accept the theory behind it, and they certainly realize how Limo's lack of activity contributed to his weight gain and related medical problems. On the other hand, the idea of creating and implementing an exercise program for a cat seems somehow *unnatural*.

When I first began working on this chapter and friends and colleagues would ask what I was writing, I initially found myself hesitating to tell them. *I* knew exercise was important, particularly for the housebound cat, but I wondered if busy owners might see this discussion as just one more entry from the lunatic cat fringe.

However, as I sorted through all the material, two concepts kept recurring to me. One, the more we and our cats need to know, the more we need to play. Two, play is the hallmark of individuals in harmony with their environments. No matter how we cut it, the housebound cat lives in an unnatural environment. While we may believe that environment spares our pets from all sorts of evils, it also forces the cat to develop a whole new set of skills quite alien to its natural roots. The more our cats can play, the more easily they can master those critical modern survival skills.

Can we use exercise and play to *create* an optimal environment for a cat in a less than perfect one? Based on mind-body studies, I believe we can. When Max plays with Minnie, he doesn't think about all she learns and how it relaxes her to the point that her once frightening new space becomes a cherished playground. When Erica and Julie initiate Limo's exercise program primarily for health reasons, they notice something more than the loss of those extra pounds.

"He's so much happier, I can't believe it," Julie marvels as she watches the sleek mini-panther stalking his favorite toy. "And he's so smart! We never realized that before."

So, let the neighbors laugh at your dumb cat games. It takes a special person to create an environment in which a cat can learn and grow in a small apartment or condo. That's something for both owner and cat to celebrate.

Before you get out the ice cream and cake to celebrate your liberated exercise program, though, better read the next chapter on all the factors that may affect what and how we feed our cats.

# 8

# A Loving Spoonful

## *Selecting Healthy Feline Foods and Feeding Rituals*

Vic and Tammy Bouden visit their local animal shelter with the idea of adopting a kitten. However, so many alluring furry faces greet them that they adopt two new pets instead of one: Fred, a gray, longhaired male, and Wilma, a white, shorthaired female. In no time, the two kittens and their playful antics become the center of the Bouden household.

"They're both so smart, let's teach them to do tricks," Vic announces the day Fred retrieves his toy mouse. "We can use food treats."

"What a wonderful idea!" Tammy exclaims as Fred lays his mouse gently at her feet. "I'll get them some special shrimp-flavored cookies to reward them for being so smart."

However, while Vic and Tammy do spend time teaching Fred and Wilma to do tricks, the owners both work, and much of their interaction with their pets centers around mealtime.

"You want some of this roast beef?" Vic asks the two cats staring at him while he eats, then immediately answers his own question, "Of course, you do."

Over the next five years, the Boudens and their cats experience a fairly typical human-feline relationship. The owners neuter their pets, continue teaching them tricks, and share snacks and treats with them. Although Fred remains thin as a rail, Wilma gets fatter and fatter.

"I don't understand," Tammy tells a friend. "We feed them both the same thing."

When the couple tries to cut back on Wilma's food, they fail miserably. She pesters them unbearably at mealtimes or repeatedly brings her toys to them, then stares up at them mournfully until they cave in and give her a treat. However, their own lack of willpower troubles the owners so much that they decide to take drastic action before their beloved pet develops serious weight-related problems.

"You're only getting this weight-reducing diet, and if you don't eat it, tough," Vic tells the cat. "We're doing this for your own good."

"And it worked," Tammy later reports to a neighbor. "Wilma hardly eats anything anymore, and she's losing weight like crazy."

Unfortunately, the owners feel so good about Wilma's increasingly sleek silhouette that it takes several days for them to realize that she's not eating at all.

"I bet she just needs some sort of dietary supplement," Tammy tells Vic as she cradles the limp cat in her arms in the veterinarian's waiting room. "You know, some vitamins or minerals."

However, the veterinarian takes one look at Wilma and knows she's critically ill. Six weeks later, the Boudens still aren't sure if their beloved pet will make it.

---

Just as problems involving cats not using the litter box have cropped up more than once in this book, so do those involving overweight animals, and for the same reason: Not using the litter box ranks as the number one feline behavioral problem, and obesity ranks as the number one nutritional problem plaguing contemporary cats. And just as many factors may lead to inappropriate elimination, obese cats may result from different feeding practices.

In the most simplistic terms, we can say that cats gain weight because they eat too much and exercise too little. Therefore, the Boudens needed only to decrease the amount they fed Wilma and increase the amount she exercised to solve her problem. However, we need only look at the glut of human diet books on the market to realize that effectively applying this scientific principle involves more than these two basic steps. Because our beliefs may strongly affect what happens to our pets, it pays to explore some of the other factors that come into play when we feed the cat.

We can divide these many factors into two main categories:

- the food
- the feeding ritual

By understanding the role these play in any existing or proposed food-related interaction, owners can prevent or treat many of the food-related problems that plague human-feline relationships.

Before we begin, though, think about what "feeding the cat" means to you.

## Feline Feeding Basics

Imagine a typical weekday and weekend day with your current or future cat. How much of your interaction with your pet centers around food? Do you offer your cat specific meals or leave food down all the time? What do you feed your cat? Do you offer your pet human food? Do you give it special cat treats? Under what circumstances do you feed your pet something other than its regular fare?

As soon as Vic and Tammy begin working on this exercise, they realize that their food-related interactions with Fred and Wilma take one of two forms.

"We usually don't make a big deal about feeding them their regular cat food," Tammy explains. "We feed them in the morning when we're pretty rushed, so we just put some dry food in their bowls and don't think much about it. I can't even remember the name of the stuff we feed them. It was something the clerk at the pet store recommended."

"But when they hang around the table while we're eating or when they're doing tricks, that's a different story," Vic adds, describing the second half of the Boudens' cat-feeding routine. "In both cases, I care a lot about whether they eat what I offer them then. It makes me feel good when they gobble their treats down."

Carole Simniak, the Boudens' neighbor and proud owner of a British blue named Charlie, finds their responses horrifying.

"From day one, I've only fed Charlie a premium, all-natural diet," she states. "He gets the same thing every day, and I'd never dream of giving him any treats. Only the best for *my* cat!"

While we know that the Boudens' approach to feeding created problems for at least one of their cats, does Carole's offer a cure or merely pose different problems? To answer that question, we need to know more about what cats eat.

## Traditional Feline Cuisine

Before we can discuss all the different kinds of cat foods available, we need to consider a most troubling reality of feline nutrition: given the cat's recent domestication as well as its natural diet, *everything* we feed it is unnatural. The pet food industry spends millions of dollars trying to create a humanly acceptable mouse-in-a-can, using poultry, fish, beef, corn, wheat, rice, vitamins, minerals, and whatever else it takes to fulfill the current definition of what constitutes a well-balanced feline diet. Those who champion home cooking basically try to achieve this same goal on a smaller scale.

"What do you mean the 'current definition of what constitutes a well-balanced feline diet'?" asks Carole as she opens a bag of top-of-the-line food for Charlie. "Don't we know this?"

Yes and no. We know the basic nutritional requirements for the average cat, but these may or may not hold true for an individual animal. For example, even if we somehow could figure out how to accomplish a direct cow- or chicken-to-mouse conversion when making cat food, my New Hampshire mouse doesn't eat the same things as the New York City or South Dakota farm mouse. Thus, subtle but real nutritional differences may exist among mouse populations; when we compare the New Hampshire mouse with the one living in New Delhi, India, or Manchester, England, these differences could become even greater.

Because predators and prey evolve together in a particular environment, wildcats adapt to accommodate any idiosyncrasies in the existing food supply. However, among purebred cat populations in which breeding for looks may concurrently alter an animal's physiology, or in which breeders create new breeds using cats from other geographical areas, any definition of a well-balanced diet represents an educated guess at best. Breeders tell of cats in one line who thrive on a diet that causes all kinds of problems in another. While most cats can't claim any direct dietary links to fish, the Singapura can because it evolved on a small island where fish played a significant dietary role. That difference, in turn, also affected the Singapura's requirements for certain minerals, such as potassium. When it comes to adding or subtracting ingredients to or from the feline diet, the old adage says it all: You tug on one corner and the whole universe moves!

Put another way, trying to make a nutritionally perfect mouse out of cows or chickens and corn embodies all the challenges encountered when making silk purses out of sows' ears—and more. Consequently, two basic rules of thumb apply to cat nutrition. Rule One: Keep your ears open. As the purebred cat population grows and evolves and more cats become strict house pets, expect changes to occur in the definition of a well-balanced diet. While some people may label any announced changes as conspiracies or sloppiness on the part of the pet food industry, such changes are perfectly natural given the cat's state of flux. If sensational news stories regarding the inferiority or superiority of certain diets crop up, check with your veterinarian for the latest scoop.

Rule Two: Even though dogs function better when fed the same food, cats do better when fed a varied diet. Because many ingredients found in cat food rarely, if ever, showed up in the domestic cat's wild ancestor's diet, food allergies do occur in cats. These include allergies not only to basic ingredients such as beef, fish, and dairy products, but also to the dyes and preservatives used in certain products. Still other cats may develop medical problems that necessitate dietary changes as they get older. In both cases, eliminating a troublesome food from a variety poses fewer problems than making a total dietary change.

"How come?" Carole wants to know.

Recall what we said about the cat's solitary nature and how that leads to early experiences becoming more firmly entrenched in the feline mind. The queen spends a great deal of time teaching her kittens what's safe to eat because, once she weans them, they're on their own. While this protects the wild animal from eating the wrong thing, it also makes it very difficult to induce a cat to eat the *right* thing if food-related problems arise. Suppose Charlie develops an allergy to one of the ingredients in his food. Because he accepts only that food as *right*, he strongly resists any new food even though the old diet makes him seriously ill. If Carole fed him a variety of nutritionally balanced cat foods, though, she could simply eliminate the problematic food from the group.

How do your ideas of the ideal feline diet mesh with what you know about your pet's heritage?

### Wild Cuisine Check

Summon an image of what you consider the ideal food for your cat. Now imagine what a small wildcat or feral cat in your area would eat. What similarities exist between the two diets? What differences? How do you feel about this?

"As far as I can tell, the only thing Charlie's diet has in common with any wildcat's is water," Carole admits. "But I don't feel the least bit guilty about that. Considering all the pollution, fertilizers, pesticides, and everything else out there, I can't imagine that eating any mouse running around this town would be healthier for Charlie than what I feed him now."

"I agree with Carole as far as there being no similarities," Vic Bouden declares. "And I sort of agree about the problems with the local mice. But I also know that what we fed Wilma made her fat, and our attempts to correct that almost killed her."

Although Vic blames Wilma's illness on what he and Tammy fed her, remember that feeding the cat consists of a two-step process: what we feed the cat and how we feed it. Before owners can select a feeding program that will best meet their and their pets' needs, they need to understand all aspects of both of these components.

# Contemporary Feline Chow

As more and more cats switched from dining *au naturel* to eating à la shopping cart, myriad feline feeding options flooded the market, and more new entries—and entrées— arrive every day. We can divide this rising tide of contemporary cat foods into four basic groups:

- regular
- premium
- home cooked
- therapeutic

*Regular* diets make up the bulk of the hundreds of cat foods you can find on grocery store shelves. Primarily produced by national manufacturers, these come in life-stage varieties, such as those developed to meet the nutritional needs of kittens, adult cats, feline senior citizens, and overweight animals. *Premium* foods theoretically provide your cat with something above and beyond fulfilling those basic feline nutritional needs. Some premium foods may use higher-quality meat, or more meat than grain or soy, as protein sources. Others claim fewer preservatives and/or dyes. Still others vow to give your pet an acid urine or fewer problems with food allergies. Whether such products constitute a premium diet depends on your cat's particular needs. *The Cat Food Reference* by Howard D. Coffman (PigDog Press, 1997) not only will help you understand what all of the fine print on cat food labels means, but it also compares 347 regular and premium canned, dry, and semimoist foods so you won't feel overwhelmed when you face that array at the store.

Owners who feed their pets home cooking fall into several categories. Some cook for their cats because they consider the ingredients used in human food superior to those used in cat food. While some, like the Boudens, may feed their pets directly from their plates or use the same-quality ingredients in their pet's food as in their own, others will buy cheaper grades of meat for their pets. Still other owners who worry about the additives found in much human food use organic ingredients when cooking for their pets as well as themselves.

Cats with specific medical problems—such as those involving digestive, kidney, or heart function—may require a *therapeutic* diet that spares the affected organ(s). Because these diets meet the special nutritional needs of a highly specialized segment of the feline population, they should never be fed without veterinary supervision.

Products comprising another category of foods—commercially available treats—don't rank as cat foods at all because none of them claim to meet the cat's nutritional needs. However, they play an increasingly important role in some owners' relationships with their cats, particularly with housebound animals. Like cat foods, treats come in regular, premium, and homemade varieties. While I don't recall seeing any manufactured therapeutic treats, I do recollect several recipes for "cookies" for cats on low-fat or low-salt diets.

Where do your ideas of the perfect cat food fall within the contemporary spectrum?

### Cat Food Evaluation

Review your notes about what you feed or plan to feed your cat. In what category does your pet's food fall?

"We feed Fred and Wilma dry food," Tammy reports after completing the exercise. "And we use our own food for treats."

"Except we do give them prepared cat treats when they do their tricks," Vic reminds his wife.

"I feed Charlie a premium, all-natural diet and no treats," Carole reports. "But now I'm not so sure what 'all natural' means and whether it's good for him or not."

Before we can help Carole with her dilemma, though, we need to look at one more critical ingredient in the feline diet that many owners often overlook.

# Water, Water, Everywhere

Most owners give little thought to how much, if any, water their cats drink. I didn't give it much thought, either, until I realized how many water-related stories owners of house cats recounted. The first wave involved increasing numbers of tales about cats drinking out of sinks, tubs, and toilets, often much to their owners' disgust. The second wave consisted of animals who learned how to turn on faucets but rarely turned them off. The third group, who I dubbed the Polluters, would put various objects ranging from priceless antique knickknacks to used tampons in their water bowls. Why were these cats doing this?

As so often occurs when I can't figure out what cats are doing, the answer comes from the cats themselves, this time from a cat of mine named Maggie. About the time I began collecting all these water tales, age caused Maggie to curtail her outdoor activities considerably. Because she was the sole cat in the household at that time, I kept a bowl filled with dry food and another filled with water for her on the counter safe from curious canines, and I cleaned and refilled these every morning. Periodically, I'd find Maggie sitting on the counter staring at her water bowl so intensely that I felt compelled, in that somewhat irrational way of all cat owners, to do something. Although the water in her bowl appeared perfectly clean, I'd rinse her bowl and refill it because I couldn't think of anything else to do. Thereupon, she would turn her back on the water and begin to *eat*.

My first reaction was, "Well, isn't that just like a cat! They make you jump through hoops, then they snub you!"

However, when the behavior kept occurring, it dawned on me that Maggie wouldn't eat unless she had access to fresh water. Before age and arthritis slowed her down, she drank from the shallow river that borders my property when she was outdoors and from the toilet when she stayed inside. While my more aesthetic nature blanched at the thought of the latter, I had to admit that the water in my toilet was fresher than that in my cat's dish because I flushed the toilet more often on any given day than I changed her water.

Once I had observed Maggie, I saw those water-related tales in a whole new light. Had I not been home to change her water when she wanted, I had no difficulty at all imagining her teaching herself to turn on the faucet in the kitchen sink. In fact, I recalled seeing her sitting in the kitchen sink about the time I noticed her staring at her dish. And for sure, no matter what the Polluters put in their water bowls, the result remains the same: the owner changes the water, albeit with more or less negative actions and emotions aimed at the cat. I can even appreciate the creative brilliance that leads one cat to fly into the bathroom and perch on the rim of the toilet bowl, anticipating the flush every time her male owner gets up in the middle of the night to use the facility. While he considers her behavior most diabolical—once he gets over his shock at the sight of this fur-covered projectile flying at his most vulnerable parts in the dim light—it does possess a certain logic. When he answers nature's call, his cat answers one, too.

Where before I classified Maggie's behavior as further evidence of a bored house cat's cleverness, I now view it as an intelligent self-domesticated creature's attempt to fulfill a basic need for fresh water any way possible. Although all cats might not experience this, owners of cats with urinary tract problems surely should pay as much attention to their pets' drinking habits as they do to their food.

If your cat pollutes its water, drinks out of the tub, sink, or toilet, stares at its water bowl, or turns the faucet on, change your cat's water more frequently. If you're not home to do that or it doesn't solve the problem, consider the Drinkwell Pet Fountain (800-805-7532), a self-contained drinking fountain that aerates your pet's water and keeps it fresh.

The cat's water bowl as well as the amount of water in it also may contribute to feline drinking problems. The tips of cat whiskers contain highly sensitive pressure receptors, and some cats won't drink out of bowls whose rims touch their whiskers.

Other cats will drink only the top inch or so of water in the bowl, then quit. This might occur because the cat initially drinks without its whiskers touching the bowl. It also may occur when the animal feels reluctant to bend its head too much for some reason, most commonly because of its concern that other cats, dogs, or people in the household could sneak up on it.

Cats with bowl aversions often will scoop the water with their paws and either lick it from their feet or fling the water onto the floor and lap it up from there. If you notice these behaviors in your pet, keeping a wider, shallower bowl filled with fresh water in an area where the cat feels secure will usually solve the problem.

By paying attention to this often-neglected part of your pet's nutritional needs, you can prevent your cat from joining the ranks of the Ancient Mariner who saw water everywhere, but not a drop to drink.

Does your cat have a drinking problem?

## Feline Water Analysis

How often do you change the water in your cat's water bowl? Does your cat drink from its bowl or from somewhere else? If from somewhere else, where? How do you react when you find your cat drinking from anywhere other than from its bowl? If your cat suffers from urinary tract or kidney problems, or comes from a breed or line prone to these conditions, what can you do to make sure your pet drinks enough?

"Both Wilma and Fred drink from the sink and tub as well as their bowls and it never bothered us," Tammy announces after she completes the exercise. "When Wilma got fat, though, she only drank from her bowl. I never thought about it before, but I bet that was because she couldn't get into the tub and sink as easily."

"Charlie used to drink from the toilet," Carole shyly admits. "But then one day he slipped and fell in, and that ended it. Now he only drinks from his bowl, and I change the water in it twice a day."

While the idea of a cat's falling into a toilet may elicit snickers, barring the presence of an equally acceptable fresh water source, house cats who have such an experience could find themselves in trouble. Similarly, owners who teach their cats to eliminate in the toilet (but not to flush like the clever cat in Chapter 7) also may cut their pets off from a fresh water supply.

Given these basic food and water ingredients, we now need to examine how the cat, environment, and owner beliefs and limits add their own special flavors to the feline feeding process.

## The Furry Diner's Club

Not only do the foods we feed our cats rank as unnatural from a nutritional point of view, but they also flunk the behavioral test. In Chapter 1 we learned how the cat responds to the sound, motion, odor, texture, and taste of its prey in roughly that order, depending on the amount of light and wind present during the hunting spree. While this system of appetite stimulation serves a marvelous survival function in the wild, cat food typically doesn't trigger the system, and the cat winds up with a totally unwarranted reputation as a fussy eater.

For example, when the Boudens first got Fred and Wilma, like many cat owners they decided to feed the kittens dry food and didn't place much of an emotional charge on the process—until their pets exhibited a lackluster response to it. Regardless of what the owners thought the behavior communicated, we can say several things for sure about that food. It:

- makes no noise
- doesn't move

- emits minimal odor
- possesses nothing resembling a preylike texture

Given this lack of necessary appetite-stimulating factors, the oddity isn't that Wilma and Fred didn't show much interest in their food, but rather that so many cats in that same situation do.

In what may be seen as a tribute to both human and feline self-domestication, most cats and owners consciously or subconsciously find ways to fill this stimulus void. The sound of a rattling bag or can opener may trigger some cats, who then leap in anticipation or take off after each other or the dog. When the owner pours or spoons the food into the dish, more sound and motion embellishes the process. If this suffices to get the cat to first pick up and then eat the food, we say the cat likes it. If the cat doesn't, we say there's something wrong with the food.

Vic and Tammy stuck with dry food because they don't like the smell of canned food. However, they also fed their pets immediately before they ate their own meal. Now Fred and Wilma face a choice: they can eat the silent, motionless, odorless dry food in their bowls, or they can pester their owners for a piece of that aromatic roast beef that moves from plate to human mouth accompanied by all the sounds and motions of mealtime. When the stimulated animals then sink their teeth into the textured meat their owners offer, does it come as any surprise that they gobble it down so much more eagerly than their own food?

"But how come Charlie eats his dry food?" Carole asks as she fills her pet's bowl. "He did pester me a little when he was a kitten, but I told him 'no' and he stopped."

Unlike Fred and Wilma, who came from barn cat litters raised on a combination of cat food and prey, Charlie comes from a long line of show cats. Consequently, until the day he encounters his first mouse or other live edible, he'll probably munch his crunchies contentedly. Also, Carole lives in a crowded condo complex where many residents own cats. Although Charlie takes his territorial duties in stride, these occupy many of his waking hours, and eating doesn't rank as a top priority. Compare this with Fred and Wilma, who don't do much but sleep and eat in the Boudens' quiet home. Even their exercise in the form of their many tricks revolves around food.

Like people, cats have different nutritional requirements based on their age, sex, breed, and lifestyle. Because of this, we can take three cats with the same optimal weight, feed them the same amount of the same food, and one will lose weight, one will gain weight, and one will remain just right. Consequently, owners must go by how their cats look rather than how much they eat. Although Fred and Wilma shared similar barn cat roots, they came from two different litters. When the Boudens fed the two cats equally, the more mellow Wilma put on the pounds.

Because obesity ranks as the number one feline nutritional problem, weight-reduction diets claiming to resolve this problem exist in regular, premium, and therapeutic forms. For every owner and veterinarian who say these diets work, you can find one who insists that cats will do better fed less of their regular food. Once again, it depends on the cat. Reducing diets work on the principle that animals who don't feel satiated when they eat will keep pestering their owners for more food. By providing the cat with a food that contains "empty calories" from carbohydrates rather than fats, owners theoretically can avoid this troubling response.

However, this works only if the cat will eat the food in the first place, which some cats won't do, for all the behavioral reasons mentioned previously. Wilma found the reducing diet so dull compared with her usual fare that she refused to eat it. Her owners opted to take a "tough love" approach and wait her out, seeing this tactic as a quick way to eliminate the unwanted weight.

Unfortunately, some obese cats thrust into the starvation mode may succumb to a devastating disease called hepatic lipidosis, in which excessive fat accumulates in the liver and inter-feres with the organ's normal function. Saving these animals' lives requires getting them to eat, which they won't. The only way to ensure life-sustaining nutrition in these cases involves feed-ing multiple small meals via a tube that opens directly into the cat's stomach, a process that must continue for 2 to 20 weeks until the appetite spontaneously recurs.

Because of this, owners of cats whose extra pounds result from highly palatable people food and treats should monitor their pets carefully if they choose to make a total dietary switch. Cats who refuse the new food may do better fed less of the usual fare, with the owner gradually deleting any nonnutritional ele-ments of the diet over time.

"But what if the cat keeps pestering the owner like Wilma did?" Vic asks. "That's why we tried that reducing diet."

Two techniques can help here. You can fool some cats into thinking they're getting the same amount of food by setting up mealtimes in such a way that it takes the animal the same amount of time to eat a lesser amount. When the Boudens distribute a lesser amount of Wilma's dry food in an assortment of paper bags spread throughout the house, they gain two benefits:

- She doesn't notice she's getting fed less.
- She gets more exercise.

Owners who feed canned food can achieve the same effect by adding water to a lesser amount of food or sprinkling it among a collection of empty plastic containers in a plastic dishpan.

A second approach involves a technique I call confuse-a-cat in which the owner offers the cat less than the usual amount of food but in *more* meals. Thus, the cat accustomed to getting fed twice a day gets fed four to six times instead. For some animals the change in schedule suffices to distract them from the fact that they're getting less.

What about treats? First, as far as rewarding animals for doing tricks with treats, we know that once an animal learns a new behavior, inconsistent rewards *reinforce* the display, so there's no sound behavioral reason to give a treat every time. Second, if the treats carry such a strong emotional charge (more on this later) that the *owner* can't give them up, then setting aside some of the cat's regular food for this purpose will enable the owner to continue the practice without adding to the cat's weight. Third, because animals often learn and internalize lessons more quickly when given a choice, allowing the cat to choose between a low-calorie treat such as a tiny piece of shredded lettuce or carrot or nothing may induce some cats to give up begging. However, if they choose to keep begging, at least the offering doesn't add much in the way of calories.

Another feline nutritional idiosyncrasy concerns those premium diets that boast less stool production. While that sounds wonderful to owners who hate to clean the litter box, these more-concentrated diets may constipate some cats. When Charlie becomes constipated and requires medical care, the expense and inconvenience of treating him obliterates any litter box advantages the food offers.

If you own or are considering a purebred cat, the best source of information regarding any dietary idiosyncrasies remains a knowledgeable breeder and others who own similar cats. Regardless of whether the cat comes from a top-of-the-line breeder or a junkyard litter, the first question shouldn't be, "What should I feed this cat?" but rather, "What has this cat been eating?" A basic rule of nutrition maintains that nothing is nutritional if the animal won't eat it, and this holds particularly true for cats. By keeping your pet's wild and domestic roots as well as any individual food-related quirks in mind when you select or change a feline feeding program, you can avoid many feline food-related problems.

Think about what and how you feed your cat strictly as it relates to the animal.

## The Feline Factor

Once again, summon the image of any food-related interactions you experience with your cat on an average day or weekend. This time, however, focus your attention on the cat. Does it appear excited, anxious, or disinterested in food? Does it nibble or gulp its food? If you own more than one cat, how are their food preferences and feeding styles similar? How do they differ?

"From the beginning we noticed that Fred and Wilma didn't approach food the same way, but we never put it in the context of their different needs," Tammy admits as she studies her notes. "It seemed both natural and right to feed them both the same way when we got them."

"They both used to pig out when we first got them," Vic adds, "but as they got older Fred became more of a nibbler."

Vic describes a feeding pattern not uncommon in multiple-cat households where the cats maintain a more social than solitary existence. While Wilma claimed a small space in her owners' bedroom as her own, Fred staked out the rest of the house, and patrolling it took a fair amount of time and energy. The only place Wilma could "dominate" occurred at the food dishes where she ate not only her own food, but also any tidbits Fred left.

"We realized that, too," Tammy declares. "But it's darn hard to keep one cat out of another's food."

Feeding the cats in separate rooms at specific times offers the simplest solution when cats in the same household experience different dietary needs. Owners who prefer something a bit more high-tech might consider the SmartBowl, which works on the same principle as those cat doors that admit only the cat wearing a special collar. In this case, all the other cats in the household wear a collar that causes the bowl to emit a high-pitched irritating sound, whereas the collarless individual who requires the special diet can approach it with no problem.

Carole's reflections on Charlie's feeding practices yield quite different results.

"When I got Charlie, the breeder gave me a long list of things she said I should feed him to keep him healthy," she reports. "I couldn't be bothered with that, plus my veterinarian said it was excessive, so I gradually weaned him off them. Now I think I ought to broaden his selection, but I'm not sure how to do that. According to the breeder his line suffers from a sensitive gut."

Cats locked in to one diet for a long time should be offered any new ones very gradually. Although the rule of thumb for dogs says to mix one-quarter of the new with three-quarters of the old for a week, then mix half new with half old the second week, then three-quarters of the new with one-quarter of the old the third week, then all of the new diet the fourth, the process might take much longer for a cat. I know of one owner who had to introduce new foods to her cat in eighth-teaspoon weekly increments over several months. If she tried to substitute any more than that, the animal rejected the entire bowl.

Once we figure out the feline factors, we need to analyze what role a particular cat's environment plays in its feeding program.

## The Feline Café

By now the idea that how comfortably a cat may eat and drink depends on how comfortable it feels in its territory should come as no surprise.

"But how do you know if a cat isn't eating for medical reasons rather than behavioral ones?" Vic asks. "We thought Wilma wasn't eating because she didn't like the food, which I think was true at first, but then she developed horrible medical problems, too."

Like urinary problems, problems related to feline digestion—such as hepatic lipidosis, recurrent vomiting, diarrhea, or constipation—increasingly earn the label "idiopathic," which means we don't know the cause. When we don't know what causes a problem, the best approach involves covering all the physical, behavioral, and bond bases. Fortunately, our cats often give us clues, so we need only train ourselves to look for them.

Consider these quite different behaviors, all of which the Boudens might sum up by using the phrase "Wilma's not eating." In the *first*, Wilma ignores her food completely. Not only won't she walk from her bed in the living room to her bowl in the kitchen, but she also ignores the food when the Boudens take it to her. In the *second* situation, Wilma goes to the food, puts her head down as if she might eat, then she backs off. In the *third*, she picks up a bit of food, then drops it and wanders away. In the *fourth*, she tries to cover her food with a dish cloth that fell on the floor.

The first behavior occurs in cats who feel so sick that they don't even want to think about eating, such as animals with high fevers or in a lot of pain. The second pattern often arises in cats with upper respiratory problems. Because cat food doesn't make noise or move, the animal must depend on its sense of smell to stimulate its appetite. A stuffed-up nose can effectively knock out that source of stimulation. Throw in a sore throat that causes the cat discomfort when it bends its head down to eat, and it will give up. On the other hand, offer these cats some smelly canned food warmed to room temperature, thinned with water and elevated on a box so they can lap it up without bending their necks, and many of them will begin to eat immediately.

If a cat acts as if it wants to eat, picks the food up, then drops it, think about tooth, gum, tongue, or other mouth problems. In this third situation, the cat can both receive and process the stimuli that trigger its appetite, but the pain it experiences when it tries to alleviate its hunger terminates the response.

Attempts to hide the food—the fourth behavior—harken back to the wild animal's habit of caching. Leopards rank as the most familiar feline cachers, dragging their kill into trees so that other animals can't steal it. Hospitalized or kenneled animals may shred the paper lining their cages and/or any bedding and use this to cover their food. Unlike the other noneating cats, these animals clearly communicate that the environment, not their health or the food, keeps them from eating.

"I can see a cat doing that in a veterinary hospital or kennel," Carole admits. "But what would make it cache its food at home?"

Anything that the cat considers a territorial violation may lead to food caching at home. Some owners report it happens only when certain people come to visit. In these cases, the cats merely try to hide their food until the intruder goes away and they can eat in peace. Animals who feel truly threatened, however, will urinate on their food.

More commonly, though, we see a variation of caching in multiple-cat households that usually involves treats, such as pieces of meat, rather than the cats' usual food. Although Fred and Wilma appear to get along wonderfully, when Tammy puts some scraps of turkey in their bowls, Wilma immediately snatches hers and disappears under the couch with it. Whether the odor and texture of these foods trigger this behavior or the cat perceives these particular offerings as worth hiding remains open to debate.

Cats who flip their food or water out of the bowl and eat it off the floor also should lead owners to conduct an environmental analysis. As mentioned, bowls with rims that stimulate pressure-sensitive whisker tips may trigger this behavior. Likewise, cats unwilling to lower their heads or turn their backs on other cats or perceived threats in the environment may react in this manner.

Regardless of how enchanting the behavior may be, we can't ignore the fact that cats who bury, flip, or cart off their food do so not to entertain us but rather because something about the feeding environment troubles them. For some cats, simply moving the food and water bowls away from the wall so they can eat facing out will solve the problem. Others may prefer their own private space for dining. While free-access crates can provide the necessary privacy, owners who keep these in their bedrooms can become lax about keeping bowls clean and changing water frequently enough. Under those circumstances, an upside-down cardboard box with a cat-sized opening cut in one side tucked into a quiet corner of the kitchen makes a convenient private dining room.

If dogs, kids, and other cats bully your cat while it tries to eat, by all means do everything in your power to stop this behavior. However, while you're training the miscreants, feed your cat in a separate room. The last thing Charlie's sensitive gut needs is for Carole to scream, "Don't bother the cat!" at her niece every two minutes while Charlie is trying to eat.

How many stars would you give your household as a feline eatery?

---

## Feeding Environment Evaluation

Examine the places where any food-related activities occur or will occur with your cat(s). How accessible are these areas for your cat? How much privacy do they afford your pet? Can you easily clean these areas? How often do you clean them and your pet's bowls?

"I was doing pretty well until I got to that last question," Carole reports with a laugh. "Charlie eats in a quiet nook in the kitchen, away from the door and appliances where he might be disturbed. And I have vinyl flooring and washable walls, so keeping it clean poses no problem." Carole pauses long enough to look at Charlie sheepishly. "But because he eats dry food, I honestly can't remember the last time I washed his dish."

Although the Boudens find Carole's confession horrifying, they admit to a few environmental failings themselves.

"I can see now how we chose Wilma's and Fred's eating areas to meet our needs rather than theirs," Tammy admits. "We enjoy watching them eat, so we put their bowls right next to the table."

"Where there's always something going on," Vic adds.

While this feeding area led Fred and Wilma to beg for table food, other cats who find the human mealtime activities stressful may vomit or experience diarrhea. Obviously, providing more serene surroundings can help make these animals feel more comfortable. Serene or not, the presence of the Bouden cats' feeding area so close to their owners' definitely made it easier for Vic and Tammy to project their own food-related beliefs on their pets.

## Food from the Master's Table

Even though anthropomorphic beliefs permeate all levels of the human-feline relationship, they seem more glaringly obvious when related to food. I will never forget how mortified I felt when I discovered that the producer of a live television show had assigned me the role of a *judge* in a fat cat contest. How could these seemingly intelligent and caring people glorify one of the most heartbreaking feline problems?

Needless to say, I declined the honor. When I explained my reasons to the producer, she immediately understood. She didn't hate cats or wish them the least bit ill. She just got so caught up in the notion of a fat cat as a symbol of the good life that it never dawned on her that this didn't comprise a positive experience for a cat at all.

While we never hear of fat dog or canary contests, owners of pets of all species may fall victim to the belief that stuffing a pet with human food is the right thing to do. Cat owners, though, get an extra nudge in this direction thanks to their pets' recent domestication and food preference. When we watch nature films of African wild dogs or wolves bringing down wildebeests or caribou, few of us make any connection between those wild canines and the poodle sleeping on the couch beside us. Moreover, most dog owners will never see their pets kill another animal, let alone eat it, and those relatively few who do often view it as "problem" behavior and try to stop it.

Compare this with cats, most of whom will hunt at the drop of a hat if given half a chance. Even owners of the most sheltered cats harbor no illusions about what their cats would hunt and eat outdoors. Not only do we know what they'd eat if left to their own devices, but more to the point *we don't like it*. So, unlike members of other species who may wind up on human food because their owners don't know what their pets should eat, cats may wind up on human food because their owners *do* know.

"But none of the cat foods contain mice, birds, and all of the other things outdoor cats eat," Vic quite correctly notes.

However, for anthropomorphic owners seeking to put as much distance between themselves and their cats' predatory roots as possible, the whole idea of a *natural* cat food strikes a negative chord because they don't want to think about their pets' natural diet.

As long as owners realize this and provide a food that meets their pets' nutritional needs some other way, no problems arise. However, anthropomorphic owners who don't realize this may succumb to advertisements that portray cat foods as human foods, complete with china and crystal. "If feeding a cat something that looks like a human food is good," they rationalize, "then feeding real human food must be even better."

Anthropomorphic feeding rituals can cause as many problems for cats as their owners' anthropomorphic beliefs about cat food. When Fred and Wilma were young kittens, their natural instincts would have led them to respond to Vic and Tammy in a loving manner, so no need existed for their owners to reward them with food treats for this behavior. Nonetheless, that's how the Boudens believed *they* would want to be treated if they were cats. Similarly, when Fred and Wilma first displayed the retrieving behavior, they didn't connect this behavior to food at all. The owners, not the cats, linked food to this charming display. Unlike the Boudens, many owners of retrieving cats reward the behavior with nothing more than praise or petting.

Because of the cat's tendency to internalize early experiences so strongly, owners should initiate only diet and feeding rituals that they can implement throughout the cat's life. Don't wind up like the owner who cooked for her cat and evolved such a complex feeding ritual that the cat not only wound up on an unbalanced diet, but it wouldn't even eat that for anyone else.

Before reading on, think about how any anthropomorphic views you maintain could affect what and how you feed your cat.

## Anthropomorphic Checkup

Again, review your notes about the ideal cat food. If you picked it because you think your cat would like it, was this based on your knowledge of cats in general and your cat in particular? Or was it based on your feelings about what you'd like to eat if you were a cat?

"We definitely took an anthropomorphic view of what and how we fed Fred and Wilma," Vic readily admits. "They were so tiny when we got them, it was hard not to think of them as babies."

"I thought their food looked so dull, so I'd give them some of our dinner instead, telling myself it had to be better than that stuff," Tammy confesses. "I didn't give a thought to whether what I was feeding was a balanced diet at all. All I knew was that it looked and smelled better *to me*."

"No wonder you got into so much trouble," Carole tells the Boudens. "If you just put the food down and let the cats eat what they want, you wouldn't have had any problems. Cats can take care of themselves."

That sounds like good advice, but such chattel views can cause owners problems, too.

## The Self-Feeding Cat

While I know of no data to prove this, I suspect that for every cat who gets into food-related problems thanks to its owner's anthropomorphic views, we can find one whose problems trace back to the owner's chattel orientation. Recall how, when the Boudens decided to get the excess weight off Wilma for her own good, they switched from an anthropomorphic to a chattel orientation. While they initially anthropomorphically attributed her failure to eat the food to her stubbornness and a desire to make them feel guilty, they then assumed a chattel orientation, telling themselves that she wouldn't make herself sick, so they needn't worry about it.

Busy owners who feed free-choice (always available) dry food may submit as easily to chattel food-related beliefs as those who opt for home cooking may succumb to anthropomorphic views. Carole looks like a human whirlwind as she gets ready to go to work in the morning. She dumps the food in Charlie's bowl after she starts the coffee and before she showers. Evenings and weekends, the cat spends much of his time with her. If asked how much he eats and when, she hasn't a clue. Although she loves her pet and selected what she considered the best food for him, once she did that she placed no emotional charge on the feeding process whatsoever.

Like anthropomorphic views, chattel views appear to work quite well until they result in problems. When Charlie begins to gain weight at middle age, Carole doesn't know where to begin. She can't feed him less of his regular food because she has no idea how much he eats. Nor can she can gauge the correct amount of some low-caloried diet. Even if she did, what if he started eating her plants or tearing things up in her absence because he still felt hungry?

"But I don't have the time to play 'confuse-a-cat' or use any of those other weight-reduction tricks, either," she moans.

In this situation, Carole's choice to dissociate herself from her pet's feeding program results in problems that will cause her to think of little else.

Recall any chattel tendencies you discovered about yourself in Chapter 4 and apply them to your ideas about feline foods and feeding rituals.

## Chattel Check

Summon the image of the ideal cat food and feeding ritual, this time with an eye toward picking up any chattel elements in it. Do you detect any? If you do, where do they occur? When do they occur—all the time or just under certain circumstances? When could a chattel orientation enhance your feeding program? When could it detract from it?

Even though Vic and Tammy approach feeding quite differently from Carole, all three owners discover that they lean toward the chattel approach when they want to avoid some aspect of the process rather than because they believe it best meets their cats' needs.

"We wanted to believe that it was okay that Wilma wasn't eating her food because we couldn't bear the thought that she might be ill," Tammy explains.

"And I fed Charlie the way I did because I didn't have time to regulate what he ate, let alone change his diet," Carole volunteers.

Compare these chattel views with those that would lead Vic and Tammy to ignore their young kittens' pleas for treats and table food. In the latter case, a chattel orientation could have saved these owners and their pets a lot of problems.

One final note to remind you how owner orientations can flip-flop and complicate human-feline relationship. Granted, the Boudens' anthropomorphic views led to Wilma's obesity, but their chattel views set her up for a serious illness, the recovery from which relies on the veterinarian's success at getting the cat to eat again. In a matter of days, the owners go from praying their fat cat won't eat to praying she will. In the meantime, their concern about Wilma leads them to ignore Fred much of the time. What happens when they realize what they're doing?

"My immediate reaction was to fix him something special to eat because that's what I do when Vic and I are down in the dumps," Tammy confesses solemnly. "But then I picked him up and hugged him instead."

Once again we see that the issue isn't the rightness or wrongness of a particular view, but rather whether it springs from emotion or solid knowledge of the cat's needs. The same holds true for any time limits we may apply to the feeding process.

## Time to Eat

Most cat owners don't give much thought to the timing of their pets' meals until something goes wrong. The Boudens and Carole maintained their quite different feline feeding schedules based on what worked for them. When problems arose, though, their concern about these problems took up a great deal of their time. For the Boudens, that meant coping with a complete upheaval in their schedule until Wilma finally began eating on her own, not to mention all the time it took to implement a more healthy feeding program. On the other hand, when Charlie begins to gain weight on his free-choice feeding schedule, Carole anguishes over how she can make any changes because she spends so little time at home.

So, what to do? While prevention always pays, it really pays in the feeding arena. I used to embrace the theory of free-choice feeding, and I still do like it for single animals capable of regulating their own weight. However, I find that fewer and fewer cats fall into this category. Consequently, a combination of a *measured* amount of dry food left down and two feedings of canned food per day appears to be the best across-the-board approach for most cats and owners.

This schedule confers three benefits. First, owners know exactly how much their pets are eating, a valuable clue to the animal's health. Second, because the odor and texture of canned food tend to appeal to most cats more than dry, owners who work or spend a lot of time away from home can use this appeal as another indicator of the pet's well-being. If Wilma always eats all of her canned food immediately, Vic and Tammy will immediately notice when she doesn't. By the same token, when Fred uncharacteristically starts gobbling his food and looking for more, that will set off alarm bells, too. Third, this schedule makes it easier to institute dietary changes because owners know exactly when and how much food the cat eats and therefore can come up with a feeding regimen that meets the pet's specific needs.

"That's all well and good, but what can I do to get the weight off Charlie now?" Carole wants to know. "I'd die if he got as sick as Wilma."

In the past, owners in Carole's position had only two choices. They could put down a smaller amount of the cat's regular food or the prescribed amount of a therapeutic one and hope it satisfied the cat until they got home, or they could ask a neighbor to come in and feed the cat small amounts during the day. In general, the latter approach worked better because the distraction posed by the arrival and departure of the cat feeder helped take the animal's mind off its diminished food supply.

Thanks to high-tech cat lovers, two other options now exist. The first, the Cat Mate Automatic Feeder, serves up to five meals at preset times. It even contains two ice packs so you can offer canned as well as dry food, a good way to both intrigue and confuse a chubby feline. The PetJoy Automatic Feeder expands on this concept. At the owner-designated times, an electric motor lowers the food bowl and fills it with the desired amount of dry food *and* plays the owner's prerecorded message twice. One hour later, it raises the bowl and empties any uneaten food back into the reservoir.

While these and other manual and automatic feeders can help time-crunched owners, two caveats apply:

- Never rely on this method until you're positive your pet is using it without any apprehension.
- Keep track of how much food you put into it and when.

While Charlie sees his talking automatic feeder as the best cat toy ever invented, the mere sight of it might make Fred dive under the couch.

Think about your schedule and how it might affect your pet's eating habits.

## Feeding Time Check

Review any time limits you noted in Chapter 4. How do they influence how and when you feed your cat? If you leave food down at all times, do you know when and how much your pet eats?

Once again the Boudens realize how their own views about the "right" time to eat their own meals affected when they fed their pets. However, they also picked up a different pattern, one that Carole noticed too.

"If we have a lot of company, Fred hardly eats anything," Tammy reports. "But I'll see him at his dish after they go."

"Every once in a while I hear Charlie crunching away in the middle of the night," Carole adds.

Indeed, some cats in stressful environments will eat more freely at night than during the day, something owners of animals with recurrent medical problems should keep in mind. In addition to providing these animals with a private eating space, supplying them with fresh food and water right before you go to bed might meet their needs much better than feeding them when you get home from work.

All this talk of special diets and automatic feeders raises the obvious question: How much does it cost to feed a cat?

## Picking Up the Tab

In a nutritional nutshell, you can pay anywhere from less than a quarter to more than a dollar for a can of cat food. Dry foods run about 50¢ per pound and up.

"That's not very specific," Carole points out. "Can you at least say that I'll get what I pay for?"

Unfortunately, I can't. First, by taking advantage of sales, coupons, and manufacturers' promotions, careful shoppers can get some of the more expensive foods relatively cheaply. Second, sometimes the more expensive products capitalize on owners' fears more than solid nutrition. Foods that guarantee to acidify Charlie's urine will help him only if he's prone to urinary problems that can be thwarted by that state. If not, the extra cost of the food gains Carole nothing and may cost her if it promotes problems related to acid urine. Third, as noted, even the highest-quality commercial, therapeutic, or home-cooked diet won't benefit your pet if the animal won't eat the food or it doesn't meet its needs. Fourth, a higher price may reflect advertising costs or those incurred when producing smaller amounts of a limited-edition product, rather than the price of higher-quality ingredients.

Buying in bulk also may cost rather than save you money. If you buy a case of mackerel canned food and your cat develops an allergy to it after the sixth can, you're out the cost of the other cans (unless you can sell them to some other cat owner) as well as the cost of veterinary treatment. As an alternative, you may be able to find a service-oriented grocer who will sell you a case of mixed varieties, a real advantage for cat owners. Buying dry food in bulk offers the additional problem of providing proper storage. Transferring the food to a plastic container with a secure lid not only will help maintain the food's freshness, but also will protect it from curious kids, cats, and other animals in the household.

When buying in bulk, and especially if the price seems too good to be true, be certain to check the date of manufacture and shelf life. Most products have a shelf life of a year, but some of the so-called natural ones without preservatives may last only four to six months. Stores often lower the price of products nearing their expiration dates in an effort to move them. That poses no problem if your 10 cats can consume the food in that shorter span. However, if it takes six months for Charlie to eat all the food Carole bought for half price because its dating expired at the end of a month, that's no bargain.

If you want to cook for your cat, be sure to add $100 to $150 for a good feline nutrition text, such as Case, Carey, and Hirakawa's *Canine and Feline Nutrition* (Mosby, 1995) and several cat cookbooks. Also, depending on the recipe, don't forget to add the cost of any vitamin, mineral, and other supplements necessary to meet the cat's requirements to the cost of the other ingredients.

You can offer your cat food and water in dishes from your own set ($0) or buy special kitty dinnerware. The former offers the added advantage that you can switch from a cereal to a soup bowl or even a salad plate if your cat wants more whisker room. Plastic dishes tend to cost the least (around $1.25 to $1.75), but I'd recommend paying the additional dollar or so for skidproof ones. Although your cat might not mind eating from a moving bowl, this spreads out any meal-related debris, makes noise that some owners find disturbing (especially at night!), may scratch your floors, and increases the probability that someone will stumble over the dish. If you prefer a combination food and water bowl, add anywhere from $1 to $5 to the price. Bear in mind that these can make changing the water a hassle if the cat prefers to snack rather than eat all of its food at one sitting.

Consider stainless steel or ceramic dishes for cats prone to allergies. The former cost about the same as good-quality plastic or polymer bowls. Because ceramic lends itself more to the whims of cat lovers, bowls in this category range from $3.50 for one decorated with paw prints to color-coordinated food and water bowls with a matching place mat for about $20. Also, while that antique bowl might seem like the perfect food dish for little Sneezums, stay away from ceramics of unknown origin whose paints or glazes may contain lead or other harmful substances.

If your cat prefers to eat at a level above the floor, it won't cost you anything to put its feeding dishes on a cardboard box or upside-down cake pan or pot. However, if you can't guarantee the stability of such a homemade system or feel the need to whisk the pot or pan away for your own mealtime preparations, spend the $6 or so for a wall-mounted dish such as the Corner Diner.

Within the high-tech realm, the SmartBowl for cats on special diets costs about $45, as does the Drinkwell water fountain.

The simplest gravity-fed feeders and waterers cost between $5 and $10. Programmable ones that allow you to regulate both the timing and amount of food range from $40 to more than $250, depending on their features.

If you want your cat to enjoy safe access to its food and water outdoors, consider spending about $30 for Le Pet Cafe. When the pet steps on the treadle plate in front of the bowls, the clear plastic shield covering them lifts up. Owners of housebound cats who dislike the odor of canned cat food might also appreciate this dinnerware option. Several manufacturers offer automatic waterers in the $25 to $35 range, all of which hook up to a hose. Bear in mind that, while these products are sound in principle, cats might not accept them as readily as dogs for two reasons. One, the shape of the bowl might put them off. Two, the water level might need to drop too low before triggering the refilling mechanism to meet some cats' needs. An inexpensive (less than $10) device called the Lixit Dog Waterer screws onto a water faucet or garden hose. When the dog licks it, it releases the flow of water. While the device is labeled for dogs, the distributor I spoke to claims that cats can trigger it, too.

Can you afford to feed your pet in a style that pleases you both?

## Balancing the Feeding Budget

Recall any financial limits you placed on your relationship with your cat. Can you afford the kinds of foods and/or feeding accessories you feel would benefit your cat? If not, can you free up these additional funds somewhere else?

"All in all, I think it's safe to say that we spent a lot more than we needed to to create problems that cost us even more to solve," Tammy decides after she tallies up the cost of all the food and food-related items as well as the resultant veterinary expenses that played such an important part in the Boudens' relationship with Fred and Wilma.

Carole fared much better and even found herself looking forward to purchasing a few high-tech items to fulfill Charlie's food-related needs.

"I never realized something as mundane as feeding the cat could be so emotional, though," she remarks after she completes the exercise.

Indeed, feeding the cat probably ranks as one of the most emotional human-feline interactions.

# A Loving Spoonful

A friend once asked if it would be possible for me to talk about feeding pets without ranting about all the problems that arise when owners equate love with food. In a word, no, because too many animals succumb to the effects of this human emotional connection. Such food-equals-love thinking leads people to stuff their cats like Christmas turkeys; after all, the fatter the cat, the more loved. This belief remains so firmly entrenched in our society despite all of the data arguing against it that it surely reflects something far deeper.

Consider the Boudens. They obviously didn't set out to kill their cat with kindness. In fact, they were ambushed by some very old as well as some very contemporary food-related emotions. Enter their home and you barely say hello before Tammy or Vic offers you something to eat or drink, a carryover from the days when people might walk miles to visit each other. However, just as the adult wildcat's kitten-saving retrieving ability yielded to Wilma's retrieving toys for fat-laden treats, the original, very practical and health-sustaining reasons behind offering guests food gave way to a potentially unhealthy ritual.

In addition to succumbing to this age-old urge to offer food to signal our hospitality, working contemporary pet owners fall into the guilt trap. No matter what problem befalls Wilma and Fred, Tammy believes it wouldn't have happened if she or Vic had been home. She knows this is totally irrational, but she also knows that's how she feels. Because she doesn't like the way the guilt makes her feel, she seeks to dissipate it by offering her pets food to atone for her absence. She rationalizes this by saying, "Everyone knows a cat who eats well is healthy."

Thus, the food she offers her cats provides three emotional benefits:

- It demonstrates her love.
- It alleviates her guilt.
- It proves her pets' health.

Given all this, we can see why trying to get the weight off fat cats can prove as traumatic for owners as for their pets. If the owners feel inadequate to begin with and we take away what they consider the best way to communicate love, the whole relationship crumbles. Consequently, in order for any dietary changes to work, owners must replace these beliefs with something else— a task that proves so daunting for some that they simply can't do it.

"That's terrible!" Carole exclaims. "How could anyone be so selfish."

"It's not that simple," Vic protests. "The first time Fred retrieved his ball and I didn't feed him, I felt like a rat. Even when he purred and batted my hand for more petting when I petted him, I felt I should be doing more. It took a good six weeks for that feeling to pass."

None of this means you shouldn't experience joy when you feed your pet. It just means that your joy should come from your awareness that you're meeting your pet's nutritional and food-related behavioral needs to the best of your ability. Put another way, the joy should spring from solid knowledge: it shouldn't replace it. As in all other aspects of cat ownership, when it comes to feeding programs, love can't and won't conquer all unless it's grounded in knowledge.

What emotions do you attach to feeding your pet?

---

## Psyching Out the Server

**Recall any emotions you experience when you offer your pet food. Do you feel better about feeding premium versus regular food? Does people food seem more special than cat food? Does guilt play any role in your feeding process?**

Carole begins chuckling the instant she reads the exercise.

"I thought my emotions didn't affect what I fed Charlie at all," she confesses. "But that's not true. I buy that food because it makes *me* feel better, not because it meets his needs. And even though I don't feed treats like Vic and Tammy, I'll fill his bowl extra full if I'm going to get home later than usual."

Fortunately, when the Boudens also realize how much their emotions dictated what and how they fed their pets, they vow to make the necessary changes.

"We just have to keep reminding ourselves that Fred and Wilma know we love them even if we don't feed them," Tammy explains as the two cats chase each other gleefully around their owners' home three months after Wilma's near-fatal illness. "It's not their problem. It's ours."

Considering the amount of emotional agony that feeding the cat can cause some owners, it's good to know that any owner physical limitations seldom create problems.

# Crunchie Chin-Ups

Aside from lugging cat food and fat cats around, feline feeding doesn't put much of a physical strain on most owners. However, your beliefs about your own physical fitness and health can definitely influence what you feed your cat. For example, if the Boudens routinely ate rodents or a nice variety of cat food, it wouldn't matter if they shared their food with their pets. Although this sounds ludicrous, feline nutritional requirements sufficiently differ from human ones that owners can't afford to make the connection, "What's good for me is good for my cat."

Many times health-conscious owners become so focused on phrases such as "all natural" or "no preservatives" that they lose sight of what the food contains relative to the cat's nutritional needs. Several very expensive diets and recipes for home cooking boast ingredients that seem more designed to meet the needs of the owner than a newly domesticated carnivore. As one knowledgeable breeder put it, "Better the owners should eat the food themselves and let the cat fend for itself!"

Also, owners with physical disabilities that they believe undermine the quality of their relationship with their pet may succumb to food-equals-love beliefs. When Carole winds up in bed with the flu for a week, she feels so guilty about ignoring Charlie that she feeds him foods she never would feed him under normal circumstances. While her illness results in only a temporary dietary lapse for her pet, cat owners with chronic ailments may need to deal with this side effect daily. Because few bond issues can rival the dilemma posed by those who claim that feeding the cat constitutes one of an impaired loved one's few joys in life, it makes sense to link expressions of love to some other activity such as game playing or grooming.

How might your own health affect your cat's?

---

## Owner Physical Feeding Checkup

Mentally review your own physical history as well as any problems that might crop up in the years ahead with your pet. How do your own food preferences affect what you feed your cat? If you feel under the weather, does this affect what and how you feed your pet? In what ways?

Once again, the Boudens and Carole come down on opposite sides of the fence.

"We're pretty much meat and potatoes and apple pie," Vic
elaborates. "While Fred and Wilma didn't eat everything we ate,
it wasn't because we didn't offer it to them. Tammy and I are
both very healthy and active, so it seemed like a natural thing to
do, since we wanted the cats to be healthy and active, too.
Besides, even though we now realize our food became a very big
part of their diets, in the beginning we only thought of it as
upgrading their cat food. Then our emotions got all tangled up
in it, and we were sunk."

"I'm very careful about what I eat, and I probably would have
cooked for Charlie if I'd had more time," Carole explains. "All
the chemicals in much of today's food concern me, and I rarely
eat meat. I know I definitely feel better for the changes I made
in my own diet. My mistake was believing that we know as much
about feline as human nutrition. What I considered an all-natural
product wasn't necessarily natural for him."

Even though these loving owners took quite opposite views
of their own dietary needs, they erred equally when they pro-
jected these views onto their pets.

Given all of the complexities involved in the simple phrase
"feeding the cat," can any basic guidelines sustain busy owners
who want to do the best for their pets?

## A Recipe for Success

In spite of the fact that owners routinely may flip-flop from
anthropomorphic to chattel orientations and apply varying limits to food-related interactions with their cats, most people define
their response as one or another. The Boudens saw mealtime as
one of the most special times they spent with Fred and Wilma.

"Tammy and I both work, and our lives are pretty hectic, but
we always made a special effort to eat dinner together as often

as possible," Vic explains. "Because Fred and Wilma are so much a part of our lives, it was only natural that we'd include them."

Compare the Boudens' ritualistic approach to mealtimes with Carole's more mechanical view.

"I rarely ever sit down and eat a meal myself, and even though I only eat healthy food, I honestly don't give much thought to the process of eating," she says as she munches an apple while she opens her mail. "I can't imagine making a big deal out of mealtimes."

The irony is that even though these two orientations and their resultant feline diets differed considerably, in both cases the feeding practices reflected the owner's rather than the cat's needs.

While I normally take an "If it isn't broken, don't fix it" attitude toward interactions that appear to work, I do believe that feline nutrition poses so many complex and variable problems that it behooves owners to recognize how what they feed their pets may affect the animals' health.

Similarly, the environment (territory) may so strongly influence a cat's food and water consumption that all owners, especially those of housebound pets, also must consider how the physical setting and any human-feline relationships and related feeding rituals in the household may enhance or undermine the feeding process. Because deficiencies in either of these areas may lead to serious health and/or behavioral problems, it makes sense for owners to make the necessary changes in their own beliefs, then gradually change the cat to a more healthy diet and feeding ritual.

For owners who believe they can't find some way other than food to express love for their pets, I can only say, don't feel guilty about it. Guilt will only complicate matters. On the other hand, don't boast about it, either, because people who are aware of normal feline nutritional needs and the problems associated with overweight cats don't consider such feeding practices loving at all.

The basic guideline when selecting a diet and creating a feeding ritual can be summed up in one word: knowledge. By feeding your pet a varied nutritionally balanced diet that meets its nutritional needs and using a ritual that works for your pet and you under a wide range of circumstances (including your absence), you can make feeding your cat a picnic for both of you.

All this talk of urinary tract problems and obesity naturally raises the issue of what to do when Puff gets sick: Call the veterinarian? Reach for a book? Pull out the herbs? Or hope Puff gets better on his own? The next chapter will discuss these and other medical issues facing contemporary cat owners.

# 9

# Prevention and Cure

## *Formulating a Feline Health-Care Plan*

Toby and Lisa Buchanan and their children immediately fall in love with the bedraggled orange tiger who shows up on their porch in the middle of a blizzard. A few good meals, a strong dose of love, and some of Lisa's herbal remedies and he soon looks as good as new.

"That cat's as tough as nails," Toby boasts to his neighbor Clark Gilman as the newly christened Butch prowls the yard. "Doesn't look at all like yours, does he?"

Clark nods his head in agreement as he mentally compares the battle-scarred young tom sporting the notched ear with his svelte female Sphinx, Delta.

Over the years, the Buchanans and Clark take quite different approaches to feline health care. If anything happens to Butch, the Buchanans take a wait-and-see approach or Lisa uses her herbal remedies. One sneeze from Delta, on the other hand, and Clark whisks her off to Mountainview Veterinary Hospital, a state-of-the-art veterinary facility 30 miles away.

"That's what you get for owning a naked cat in Minnesota," Toby teases his neighbor.

"Maybe I should have learned more about the breed before I got her, but I was living in Florida at the time and didn't give it much thought," Clark admits candidly. "All I can say now is, thank God I have health insurance for her."

Toby stares at his neighbor dumbfounded, then begins to laugh until tears run down his face.

"You have health insurance for a cat?" he asks when he regains some semblance of composure. "I mean, I like Butch and all that, but he's just a cat."

"Well, I think it's a good idea in Delta's case," Lisa says in defense of Clark. "We certainly wouldn't need it, but I can see how it could come in handy with a rare breed like a Sphinx."

A month shy of his 13th birthday, Butch stops eating. Lisa tries every home remedy she can think of, but nothing works. After taking him to the veterinary clinic and then on to a specialist, they get the bad news.

"Butch's kidneys are failing, and the only chance of a cure is a transplant that will cost about $10,000 to $15,000 for everything," Lisa explains to Clark. "I have no idea how we're going to pay for it, but Toby insists we do it."

When Clark's mouth drops open in disbelief, Lisa immediately answers his unasked question.

"I know what Toby used to say, but things are different now," she continues. "His dad was just diagnosed with the same problem as Butch, and Toby can't deal with that right now."

---

As with cat foods, a new feline health-care option seems to crop up every day, promising all sorts of benefits for cat and owner alike. Fortunately, as different as these approaches may appear superficially, they all fall into one of two basic categories:

- traditional
- alternative

Traditional medicine represents the familiar "team in white" concept. In spite of its name, traditional medicine represents the more recent addition to the medical lineup, one springing from late-18th-century Western scientific thinking and technology. American veterinary education remains basically traditional, although increasing interest in alternative approaches among both the animal-owning pubic and veterinarians themselves gradually has resulted in an expansion of this view.

Alternative medicine applies to everything not considered traditional, such as acupuncture, homeopathy, chiropractic, and massage therapy. However, as more and more veterinarians incorporate alternatives in their medical repertoire, the term *complementary* rather than alternative has become more popular.

Books for cat owners who prefer a more traditional approach include Carlson's and Johnson's *Cat Owner's Home Veterinary Handbook* (Howell/Macmillan, 1995), McGinnis's *The Well Cat Book* (Random House, 1993), and Ackerman's *Owner's Guide to Cat Health* (T.H.F. Publications, 1996). Books with a more alternative slant include *Dr. Pitcairn's Complete Guide to Natural Health for Dogs and Cats* (Rodale, 1995), Stein's *Natural Remedies for Dogs and Cats* (Crossing Press, 1994), and Frazier's *The New Natural Cat* (Plume, 1990).

In addition to representing two different medical orientations, health-care programs also take two different approaches to maintaining health:

- problem oriented
- prevention and wellness centered

Problem-oriented programs focus on the sick individual, seeking to determine the cause of the problem and the best treatment for it. Prevention/wellness programs, on the other hand, focus on ways to keep an animal healthy. While both owners and veterinarians may lean in one direction or the other, they may opt for the opposite orientation in certain situations.

The Buchanans did just that. As for Clark, under normal circumstances he routinely bathes Delta to control the oiliness in her skin and prevent any problems. However, when his boss saddles him with a major last-minute assignment, he forgets all about her baths. Then, when she develops an infection, he focuses all of his attention on treating that problem. Clark likes Mountainview's Dr. Solomon because she shares his desire to prevent rather than treat problems. However, if Delta required surgery, he'd opt for her problem-oriented colleague, Dr. Jacobs.

Problem-oriented traditional books often tackle emergency situations, such as Bamberger's *Help! Quick Guide to First Aid for Your Cat* (Howell, 1994) or Hawcroft's *First Aid for Cats* (Howell/Macmillan, 1994). Others, such as *The Doctors Book of Home Remedies for Dogs and Cats* (edited by Matthew Hoffman, Rodale Press, 1996), briefly discuss numerous problems, while still others focus on specific body parts, such as Mellman's *Skin Diseases of Dogs and Cats* (Doral, 1994). Another group of books concentrates on specific life stages, such as Anderson's and Wrende's *Caring for Older Dogs and Cats* (Williamson, 1990), or specific medical problems, such as Simpson's *Management of Diabetes Mellitus* (Veterinary Behavior Development, 1994).

While many alternative texts take a problem-solving approach, most describe the use of one alternative method to treat an array of conditions. Examples of these texts include Levy's *The Complete Herbal Handbook for the Dog and Cat* (Faber and Faber, 1991), Brock's *How to Massage Your Cat* (Chronicle Books, 1992), and Schwartz's *Four Paws, Five Directions: A Guide to Chinese Medicine for Cats and Dogs* (Ten Speed Press, 1996).

Owners seeking a general overview of the world of animal health care might enjoy exploring the American Veterinary Medical Association's public Web site at http://www.avma.org/care4pets.htl. In addition to offering a wide range of pet health information, the site includes a children's area and a place where you can share comments about yourself and your pet.

Even though cat owners may take either a traditional or alternative, problem-oriented or preventive approach, depending on the particular situation, most favor one kind of medicine and approach to their pet's health. Consequently, recognizing any such preferences ranks as the first step to selecting the best health-care program for you and your cat.

## Health-Care Preferences Evaluation

Think about what you consider the ideal health-care program for your cat. Do you lean more toward traditional or alternative methods? Do you prefer to focus on problem solving or prevention?

When Toby performs this exercise, he discovers that he didn't think much about his pet's health-care program at all.

"Until Butch got sick," he adds ruefully. "Before then, I just figured he'd take care of himself like he always did."

Lisa, however, much prefers a problem-oriented alternative approach.

"I'm not much into special diets and supplements and all that preventive stuff," she admits. "But when Butch had bite wounds and other simple problems, I think the herbal remedies worked very well."

Clark rounds out the typical owner spectrum of health-care approaches.

"I'm a big fan of the latest science and technology, and I'd much rather prevent than treat problems," he declares with certainty. "However, if that didn't work for some reason, I'd try anything I thought would."

Given that veterinarians can maintain the same orientations as cat owners, as well as some very special orientations of their own, we need to take a closer look at the veterinary part of the health-care equation.

# Finding Dr. Right

Even though few owners give it much thought, every veterinary interaction consists of three components:

- the animal
- the owner
- the veterinarian

And while studies indicate that people take their animals to the most conveniently located veterinarian, that person might not always be the *best* practitioner for a particular owner/animal combination. As long as the animal remains healthy and well behaved, most owners will accept this trade-off. However, when problems arise, most regret they didn't put a little more effort into finding Dr. Right.

In addition to maintaining the same traditional/alternative, problem/prevention orientations as pet owners, veterinarians may assume one of three basic roles when interacting with clients and animals:

- god-player
- best friend
- facilitator

While most practitioners may don all of these professional hats on occasion, most prefer one on which they also tend to fall back in times of stress. Because this may include those times when the owner and/or the animal experiences the most serious problems, selecting a veterinarian whose approach relieves rather than adds to your own and your animal's stress can benefit everyone.

Many people associate god-players with traditional medicine. These veterinarians basically see their job as making the best possible diagnosis and prescribing the best possible treatment for the problem. They then expect you to do what they say and pay for it without question.

Although some owners blanch at what they consider a very patronizing approach, others like it because they lack both the time and the interest to become more deeply involved in the process. In other situations—such as when the animal becomes seriously ill or injured—owners may prefer a god-player because the event so overwhelms them that they want someone to take it out of their hands completely. Still other owners like the approach sometimes but not always. While Toby preferred Dr. Jacobs's god-player approach when Butch needed only routine care for a cut foot, he dislikes the veterinarian's reluctance to include the family in the treatment process when Butch becomes critically ill.

Compare Dr. Jacobs's approach with that of his colleague, Dr. Solomon. In her role as a best friend, Dr. Solomon asks Toby about his family, where he works, what hobbies he enjoys, and a host of other topics that he finds time-consuming and totally unrelated to his cat. On the other hand, the Buchanan children adore Dr. Solomon's friendliness and much prefer her to Dr. Jacobs.

Dr. McFadden, the third veterinarian in the practice, prefers the facilitator role, which gives owners a wide range of options to treat their pets' problems. Lisa prefers this approach because it takes into account her interest in alternatives as well as any fluctuations in the Buchanan family finances. However, when Delta succumbs to another skin problem and Clark sees the deadline for that big project looming on the horizon, he finds this approach maddening. He really doesn't care about the name of the particular bacteria causing *this* infection, or what makes antibiotic A different from B, C, and D. He just wants to get the medication and get out of there as quickly as possible.

Though evaluating a veterinarian in terms of these approaches may seem like a lot of work, in reality most owners automatically make such judgments. However, they do so primarily in terms of noting that they like this and don't like that, rather than with any awareness of why the veterinarian's approach appeals to or bothers them—or their pet—and what might better fit their needs.

Because most practitioners adopt a particular orientation based on the assumption that it works for their patients and clients, sometimes simply telling that person what you like and don't like can benefit the relationship enormously. When Lisa finally musters the nerve to tell Dr. Jacobs that his god-playing role makes the Buchanans feel isolated at a time they want and need to feel intimately involved in Butch's treatment, he apologizes profusely.

"I was so concerned about Butch" he explains. "Plus Toby never expressed much interest in what I did to Butch in the past."

Remember that you pay the veterinarian for his or her services and that, as an informed consumer, it's your responsibility to make your needs known. While a few veterinarians may claim clairvoyant as well as medical skills, most rely on their clients to tell them if their orientation creates problems. Owners who can't do so should consider selecting another veterinarian because the negative effects of a mismatched owner/animal/veterinarian combination will undermine even the simplest treatment.

Finally, cat owners in some areas also may opt to go to a veterinarian who specializes in cats. Just like other practitioners, these veterinarians may assume the same roles and maintain traditional or alternative views and problem or prevention orientations.

"What if you like the idea of a cat specialist, but you don't like that person's approach or don't feel you can communicate with him or her?" Clark asks.

The answer to that question lies in the answer to another: How much do you *want to* communicate? Given Delta's somewhat complex medical history and Clark's hectic schedule, probably no amount of specialized feline knowledge would compensate for a veterinarian's lack of communication skill. Compare Clark's ongoing veterinary relationship with that which arises between the Buchanans and the surgeon who would replace Butch's kidney. If the surgeon can't communicate, Dr. Jacobs or one of his colleagues can serve as an intermediary during the relatively brief period during which the surgeon will play an active part in Butch's care. On the other hand, if Clark can't easily communicate with the veterinarian responsible for every routine vaccination, physical examination, or skin problem Delta experiences, that could take its toll on this human-feline relationship—and thus her health—over the years.

"So, how do you know who's good?" Toby asks the question on every pet owner's mind.

Even though studies indicate that owners typically choose veterinarians based on location, discussions with other pet owners, shelter workers, groomers, and other animal-care folks can provide a wealth of information about the local veterinary population. If you maintain strong views about holistic or alternative approaches, contact the American Holistic Veterinary Medical Association (2214 Old Emmorton Road, Bel Air, MD 21014) for the names of practitioners in your area.

Because your cat relies or will rely on you and your veterinarian to fulfill its health-care needs, take a moment to think about what you consider the perfect veterinary relationship. Even if you don't own a cat yet, the exercise will help you recognize Dr. Right when you get your pet.

---

## Dr. Right Evaluation

Imagine taking your cat for a routine examination. How does your veterinarian respond to you and your pet? How would you like your veterinarian to treat you and your pet? Next imagine that your cat experiences some serious illness or injury. Does your veterinarian treat you and your pet the same way? How is it the same? How is it different? In either of these situations, what would you change? Have you discussed this with your veterinarian? If not, why not?

"It's tough looking at this after the fact," Lisa confesses. "But in retrospect, I wish Toby had taken Butch to see Dr. McFadden rather than Dr. Jacobs when he first got sick. I'm not saying that we wouldn't have done the same thing, but I would have felt a lot more comfortable knowing all our options up-front."

"I don't know if I agree with that," Toby counters. "I know I felt much better once we had more say in what happened to Butch, but at first I was so stunned when I realized how sick he was and how much he meant to me that I don't think I could have dealt with a bunch of options on top of everything else."

"I sort of agree with Toby," Clark adds. "I like Dr. Solomon's friendliness for routine stuff, and Dr. McFadden's options when Delta comes down with something not life-threatening that may require long-term treatment. But were she to get *really* sick, I think I'd prefer Dr. Jacobs's can-do attitude."

Fortunately, most veterinarians can and do adopt any one of these orientations, depending on what they perceive as the client's and/or animal's needs. However, like Dr. Jacobs, occasionally they do misread the situation. When that occurs, it's up to owners to make their wishes known. Just as a particular owner may respond differently to a particular veterinarian's orientation, the cat may, too. Because of this, we can't forget the four-legged component of the health-care issue.

## The Feline Patient

Even though cats outnumber dogs in the United States, fewer cats than dogs receive routine medical care. Does this mean that owners love their cats less? I doubt it. More likely the discrepancy arises from one myth and one reality. The myth maintains that cats can take care of themselves and thus don't need regular checkups and other health-care assistance the way dogs do. The reality, visible in practically any veterinary clinic waiting room in the form of all those terrified cats, contends that taking the cat to the vet is not a fun experience.

Riding in a car with a yowling, drooling, vomiting, urinating, and/or defecating cat who then either sits petrified in the waiting room or tries to kill everyone in sight, then proves impossible to medicate at home, usually provides the average owner with more than enough good reasons to avoid routine feline health care like the plague. To ensure that this doesn't happen to you and your pet, let's examine the major factors that affect the success of any feline health-care program:

- a private space to which the cat can retreat when ill or injured
- a calming environment in which to examine the cat
- a veterinarian whose orientation calms and reassures the cat
- an owner who knows what's normal for his or her cat
- an owner who can properly handle his or her cat

Chapter 3's discussion of free-access crate-training mentioned two aspects of the process that relate directly to feline veterinary care. One, cats who accept their crates as a private space arrive at the veterinary clinic in a much calmer state than those who hate them. Second, cats who have had negative crate/veterinary experiences will resist crate-training more than others. Still, the benefits of free-access crate-training for the sick cat, in particular, make it worth any extra effort necessary to train the crate haters to view this space positively.

Cats with limited exposure to other people or environments who become traumatized when taken for veterinary care also may benefit from a veterinarian who makes house calls. When Dr. Solomon comes to Clark's home, Delta purrs and rubs while the veterinarian examines her. When Dr. Solomon performs that same procedure in the veterinary clinic, Delta quakes and tries to run.

Of course, different cats respond differently. While Delta prefers home visits, Butch sees them as a territorial violation. He accepts handling by strangers much more readily away from home because he feels no need to mount a protective display in that environment.

Other cats resist veterinary care because the veterinarian's orientation upsets rather than comforts them. Delta normally perceives Dr. Jacobs's god-player approach as dominant, and, because cats normally don't play by social, dominant and subordinate pack rules (especially when stressed), his approach makes her defensive rather than compliant. On the other hand, the cheerful chatter of best friend Dr. Solomon may frighten or confuse a shyer animal. Meanwhile, facilitators who take an optional—Should I hold Delta firmly or let her move about?—approach toward cat handling come across as indecisive, an orientation that also may confuse or upset some animals.

I suspect that the hassles associated with taking a cat to the veterinarian also lead many cat owners to consider at-home remedies. Whether these will benefit or harm the cat depends on whether these treatments come from someone with a sound knowledge of *feline* anatomy, physiology, and diseases. Just as people who apply traditional treatments to cats based on what works in humans or dogs can get themselves in a great deal of trouble, so can those who apply similar other-species knowledge of alternatives. In the latter case, people often equate "alternative" with "safe." However, even the safest herb given in the wrong dosage or under the wrong circumstances can create problems. When Lisa decides that Butch's problems originate in his bladder, she gives him a "natural" remedy that increases the load on his damaged kidneys and precipitates a crisis for her pet.

Knowing what constitutes normal for your pet enables you to detect any abnormalities sooner. This is so crucial in a quality human-feline relationship that we'll discuss how to do this at length in the next chapter. However, as noted in Chapter 2, individual breeds and lines may be predisposed to certain health problems, and it pays owners of these animals to know this. Because any cat may experience breed- or line-specific problems, find out as much as possible from the breeder and those who own other cats (of all ages) from your cat's line. While annual or biannual anesthesia for teeth cleaning may pose few problems for most cats, wise owners of pets with a tendency toward liver, kidney, or heart problems may want to focus more on brushing as the way to maintain their pets' dental health.

Nor should owners of mixed-breed cats ignore their pets' heritage when it comes to health care. In my area, a lot of people consider cats with extra toes (called *polydactyly*) lucky. Whether the cat shares that view depends on whether the owner recognizes that the cat may experience difficulty keeping these extra claws and digits properly groomed. This may mean no more than checking the paws every week to make sure everything looks clean and healthy. On the other hand, it may mean regularly clipping these extra nails and removing any debris that gets caught between them that the cat can't or won't remove by itself for some reason.

Also, as more and more people get purebred cats, we can expect to see more purebred genes in the general feline gene pool. Where 30 years ago most of the longhaired domestic cats in the free-roaming population probably owed their long locks to mutations within their local gene pools, now many owe the trait to planned or unplanned matings with Persians.

Handling the cat poses another aspect of feline health care that may foil even the most dedicated owner. After spending three hours fighting to get a pill into Butch, the Buchanans decide he can't be all that sick. The haphazard administration of the treatment not only delays his recovery from the problem, but it can also make the problem worse.

"How so?" asks Toby as he examines the scars on his hands from numerous unsuccessful attempts to medicate his cat.

Pathogens (disease-causing organisms) exposed to lower levels of drugs can become resistant to those drugs a lot more quickly and easily than those exposed to the proper amounts. When the Buchanans medicate Butch erratically for a minor medical problem, Dr. Jacobs must switch him to a much stronger—and more expensive—drug when the problem not only doesn't resolve, but also becomes more serious.

In a nutshell, we can say that cats respond best to two kinds of restraint: all or nothing. If you do it, do it right and do it well. Often, snugly wrapping the cat in a towel so that only the head sticks out will allow the owner to medicate ears or eyes, or stuff a pill down the animal's throat.

"You make it sound so easy to stuff a pill," Toby says ruefully. "There's really some trick to it, isn't there?"

Actually, you can use several tricks. The first involves curling the cat's upper lip over its upper teeth when you open its mouth with your left hand (if you're right-handed) pressing down on the lower jaw with the index finger of your right hand, then stuffing the pill as far back into the mouth as you can get it with that same finger. The trick here is to do it so fast and smoothly that the cat doesn't realize what's happening until it's swallowed the pill.

"What if you're afraid the cat will bite you?" Lisa asks, a question familiar to many cat owners.

You can cover the tips of a pair of tweezers or small forceps with tape (to protect the cat's mouth) and hold the pill with that, or you can use a device made especially for this purpose. (Many veterinarians and pet stores carry these.)

Another technique, which requires a bit more practice, involves facing the cat and gently but firmly grasping the skin at the base of the cat's skull and its left ear with the fingers of your left hand (if you're right-handed), then rotating the head toward the cat's left (your right) and slightly upward. When the technique is done properly, the lower jaw will drop open, and you can pill the cat with your right hand.

However, because the proper grip and right amount of pressure are crucial to the success of both of these approaches, ask your veterinarian or vet tech to demonstrate these procedures for you before trying them yourself.

"Why not just put any medication in the cat's food?" asks Clark.

Two reasons argue against this approach. First, many cats who require medication feel too sick to eat. Second, if the cat does feel like eating, any change in the odor, texture, or taste of the food produced by the medication may cause the animal to stop eating, the last thing we want any sick animal to do. Unlike dogs who will gulp their food, cats nibble and chew, making it much more difficult to sneak alien substances into it.

Mesh bags designed for washing lingerie, or those specifically designed to hold cats, do the same job as towels but without the bulk and offer the additional advantage of allowing owners to bathe the cat without getting scratched. Likewise, fabric bags with strategically placed zippers allow owners access to virtually all parts of the cat's body without fear of teeth or claws. A variation on this theme, the solid-plastic Pet Bath Treatment Spa, comes with a rinse hose and showerhead. A quick-release collar securely restrains the standing cat's head, enabling owners to bathe, dip, and medicate the animal without worrying about its moving around.

Another form of restraint—none at all—strikes some owners as suicidal, but it works remarkably well with certain animals. Even though Butch will squirm and struggle and resist every attempt to hold him, the Buchanans can do just about anything to him if they just let him go. In this instance, owners place the cat on a hard, smooth surface (such as a table or counter) and move when the cat moves. While it does take a while for owners to discern a pet's natural rhythm and then match their own to it, the technique can save both owner and cat a lot of needless stress.

Whether performing routine care or treating a cat with a special problem, always strive to accomplish this as quickly and effectively, and with the least amount of trauma to your pet and yourself, as possible. If your veterinarian asks you to do something to your cat and you don't have a clue how, for heaven's sake say so. When Clark voices his concerns to Dr. McFadden, the veterinarian suggests different medicating techniques that Delta might accept more readily. If Clark believes these won't work, Dr. McFadden might opt to use medicated baths rather than pills to treat the cat's problem, or a liquid medication instead of a tablet. If no options appeal to the owner or no other good ones exist, he may suggest that Clark take advantage of the clinic's day-care treatment plan and drop Delta off on his way to work in the morning. The clinic staff will then treat the cat, and Clark can pick her up on his way home.

Regardless of what type of health-care program you choose for your cat, you should recognize your cat's special needs when you make your selection.

## Feline Factor Analysis

Think about how any existing or dream cat's breed and personality could affect its health care. Does your pet travel well? Would your cat fare better if the veterinarian came to your home? What health idiosyncrasies occur in your cat's particular breed (or mix) or line? How comfortable do you feel handling your cat? Can you give your cat medication?

"It seemed so obvious that someone with a purebred like Clark would pay attention to all these things, but I never gave it a thought when we took in Butch," Toby admits frankly. "In retrospect, I can see now where he gave us a lot of little hints about his kidney problems the past few years, but we missed them. Because we expected him to be so healthy, we never bothered much with any handling. Then when he got really sick, we had to fight with him on top of everything else."

"I feel pretty good about my ability to handle Delta," Clark observes. "But I never really paid that much attention to which one of the vets she liked best. All I cared about was whether *I* liked them."

By seeing their chosen health-care programs through their cats' eyes, these owners saw their many options in a whole new light. For the ailing cat, though, a bit of darkness rather than light might work better.

# A Healthy Health-Care Environment

Two kinds of environments exert the greatest effect when it comes to preventing or treating feline health problems:

- the caregiver's facility
- the owner's home

The old saw maintains that cleanliness ranks right up there with godliness, and that certainly applies to any veterinary hospital, groomer, or kennel where you take your cat. Given the cat's solitary and territorial nature, *any* space away from its home base generates stress, and, depending on the cat's personality, that can interfere with its immune response. A poorly cleaned and/or ventilated space will increase the chance that the cat will contract some illness there. If the cat entered that space with an existing medical problem, the unclean environment will only make that problem worse.

Give any caregiver's environment the sniff test. Granted, busy health-care workers can't clean up every molecule of urine, stool, or vomit the instant it appears. On the other hand, routine checks should keep this at a minimum, and a good ventilating system should control the few odors that do occur.

Also beware of dirty cotton balls or other debris strewn on counters, as well as the presence of uncovered cans of food, dirty clipper blades, and cages with malfunctioning doors or bent wires. While caregivers who don't care about keeping their physical facilities sparkling clean might become scrupulous when they interact with your pet, that seldom occurs. Even if they did, habitually using dirty equipment, putting animals in dirty cages, or feeding improperly stored food will undermine any treatment.

"What if you have the choice between a slob you like and a neatnik you can't stand?" Lisa wants to know.

In this situation, focus on the result. If you like the slob, you receive satisfactory service, and your cat stays healthy, don't worry about it. But if your cat comes down with a cold, a urinary tract infection, or some other problem within a week or so after your pet visits that facility, then the neat grouch might be the lesser of the two evils. Better yet, talk to other pet owners and find yourself an animal health-care professional who can give you both.

On the home front, previous chapters described the role the cat's intimate environment can play when the animal experiences a wide variety of medical and behavioral problems. Time and time again, we saw how providing the cat with a private space to which it could safely retreat could help the healing process. When Butch goes into his special nook in his owners' bedroom, the Buchanan children know not to bother him there.

Crates also can help owners of multiple cats determine to which cat the vomit, diarrhea, or bloody urine belongs. If the cats don't feel comfortable in their crates, keeping the animals in separate rooms with their own food and water dishes and litter boxes or hospitalizing them all for that same purpose may offer the only other alternatives.

"Wouldn't it be simpler just to medicate all the cats?" Clark asks.

Although harried owners of multiple cats trying to identify the phantom barfer often feel tempted to do exactly that, medicating healthy animals can lead to drug resistance or intolerance the same way that improper use of drugs can in sick animals. This seems too high a price to pay for a bit of short-term convenience.

Of course, any kind of private space works only if owners also keep track of the pet's activities—or lack thereof. If not, the cat's retreat could complicate rather than simplify its problems. In the two days it takes Lisa and Toby to notice that Butch isn't eating, drinking, or urinating, their pet becomes one very sick cat.

Needless to say, cleanliness applies to the home environment, too. While always an issue, it becomes particularly important when the cat becomes ill. Whatever comfort a fuzzy sweater and sweatshirt used as bedding provide a sick animal, the benefit wanes dramatically when these articles become soiled and pose an additional health threat. To avoid this, change the sick animal's bedding daily. Similarly, make a special effort to keep food and water dishes, crates, and any other special places particularly clean during the period of recuperation.

## Environmental Health Check

Think about the veterinary clinic, grooming facility, or kennel where you take or plan to take your cat. Do they pass the sniff test? Does anything about them make you question their cleanliness? Do you feel comfortable discussing this with the caregivers?

Next, take a quick tour of your cat's favorite haunts in your home, or those areas you'd like any new cat to claim. Could you easily clean these areas if your pet vomited or had diarrhea there? If your pet required medication or other special care, such as hand-feeding, could you accomplish this in this space?

"The first thing I noticed about the veterinary clinic where we take Butch is how nice it smells," Lisa reports after completing the exercise. "The examination rooms are always clean, and every time I visited Butch when he got really sick, he was very clean, too."

"I noticed those same things," Clark adds, then grins sheepishly. "But I never paid that much attention to how clean Delta's areas were at home. She sleeps on my bed on a towel that I toss in the wash once a week or so. It's big and thick enough that if she ever threw up or had diarrhea on it, it would protect the bed. I do know from a lot of practice that it's much easier to medicate her there. She digs her claws into that towel rather than me, and I can easily move around her if I have to."

Once again we see that no right or wrong answers exist. What works for one owner and cat may not work for another. However, because health problems invariably upset pet owners, it makes sense to evaluate all the factors that may come into play before the fact rather than try to deal with them *and* a sick cat at the same time. That way you can forget about the environment and focus on ensuring the best possible care for your pet—and yourself.

# A Crack in the Furry Mirror

Anthropomorphic and chattel views may manifest very strongly in the health-care arena. When Butch becomes critically ill, Toby immediately thinks of his own father, who suffers from a similar problem. Even though the owner's response seems totally out of character given his previous view of his pet as more than capable of taking care of himself, such dramatic shifts in orientation can and do occur.

Regardless of what orientations owners adopt toward their cats, they do it for one reason: it works. Clark took a highly anthropomorphic view of Delta when he moved to Minnesota, because her increased medical problems bothered him greatly.

"I felt so helpless at first," he explains. "There aren't a lot of Sphinx around, and Delta was the first one my vets had ever seen. I didn't want to ignore some little sign and have it explode into some big problem. On the other hand, I rushed her to the clinic in a panic a few times for nothing, and I didn't like making a fool of myself, either. Now I just keep a close eye on her and evaluate what she does in terms of how I'd feel under those same circumstances. It's not accurate by any means, but it seems to work. Plus I'm really health conscious and into prevention myself," he adds. "So, that's where I concentrate most of my effort."

Compare the evolution of Clark's orientation with Toby's. Much of Toby's admiration for the battle-scarred Butch springs from his belief that the cat could take care of himself. When Lisa would worry if Butch didn't come home every day, Toby would dismiss her concerns with a "That's how cats are." His description of his relationship with his cat prior to Butch's illness sounds quite different from Clark's.

"What attracted me to him is the fact that he didn't need anything," Toby recalls of their early days together. "I cared for him, but mostly as a curiosity. He was such a grub ball compared with Delta and didn't seem to depend on us at all. I guess in a way I admired him for that."

And how did Lisa feel about Butch?

"Oh, he did a number on me from day one," she says with a laugh. "I felt so sorry for him because of the rough life he'd obviously lived. In spite of that, though, he was always gentle with kids. And even though I never tried to keep him inside or anything, he really was my baby, and I wanted to do the best I could for him. I knew how Toby felt about taking him to the vet for every little bite wound, but I've always been interested in alternatives, and I relied on these. Up until the end, it seemed to work."

Now let's see how these owners' orientations changed over time and the effect these changes had on their views toward health care and their cats' health.

"I know I take a much more balanced view toward Delta's health now," Clark declares candidly. "Since we moved here, her vets have developed contacts with people who know a lot about the breed. The fact that they were willing to do that took a tremendous amount of pressure off me. Now when she develops a problem, I try to look at it the way she would, rather than the way I would. I also give her credit for being a lot healthier and better able to cope with the weather here than I did at first. To tell you the truth, I think *I* had more trouble coping with all that snow than she did."

In this situation, Clark slowly relinquishes his anthropomorphic view as he gains more concrete knowledge about his pet and faith in her veterinarians. As he does this, his confidence in her grows and his fears for her health diminish. Because he no longer hovers over her, his cat can relax, and her quality of life improves. It's no surprise that her health does, too.

Next door at the Buchanans', the pendulum swings in the opposite direction.

"When Butch came down with the same problem as my dad, it hit me like a ton of bricks," Toby recounts softly. "The two of them are so much alike, I couldn't understand why I didn't see it sooner. As soon as I did, though, that was it. I felt I just couldn't let Butch die, no matter how much it cost."

When Butch became ill and Toby links his pet's condition to his father's, the result ranks more as a displaced than true anthropomorphic projection. Toby doesn't react to his cat's problem as if he experiences it himself or make any decisions regarding Butch's care based on that. Rather he sees his pet as suffering from the same condition as his father in the same way. Once he makes that link he *must* do everything possible because that's what he wants for his father.

I mention this anthropomorphic variation here because it most commonly occurs when pets become ill or injured. Owners rarely pay much attention to any connections they make between the cat and any other person when they choose exercise or feeding programs. Nor does this become an issue when deciding whether to opt for traditional or alternative, or problem-oriented or preventive medical approaches. However, when a crisis occurs, when the cat gets hits by a car or succumbs to a serious infection, the memory that a now-grown child smuggled that cat home from summer camp or a now-departed spouse gave it as a gift suddenly inundates these owners. In that instant, the cat ceases to be a cat and becomes a symbol.

Nor is it unusual for some owners to swing in exactly the opposite direction, doing everything in their power to divorce themselves from the painful situation.

"You do whatever you want. He's just a cat. I can't deal with it!" Lisa shouts at Toby and Dr. Jacobs as she runs out of the room.

Take a few minutes to think about how your own anthropomorphic or chattel views could affect your pet's health. Then run a few worst-case scenarios so you won't find yourself floundering like the Buchanans when your pet needs you the most.

## *Owner Orientation Checkup*

Imagine both a routine and an emergency pet health-care situation. Which, if any, of your responses arise from anthropomorphic views? Do any chattel views affect your response? Do your anthropomorphic or chattel views arise from solid knowledge of your cat and the situation? Or do they arise from emotion?

"Even though Lisa opted for those herbs of hers almost every time, I think she consistently took a much more balanced view of feline health than either Toby or I," Clark declares after some thought. "She didn't just give Butch something because the book said to or because she knew it would work for her. She tried to understand what was going on in his body. It didn't matter whether it was just a little bite wound or something more serious. She gave all of his problems her complete attention."

"Until the end." Lisa shakes her head disgustedly. "Then I lost it."

Maybe, but even the most loving cat owners have their limits.

## A Stitch in Time

Owner time limits can exert many surprising direct and indirect effects on the average cat's health. For example, when asked about any preferences regarding their cats' health care, many owners will mention that they don't have the time to think about it.

"I'll think about it when the need arises," they say almost apologetically.

Naturally, they hope the need never does arise because that most likely would mean that the cat has developed a medical and/or behavioral problem that requires treatment. That, in turn, would mean they must find the time to decide what kind of approach would best fit their and their cats' needs, as well as find the time to implement any treatment.

Consider what happened to the Buchanans and Butch. Butch's vigor initially strongly reinforces Toby's belief that his pet could take care of himself.

"I took him in for one dose of vaccine, but he's so healthy I don't even do that anymore," he brags to his friends. "I get the vaccine through a mail-order company and do it myself. Saves me tons of time."

Toby's "time-saving" approach to feline health care produces one immediate time-*consuming* result: Lisa spends a great deal of time reading about alternative treatments and home remedies so she can treat Butch at home if any problems arise.

"I think Butch is pretty darned healthy, too," she confides to Clark. "But I want to be prepared, just in case."

When Butch becomes seriously ill, Toby and Lisa must grapple with where to take their pet. They know Clark likes the staff at Mountainview, but it will take them 45 minutes to get there. On the other hand, Lisa's recollections of her one experience at the closest clinic when Butch was neutered don't bode well, either.

"The place was dirty, and I don't think the veterinarian likes cats very much," she reminds her husband. "Besides, Mountainview has office hours that fit into our work schedule. One of us would have to take time off from work to take him to the other place."

When the Buchanans first meet with Dr. Jacobs, the veterinarian immediately recognizes the seriousness of Butch's condition. As Dr. Jacobs endeavors to learn as much about the 13-year-old cat and his activities as possible, Toby struggles to remember what he vaccinated Butch for, when. Meanwhile Lisa wracks her brains trying to remember if she treated the cat two or three times for vomiting during the past month, and what herbs she used. Neither owner can offer anything but the roughest estimate of how much the cat eats and drinks.

Compare this with what happens when Clark takes Delta to Mountainview with a problem. Because she receives her annual checkups there, the staff knows her medical history and can access it on their computer system almost instantly. They also know Clark and his limits as well as Delta and her little idiosyncrasies. Clark, meanwhile, knows to monitor how much his pet eats and drinks, as well as to keep track of her urine and stool production. Because Dr. Jacobs knows none of this about Butch and given the cat's critical condition, he must try to sort through a decade of vaguely recalled feline and owner history as quickly as possible.

Treatments also may pose time problems for cat owners. When a battery of tests confirms Dr. Jacobs's diagnosis of renal (kidney) failure and Toby goes to pieces, the veterinarian refers the Buchanans to a veterinary teaching hospital, a five-hour drive from their home. As veterinary care becomes more sophisticated, more owners face similar dilemmas.

More commonly, though, treatment time-crunches hit closer to home. Whether the treatment is traditional or alternative, its effectiveness depends on its administration at the proper times. If the directions say, "Give one tablet every eight hours for ten days" and Clark gives Delta one tablet before he leaves for work at 7:00 A.M., the second when he gets home at 6:00 P.M., and the last four hours later before he goes to bed (except for those five days when he falls asleep on the couch and she doesn't get anymore), the medication may do more harm than good.

Fortunately, twice- or even once-daily administration of some drugs will do the job. However, others require more frequent administration. Because of this, if your veterinarian prescribes something you know won't fit into your schedule, say so. If other options don't exist, more and more veterinarians now offer daycare service for busy owners. When Delta develops an eye infection, Clark medicates her first thing in the morning, then drops her off at Mountainview on his way to work. The technicians medicate her during the day, then he picks her up on his way home and administers the last dose that evening. Other working owners depend on cat-loving neighbors for this service.

Every medical problem also contains its own time element. *Acute* problems arise suddenly and resolve relatively quickly, with the animal's either getting better or dying. *Chronic* problems may arise suddenly or gradually but tend to persist for a long time. Thus, Butch's wounds from his fights with other cats comprised an acute problem because they occurred quickly and healed in about 10 to 14 days. On the other hand, when one of those bite wounds became an abscess that swelled and drained just enough pus to take the pressure off, then swelled and drained again two weeks later, and then three weeks after that, it became a chronic strain on the cat, whose temperature and appetite would wax and wane with each episode. However, while surgically lancing and thoroughly draining the abscess would resolve that problem once and for all, no such treatment can revitalize the old cat's kidneys when they lose irreplaceable functional cells over time.

Unfortunately, many times owners prepare themselves for two results when their pets become seriously ill or injured: the cat will die, or it will become completely normal again. However, sometimes the cat survives but needs constant care. This may mean little more than a special diet, but it also may mean daily medication and nursing care of one sort or another. Owners who didn't consider their time limits when choosing a treatment may find that their joy at having their pet home turns to frustration and resentment when they can't accomplish the necessary aftercare.

Review your notes about any time limits that might affect your relationship with your cat, then apply them to health-care issues.

## *Health-Care Time Check*

Think about your preferred form of health care and Dr. Right. How well do your preferences and schedule mesh for routine health care? Would these work as well in a crisis situation? If your pet needed long-term home care, could you fit it into your schedule? If not, could you free up more time to do this?

Clark experiences little difficulty with this exercise because Delta's minor problems over the years caused him to confront the issue early in their relationship.

"At first I used to get really irritated with her when her problems upset my schedule," he confesses. "But then I realized I was just taking my frustration out on her. Once I explained my situation to the vets at Mountainview, they were very understanding and found all kinds of ways to help me fulfill her needs even with my hectic schedule."

Because Toby gave no thought whatsoever to how his time limits might affect his cat's health, he had to juggle this aspect along with everything else.

"An endless nightmare," he described it later.

Because Toby had convinced himself that Butch would always take care of himself, he never gave a thought to how he could fit caring for his pet into his schedule. Without that basic awareness, he found himself reacting subjectively rather than objectively, a choice that cost him dearly in more ways than one.

## The Cost of Feline Health Care

Dare I say it again? I must because, especially when it comes to health care, it *always* costs less to prevent problems than to treat them. How much does it cost to keep a cat healthy? That depends on what you mean by "healthy," where you live, and your pet's lifestyle (housebound or in-and-out). The charge for a veterinary visit averages about $52 (and roughly double that for house calls) nationwide, with veterinarians in some areas charging anywhere from half to twice that amount. In addition, the definition of what owners must do to ensure their pets' basic health changes almost daily.

Take, for example, something as seemingly necessary and mundane as vaccinations. A co-worker of Toby's vaccinates her 10 cats using vaccine she purchases from a mail-order catalog.

"It's the same stuff the vet uses, but it's much cheaper," she informs him. "I'll help you if you want."

Toby takes a "more is better" approach, selecting a vaccine guaranteed to provide protection from the most feline diseases and religiously giving it to Butch every year. As more vaccines for more diseases come out, he adds these to his shopping list, each time congratulating himself for this money-saving habit.

However, had he taken Butch to Mountainview for annual checkups instead, the veterinarians there would have informed him of the growing reservations about the need for all those vaccinations and the risks of overvaccination. While Toby was vaccinating his pet more and more, the veterinarians at Mountainview were vaccinating less and less. For most adult cats, one dose of the standard feline combination vaccine plus one dose of rabies vaccine every three years offers adequate protection. While we don't know what negative effects overvaccination may have on cats as they get older, we do know that some cats may develop allergic reactions and even cancers at the injection site. While this happens to only a small percentage of animals, it still makes sense to vaccinate only when necessary.

Toby initiated his program of home medical treatment because he thought he paid the veterinarian only to stick a needle in his cat, which he could do himself. He saw this as a simple mechanical act rather than the result of the veterinarian's physical examination of that particular cat coupled with the latest scientific knowledge of what vaccines to administer, when, and where. Consequently, if you plan to treat your cat yourself, set aside $100 to $150 for basic feline anatomy, physiology, and disease texts. Because our knowledge of feline health problems and their treatments changes so rapidly, also plan to update your medical library every two to three years.

In general, alternative and traditional options cost about the same when you take all the factors into account. Although acupuncture certainly ranks as a less complicated treatment than surgery, the cat may require regular acupuncture for some conditions for the rest of its life. Moreover, whether one opts for a traditional or alternative treatment, its success relies on a quality workup to determine the exact nature of the problem. Because both approaches use many of the same diagnostic tests, this cost will remain the same.

For those who find their cats a bit too rambunctious to treat, mesh lingerie laundry bags cost around $5. For about twice that amount you can get a heavier version designed especially for cats.

Not only does the latter permit you to medicate and bathe the cat, some cats who resist carriers will happily crawl into the bag and allow their owners to carry them. Heavy nylon bags with strategically placed zippers range in price from $24 to $32, depending on the size. Owners whose pets suffer from painful ear or paw problems might find that a nylon cat muzzle (approximately $10) enables them to accomplish any treatments much more quickly and safely. Some veterinarians offer some or all of these products for sale to their clients with difficult pets, while others will order them if asked.

For owners of pets requiring medicated baths or dips, or those who would like more, but still humane, restraint to brush kitty teeth, administer pills, or medicate eyes or ears, the Pet Bath Treatment Spa is available at $69.95 plus shipping and handling. (Call 800-636-8080 for more information).

A recent addition to the veterinary scene in many areas takes the form of the pet superstore, complete with veterinarians ready to meet your pet's health-care needs. Whether any reduced fees charged by such places will save you money depends on the service you get. While some owners appreciate both the convenience and lower fees, others complain about high staff turnover and feeling pressured to buy products they don't want.

"I've experienced those same problems at regular vets' offices," Clark points out. "The reason I chose Mountainview was that they're capable of doing a lot more sophisticated work."

Clark makes a valid observation. Some practices focus primarily on routine work and offer no emergency coverage, whereas others consider themselves full-service facilities. If you lean in one direction or the other, find a practice that meets your needs even if it means traveling a few extra miles. As Butch's illness progressed, Toby truly appreciated knowing he'd see a familiar person in a familiar place when problems arose in the middle of the night.

"Mountainview had all of Butch's records, and everyone there knew him and me," Toby points out. "It would have been extremely difficult for me to try to explain all that to a stranger."

I said it before and I'll say it one last time. Regardless of where you take your cat for what kind of treatment, ask about the cost and any payment policies (cash, credit card) or payment options *before* you agree to any treatment. When Dr. Right recommends a particular treatment for your pet, bring up the cost if he or she doesn't. If you would need to make special payment arrangements in order to afford it, say so and make those arrangements beforehand. If you can't afford it, ask Dr. Right to describe your other options, and *don't* feel guilty about doing this. Maybe some god-players will look askance at you for bringing up money, and some unfeeling dolts might even imply that you don't love your cat. However, agreeing to a treatment you can't afford definitely will undermine your relationship with your pet as well as with your veterinarian. When Toby found out how much the kidney transplant and aftercare for Butch would cost, he couldn't look at his pet without feeling despair over the financial burden this would place on his family.

Pet health insurance offers another financial option for contemporary pet owners. Although those unfamiliar with the concept may laugh, many who subscribe to the service swear by it. The oldest program, Veterinary Pet Insurance, charges an annual premium ($49 and up) plus a specific deductible ($20 to $40) for coverage of everything from skin rashes to cancer. However, it doesn't cover routine preventive care or existing conditions. Because pet health insurance companies must meet individual state requirements like human health insurers—a costly venture—pet health insurance programs have a way of coming and going. A program that disappears after two years won't help you or your pet, so make sure you pick one with a proven track record.

Also discuss this option with your veterinarian. Those who participate in these programs can give you further insight. Those who don't may lack familiarity with the process, and you may need to explain it to them. Still others hate to do paperwork of any kind, and your willingness to select a program that makes this as easy as possible for them may mean the difference between their accepting or resenting the program—and you.

With all this talk of the cost of medical treatment, don't forget all the things you can do to keep your pet healthy. Even at the high end of the veterinary scale, proper vaccination of young and adult animals remains a great bargain compared with the cost of treating your pet for preventable diseases. While tests for heartworm disease in cats aren't as reliable as those for dogs, if this disease occurs in your area, it will definitely cost less to prevent than treat it. Owners who walk their cats on leashes ($10 to $15) and carefully monitor their paths don't need to worry about cut foot pads ($50 and up) or their pets' getting hit by cars ($150 and up). They can control fleas by combing their cats with a flea comb ($5 to $10) and vacuuming their homes ($0), or by regularly using some sort of chemical flea protection ($10 to $50). Owners who do nothing to control fleas, however, can easily spend $100 or more to subdue a houseful of fleas, then spend another $10 or so to treat the tapeworms the fleas may transmit to their pets when they bite them. Owners can brush their pets' teeth with a washcloth moistened with warm water ($0), use a pet toothbrush and toothpaste (roughly $10), or spend $150 or more for anesthesia, professional cleaning, and medication when their pets develop a gum infection.

How does your approach to feline health care balance with your checkbook?

---

## Health-Care Financial Analysis

Review any financial limits you determined in Chapter 4. Deduct those amounts you already allotted for any exercise and feeding programs and related paraphernalia. What kinds of routine health care do you want for your pet? Can you afford this? If your cat became seriously ill or injured, how much could you afford to spend? What kind of payment options would you consider? Does your veterinarian offer different payment options to owners of new kittens or in cases of serious illness or injury? Talk to other veterinarians, cat owners, breeders, shelter personnel: Can you find less expensive health-care options that would meet your needs? If not, could you free up the money from another area to provide the quality of health care you want for your pet?

"In those last weeks with Butch, Toby and I agonized over how much his surgery would cost," Lisa admits. "The specialist didn't say anything about the cost until Toby brought it up. It was really hard for Toby to do that, but I'm glad he did."

"Me, too," her husband agrees. "At the time I felt like I'd been hit with a bucket of ice water when I heard how much a transplant and all the aftercare would cost. It never dawned on me that something for a cat could be so expensive, but when the specialist explained all that was involved, well, it really wasn't much different from doing all that to a person."

"Initially I got insurance for Delta more as a lark," Clark admits. "Everyone was teasing me so much about having a hairless cat and moving to Minnesota, but it still seemed like a good idea. All things considered, I probably break even having it."

But how would Clark feel if Delta got as sick as Butch?

After a long pause, he finally answers.

"If she got really sick, a lot of other factors would come into play besides money," he solemnly replies. "How I feel about her and her problem would play a really big role."

## Emotions and Health

When I surfed the Net looking for the latest information on pet health insurance, I came across a reference to "financial euthanasia" as the number one killer of pets in this country. Perhaps I live in a unique part of the world and know unique pet owners nationwide, but I think my overall experience is fairly common. Granted, when pet owners try to explain to nonowners or others whom they don't believe will understand their reasons for choosing euthanasia, they may give cost as the issue. "I couldn't afford the $1,000 it would have cost to treat him" takes less time to explain than the myriad reasons that often underlie this painful decision. While cost may be among those reasons somewhere, it rarely heads the list.

What does head the list? When their pets become ill or injured, most pet owners voice concern about issues that fall under the heading "quality of life." Moreover, these concerns address the quality of both the cat's and the owner's life. While some cat lovers may cringe at the idea of asking the question, "What does my cat's problem mean to *me*?" and dismiss any owner who would ask it as disgustingly selfish, it represents a loving as well as necessary first step when considering any health-care options. If the approach doesn't sit well with the owner for any reason, it can produce a host of negative effects on the cat and the relationship.

For example, suppose Dr. Jacobs prescribes an antibiotic for Delta's recurring skin infection, but Clark doesn't believe it will work. If he doesn't discuss his feelings with the veterinarian and accepts a treatment in which he doesn't believe, this could affect how he gives the medication. Perhaps he skips a few tablets or forgets to take them with him when he and Delta go to visit his folks one weekend. Or maybe he experiences guilt or other negative feelings when he gives the medication to his pet.

"Poor Delta," he apologizes as he stuffs the pill down her throat. "If I weren't such a spineless blob, I'd be giving you something that works."

Suppose Delta resists his attempts to medicate her, or her condition gets worse rather than better. Now Clark will pour even more negative feelings into the process, creating even more problems. If Clark doesn't tell Dr. Jacobs that Delta didn't get the medication as directed and why (be it because he forgot, couldn't fit it into his schedule, or didn't want to), the veterinarian most likely will prescribe another round of that *same* treatment when the cat doesn't get better.

"Sometimes it takes a little longer for these conditions to respond," Dr. Jacobs tells Clark, handing him another container of tablets. "If there's no improvement this time, though, I'll need to do some blood work and maybe some other tests."

Because Clark didn't discuss his feelings about the treatment, he created four problems for his cat:

- She didn't respond to the erratic treatment.
- The erratic treatment prolonged the course of her problem.
- She may develop a resistance to that particular drug.
- She may need to endure additional veterinary procedures.

Nor does Clark get off scot-free, either. His unwillingness to communicate with Dr. Jacobs causes him a lot of mental anguish in addition to costing him a lot of time and money.

In addition to a need for owners to openly communicate their feelings about any aspect of their cats' treatment that bothers them, how owners feel about the cat with problems also can make or break a health-care program. As I worked with and talked to owners of sick pets (including animals with behavioral problems) over the years, yet another surprising paradox emerged. The owners who experienced the fewest negative emotions about themselves and their cats and who did the best job treating their pets invariably viewed the animal's problem as normal.

"Surely you're joking!" Toby exclaims. "How can anyone view an animal with a problem as normal? That doesn't make any sense."

"Yes, it does," Clark says thoughtfully. "When Delta first started having her little skin flare-ups, they bugged me a lot because I saw them—and her—as complicating my life. But once I learned to accept that this is just the way she is and that it doesn't matter because she's such a neat cat, I just took it in stride. Now if she needs medication, it's just something I do automatically, like brushing my teeth. I don't even think about it anymore."

The best support groups for owners whose pets suffer from a particular serious disease, such as diabetes or cancer, see these conditions as normal challenges rather than problems, too. Because everyone in the group experiences the same challenges, this lends a certain normalcy to the everyday ups and downs of living with these animals which, in turn, helps smooth things out. In addition to sharing information and support, group members often pet-sit for each other, a real blessing for owners reluctant to leave a pet in the care of an inexperienced person. Some veterinarians maintain informal support groups within their practices in which owners of animals with a particular problem can exchange information as well as work through their feelings. Other owners report finding kindred spirits in pet- and cat-related groups on the Internet. No matter where the support comes from, though, those who seek and find encouragement to incorporate the animal into their lives with the least drama benefit the most, as do their pets.

Speaking of drama, we left Toby on the verge of giving the go-ahead for a kidney transplant on his 13-year-old cat, who suffered from the same degenerative disease as Toby's father. The resolution of this particular tale underscores a point I can't overemphasize: when it comes to your feelings about your pet's care, and especially when your pet suffers from a serious illness or injury, you *must* openly communicate your feelings to your veterinarian for your cat's sake as well as your own. If you don't believe you can talk to your veterinarian, find another one.

When the still-dazed Toby stopped in at the Mountainview Veterinary Clinic to arrange for time payments after his visit to the specialist, Dr. Solomon invited him into her office to discuss what lay ahead for him and his pet. Although the specialist had described the surgery in detail, he didn't say much about the aftercare. However, because much of the responsibility for the aftercare would fall on Toby and Lisa, who both worked, Dr. Solomon focused the discussion on this.

"The more I talked to her, the more I realized I was one of those people who thought that any treatment that cost that much would make Butch perfect again," Toby recalled later. "Heck, I expected it to make him a *kitten* again. I really wasn't thinking of him at all, though. I leaped on the idea of the surgery because of my dad."

After his meeting with Dr. Solomon, Toby, Lisa, and the children discuss their feelings about Butch and his treatment as well as all the other factors involved in it. In the end, they opt for a more conservative approach, treating their pet symptomatically, keeping him comfortable and with them at home as long as possible.

Whether you maintain strong feelings about the use of traditional or alternative approaches, or whether you adopt a "do everything possible" versus a more conservative approach, you owe it to yourself and your pet to recognize and understand the source of those feelings.

## Health-Care Feelings Evaluation

Recall your description of the ideal health-care program for your pet and your selection of any Dr. Right. Do your choices arise from solid knowledge of your pet's and your own needs, or do they arise from emotion? Now imagine a routine health-care event and a worst-case scenario again, this time paying particular attention to your feelings. Does visiting your veterinarian make you feel apprehensive, regardless of the circumstances? Does the idea of your cat's succumbing to an illness or injury leave you feeling numb? Frightened? Something else?

"I feel comfortable that the alternative approach I took with Butch was based on knowledge rather than emotion," Lisa declares with certainty. "While herbs have always interested me, I studied a lot before I used them on Butch, and I think I did a good job."

"To tell you the truth, I never gave a thought to Butch's health until he got sick," Toby confesses. "Then I felt really uncomfortable with the vets at Mountainview at first, because I hadn't taken him there for regular checkups. After I got the diagnosis, my response was even more emotional, and none of it had anything to do with Butch until Dr. Solomon talked to me. Once she gave me some solid facts, then I was able to see things in their proper perspective."

"This may sound silly, but I used to feel as uneasy taking Delta to the vet as I did going to the doctor myself," Clark notes, contributing his share to the discussion. "But then I met the whole Mountainview staff at an open house they held at the clinic, and that changed everything. Now I'm on a softball team with one of the techs, and I see two of the vets at my health club every week."

Three different owners with three very different emotional views of their pets' health. Fortunately, all of these people are hale and hearty, but what if they had physical problems as well as their cats?

# The Physical Limits of Feline Health Care

Much literature contains glowing accounts of how cats provide a special and welcomed dimension to owners with problems of their own. However, what happens when the cat belonging to such a person becomes ill or injured? The case that immediately springs to mind concerns the owner with an impaired immune response whose cat begins vomiting and develops diarrhea. While some health-care professionals often portray this as a disastrous event and even point to it as a reason why these people shouldn't own pets, those trained in human, veterinary, *and* immunodeficiency diseases don't share this view. Those with an understanding of both human and animal problems echo the common theme repeated to *all* owners of sick cats: prompt action and cleanliness.

If you suffer from any ailment yourself, you should pay particular attention to your cat so that some little problem doesn't become a big one for both of you. You, or someone else if you're not able, should keep your pet well groomed. Not only will this enable you to pick up any evidence of fleas or other skin problems, but it also will reduce the amount of hair and dander floating about that may aggravate human problems. If your pet uses a litter box, keep it scrupulously clean. Your cat will thank you, and your efforts will greatly limit the chances of any feline waste serving as a source of human disease. Naturally, if your physician tells you to stay away from the box entirely, you should arrange for someone else to clean it.

Owners whose physical limitations make them hesitant about medicating their pets should ask someone else to do this for them, too. Confidence and speed form the foundation of any successful cat-treatment protocol. If Delta senses any hesitation on Clark's part, that will make her feel more apprehensive herself, thereby increasing the likelihood that she will struggle or try to get away and scratch him in the process.

While different owners may experience different physical problems, feline health-care issues revolve around the owner's ability to attend to the cat's basic needs (and thus prevent problems) and provide the proper treatment when problems arise.

## Owner Physical Evaluation

Evaluate your feline health-care preferences as they relate to any physical limits you may experience. Could these limits interfere with your pet's routine health-care needs? How? What effect could they have if your pet became critically ill or injured? How can you avoid any problems that might arise as a result of your physical limits?

While Toby, Lisa, and Clark all pride themselves on their health, they realize that their lack of awareness of this aspect of pet ownership would cause their pets to fare worse than those belonging to owners with known physical limitations.

"My dad has a neighbor who will come in and take care of his dog if anything happens to him," Toby states. "But I never gave a thought to who would take care of Butch if something happened to Lisa and me."

"I'd take care of him," Clark volunteers immediately. "And I know you'd help me with Delta, too."

Like most other cat owners, the three friends not only find others ready to help them if they only ask, but they also help ensure the quality of their pet's life even under the worst of conditions.

# Quality Health Care

No matter what kind of health-care program you select for your pet, two factors will determine its success:

- knowledge of your cat and yourself
- your willingness to communicate your own and your pet's needs to any health-care provider

Many times owners expect their veterinarians to tell them everything they need to know, something most veterinarians will attempt to do. However, each cat and owner forms a unique unit. While sometimes it takes a bit of courage to get the dialogue going, and you may even need to hunt for a veterinarian and/or other health-care professionals with whom you feel comfortable, it's definitely worth the effort.

When Toby stops in at Mountainview to make the final payment several months after Butch dies, the receptionist greets him with a big smile.

"Wait here a minute," she cheerfully orders him, and disappears only to return a minute later with Dr. Solomon who holds a little tiger-striped fuzz ball.

"He needs a good home," the veterinarian explains as she hands the kitten to Toby. "I thought you might be interested."

"I . . . I don't understand," Toby stammers. "I thought you people would think that we were irresponsible owners after we let Butch get so sick."

"We never thought you didn't care," Dr. Solomon assures him as the kitten crawls up Toby's sweater and licks his chin. "It was just that you didn't know."

While Toby makes an appointment to get his new pet off to a good start, let's look at what you can do at home throughout your cat's life to help ensure a long and healthy relationship.

# 10

# Forever Feline

*Creating a Lifelong Living-Learning Program for You and Your Cat*

S hortly before they split up, Nicole Corry and her ex-husband, Steve, got two longhaired kittens from the same litter. Nicole kept the orange male, Freebie, while the tricolored female, Elspeth, remained with Steve.

Over the years, Freebie succumbs to one medical or behavioral problem after another while Elspeth and Steve enjoy a most rewarding relationship.

"I don't understand it," Nicole complains. "Freebie and Elspeth are littermates. How can two cats be so different?"

Although Steve knows that cats from the same litter can display quite different physical and behavioral traits, he also recognizes the role the owner and environment play.

"Because of my crazy schedule, I decided to learn everything I could about cats, and I've been giving Elspeth routine checkups since I got her," Steve tactfully reminds his ex-spouse. "I think that's helped a lot."

"But I can't afford to run to the vet every time Freebie sneezes," Nicole counters.

"I don't run to the vet," Steve replies. "I do it myself."

"You're kidding!" Nicole scoffs.

"No, I'm not. And you can do it, too," Steve encourages her as he picks up the reluctant Freebie and hands him to her. "I'll show you."

---

In the preceding pages, we examined some of the most common feline behavioral and medical problems and their effect on the cat, the owner, and their relationship. And throughout this material, the same theme repeated itself again and again: prevention always takes less time and costs less than treatment.

Consider what led up to Nicole's conversation with Steve. From the day she introduced him to their new home, Freebie urinated by the back door. However, because Nicole seldom used that door, she missed this valuable indicator of how her pet perceived his new environment. The only time she actually saw him not using his litter box was when he went on the floor right in front of her.

Nicole then took Freebie to Dr. Guyer, her veterinarian. When Dr. Guyer asked Nicole to describe the problem, Nicole could offer only the sketchiest details.

"How much urine, and was there any blood in it?" she echoes Dr. Guyer's questions as she ponders the event in question. "To tell you the truth, I don't have a clue. I was so disgusted I just wiped it up as fast as I could."

When the veterinarian asks the owner to describe how much the cat eats and drinks, Nicole hesitates again.

"I honestly don't know," she finally admits.

As if all this doesn't complicate the situation enough, Nicole's hands-off approach to her pet makes him resist handling. After several futile attempts to examine Freebie, the veterinarian suggests hospitalizing and anesthetizing the cat to get a urine sample as well as conduct any other tests that might help determine the cause of the problem.

"I don't like to do so many tests based on so little information," Dr. Guyer admits to Nicole. "But it's better than putting him through hospitalization and anesthesia again if the preliminary tests are inconclusive."

"Do everything you can now," Nicole heartily agrees as she dabs at one of the many scratches with which Freebie has decorated her arms since they left home that endless day. "I hate the thought of going through this again myself."

Three hundred and fifty dollars later, Dr. Guyer pronounces Freebie free of any medical problems and concludes that the problem is behavioral.

"And that means doing a complete behavioral workup next," she advises her client.

"I've heard they're using drugs to treat behavioral problems in animals," remarks Nicole, hoping for something that doesn't take a lot of time. "Can't you give him something like that?"

"We still need to know what's causing the problem so you can make the necessary changes to ensure it won't recur when we take him off the drug," Dr. Guyer explains.

"But why take him off the drug if it's working?" Nicole reasonably wants to know.

"Practically all of the drugs used to treat behavioral problems in animals are experimental, so we don't have any good data about any negative side effects of long-term use," the veterinarian elaborates. "That's why you'll need to monitor Freebie very closely while he's on the medication, and I'll need to run tests periodically to make sure he's not getting into any trouble."

"You make this sound like a long-term project," Nicole notes as she envisions her quick fix going down the drain.

"It can take up to four to six weeks to see a response to some of the drugs," Dr. Guyer explains.

"And if he doesn't respond?" Nicole asks.

"We can try another drug."

Later, a dejected Nicole describes Freebie's problem to Steve.

"It's a no-win situation as far as I'm concerned," she tells him as she strokes Elspeth sleeping on her lap. "The drugs are experimental and expensive, and they only work as long as I give them, if they work at all and if I can get them into Freebie, which is pretty iffy right there. Any behavioral changes will take Freebie—and me—at least four to six weeks to get to the point that they're second nature to both of us and we don't have to think about them all the time. I don't have the time and money for that. I don't know what to do!"

This worst-case scenario unfortunately plays itself out in numerous households as owners face many common medical, behavioral, and relationship crises. In Nicole's case, this serious behavioral and relationship problem didn't begin the day Freebie squatted and urinated practically on her foot. In reality it began years before, when she and Steve first got the kittens.

The Corrys adopted their two kittens just as their marriage began to fall apart. Whereas Nicole consciously or subconsciously rewarded any signs of dependency and almost welcomed Freebie's early ailments and behavioral quirks because they took her mind off her other problems, Steve decided he wanted a cat who could deal with just about anything. To that end, he systematically examined Elspeth daily until she was 16 weeks old, then biweekly until six months of age, weekly until a year old, then monthly after that. However, at the time he didn't see this as giving her a physical examination. To him, it was just a way of getting to know his pet and getting her used to being handled.

Regardless of his motives, Steve's approach did a great deal to ensure his pet's physical and behavioral health.

Let's begin with an overview of the basic steps of an at-home examination, then consider some of the more common hot spots that may arise during various feline life stages.

## *Fact-Finding Want List*

Think about what you consider the most important health, behavior, and bond aspects of your relationship with any existing or future cat(s). What signs do you equate with feline physical health? Behavioral health? A healthy relationship?

When Nicole performs this exercise she realizes that she can easily describe what she considers Freebie's medical and behavioral *problems*, but she has little or no clear ideas about his health. While you would think that this focus on the abnormal would enable her to respond more quickly when problems arise, Nicole's lack of awareness regarding what constitutes her pet's *normal* physical and behavioral state causes her to miss the early, much more easily treated conditions that presage Freebie's various crises. Elspeth experiences just as many early symptoms as her littermate, but because Steve notices and treats them immediately, they never escalate into serious problems. Thus, even though both cats have the same potential to develop problems, how the owners respond to their pets determines whether or not they do develop problems.

# The At-Home Basics

Examining cats poses its own special challenges, not the least of which is getting them to cooperate. As mentioned in the preceding chapter, either complete or no restraint works best on cats. Because the more relaxed the cat, the more information you can glean from your examination, you should aim for minimal rather than maximum restraint.

"Oh, sure!" laughs Nicole, pointing to her scratches.

Granted, once problems arise and medication becomes necessary, maximum restraint may be your only option. However, when doing an at-home exam, you can take your time and ease your pet into the experience under the best possible conditions.

For example, although Freebie normally resists handling, he does like to snuggle next to Nicole on the couch where she normally pets him while she reads or watches television. Because a physical examination really consists of little more than purposeful petting, she's a lot further along in the process than she thinks.

Pause here a moment and give some thought to the best way to examine your own pet.

## Setting the Physical Stage

Think about your cat's personality and activity level. Where would your pet feel the most comfortable receiving a physical examination? On the floor? A table? Your bed? Where would you feel the most comfortable giving your pet such an exam?

Although Nicole felt that both she and Freebie could accomplish the most on the couch, Steve prefers to put Elspeth on a table for her routine examinations.

"It's easier for me because I don't have to hunch over," he explains. "At first she didn't like it because of the hard, smooth surface, but then I put a rubber-backed rug on the table, and that made her feel more secure. It's also easier for me to move with her when she's on the table. Plus I always do the exam after her playtime when she's tired. That helps a lot, too."

Bear in mind that if you're new to the cat physical game, you don't need to do it all at once. Until you and your cat get the hang of it, do ears one day and eyes the next. If you don't own a cat but plan to get one (as much as anyone can ever plan to get one!), borrow a friend's cat to master the basic techniques. And don't forget to examine any cat you plan to buy or adopt before you sign any papers.

Let's watch Steve examine Elspeth and see what we can learn about the process.

# The At-Home Examination

To begin the physical examination, Steve pets Elspeth's head, then peers in each of her ears with three points in mind:

- color
- odor
- discharge

The insides of cat ears normally range from pale pink to grayish-tannish white and sometimes combinations thereof. Different cats may display more or less pigment, so you need to know your pet's normal coloration to pick up any changes more quickly. Because Steve knows that Elspeth's ears normally appear grayish white, he immediately notices the pink that results when she begins scratching one.

Feline ears normally exude an odor that strikes many as *faintly* musty or oily, and distinctly catlike. Although I don't mind the scent in the least, I know it does bother some owners. Regardless of what you think your cat's ears smell like, though, the odor should be subtle. If you can smell them from two feet away, schedule a visit to the veterinarian.

Normally you shouldn't see any discharge in your cat's ears, and you should never put anything (such as a swab) into your pet's ears to check for one. Doing so will only ram any debris deeper into the ear canal and create far more problems than it solves. If you notice debris in the ears of a prospective cat or kitten, beware of responses such as, "All cats have ear mites, it's no big deal" from breeders, pet store clerks, or other feline sources. While ear mites aren't an uncommon problem, their very frequency and ease of treatment argues against offering such an animal for sale or adoption. Also, unknowledgeable people often blame any dark brown debris on mites when other causes, such as a yeast infection, may be the real culprit. If that's the case, no matter how long you treat the animal with ear mite medication, it won't get any better.

Before continuing, think about examining your own cat's ears.

## Feline Ear Check

Assume your most cat- and owner-friendly position, and examine both of your pet's ears. What color is the inside of the ears? What do they smell like? Do you notice any discharge? If so, what does it look like? If you see something that strikes you as unusual, look it up in your breed book, or ask the breeder and/or your veterinarian about it. How does your pet respond to this handling? Do you feel comfortable doing this exam? If not, why not?

Continuing his physical examination, Steve cups Elspeth's chin in his hand, slowly raises her head, and looks directly into her eyes. First, he notices how bright and clear they appear. Then, he checks for any discharge. In addition to owing her long hair to her mother's Persian ancestors, Elspeth owes them her prominent eyes, a feature that interferes with normal tear draining. As a result, she normally has some clear discharge from both eyes which Steve can ignore unless the amount, consistency, or color changes, or if one eye tears more than the other. On the other hand, Freebie inherited his father's deeper-set eyes which normally don't tear at all, so any kind of a discharge from them should draw Nicole's attention immediately.

Needless to say, if you notice anything that strikes you as out of the ordinary in a dream-cat candidate, not only should you have your veterinarian examine the animal, you also should check with owners of other animals from that breeder to make sure more serious eye problems don't tend to develop over time.

To complete the eye check, Steve gently pulls down each of Elspeth's lower eyelids with his thumb, checking for color as well as any evidence of swelling. In addition to telling us about the eye's health, the soft tissue around the eye (the *conjunctiva*) provides other valuable clues to the animal's well-being. Normally the conjunctiva appears light pink and relatively smooth, whereas an infection or irritant will cause redness and swelling (called *conjunctivitis*). A relatively smooth conjunctiva with a yellowish or very pale pink to white color can indicate serious problems spanning the spectrum from liver disease to shock and blood loss associated with injury.

---

## Feline Eye Checkup

Using the process described, check your cat's eyes to determine what is normal for your pet. What color are your pet's eyes? Do they appear bright and clear? Is there any discharge? If so, what does it look like? Does it occur in both eyes or just one? What color is your pet's conjunctiva? Don't forget to jot down any notes about anything you consider unusual and consult the standard sources to find out more about it. How did your cat respond to this part of the examination? How did you feel when you did it?

Next, Steve begins examining Elspeth's mouth by wrapping his hand over her muzzle and lifting her upper lip to expose her teeth and gums without opening her jaws. He checks the color of her gums because, like her conjunctiva, it can serve as an excellent indicator of her general health. To determine Elspeth's normal color, he presses his index finger firmly on the gum just above her upper canine tooth (fang). This forces all of the blood out of that area so that, when he releases the pressure, he can see a distinct contrast between this whiteness and the natural pink of the rest of her gums. In cats whose gums normally contain areas of pigmentation that form dark spots or streaks, a change in color rather than the actual color may serve as the primary guide. Regardless of the color, healthy gums appear smooth and evenly moist, neither excessively wet nor dry to the touch.

Steve then turns his attention to Elspeth's teeth. He examines all of her teeth on the outside, making sure to pull the corner of her lips all the way back so he can see the upper and lower molars tucked in the area where the jaws converge. He pays particular attention to these teeth because cats who do a lot of marking with the scent glands on the sides of their faces may accumulate a great deal of tartar there, even though their other teeth appear spotlessly clean. Cats accustomed to handling often will let a veterinarian or even their owners remove this buildup without anesthesia. Steve also notices the normal color of Elspeth's gums immediately above the teeth because redness or swelling in this area could indicate periodontal disease.

To examine the inside of Elspeth's mouth, Steve curls her upper lip over her upper teeth, places the index finger of his other hand in her mouth, and gently but firmly presses downward until he opens her mouth. Once she does, he slides his finger farther back, pressing down on her tongue to give himself a clearer view of the inside of her mouth and throat.

Once again, what you'll see depends on your cat's breeding. Because squashed-nosed breeds such as Persians must cram all of their teeth into a relatively small space, the soft palate that forms the back part of the roof of the mouth may hang down and block inspection of everything else. In cats with longer muzzles, such as some Havana browns, that same number of teeth get more spread out to the point that spaces occasionally occur between some of the teeth.

Although you might feel tempted to hold your breath while conducting a feline oral examination, don't forget to take a whiff of your cat's breath. Kitten breath definitely smells different from adult cat breath, and if you don't know what your pet's breath normally smells like, you'll miss the change in odor that can signal liver, kidney, or digestive problems, as well as those involving the teeth and gums.

## Feline Mouth Check

Practice opening your cat's mouth. Once you feel comfortable doing this, examine your pet's gums and teeth. What color are your cat's gums? Do all of your cat's teeth look clean? What color is the gum directly above the teeth? What does your cat's breath smell like? How does your cat respond to this part of the examination? How did you feel when you conducted it? Consult the standard sources if you detect anything unusual.

To get a feel for Elspeth's general body condition, Steve next runs his hands over her body from head to tail and down all four legs several times, ending his sweep by picking up each foot. During his first pass, he checks her coat, including its odor. Elspeth's thick coat feels and smells quite different from that of a smooth-coated Siamese or even a full-coated Birman.

If Steve feels anything abnormal in Elspeth's hair, he examines it more closely. Longer-haired cats may develop tiny tangles under their ears which, if not removed, may become large mats that not only bother the cat, but also may lead to skin infections. Smart cat owners also pay particular attention to the coat and skin around the base of the tail. Dark specks in this area could mean fleas, a common cause of feline allergic reactions.

"How can you tell it's not just dirt?" asks Nicole as she parts Freebie's fur and scrutinizes the area.

If any doubt exists, place some of the specks onto a wet paper towel, and let them sit. Because fleas feed on blood, their waste, or "flea dirt," contains dried blood products. When dampened, the specks will dissolve and turn red, while dirt remains black.

The second time Steve runs his hands over Elspeth's body, he focuses on her skin and anything he can feel on or beneath it. With a little practice, he can feel the lymph nodes where her lower jaw and the neck meets, in the axillary ("armpit") area, and on the back surface of her lower hind legs. Whether he feels lymph nodes, cysts, or tumors, the basic questions remain the same:

- What's normal for my cat?
- What does this lump feel like: Is it smooth, lumpy, attached or freely moving, within or under the skin?
- What does this lump look like: Is it the same color as the skin, or does it appear darker or lighter?

During his third pass, Steve checks Elspeth's weight by placing both hands flat on the sides of her chest, then sliding them slowly forward and backward. He should be able to feel her ribs, but not any great dips and valleys between them.

"How can you tell fat from fur?" asks Nicole as she eyes Freebie's thick coat.

Although owners of all but the most smooth-coated overweight cats may dismiss their pets' pudginess with an "Oh, that's not fat; that's just fur!" the two really do feel quite different. As long as you work your fingers through the coat to the skin before conducting the test, you can feel how much fat underlies the skin.

Some people say optimum-weight cats, like dogs, have a definite "waist" area behind the ribs, too, but that's pretty subjective. While this does serve as a good indicator in cats with warm-climate conformation, many kittens don't develop these contours until they get older, and breed conformation—such as a compact Persian with a thick coat, for example—may obliterate it.

Most overweight cats, however, do develop a palpable fat pad between their hind legs. In addition to signaling weight problems, this may make it difficult for cats to groom themselves. Cats who can't keep the area around the penis or vulva clean can set themselves up for urinary tract infections or vaginitis. Overweight cats who develop diarrhea may suffer all the added problems that their inability to keep this area clean may cause, too. Few chores rival the unpleasantness of cleaning a fat cat's behind caked with stool—except cleaning one that also has maggots, a not uncommon and sometimes life-threatening complication that may occur when these animals soil themselves.

Owners who routinely bathe their cats also may use this opportunity to check for any fat pads, lumps, and bumps, because these will show up more clearly on a sopping wet animal and especially a thick-coated one.

---

## Cat Coat, Skin, and Weight Check

Evaluate your cat's coat, skin, and weight as described. What does your pet's coat feel and smell like? Can you find your pet's lymph nodes? Can you see or feel any other lumps or bumps? What about fat pads? Once again, note anything you discover that requires further explanation. How does your cat act during this part of the examination? Did any part of this procedure bother you?

The final part of the physical examination involves palpating your cat's abdomen to feel what's going on inside.

"Be serious!" Nicole exclaims with a laugh.

That's what Steve said, too, when he started giving Elspeth her kitten checkups, but now he can feel all sorts of things.

"It's easy," he encourages his ex-spouse. "Close your eyes and imagine you're trying to feel what's inside a soft bag. Put your hand flat against the bottom of Freebie's belly when he's standing, press firmly and gently upward toward his spine as far as you can, then bring your fingers and thumb together and let the abdominal organs slowly slide between your fingers as you move your hand down from the backbone."

"What if Freebie won't let me?" Nicole asks, eyeing her less-than-agreeable pet.

Making it a positive—or at least a passive—experience for owner and cat alike remains the key to a successful at-home examination. Some owners whose cats won't stand for the procedure wait until their cats fall into a deep sleep to palpate them. By the time the cat wakes up enough to realize what's going on, the owner has finished the task. Others gradually apply more pressure as they stroke the abdomen of the cat lying on the bed or couch beside them. While such a one-sided approach won't allow you to feel various internal organs as thoroughly, once the cat accepts this you can slide your fingers beneath your pet's reclining body and slip the abdominal contents between your fingers and thumb.

Focus on learning how a relaxed cat abdomen feels, and how your cat looks and acts while you palpate it. If you want to know the exact names of the various structures, refer to a feline anatomy text or ask your veterinarian or veterinary technician to help you.

Remember that the goal is to establish a reliable mental image of your pet's normal abdomen that will enable you to detect any signs of change. The sudden appearance of a distended abdomen requires immediate attention, as does one that gradually becomes larger over time. Similarly an abdomen that one day feels tense or a cat that suddenly expresses displeasure when palpated also warrants a trip to the veterinarian. If Nicole doesn't know what Freebie's abdomen normally looks like, let alone feels like, she'll miss these crucial early signs.

## Feline Abdominal Check

Palpate your cat's abdomen as outlined in this section. What can you feel? How does your cat respond? How do you feel about doing this part of the examination?

When Steve finishes Elspeth's checkup, he lifts her an inch or so off the table and returns her to the floor.

Although it may seem hard to believe, once you get used to handling your cat in this manner, you can accomplish this entire examination in one smooth motion that takes about two minutes. Even more amazing, we've discussed only a third of the information you can collect during that brief interval.

## The Behavioral and Bond Checkup

The at-home physical examination incorporates behavioral and bond facets, too. Consider this list of different ways Steve interacts with Elspeth during a routine at-home examination:

- placing his hands on her head, neck, or shoulders
- establishing eye contact
- wrapping his hand around her muzzle
- opening her mouth
- holding her paws
- lifting her

Virtually all of these displays communicate dominance.

"So what? Cats are solitary animals who don't play by pack rules," Nicole points out.

Yes and no. Ideally cats respond to us enough as their mothers to ensure that they maintain a social orientation toward us, but not so much that they become overly dependent. That being the case, we want our cats both to recognize and to accept our authority. Queens normally carry their kittens by the scruff of the neck when moving them, and will mouth—but not shake—them when they get out of line. Consequently, when Steve gives Elspeth those first kitten examinations and she resists, he realizes she could become a holy terror if he doesn't do something.

"I entertain a lot and wanted a cat who would enjoy my friends as much as I do," he explains. "Besides, I had no intention of fighting with her to groom that long coat."

In addition to initiating an exercise program that utilizes Elspeth's high energy level and intelligence, Steve gives her the at-home examination at first daily until four months of age, then twice weekly until six months, then weekly. Although he does look for any physical changes, he performs the examination primarily for behavioral and bond reasons. By the end of that time, Elspeth stands patiently for her checkup, even when a visiting child performs it. Needless to say, Dr. Guyer and all the vet techs can handle her effortlessly, too.

Compare this with Nicole's experience. After she gets Freebie, she never finds the time in her busy schedule to master the basic skills of the at-home checkup.

"That's why we have vets," she explains as she rushes off to her ceramics class.

Nicole's failure to make this initial few minutes' investment coupled with her desire to baby Freebie produce the following results:

- Freebie develops all of the problems associated with overdependency.
- Nicole misses the early signs of medical problems.
- She can't properly groom him.
- She can't properly medicate him when he becomes ill.

In addition to all of this, Dr. Guyer dreads seeing Freebie because she knows she'll need to use heroic methods to restrain the cat. When she does, Freebie sets up such a fuss that it upsets Nicole, which further upsets the cat. All of this, in turn, makes it very difficult for the veterinarian to determine which of Freebie's physical signs relate to any medical problem and which arise purely as a result of his behavior. To put it mildly, Nicole's failure to find the time to examine Freebie as a kitten can cost her dearly throughout her pet's entire life!

Recall how I asked you to keep track of your cat's behavior and your own feelings as you conducted each part of the physical examination. These notes can give you valuable insights about your own orientation toward your pet. Let's ask Nicole to give Freebie an examination and see what her comments reveal about her and her relationship with her pet.

*Ears*

"Freebie acted surprisingly good, but I felt a little queasy about sniffing his ears."

*Eyes*

"Freebie wouldn't let me pull his lower lids down. I was afraid I was hurting him, and that made me feel *really* queasy."

*Teeth and Gums*

"Freebie kept pulling his head away, and once I think he wanted to bite me. I was very uncomfortable and a little scared, and I'm positive that wrapping his upper lip over his teeth hurt him."

*Coat, Skin, Weight*

"Freebie kept trying to get away and hated it when I touched his feet. I knew I wasn't hurting him, and I got so frustrated and angry when he wouldn't hold still, I yelled at him and almost smacked him when he tried to pull away. That made me feel so guilty, I gave him a treat."

*Abdomen*

"Freebie resisted a little at first but then settled down. I was very pleased with the way he acted but frustrated with myself because I couldn't feel anything."

From these remarks, we can see that Nicole approaches the project anthropomorphically as well as emotionally. Because she doesn't feel comfortable examining Freebie's eyes and mouth, she attributes his resistance to discomfort rather than his reluctance to accept handling. However, when she does something she considers innocuous, such as checking his coat and lifting his feet, she becomes angry and frustrated when he fights her. Instead of asking herself what she and her cat communicate to one another via their behaviors, she yells at him and then feels guilty and gives him a treat.

Let me briefly pause for a few comments about people who give ill-mannered pets treats. Sometimes out of ignorance but usually because they feel bad about the experience, some animal-care folks as well as owners will give treats to animals who misbehave when they try to work on them. Somehow these people assume that the treat will make the animal decide to act better the next time. However, such thinking contradicts everything we know about conditioned responses in all animals, including people. The treat *reinforces* the behavior that preceded it. Consequently, giving an unruly or obnoxious animal a treat loudly and clearly communicates, "I simply *adored* the way you tried to bite the veterinarian. Please do it again the next time, too!"

So, if the groomer, veterinarian, or some member of the clinic staff offers you a treat for your cat, save it until your pet does something that truly merits a reward. And if your pet acts like a jerk when you handle it, skip the treats when you finish.

## Feline Behavioral Checkup

Review the notes you made regarding your cat's behavior during the examination. Did your cat display any behaviors that upset you? If so, did they upset you because of what they communicated, such as fear or anger? Or did they upset you because they interfered with your ability to conduct the examination? Did the cat's behavior make it impossible for you to continue the examination? Or did you stop because of your fears about what the behavior communicated?

When Nicole first tried to examine Freebie as a kitten, he resisted just as Elspeth initially did. Rather than working with her pet as Steve did, though, Nicole decided Freebie's behavior meant that something about the examination bothered him, and she didn't want to cause her pet any discomfort. However, did she really believe this?

"Not really," she confesses. "To tell you the truth, he was so crazy that I was a little afraid of him."

Because of this, Nicole avoided handling her pet, who naturally became even more resistant to handling as he got older.

---

## Bond Checkup

Review your notes about your own feelings as you examined your cat. Did any parts of the examination make you feel uneasy? Did any parts of it make you feel frightened, frustrated, or angry? If so, did these emotions arise from solid knowledge of yourself and your cat?

Nicole quickly recognizes that most of the feelings she experienced during Freebie's checkup not only arose from emotion rather than knowledge, but also contributed to his negative behavior. Once she realizes this, she takes a two-pronged approach to the problem. First, she reviews how her orientation affects her pet.

"I now know that I can't afford to be as anthropomorphic as I thought I could," she remarks as she gradually accustoms Freebie to more handling.

In addition, Nicole employs an extremely useful self-help technique alluded to in previous chapters called *imaging*, a technique used in areas as diverse as medicine and sports. Basically, while Nicole sits in a boring meeting, or as she lies in bed at night or first thing in the morning, she imagines herself examining Freebie in a confident and deliberate manner. Like imaging golfers who improve their scores almost as much as their friends who practice every day, all of Nicole's mental training pays off. Using this approach, she previews every step of the process in minute detail, focusing on any potential trouble spots. She imagines herself conducting the examination at a slower or faster pace to determine the rate that will enable her to do her part most naturally.

"But what if Freebie doesn't respond as perfectly as he does in my images?" Nicole asks as the cat streaks through the house.

This question raises two points. First, because imaging occurs within the safety of your mind, you can easily cover all the worst-case scenarios—and I strongly recommend you do. The more problems you anticipate, the more you prepare yourself to respond in a knowledgeable rather than emotional manner. Second, the very act of imaging generates confidence, and that enhances your presence. Consequently, the more you envision yourself confidently examining your pet in one fluid motion that you both enjoy, the more confidently you'll approach your pet and this task.

Rather than worrying about how she and Freebie will react to every step of the process, when Nicole next examines Freebie she simply recreates the scene she's experienced so many times in her mind's eye. She smoothly and confidently picks him up and talks to him soothingly as she looks in his ears and eyes, examines his teeth and gums, calmly runs her hands over him, palpates his abdomen, gives him a hug, and puts him down on the floor. Just like that. The very smoothness of her actions communicates authority, and Freebie responds by quietly accepting a process he previously fought.

Admittedly, teaching older cats to accept at-home checkups requires a certain amount of patience and commitment. Recalcitrant older animals don't become placid overnight, and their early experiences can make them highly resistant to change. On the other hand, when such experiences set the animal up for recurring medical and/or behavioral problems as it gets older and make it difficult or impossible to treat these when they occur, anything the owner can do to lessen this burden would seem more than worth the effort.

## Young Kitten Concerns

In addition to paying big human-feline dividends, routine at-home examinations provide owners with an opportunity to address specific life-stage issues.

While puppy development adheres to a more-or-less predictable timetable, kitten development may or may not. Even more maddening, kittens raised in the same litter with the same early experiences may grow into quite different adults. The cat's self-domestication plays as much of a role in this phenomenon as does its solitary nature. Give three kittens the same toy to play with and one may display typical predatory behaviors, a second may carry the toy to its owner, and the third may cache the object in the owner's shoe or under her pillow. While predatory, retrieving, and caching all represent part of the wildcat's behavioral repertoire, we can't say with any certainty that cats will always display these behaviors at specific times.

However, even if we may not know exactly why cats do what they do, most of us do recognize those behaviors that make living with a cat a pain rather than a pleasure. Realizing how firmly entrenched any early negative behaviors may become, it makes sense to respond constructively rather than hope that the kitten will outgrow them or that they'll otherwise miraculously disappear.

Consider what happened to Nicole and Steve. They got Freebie and Elspeth from a private home when the kittens were about nine weeks old. Nicole immediately fell in love with the shy little kitten huddled in the corner while Steve immediately felt drawn to the way Elspeth studied him quietly, then scampered to him when he called her. Once the couple got the kittens home, they set about consciously or subconsciously reinforcing those feline behaviors that they personally found most enjoyable.

Steve didn't deliberately set out to routinely handle and examine Elspeth. He merely found the little bundle of fur so fascinating that he wanted to know more about her. That led him to look in her ears, open her mouth to see her permanent teeth replacing her baby ones (a process that isn't complete until around six months of age), and gently press her paws so he could see her claws.

However, this early handling and, above all, the owner's desire to know more about his pet greatly benefited both of them. While Nicole agonized over when and if to neuter Freebie, Steve felt comfortable with his choice.

"Dr. Guyer told me she could spay Elspeth right after I got her, but I saw no need for that," he explains. "I felt that coming into a new home, teething, and her vaccinations were enough for her to handle without adding the stress of surgery. As long as I got her spayed before she came into heat, that was fine with me."

Other owners opt for early neutering, and still others adopt kittens from shelters where early neutering is the rule. These programs remain sufficiently new that we don't have any data on if or how the surgery may affect the animals as they get older. However, it seems safe to say that knowledge and cleanliness should rank as the top priorities of any animal-care facility or individual who takes this approach. No matter how we cut it, anesthesia and surgery stress an animal, and it behooves us to do it under the best circumstances.

As far as breeding goes, I think we can safely say that far too many people are breeding far too many cats. This statement doesn't refer solely to mixed-breed animals, as some purebred fanciers would like to believe. I suspect that if the purebred associations would accept only the most physically and behaviorally sound cats for showing and breeding, the number of purebred animals would plummet dramatically. Until that happy day, it falls within the realm of responsible cat ownership for *anyone* who considers breeding his or her cat(s) to ask, "Why do I want to do this?" If the answer is anything other than because this animal represents the very best in terms of physical soundness, intelligence, and behavior, then the endeavor reflects concern for human far more than for feline needs.

During their pets' kittenhood, owners should think about the animals' claws as well as reproductive organs. Although Steve didn't want to declaw Elspeth, he did have some major concerns about her scratching.

"I don't like the idea of her ruining my furniture, but I worry a lot more about her scratching a friend of mine with an immune problem," he tells Dr. Guyer. "But isn't there anything else I can do besides declaw her? I really don't like the idea of that."

Because Steve recognized this potential problem immediately, Dr. Guyer could offer him several options that his more malleable kitten might accept. First, Steve could teach Elspeth what she could scratch and what she couldn't. In addition to providing her with a suitable scratching post, that meant stroking and playing with her in different ways to determine what would cause her to swat him with her claws, then extinguishing those responses as discussed in Chapter 1. Second, he could place specially made protective covers over her claws to prevent clawing. While these do prevent some cats from clawing, they require periodic replacement as the cat's claws grow. Also, some question exists about whether the covers may interfere with regular feline nail grooming. The third nail option consists of Steve's periodically clipping Elspeth's claws.

"I opted for clipping because I'd handled her feet and knew I could easily see the blood vessel at the base of each claw," he later explained. "I used a regular nail clipper on her when she was a kitten, but as she grew older I bought one made specifically for cats. I just remove the points so her nails look—and feel—like rounded triangles."

Meanwhile, Nicole didn't give neutering a thought and totally dismissed any consideration of claw-related issues because she found "declawing too horrible for words." It's not surprising, then, that when that first breeding season rolled around and Freebie marked his territory with urine and claw slashes, she wished she'd paid more attention to these behaviors earlier.

I won't open the Pandora's box of declawing except to say that nowhere else does the human self-fulfilling prophecy so come into play. Cats who belong to owners who maintain any negative feelings about the process almost invariably experience more problems than those who don't. Owners who enjoy good, stable relationships with their cats and make an informed choice to declaw because they believe it the best option for them and their particular cats in their particular situation fare much, much better than those who feel guilty or pressured by others to seek the procedure.

Also, while declawing may end the damage, it won't remove any territorial pressures that may have led the cat to claw in the first place and may, in fact, make the cat feel more vulnerable. Consequently, owners may see gray smudges (from the scent glands in the cat's paws) on furnishings rather than slashes. Even if owners find this acceptable, they should provide the cat with a safe space, exercise it more, and otherwise help the animal dissipate any stress. Otherwise they may swap clawing for another behavioral or medical problem.

Think about kittens and all the ways they may change and grow during their first six months or so.

## Kittenhood Checkup

Think about any kittens you know or have known. What about them attracts you? What bothers you? What is the kitten communicating via these behaviors? Does your response to it arise from knowledge or emotion? How do you feel about neutering and declawing? Do these views arise from knowledge or emotion? If you plan to breed your cat, why do you want to do this?

Because Steve maintained very clear ideas about his cat's behavior based on what he read and his discussions with his veterinarian, he felt completely comfortable with the decisions he made regarding his pet. However, because Nicole lacked this knowledge, her relationship with her pet consisted of one emotion-laden minidisaster after another. Naturally, when a real disaster struck, she wasn't prepared for that, either.

# When Disaster Strikes

In just the course of my writing this book, various parts of the country experienced hurricanes, mud slides, blizzards, floods, ice storms, and fires, among other disasters. Each one generated its complement of photos of lost pets and heartbreaking stories of owners whose animals fled during the chaos or were turned away from crowded human shelters. Such events now occur so frequently that a pet disaster kit should rank as a norm rather than an exception for every pet owner.

"I can't imagine me and Freebie going through something like that," Nicole says, immediately assuming her head-in-the-sand position yet again. "I don't even want to think about it."

Few pet owners do, but once again prevention can save the day. Consider the following contents of Steve's do-it-yourself pet disaster kit:

- two days' supply of dry cat food
- several cans of cat food
- a can opener
- a gallon jug of water
- plastic food and water bowls
- copies of Elspeth's vaccination records
- a photo of Elspeth
- a week's supply of any medications she needs

- a first aid kit including:
  rectal thermometer
  clean washcloths or gauze sponges
  1″ adhesive tape
  2″ elastic bandage
  Kaopectate (for minor digestive upsets)
  hydrogen peroxide (to clean wounds)
  a muzzle
  a towel or mesh bag for restraint
  a first aid manual

In the worst-case scenario, a major flood rolls toward the Corrys' hometown. While Nicole races around frantically, Steve picks up the large plastic bag containing Elspeth's disaster kit, pops her into her crate, and heads for higher ground. Some disaster shelters now accept animals in crates; if they don't, emergency facilities set up by animal shelters certainly do. Naturally, shelter personnel want and need to know the vaccination history of any animal guests, and Steve can provide this information immediately.

If Elspeth did happen to get loose, her photo will help others identify her. More and more owners also now have their pets injected (in a simple procedure) with a microchip, whose identifying numbers animal shelter personnel or others armed with electronic scanners easily can read. They then call a national registry for the owner's name and address. Still other owners tattoo their pets and enroll them in similar national registries.

In both cases, the person who finds the cat must know to look for such identifiers, and the cat must allow that person to do this. Consequently, in addition to selecting stable animals, socializing them well, and identifying them with microchips or tattoos, pet owners in disaster-prone areas often use distinctive collars to further help distinguish their animals. Although most of Steve's neighbors can't tell one cat from another, they all remember Elspeth's bright red plaid collar.

The photo also helps because, although it seems hard to believe, a lot of owners can't describe their cats in much detail, especially when caught in the throes of a disaster.

"She's tricolor, but more orangish, well, actually more red, with two, no, make that three white feet. I think," a flustered Steve tells the overworked shelter volunteer. "Her eyes are sort of greenish yellow. No, probably more yellowish green, come to think of it."

Obviously the emergency food and water supply in the disaster kit won't last forever, but at least it will provide Elspeth with some familiar nourishment. The last thing she needs as she copes with all the other changes is a new kind of food.

"Why the muzzle?" Nicole asks apprehensively as she peers at the contents of Elspeth's kit.

Every first aid kit should contain one because a frightened or injured cat may bite; and even if it wouldn't, owners who fear this will respond less confidently at a time when the animal needs the owner's reassurance the most. If the injury occurs in the animal's back end, you can bundle the front end in the towel or mesh bag to immobilize the head and front claws. However, if you need to work around the front end, a lightweight nylon muzzle specially designed for cats works the best. In a pinch you can also use a strip of gauze bandage long enough to loop around the cat's nose, tie in a half hitch under its chin, and then tie behind its ears. Pass a second strip of gauze under loops encircling the nose and neck and tie it in a knot between the cat's eyes to keep the nose loop from sliding off.

By replacing the food and water and updating his kit routinely (some owners do this when they change their clocks in the spring and fall), Steve takes some of the worry out of a worrisome situation. Such kits are also a boon to people who travel with their pets. Rather than packing for Elspeth as well as for himself when he goes to visit friends, Steve takes her disaster kit and then replenishes it when they return.

In environments where fire poses a threat, consider adding a Pet Saver Tote to your kit. This heavy, flame-retardant canvas bag not only protects the animal, but also is designed to be slung over your shoulder, thus leaving your hands free to negotiate fire escapes or environmental hazards. For further information, call 800-326-5708.

How prepared are you and your pet for a disaster?

---

### Disaster-Preparedness and Travel Check

Imagine that you and your cat must make a sudden trip away from your home, possibly to a strange and limited environment. What would your pet need? How easily could you pack and transport these items?

## Coming of Age in CatLand

Once again, the stages that mark adult feline development occur neither as frequently nor as predictably as they do in dogs. Rather, adulthood serves as a time when all the idiosyncrasies of kittenhood manifest. Let's create another worst-case scenario for Nicole and Freebie in order to explore what this can mean for the unknowledgeable owner.

After Nicole and Steve divorce, Nicole spends several quiet months just trying to get her bearings. She also fosters any signs of dependency in Freebie, because doing so makes her feel needed during this difficult time. However, as she grows more confident in her new, single role, her lifestyle changes. She entertains and goes out more often, both of which upset Freebie, who begins marking his territory and experiencing intermittent bouts of diarrhea. Because the cat resists even the most basic workup, Dr. Guyer suggests feeding Freebie a special diet to eliminate food allergies as a cause of the diarrhea. Nicole quickly discovers that whatever time or energy she saved by always feeding Freebie the same food evaporates as she tries to gradually trade him over to a new food.

How successfully owners can medicate adult cats also depends on how they—or others—treated the animals when they were young. Because Nicole never thought to open Freebie's mouth under ideal circumstances, she has no success doing so on an animal made vulnerable and defensive by illness. The more he resists, the more she fears he'll bite her. This fear, in turn, undermines what little presence she radiates, further upsetting her pet.

Granted, an ounce of prevention can save cat owners a ton of grief, but Nicole's failure to take a knowledge-based approach to kittenhood doesn't mean she must write him—and their relationship—off when he becomes an adult. However, it does mean that she'll need to use different techniques with *confidence* even under the worst conditions.

"How can you do anything with confidence to a cat who's trying to kill you?" Nicole rightfully wants to know.

Recall the first step when dealing with an aggressive animal: wear whatever protective clothing or gear you must to feel totally safe handling that animal. Second, do what you must do, and do it smoothly, quickly, and quietly. Using this approach, Nicole dons thick jeans, a canvas apron, boots, a long-sleeved denim shirt, a heavy jacket, and two pairs of gloves, the ones she uses to prune roses over the fitted leather pair she uses for driving. Then she drops a towel over Freebie and wraps him snugly in it so that only his head sticks out. Next, she sheds the outer, bulkier pair of gloves and opens his mouth wearing only the inner, fitted leather pair. She stuffs the pill as far back into his mouth as she can, verifies that he swallowed it, and turns him loose. Although it took her quite a while to prepare herself both mentally and physically for this ordeal, her actual interaction with

Freebie lasted only about a minute, far less than her usual unproductive encounters. By the end of a week of successfully medicating him, she wears only the light gloves for protection, and she eventually sheds these, too.

As all of those early-kittenhood experiences converge to create the adult animal, a new creature emerges. Freebie loses his kittenish roundness and develops the sleeker silhouette of an adult. With this new body comes a new set of physical and behavioral norms, too.

As cats mature, some physical changes may happen so gradually that even the most attentive owner may miss them. Most of us rationalize this, saying that, if the cat becomes ill, blood and other tests will detect any abnormalities. However, two changes in the human-feline population make more veterinarians and owners take a different view of this approach. First, as owners' lives get busier, prevention and wellness become even more crucial, and that means gaining the clearest sense of normal for one's specific animal as possible. Second, as more and more purebreds enter the domestic cat population, the "average-cat" values associated with most tests might not give that accurate a picture of what's going on in a particular cat of a particular breed. A normal value in one individual, breed, or line of cats might signal problems in another.

To see how this works, consider "normal" body temperature for a healthy cat which ranges from 101 to 102.5°F. If Freebie's temperature normally runs 101°, then a temperature of 103° should trigger more concern than if his normal temperature were 102.5°. Similarly, if you owned a cat from a breed or line of animals with a history of kidney, liver, or heart problems, knowing normal for your specific animal would enable you and your veterinarian to detect any warning signs sooner.

Because of this, the idea of doing blood work and other significant tests on *healthy* adult animals to establish their specific normals is gaining favor.

"What happens if I take Freebie in for these tests when he's perfectly healthy but the vet says there's something wrong with him?" Nicole asks.

The fact that Freebie gets so upset when he goes to the veterinary clinic definitely could alter his blood results. When Nicole uses a problem-oriented rather than preventive approach, this puts Dr. Guyer in the frustrating position of having to sort out which abnormal values result from the cat's behavior and which ones reflect a physical problem. While the veterinarian certainly hopes that Nicole will work with Freebie enough that visits to the clinic won't traumatize him so much, having a set of test results from a behaviorally traumatized and anesthetized *healthy* Freebie with which to compare any results from an ailing one will give her a much clearer picture of his actual physical condition.

Also, bear in mind that test results in and of themselves don't pronounce an animal sick or healthy. These must be combined with a thorough physical examination and solid information from the owner regarding how the cat acts at home. Without these, the test results are nothing more than bits of paper with numbers on them. I've seen some very sick cats with perfectly normal test results and some perfectly healthy ones whose test results the averages pronounced ill. You need to look at the whole picture.

During adulthood, feline pounds also may begin to pile up. This, too, may happen so gradually that owners don't even notice. I recall several cases in which the first awareness occurred when owners discovered a huge "tumor" between the cat's hind legs. While they felt tremendously relieved to learn it was only fat, to a one they expressed surprise that their cats, even the ones who looked like furry watermelons, were overweight.

The idea of fat cats raises the issue of exercise which leads me to mention another aspect of feline adulthood, the development of the adult cat's sense of humor. Although I do so at the risk of getting myself tarred and feathered in some scientific circles, this phenomenon comprises such an enchanting part of cathood that I'm willing to risk it. The almost nonstop play of kittens necessary for them to learn all they need to know slowly gives way to a different kind of activity. While the kitten will stalk just about anything that moves, the adult may, but it also will look for new things to stalk in new ways, just for the sheer fun of it.

I previously mentioned that the new theories of adult animal play view it as an indication that the animal perceives its environment as optimal. Needless to say, wild animals who misjudge quickly find themselves eliminated from the gene pool. However, those with the knowledge and skill to pull it off successfully radiate a presence that makes them far superior to their more somber pals.

Compare the play styles of Freebie and Elspeth. Freebie will play if Nicole initiates a play session, but he won't play by himself because he doesn't feel comfortable away from her. Under those circumstances, he'd much prefer to hide out in his private nook in her bedroom. Elspeth, on the other hand, spends a great deal of time making up new games to amuse herself in Steve's absence.

"I recall once when a friend brought his new pup over," Steve begins recounting the story with that familiar cat-lover's glint in his eyes. "Elspeth did the usual rough and tumble play with the pup until the dog got tired, and we ignored them. Then she sat there, licking one paw and studying him. When he was just about ready to doze off, she suddenly puffed herself up like a Halloween cat and charged right at him. Scared the poor pup—and us—half to death! Then she jumped into my lap and started grooming herself like nothing happened. She did that three more times before she got bored and took a nap."

Many owners, I among them, can recount similar tales of adult cat play that seems, to us at least, to radiate an added dimension. Like Steve, those who describe it often speak of the play as resulting from some deliberate thought process on the cat's part. To be sure, probably all of these displays more or less spring from the ancient feline repertoire. On my more objective, scientific days, I might even go so far as to agree (grudgingly) that these enchanting behaviors might represent nothing more than an example of what happens when primitive feline displays manifest in an environment where the need for them no longer exists.

However, such thinking just doesn't hold up in the company of an adult cat at play. These feline activities practically scream, "Optimal conditions!" and they provide us with several insights. First, the fact that Elspeth indulges in such play clearly communicates to Steve that, in spite of all the time that he's gone or the fact that he forgot to change her water or brush her, she considers her life with him more than adequate. Even if some scientists won't allow us to say that her play represents a feline celebration of an optimal state, Steve can certainly celebrate the fact that she sees their environment and relationship as optimal.

Second, as mentioned before, cats with behavioral or medical problems don't engage in this special kind of play; and when problems arise to disrupt the optimal state, a playful cat may cease playing altogether. Consequently, resumed feline play serves as one of the most delightful indicators that pet and owner have weathered the storm. While Dr. Guyer may consider it a good sign when Elspeth starts eating again after a rough time with a hot virus, Steve doesn't completely relax until he can report, "She's hiding my socks again!"

Think about past, present, and any future adult cats in your life. What about them sticks out the most clearly in your mind?

## Adult Cat Evaluation

What images come to mind when you think of adult cat health? What does the cat look and act like? What behaviors do you associate with an adult cat? Do you expect it to act more laid back and less playful than a kitten? Do you associate certain traits with a particular cat or cats in general? What do you consider normal play for an adult cat? Does your cat play as much as you'd like it to play? Or do you see its lack of play as part of the normal maturation process?

Having a clear picture of what constitutes normal for your particular adult cat can make your pet's golden years even more golden.

## The Final Feline Years

Of all living creatures, cats seem to age the most gracefully. Whereas we and our dogs get grayer and creakier as time goes on, many cats show little obvious evidence of the aging process. In fact, they adapt so well that we may miss valuable early-warning signs of change. At such times, owners who made the effort to understand what constitutes normal for their particular pets definitely hold the advantage.

For example, Steve knew that Elspeth's mother experienced kidney problems as she got older, so he pays particular attention to her water intake. When she reaches adulthood, he pours two cups of water into her bowl each morning rather than filling it directly from the tap. Then he measures how much remains that evening when he changes her water again. By subtracting the second amount from the first, he knows how much she drinks. By doing this for a week, he also discovers that she drinks more at night. This prompts him to change her water right before he goes to bed as well as in the morning and when he gets home from work. He also monitors her food intake the same way and discovers similar unique quirks.

Sound (specifically a blood-curdling cry one night) serves as Steve's first evidence that the aging Elspeth can no longer *see* as well as she once did. When he flies out of bed to determine what horror has befallen his pet, he finds her standing in the angle formed by the wall and the back of his opened bedroom door. Until then, he had no idea she found her way through his home primarily by scent. When an airborne scent trail leads her behind the door to the crack between it and the door frame, she's afraid to back up and lose her bearings.

Whether the cat's cry represents an attempt to use sound to navigate (much as bats use sonar) or merely serves to summon help remains unclear. However, owners who spray a bit of lightly scented cologne at cat-head height on the proper side of door frames and other prominent objects, as well as in lines about 18 inches from the top and bottom of stairs, can make life easier for the visually impaired pet.

For senior cats who claim territories above floor level, solid ramps leading to favorite shelves, chairs, or the owner's bed can help prevent falls. Other owners make "steps" using a series of increasingly larger cardboard boxes, which they fill with heavy books to guarantee their stability.

More and more veterinarians offer geriatric workups, and these can provide valuable medical information. However, many veterinarians and owners overlook the behavioral and bond factors that may affect the aging cat and its owners, too. I know I did until some wonderful clients pointed these out to me. Essentially, these folks asked to meet with me for the sole purpose of discussing what lay ahead for them and their pet as the animal got older. I found this such a rewarding experience for all involved that I now heartily recommend it to all veterinarians and owners.

"That's terrible!" Nicole once again exclaims, hugging Freebie protectively. "I don't even want to think about it!"

However, Steve decides that he does. He makes an appointment to see Dr. Guyer, without Elspeth because he believes this will enable him to discuss these difficult issues more objectively. During the meeting, Dr. Guyer reviews Elspeth's medical and behavioral records and notes anything that could become problematic as the cat gets older. She and Steve then discuss his options under those circumstances, given his specific time, financial, emotional, and physical limits.

"If Elspeth got really sick, I don't want to take her to a specialist or do any heroic treatments," Steve tells Dr. Guyer. "It isn't the money or the time. I just have some very strong feelings about not putting her through that. I'd rather have her home with me as long as possible."

Dr. Guyer then discusses the clinic's hospice service wherein a group of staff and volunteers assist owners who want their terminally ill pets to die at home. While always a difficult proposition for any pet owner, these final days can be particularly trying for those who own cats. So often we maintain images of an animal's dying quietly in its sleep. While some do, others may linger for days. Also, dying cats may purr or emit loud, eerie cries guaranteed to unnerve all but the most prepared owner.

Finally, Dr. Guyer discusses a subject many veterinarians find as difficult as most owners do: euthanasia. First, she asks Steve to think about whether he would consider euthanasia and under what conditions. When he says he would, they discuss those circumstances.

"Everything's the same as when we collect a routine blood sample, only this time I'd inject a small amount of highly concentrated anesthetic into her vein instead," Dr. Guyer explains. "Elspeth will fall asleep first, then her vital functions will cease."

The veterinarian then goes on to explain how some cats empty their bladders and/or defecate at the time of death, while others may give a few gasps that some owners find upsetting. If Steve chooses this option, does he want to remain with Elspeth or not? Dr. Guyer assures him that he shouldn't feel guilty if he doesn't want to stay, because Elspeth likes both her and her techs and feels comfortable with them. Dr. Guyer also offers to come to his home to perform this final service there if he desires.

"Above all, you must make this decision yourself," she cautions him. "Don't let anyone, not even me, force you to let go sooner or hang on longer than you think is right for you and Elspeth."

Finally Dr. Guyer describes Steve's options regarding what to do with Elspeth's remains: Would he want to bury Elspeth at a pet cemetery, or on his own property if local laws permit it? Or would he prefer to have her cremated? Would he like her ashes?

"I almost lost it a couple times during that meeting," Steve frankly admits later. "But when the end came, I was glad I knew what to expect. I was still very sad because Elspeth was such a wonderful cat. But I wasn't afraid, and she wasn't, either."

As we come to the end of our human-feline journey, think about old cats you have known and know, and those who will grow old with you.

## The Final Evaluation

Given your knowledge of your particular cat, its breed, or any parent history, what potential trouble spots might arise in old age? What environmental factors might complicate life for your old cat? What can you do to minimize their effects? How do you feel about euthanasia? If you wouldn't consider it, what kind of care would you want for your pet? State-of-the-art? Hospice? Would any time, financial, emotional, or physical limits affect your choice? If they might keep you from doing something you really want to do, can you think of any ways to work around it (time payments, asking friends to care for your pet when you can't, etc.)? If you would consider euthanasia, under what circumstances? Would you want to stay with your pet at this time? What would make this final farewell a quality one for you and your cat?

As a veterinarian, I've witnessed or participated in the death of many animals, including my own pets. While each inevitably leaves its own special mark, the passing of Maggie, that tough old hunter who wouldn't tolerate the hint of another cat anywhere on *her* property, sticks out. In retrospect, I was probably in denial about her fading away. I'd seen all the signs, and on some level that I didn't even recognize at the time I'd made up my mind that she would die at home. She was that kind of cat.

When the end came, I held Maggie most of that day and night, then carried her outside and sat on the stone steps and held her as the sun rose the next morning. Twice she gave out that strange, heart-wrenching cry that arises from some source beyond human comprehension.

And then she was gone.

I buried Maggie in a patch of rocky ground where nothing ever grew. Now something always grows there because that's the way cats are, too. They come into our lives and make us think and feel things we never thought or felt before. They fill a void we never even knew existed, and sometimes demand we give more than we ever knew we could. And when they go, and no matter how they go, they always leave part of themselves behind.

The day before Maggie died, she somehow caught one last mouse and laid it neatly on the doorstep as if to say, "There. Do you finally get it?"

Not yet. But given every cat's ingenuity and willingness to teach, I hope that someday I will.

# Index

Abdominal examinations, 385–86

Abyssinians, 62, 65, 75, 217

Activity centers, 266, 278–79

Acute medical problems, 356

Adult cats, 402–6

African wildcat (*Felis libyca*), 10, 57

Ageism, 163

Aging cats, 406–9

Allergies, 294

Alternative medicine, 333, 334

American curl cats, 62

American Holistic Veterinary
    Medical Association, 339

American shorthair, 65

American wirehair, 61

Ammonia, 239–41

Angoras, 64

Animal behavior,
    priorities governing, 14

Animal development, 8

Animal response, layers of, 168–69

Animal shelters, 82, 84–85

Anthropomorphic orientation, to pets
    exercise and, 268–70
    of feeding, 311–14
    health care and, 350–54
    of human feline bonds, 129–33

At-home examinations, 377–79
    abdominal, 385–86
    behavioral and bonding facets
        of, 387–90
    for body weight, 384–85
    of cat's body condition, 383–85
    of cat's ears, 379–80
    of cat's eyes, 380–81
    of cat's mouth, 381–83

Automatic feeders, 318, 321–22

Automatic waterers, 321–22

Aversion techniques, 100

Bastet goddess, 50

Baths, 360

Battables, 264, 278

Behavioral problems, 290

Belyaev, Dmitry, 7, 41
Bengals, 72–73, 218
Birmans, 53–57
Blood work, 402
Body temperature, 402
Bonds, 138
Breeders, 78
  casual, 82
  professional, 82–83
Breeding, 8, 394–95
  problems resulting from, 74–77
  for shows and exhibitions, 55
Breeding true, 72
British shorthair, 65
Budge, Claire, 127
Burmese, 70

Cabana Systems, 94–95, 102
Caching, 309
Castration, 216
Casual breeders, 82
Cat calls, 76–77
Cat doors, 101, 242
Cat environments
  cat development and, 63–67
  health problems and, 347–50
  importance of, 35–36
  space requirements for, 91–95
  tension and, 97
Cat Fanciers Association, 47, 48
Cat feeders, 318, 321–22
Cat Fence-In, 94
Cat food
  adding medications to, 345
  allergies to, 294
  cost of, 320–23
  dishes for, 321
  eating human, 311–13
  human emotional connection
    to, 323–25
  measuring consumption of, 406
  publications about, 296

  traditional, 292–93
  types of, 296–97
*Cat Food Reference, The* (Coffman), 296
Cat Hole, 104
Cat ownership.
    *See* Human-feline bonds
Cat scratch disease/fever, 285
Cat shows, 75
  breeding for, 55
  finding breeders at, 83
Cat-a-Comb, 104
*Cat-Book Poems, The*, 69–70, 71
Catching objects, 253–54
CatCliffs, 103
Catnip, 264–65
Cats. *See also* Kittens; specific breed
    or type
  dogs and, 115–16
  factors to consider in
    selecting, 78–80
  inherited tendencies, 9
  legends about, 53–56
  personality differences between
    breeds of, 76–77
  play and, 256–60
  relationships with other
    animals, 115–17
  religious role of, 49–52
  sexual behavior, 28–33
  social system of, 20–22
  sources for, 81–85
Cavada, Carmen, 35
Chartreux, 65
Chattel orientation, to pets
  of feeding, 314–16
  health care and, 350–54
  of human-feline bonds, 133–37
Chronic medical problems, 356–57
Claw trimming, 109–10
Claws/clawing, 108–12, 395
Cleaning products, use of, 239–41
Codependency, 182–87

Coffman, Howard D., 296
Color, cat, 61
Complementary medicine, 333
Confinement, 241–42
Conjunctiva, 381
Conjunctivitis, 381
Copulation, 30–31
Cornish, 61
Courtyards, interior, 98–99
Crate training. *See* Free-access
    crate-training (FACT)
Cymric, 62

Declawing, 395–96
Defecation problems.
    *See* Inappropriate elimination
Delta Society, 161–62
Devon Rex, 61
Diets
    changing, 307
    inappropriate elimination and,
      237–39
    weight-reduction, 303–4
Digestion problems, 308–9
Dips, 360
Disaster kits, 397–400
Distraction techniques, 100
Dogs, cats and, 115–16
Domestic cats, 5–6
Domestication, 8
Doors, 99–101
Double-sided tape, 15
Drinking behavior, 297–300
Dying cats, 408–10

Ears, cat's, examining, 379–80
Eating disorders, 308–9, 316–19
Effect of person, 156
Egyptian Maus, 52, 73
Elimination behavior.
    *See* Inappropriate elimination
Emergencies, 397–400

Emotional limitations, 152–57
Emotions, 131–33
Environmental enrichment, 260
Environments
    cat development and, 63–67
    cat's space and, 91–95
    health problems and, 347–50
    importance of, 35–36
    tension and, 97
European wildcat (*Felis silvestris*), 10, 57
Euthanasia, 363–64, 408–9
Examinations, 377–79
    abdominal, 385–86
    behavioral and bonding facets
      of, 387–90
    for body weight, 384–85
    of cat's body condition, 383–85
    of cat's ears, 379–80
    of cat's eyes, 380–81
    of cat's mouth, 381–83
    of kittens, 393–97
Exercise
    cat's age and, 254–55
    cost considerations, 277–80
    emotional aspects of, 279–84
    importance of, 287
    mind-body challenge of, 250–52
    owner physical limitations
      and, 284–86
    programs, 286–87
    time commitments for, 272–76
Exhibitions, breeding for, 55
Eyes, cat's, examining, 380–81

FACT. *See* Free-access
    crate-training (FACT)
Feeding
    anthropomorphic view of, 311–14
    areas for, 309–10
    chattel view of, 314–16
    free-choice, 314–15
    schedules for, 317–19

Feline space, 90–91. *See also* Territories
    furnishings in, 106–13
    inhabitants in, 113–17
    structure of, 95–106
    types of settings for, 91–95
*Felis libyca* (African wildcat), 10, 57
*Felis silvestris* (European wildcat), 10, 57
Feral cats. *See* Wildcats
Financial considerations, 139–47
Fleas, 383
Flooring, 104
Food. *See* Cat food
Foot fetish, 15
Free-access crate-training (FACT),
        13, 341
    inappropriate elimination
            and, 241–42
    for multiple-cat households, 244
    as stress reliever, 118–24
Free-choice feeding, 314–15
Furniture, 106–9

Harnesses, 279
Health care
    factors determining success
            of, 370–71
    medical approaches to, 332–34
    owner physical limitations to, 368–70
    price of, 358–63
    publications about, 333–34
    time considerations for, 354–58
Health insurance, pet, 361
Health problems, environments
        and, 347–50
Health-care programs
    factors that affect success of, 341–46
    prevention and wellness-centered
            approaches to, 333–34
    problem-oriented approaches
            to, 333–34
Heat cycles, 30
Henry Higgins Syndrome, 194–95

Hepatic lipidosis, 303–4
High-rise cats, 92
Himalayans, 71, 72, 216–17
Holistic approach, to health care, 339
Home-cooked foods, 296
Hospices, 408
Housebound cats, 172–75
Housing, pet-friendly, 98–105
Human-feline bonds, 127–28
    anthropomorphic view of, 129–33
    balancing, 162–65
    chattel view of, 133–37
    emotional limits to, 152–57
    factors affecting, 4
    financial limits to, 139–47
    integrated view of, 133–37
    limits to, 137–39
    physical limits to, 157–62
    time limits to, 147–52
Hunting behavior.
        *See* Predatory behavior
Hunting rituals, 24–28

Identification systems, 398–99
Imaging, 214–15, 391
Immunodeficiency diseases, 285,
        368–69
Inappropriate elimination,
        210, 219–22, 228–33
    cleaning products and, 239–41
    diet and, 237–39
    electrical outlets and, 242–43
    free-access crate-training, 241–42
    in multiple-cat households, 244
    Persians and, 76
    removing hot spots for, 234–36
    studies on, 212–15
    time needed for breaking cycle
            of, 243–44
Integrated orientation, to pets, 140
Interior courtyards, 98–99
International Cat Association, The, 48

Jackson, Virginia Sandford, 98
Japanese bobbed-tail, 64
Jones, Boyd, 127

Kali-Ko Cathouses, 95
Kittens, 36–37. *See also* Cats
   crate-training, 123
   development of, 34–40
   examination concerns for, 393–97
   play and, 255–60
   raising, 40–42
Korats, 52

Leashes, 274–75, 279
Lesson of Degree, 40
Leyhausen, Paul, 9, 20, 25
Litter boxes, 208–9, 216–19,
      222–28, 290. *See also*
      Inappropriate elimination
   placement of, 229–30
   two cats using, 232–33
Longhaired cats, 64
Love symbolism, 195
Lymph nodes, 384

Maine coon cats, 65–66
Malayans, 70–71
Manx, 62, 64, 74
Maternal instincts, 34–40
Medications, adding, to food, 345
Microchips, for identification, 398
Mother cats. *See* Queens (mother cats)
Mouth, cat's, examining, 381–83
Multiple-cat households, 19
   adding to, 80
   feeding in, 306–7
Mutations, 59–63
Muzzles, 399

Nail-grooming, 109
Nebelungs, 62
Negative symbolism, 192–96

Negus, Daphne, 71
Neutering, 394
Neutralizers, odor, 240–41
Nocturnal behavior, 11–13
No-kill shelters, 84–85
Norwegian Forest cats, 66, 217–18
Nutrition, 294
Nutritional problems, 290

Obesity, 290, 303–4, 384–85
Ociats, 73
Odor-elimination products, 240–41
Owner orientations, health-care
      problems and, 350–54
Owners, physically impaired, 369

Pavlov, Ivan, 155–56
Paws, 15
Pedicures, 109–10
Persians, 64
   breeding-related problems, 74–75
   elimination behavior, 76
   evolution of, 71–72
   temperaments, 76
   using litter boxes, 216–17
Personality differences, between
      breeds, 76–77
Pet carriers, 13
Pet Doors U.S.A., 101, 104
Pet health insurance, 361
Pet stores, 82, 84
Pet-friendly housing, 98–105
Pheromones, 12
Physically impaired owners, 369
Pillows, 107–8
Placebo effect, 156
Play
   cost considerations, 277–80
   emotional aspects of, 279–84
   importance of, 287, 403–6
   owner physical limitations
      and, 284–86

time commitments for, 272–76
Playground equipment, 261–67
Polydactyly, 343
Predatory behavior, 22–24
    reasons for, 25–28
    stages of, 24
    stimulus for, 24–25
Premium foods, 296
Presence, 200–203
Problem-oriented approaches to
        health care, 334
Professional breeders, 82–83
Publications
    for alternative medicine, 334
    for cat breeds, 48
    for cat foods, 296
    for problem-oriented approaches
        to health care, 334
    for traditional medicine, 333
Punishment, 100
Purebred cats
    defined, 72
    dietary idiosyncrasies of, 305
    factors for development of, 56–57

Queens (mother cats), 21
    weaning and nursing behavior, 36–37

Regular foods, 296
Reinoso-Suarez, Fernando, 35
Restraints, 344–45
Retrieving cats, 253–54
Russian blues, 62, 64

Scent hormones, 12
Scent marking, 15–18
Scottish fold, 62
Scratching objects, 111–12, 263–64
Screen doors, 99–100
Sekhmut goddess, 49–50
Senior cats, 406–9
Separation anxiety, 178, 181

Sexual behavior, 28–33
Sexually oriented symbolism, 192–94
Shelf systems, 102–3
Shelters, 82, 84–85
Shows, cat
    breeding for, 55
    finding breeders at, 83
Siamese, 52
    evolution of, 68–70
    temperaments, 76
    wool-sucking problem, 37–38
Siberians, 66
Singapuras, 66, 217–18, 293
Smell, development of, 35
Solitary cats, 19–22
Somalis, 62, 75
Sound, 406–7
Sound machines, 13
Space, feline, 90–91. See also Territories
    furnishings for, 106–13
    inhabitants in, 113–17
    structure of, 95–106
    types of settings for, 91–95
Spaying, 394
Sphinx, 62
Spicer, John, 127
Spraying, 216. See also
        Inappropriate elimination
Stalkables, 278
StGeorge, Ross, 127
Stress, 97
Stress-relievers, 118–24
Sucking behavior, 37–38
Support groups, 366
Symbolism, 187–92
    Henry Higgins Syndrome, 194–95
    love, 195
    negative, 192–96
    sexually oriented, 192–94

Tailless cats, 64. See also Manx
Tape, as training aid, 15

Tattoos, for identification, 398
Teasers, 278
Temperaments, 76
Tension, 97
Territorial personality, 18
Territories. *See also* Space, feline
  establishing and protecting, 20
  marking, 14–18
Therapeutic foods, 296–97
Time considerations
  for exercise, 272–76
  for health care, 354–58
Tonkinese, 70–71
Toys, 261–67
  prices of, 277–80
Traditional medicine, 333, 334
Training aids, 15
Treats, 305, 390
True breeding, 72
Turkish Angoras, 66
Turkish Vans, 66

Upholstery, cat-resistant, 107
Urination. *See* Inappropriate
  elimination; Spraying

Veterinarians, 82
  communicating feelings to, 366–67

roles of, 336–38
selecting, 336–40
Videotapes, 266, 279

Walking, 274–75
Wall coverings, 103
Water
  cat's attraction
    for, 252
  feline drinking behavior
    and, 297–300
Waterers, 321–22
Web site addresses
  American Veterinary Medical
    Association, 334
  Cabana Systems, 102
  Delta Society, 161–62
  Weight checking, 384–85
  Weight reduction, 303–4
Wellness-centered approach, to
  health care, 333–34
Wildcats
  adaptability of, 10–11
  behavior of, 5–6
  defined, 10
Williams, Robert, 35
Window perches, 102–3
Wool-sucking, 37–38